Freelance Journalism and Mass Communication

Freelance Journalism and Mass Communication

Shipra Chawla

Freelance Journalism and Mass Communication

ISBN 978-93-5111-388-1

Published in 2014 in India by

RANDOM PUBLICATIONS

4376-A/4B, Gali Murari Lal, Ansari Road
New Delhi-110 002
Phone : +91-11-43580356, +91-11-23289044
e-mail: randomexports@gmail.com, sales@randompublications.com, info@randompublications.com

Reprinted 2021

Type Setting by : Keystoneprintads, Delhi-110051
Digitally Printed at: Replika Press Pvt. Ltd.

Preface

Freelance journalism is one of the more hectic forms of freelance writing. If you want to become a successful freelance journalist, you'll need to be comfortable with spending much time hunting down stories, traveling from place to place, and writing under short deadlines. If you enjoy all of that, and if you're interested in some of the best opportunities for personal creativity, then freelance journalism may be for you. When we talk about freelance journalism, we need to distinguish between two types: newspaper journalism and magazine journalism.

Typical newspaper articles follow a hierarchical format: the most pertinent information first, the least pertinent last. For example, an article about a local parade would start with "The X Parade will travel down Main Street at 10:00 Saturday in support of Y," while it might end with "Onlookers are advised to bring umbrellas." Additionally, writing as a newspaper journalist means that you need the ability to find out about the news. Often, a journalist's day looks like this: the editor assigns the journalist an article topic at 6 AM. By 8 AM, the journalist is making phone calls to various parties related to the topic. For a story on rising gas prices, this may include CEOs of oil companies, local gas station owners, car owners, car manufacturers, and local policymakers.

The journalist then works on the article, fact-checking where appropriate, before submitting it for publication sometime that night, with the deadline depending on the individual paper. Then the journalist is able to go to sleep--until 6 AM rolls around again, and the next article topic comes in. More leeway is available with the larger "feature" articles. These appear in film sections, lifestyle sections, health sections or other less breaking-news-focused parts of the daily paper. Often newspapers publish these sections weekly, rather than daily, to save on printing costs. For example, the film section may only appear on Fridays, the food section on Tuesdays, etc. The upshot of this is the freelance journalist has more time to research and to work on an excellent, well-rounded article. Using the same research methods, a feature writer constructs a more in-depth look at a given topic than a news writer can achieve in a short column of text. Magazine journalism is similar to the "feature" style of newspaper journalism, albeit with much more generous word limits. The downside is that a magazine may not have as many opportunities for publishing your work.

Freelance journalism becomes successful only when you contentedly use much time chasing down stories, traveling from place to place, and writing under short deadlines. As a rule, newspaper journalism engages a much narrower range of subject matter than magazine journalism, appreciably shorter articles, and a greater focus on form. The career of a journalist isn't for everyone. Whereas many freelance writing projects are about a predictable routine of research and writing, the variety and novelty of writing news and feature articles eschew all routine in favor of a constant flurry of ad hoc interviews, phone calls, and general information-gathering. This fully up-to-date book recognizes the vast and rapid changes taking place in freelance journalism and mass communication. This book brings it into the 21 century for a new generation of students, scholars, and media professionals

I thank all members of my team who have helped in the preparation of the book. My special thanks go to "Random Publications" who have published the book.

– Shipra Chawla

Contents

1

Introduction

Freelance journalism is one of the more hectic forms of freelance writing. If you want to become a successful freelance journalist, you'll need to be comfortable with spending much time hunting down stories, traveling from place to place, and writing under short deadlines.

If you enjoy all of that, and if you're interested in some of the best opportunities for personal creativity, then freelance journalism may be for you. When we talk about freelance journalism, we need to distinguish between two types: newspaper journalism and magazine journalism. As a rule, newspaper journalism involves a much narrower range of subject matter than magazine journalism, significantly shorter articles, and a greater focus on form. Typical newspaper articles follow a hierarchical format: the most pertinent information first, the least pertinent last. For example, an article about a local parade would start with "The X Parade will travel down Main Street at 10:00 Saturday in support of Y," while it might end with "Onlookers are advised to bring umbrellas."

Additionally, writing as a newspaper journalist means that you need the ability to find out about the news. Often, a journalist's day looks like this: the editor assigns the journalist an article topic at 6 AM. By 8 AM, the journalist is making phone calls to various parties related to the topic. For a story on rising gas prices, this may include CEOs of oil companies, local gas station owners, car owners (interviewed on the street or at gas stations), car manufacturers, and local policymakers. Journalists usually interview anyone with a meaningful connection to the topic, and who can provide some good, succinct quotes and information.

Information-gathering goes on for most of the day, usually ending around evening. The journalist then works on the article, fact-checking where appropriate, before submitting it for publication sometime that night, with the deadline depending on the individual paper. Then the journalist is able to go to sleep—until 6 AM rolls around again, and the next article topic comes in. More leeway is available with the larger "feature" articles. These appear in film sections, lifestyle sections, health sections or other less breaking-news-focused parts of the daily paper. Often newspapers publish these sections weekly, rather than daily, to save on printing costs. For example, the film section may only appear on Fridays, the food section on Tuesdays, etc. The upshot of this is the freelance journalist has more time to research and to work on an excellent, well-rounded article. Using the same research methods (calling everyone connected to the topic, scheduling interviews, synthesizing succinct points from a large information pool), a feature writer constructs a more in-depth look at a given topic than a news writer can achieve in a short column of text.

A freelancer, freelance worker, or freelance is somebody who is self-employed and isn't committed to an employer for too long. The term was first used by Sir Walter Scott (1771–1832) in Ivanhoe to describe a "medieval mercenary warrior" or "free-lance".

It changed to a figurative noun around the 1860s and was recognized as a verb in 1903 by authorities in etymology such as the *Oxford English Dictionary*. Only in modern times has the term morphed from a noun (a freelance) into an adjective (a freelance journalist), a verb (a journalist who freelances) and an adverb (she worked freelance), and then the noun "freelancer." The author and poet Ernest William Hornung (1866–1921) used the term in "The Gift of the Emperor" to describe something of poor quality: "I warmed to my woes. It was no easy matter to keep your end up as a raw freelance of letters; for my part, I was afraid I wrote neither well enough nor ill enough for success."

Fields where freelancing is common include journalism, book publishing, journal publishing, and other forms of writing, editing, copyediting, proofreading, indexing, copywriting, computer programming and graphic design, consulting and translating.

Freelance practice varies greatly. Some require clients to sign written contracts, while others may perform work based on verbal agreements, perhaps enforceable through the very nature of the work. Some freelancers may provide written estimates of work and request deposits from clients.

Payment for freelance work also varies greatly. Freelancers may charge by the day, hour, or page or on a per-project basis. Instead of a flat rate or fee, some freelancers have adopted a value-based pricing method based on the perceived value of the results to the client. By custom, payment arrangements may be upfront, percentage upfront, or upon completion. For more complex projects, a contract may set a payment schedule based on milestones or outcomes.

In most professions involving creation of intellectual property, "freelance" and its derivative terms are often reserved for workers who create works on their own initiative, then look for someone to publish them. They typically keep the copyright to their works and sell the rights to publishers in time-limited contracts. In contrast, workers who are hired to create a work according to the publishers' or other customers' specifications are referred to as "independent contractors" and similar terms. They have no copyright to the works, which are written as works made for hire, a category of intellectual property defined in US copyright law — Section 101, Copyright Act of 1976 (USC 17 §101).

Freelancers generally enjoy a greater variety of assignments than in regular employment, and—subject to the need to earn a regular income—usually have more freedom to choose their work schedule. The experience can also lead to a broad portfolio of work and the establishment of a network of clients.

Sometimes a freelancer will work with one or more other freelancers and/or vendors to form a "virtual agency" to serve a particular client's needs for short-term and permanent project work. This versatile agency model can help a freelancer land jobs that require targeted, specific experience and skills outside the scope of one individual. As the clients change, so too may the players chosen for a virtual agency's talent base.

This is a common way for freelancers to get work if the non-competing freelancer in the relationship reciprocates the relevant type of work back assuming that both are in the same industry. Freelancers and clients may form a relationship based on mutual needs and the professionalism and competence of both parties.

The Internet has opened up many freelance opportunities, expanded available markets, and has contributed to service sector growth in many economies. Offshore outsourcing and crowdsourcing are heavily reliant on the Internet to provide economical access to remote workers, and frequently leverage technology to manage workflow to and from the employer.

Much of the computer freelance work is being outsourced to poorer countries outside the United States and Europe. This has spurred conflict because American and European workers are not receiving the benefits. The compromise has led to student freelancers who now provide a steady source of cheap labour while keeping jobs American and European.

As a result, freelance employment has been common in the areas of writing, editing, indexing, software development, website design, advertising, open innovations, information technology, and business process outsourcing. Changes to the publishing industry since the 1980s have resulted in an increase in copy editing of book and journal manuscripts and proofreading of typeset manuscripts being outsourced to freelance copy editors and proofreaders. The major drawback is the uncertainty of work and thus income, and lack of company benefits such as a pension, health insurance, paid holidays and bonuses. Many freelancers, especially in journalism, regard themselves as having greater income security through the diversity of outlets—the loss of any one of which leads to the loss of only a proportion of income, rather than its totality as with salaried employees. It is important to note that being a freelancer is not suitable to all people. Being a freelancer requires discipline and self-motivation along with other easier to acquire skills. If the freelancer works at home they are prone to additional stresses, that if not managed properly, could prevent them from earning an income at their profession.

Many periodicals and newspapers offer the option of ghost signing, when a freelance writer signs with an editor but their name is not listed on the byline of their article(s).

This allows the writer to receive benefits while still being classified as a freelancer, and independent of any set organization. In some countries this can lead to taxation issues (e.g., so-called IR35 violations in the UK). Ghost signing has little bearing on whether a writer is a freelancer or employee in the US. Freelancers often must handle contracts, legal issues, accounting, marketing, and other business functions by themselves. If they do choose to pay for professional services, they can sometimes turn into significant out-of-pocket expenses. Working hours can extend beyond the standard working day and working week.

In Europe, the perceived disadvantages of being freelance have led the European Union to research the area, producing draft papers that would, if enforced, make it illegal for companies or organizations to employ freelancers directly, unless the freelancer was entitled to benefits such as pension contributions and holiday pay.

In the UK, where the terms of integration into the EU have and are being hotly debated, this would lead to a significant reshaping of the way freelance work is dealt with and have a major impact on industry; employers would be required either to give freelances the contractual rights of employees or employ only freelancers already being employed by agencies or other organizations granting them these rights.

However, the White Papers that recommend such moves have not yet been adopted in the EU, and the potential impact on UK employment laws is being opposed by key UK organizations lobbying the government to negotiate over the acceptance of EU legislation in such areas. In the U.S. in 2009, federal and state agencies began increasing their oversight of freelancers and other workers employers classify as independent contractors. The U.S. Government Accountability Office (GAO) recommended that the Secretary of Labour have its Wage and Hour Division "focus on misclassification of employees as independent contractors during targeted investigations."

The increased regulation is meant to ensure workers are treated fairly and that companies are not misclassifying workers as independent contractors to avoid paying appropriate employment taxes and contributions to workers' compensation and unemployment compensation. At the same time, this increased enforcement is affecting companies whose business models are based on using non-employee workers, as well as independent professionals who have chosen to work as independent contractors. For example, book publishing companies have traditionally outsourced certain tasks like indexing and proofreading to individuals working as independent contractors. Self-employed accountants and attorneys have traditionally hired out their services to accounting and law firms needing assistance. The U.S. Internal Revenue Service offers some guidance on what constitutes self-employment, but states have enacted stricter laws to address how independent contractors should be defined. For example, a Massachusetts law states that companies can hire independent contractors only to perform work that is "outside the usual course of business of the employer," meaning workers working on the company's core business must be classified as employees.

According to this statute, a software engineering firm cannot outsource work to a software engineering consultant, without hiring the consultant as an employee. The firm could, however, hire an independent contractor working as an electrician, interior decorator, or painter. This raises questions about the common practice of consulting, because a company would typically hire a management consulting firm or self-employed consultant to address business-specific needs that are not "outside the usual course of business of the employer." International freelancing is a relatively new development in the global market. Some freelance professionals move from one country to another looking for business opportunities along with travelling experience. These individuals often use the Internet as their main communication technology for running a business. Online outsourcing marketplaces focus on assisting freelancers to find work around the world. International freelance support may differ in developed countries, as opposed to developing countries, which have almost no freelance support at all.

2

The Law of Amateur Journalism

Journalism traditionally has been a full-time job. Because printing and broadcasting require assets to reach an audience, conventional journalists have to work for newspapers or broadcasters. In this bricks-and-mortar" model of journalism, practitioners make significant investments in physical equipment, technology, office space, personnel, and goodwill. Media firms' capital and reputational assets provide a kind of bonding mechanism.

A broadcast or print media company can be expected to protect its significant investments by putting structures in place to carefully monitor its output. The downside is that the need for capital restricts entry to firms that can attract a mass audience. This restriction can filter out divergent views and prevent some markets and viewpoints from being served.

This model of journalism started to change with the rise of the Internet and the World Wide Web. Journalism was no longer exclusively the province of professionals. Anybody with a computer could launch a post to a website maintained on a server connected to the Internet and, potentially, a large audience. Viewers, however, had to find posts in the rapidly expanding heap. Some independent journalists, such as Matt Drudge, managed to be heard above the din, but most popular Internet news sites were those of professional newspapers and broadcasters.

The technology of amateur journalism has continued to develop. Amateur journalists now not only can post their thoughts cheaply on the Web, but also can get the attention of significant numbers of readers. They use devices called "weblogs" or, more popularly, "blogs."

These are, in general, series of web posts from a single web address with a common author or set of authors, often integrated with commentary on the post itself or on other blogs. According to one survey, there are over 35.3 million blogs, with the number doubling every six months.

Blogs have started to generate significant legal issues. This Chapter develops an economic framework for addressing those issues, as well as those that are likely to arise as amateur journalism continues to evolve. The central legal question concerning blogs is how to balance the need for regulation against the risk that regulation will reduce the benefits of individuals' unfiltered participation in the public debate. Critics of blogs, including many professional journalists, see blogs' low entry costs and lack of conventional intermediaries as a threat to responsible reporting.

As Jonathan Klein, now president of CNN, famously said, "bloggers have no checks and balances.... You couldn't have a starker contrast between the multiple layers of checks and balances and a guy sitting in his living room in his pajamas writing." It arguably follows that bloggers should be regulated to ensure accuracy and fairness, perhaps even more heavily than conventional journalists.

This argument erroneously views the checks-and-balances issues from the perspective of a single blogger rather than what has been referred to as the "blogosphere." Although anyone can enter the Web, not everybody can get noticed. The process of attracting attention, particularly through Google and other search engines, provides a neutral mechanism for establishing credibility that avoids conventional journalism's potentially biased filtering.

Moreover, any benefits of regulation must be balanced against the cost of over deterring speech by bloggers, who usually have weaker incentives to speak than career journalists. Regulation may sharply reduce amateur journalism's comparative advantage over professional journalism in allowing the expression of diverse views and the dissemination of specialized information.

The limited benefits and high costs of regulating amateur journalism apply most directly to regulation designed to ensure accuracy. However, blogs also present distinct problems of confidentiality and infringement of property rights that are not necessarily constrained by market mechanisms. Professionals may be more subject than amateurs to regulatory and extraregulatory sanctions for disclosing private information or disseminating copyrighted materials.

This Chapter focuses on the basic economics of amateur journalism rather than on a particular format or technology. The Chapter covers the subset of bloggers who are engaged in "journalism" in the sense that, like conventional newspaper and magazine reporters, they broadly distribute relatively short pieces that are intended to report or reflect on current events. In other words, the Article does not deal with the many people who use their blogs essentially as diaries, which usually are not intended for readers other than themselves and close friends and family.

Much of this Chapter's analysis applies to those who seek to contribute in some way to public debate rather than engage in personal reflection. Though bloggers tend to focus more on analysis or opinion than reporting of facts, they are no less "journalists" in the broad sense of the term. In any event, many bloggers do report facts or present expert analysis, whereas many conventional journalists write opinion columns. In this Chapter, an "amateur journalist" is one who either is not employed at all, or writes as a sideline to some other business. Thus, an amateur journalist may be a professional in some line of work, including a professional journalist who blogs separately from her main job.

This distinction reflects the different incentives of one who is not engaged in the relevant work as if it were a paid career. Although the professional-amateur distinction does not depend on whether the work is done on the Web, amateur journalism is currently enabled by technologies that are specific to the Web. Although the Chapter discusses the amateur-professional distinction from the perspective of recent technological developments, the same general issues will remain even as these technologies and formats evolve. Conversely, the economics of blogging may change even if formats remain the same.

For example, web pages that mimic blogs' format may involve very different issues if, like traditional journalism, they are written and managed by professionals as an adjunct to professional media. These products are interesting for present purposes mainly to the extent that they illustrate the interaction between, and potential convergence of, professional and amateur journalism.

THE TECHNOLOGY OF BLOGGING

Before developing the economic framework, a review of some salient technical features of blogs is useful. A blog is built on a web page. Dave Winer, one of the first bloggers, provides the following definition: "A [blog] is a hierarchy of text, images, media objects and data, arranged chronologically, that can be viewed in an HTML browser." Winer summarizes some important technical features shared by many blogs:

- Each blog post has a title, date, and "permalink" that gives its web address.
- The home page has the most recent posts.
- Archives include the remaining posts, usually organized by category.
- The author may permit comments below each post.
- Really Simple Syndication (RSS) feeds let people who use "news aggregators" such as "Bloglines" to "subscribe" to the blog and thereby disseminate posts quickly across the Web.
- Each blog post "pings," or notifies, change-aggregators such as "blo.gs" to signal the Web that the post has been made.
- A "trackback" linked to the blog post enables other blogs to ping blogs they link. The blog author can then track and respond to others who cite her, and readers of the linked blog can refer to the record of trackbacks under each blog post.
- Tools for recording hits and ranking blogs by popularity allow blog authors to increase or focus their audiences.
- A blog's "blogroll' establishes the blog in a community of other blogs, as well as publicizing these blogs.

At a deeper level, blogs are enabled by three technologies: the Internet, the Web, and Google and other sophisticated search engines. The Internet's and Web's roles are obvious, but that of search engines may not be. The key to understanding the importance of search engines is considering how easy it otherwise would be for a blog post to be lost among many millions of Web pages.

Google and other search engines provide a spontaneous filtering mechanism by not only finding the post but, more importantly, giving top ranking in searches to the more "important" posts. Google ranks search results according to the number of sites that link to the result and the importance of each linking site, so that links are "votes" by the linking web pages for the blog's quality and accuracy.

Bloggers have an incentive to link only to high-quality blogs because their own readers judge them by, among other things, their link's quality. The votes themselves are weighted according to the voter's importance, which is apparently a function of the voter's quality and accuracy.

Moreover, Google distinguishes more active journalists by visiting their sites, and therefore spotting them in searches, depending on how frequently they update. In general, therefore, blog authors build readership by establishing their credibility and encouraging links by other blogs. A blog's readership represents a kind of goodwill asset analogous to the audience of the conventional media. The difference is that, whereas professional media companies must make upfront capital investments, entry to amateur journalism is free but without value until the author makes the additional investments in time and credibility necessary to build readership.

Although investments may be required in both cases, the fact that no upfront investment is necessary to blog is significant. As discussed in the next Part, blog authors have "self-expression" incentives that encourage entry even without the investment necessary to gain an audience. Blogs thereby allow individuals to test their skills and marketability rather than have to get a job from one of a limited number of media firms.

This overview, of course, is only a snapshot of rapidly evolving technology. But though the technology may look very different in a few years, certain underlying characteristics, particularly interactivity, are likely not only to remain but to develop. Thus, this peek at the technology is useful in specifying the assumptions that underlie the following analysis.

THE ECONOMICS OF BLOGGING

Private Costs of Amateur Journalism

Blogs are a classic example of "cheap speech." In terms of capital investment, blogging requires no more than a computer, Internet access, and, perhaps, a blogging programme such as Typepad. This ease of access means significant diversity and nearly zero intermediation, either directly or indirectly through entry costs. However, blogging involves significant potential noncapital costs. Expert bloggers with relatively high opportunity costs likely would make the investment only with some expectation of a tangible return, including reputation enhancement.

Also, inaccurate or harmful posts could damage readership or the author's main business, particularly in reputation-intensive businesses such as professional practice. The costs incurred by amateurs depend on whether, in their nonblogging lives, they are self-employed or work for others. A self-employed blogger obviously has an incentive to refrain from expressing very unpopular opinions, irresponsible or untrue statements, or statements that disparage his own skills.

A blogger who works for others may be less concerned with the reputation costs his blog inflicts because they are incurred by his employer, unless the blogger faces firing, demotion, or other employer constraints on nonwork activities. This discipline may reduce agency costs by aligning the employed author's incentives with those of his employer, thereby making his activities similar to those of the self-employed.

But employers also might seek to discipline bloggers who disagree with them but do not injure the business. This discipline might itself be an agency cost in a large firm to the extent that supervisors create an unpleasant work environment or repel productive workers who value freedom of expression.

In a small sole proprietorship such discipline may be a consumption activity by the proprietor. Any risk of excessive employer discipline of bloggers is mitigated by the fact that bloggers are often knowledgable workers with special skills that give them some bargaining leverage with their employers.

Amateur journalists, including many, if not most, who work for others, can reduce these private costs by not identifying themselves. Indeed, current technology probably allows bloggers who are willing to pay the costs of total anonymity to avoid any constraints on their activities, including the reputational constraints discussed. However, anonymity also reduces the private benefits and therefore the incentive to blog that most amateur journalists have. This suggests that the constraints on bloggers are to some extent built into their incentives to blog.

Incentives

Blogs' private costs and minimal tangible benefits to their authors raise a question why so many millions of people find the activity worthwhile. The following are some reasons why people have been willing to commit time to amateur journalism. As discussed throughout this Chapter, one must understand the nature of these incentives in order to be able to evaluate regulation's potential deterrent effect.

- Self-expression and Communication

The original bloggers sought mainly to reflect on personal matters as they would in a diary, or communicate with friends or family. Political blogs intended for broader distribution were spurred by the coinciding development of blogging technologies and the 2004 presidential election, which elicited strong views on both sides.

Amateur journalism has developed to include many bloggers who write on particular areas of expertise rather than general personal or political views. These writers derive consumption value from expressing their views and communicating them to others. The self-expression motive is important because it explains why blogs would start up with no audience or tangible hope of conventional economic benefit. Self-expression is also important to blogs that have developed an audience.

Without a strong expressive motive, one might expect successful blogs to merge with professional media. This exit strategy could then motivate blog startups. Over the long term, therefore, blogs might be more a way to enter conventional journalism than a new medium. But a significant self-expression motive would preserve the distinctiveness of blogs.

- Cross-promotion

Blogs increasingly are used to promote paid services, most prominently by lawyers and other professionals. Blogs not only advertise the related product, but help establish its quality. Professionals sell "credence qualities" that buyers can evaluate only by experiencing the quality of the advice over time. Blogs let professionals demonstrate the quality of their advice for potential customers or clients. A blog therefore can be viewed as a kind of "loss-leader," in which giving away the free service sells the paid service.

Blogs also can be used to promote business firms. The blog can be run by the firm, with individuals acting explicitly as agents. Such a blog would not fit this Chapter's definition of "amateur journalism." In professional firms and schools, individuals more likely write blogs for themselves with spillover benefits to their employers. In either case the firms have incentives to reward their employees' blogging activities.

Many academics use blogs as a medium for presenting and publicizing scholarship. Blogs may become particularly important in academia because scholars generally need not account for their time, which is blogs' major private cost. Scholars have significant incentives to publicize their work.

For example, rankings such as those by U.S. News and World Report have focused attention on objective measures for evaluating academic performance.

One emerging measure is downloads on the Social Science Research Network (SSRN). Scholars can increase downloads by linking their articles on a widely read blog and their schools can thereby rise in the rankings. This suggests that schools might subsidize blogs and other ways of improving statistical measures of faculty performance in order to succeed in the increasingly market-driven academic environment. They also might run blogs themselves and invite faculty to participate.

- Advertising Revenue

Amateur journalism's business model is evolving. Bloggers can follow the conventional media and offer advertising. This practice was first institutionalized by Blogads, an intermediary that sells advertising on individual blogs. Advertisers can choose specific blogs and thereby engage in cost-effective micromarketing.

Several different advertising models for blogs are available. Bloggers can sign up for a service like Google's AdSense that chooses the ads that appear on the site, one like BlogAds that acts as an intermediary to sell advertisements for specific blogs, or an "affiliate network" that enables ad sales to groups of bloggers but allows the blogs to choose which advertisements they carry. Firms like Gawker and Weblogs, Inc. aggregate writers on a single blog that sells advertisements.

This format resembles a conventional newspaper except that the writers are more like independent contractors than employees. Pajamas Media, a network of leading right-leaning blogs, commits bloggers to advertising for an extended period and frees them from shaping content to attract advertising during the commitment period.

Group blogs that sell advertising can be hybrids of professional and amateur journalism. The bloggers in some ways resemble reporters employed by a newspaper, which in turn produces and sells their work. Unlike newspaper reporters, however, the participating bloggers do not work full-time under the newpaper's supervision. Although newspapers also get content from those who are not full-time employees, such as freelancers, wire services and readers, publication of this material is more likely to be subject to final review by the publisher than is the work of co-bloggers. The legal implications of these various relationships are explored below.

Advertising may affect blogs' content. News reports indicate that "many companies are wary of putting their brand on such a new and unpredictable medium." For example, Cendant pulled ads from Gawker, possibly because the site had gotten "too naughty" for the sponsor. Sponsors also might be offended by politics and political incorrectness.

Amateur journalists, in effect, may be able to capitalize their advertising revenue by selling their blogs. The important question in such transactions is whether the seller will continue to write for the blog or retain editorial control. If the original blog author continues in place after a sale of or investment in the blog, the blog's value would depend partly on the present value of past revenues, discounted for such risks to future revenues as the author's health and reputation for quality. The blog's value also would depend partly on projected expenses, consisting mostly of wages to the author. Given the small capital investment necessary for a blog, the question becomes what a purchaser or investor could contribute other than authorship that might justify a return on investment. The buyer might sell its promotion and back office services in exchange for a share in the profits. The buyer may also assume some risks of the author's health or market uncertainty in exchange for a profit share.

The buyer in this scenario is a type of risk arbitrager who offers the seller the difference between what the risk costs the blogger and what it costs the specialist, who is in a better position to diversify risk.

The buyer or investor, however, must find some way to enforce the deal given the inherent mobility of human capital, because when the original author has sold his equity stake he may be tempted to quit or shirk. More importantly, the contract has to be designed to provide incentives as it lifts the fear of failure. The sale or investment scenario is more complicated if the buyer expects the seller to leave the blog. The seller might not be able to deliver anything to the buyer in this situation other than a trade name and web address. Although the seller can license rights to any copyrighted content, the material is unlikely to be worth much on this basis because it has been available for free and is time-sensitive. However, the blog's web address and back blog posts may have some continuing value as they will continue to attract viewers and therefore potential advertising revenue.

Similar issues arise in the sale of any service business such as a professional firm, including the constructive sale of the business that occurs when a partner retires. The retiring partner arguably should be entitled to a share of the value that inheres in physical assets, client lists, and the organization of the firm, but not the continuing partners' personal reputations. Courts traditionally have assumed that a continuing professional firm has little, if any, value.

Although this assumption may make little sense as applied to modern, heavily institutionalized, professional firms, it makes more sense for a blog that is little more than the writer's individual contributions.

A substitute blogger might expect to capture something like the same audience if he had been introduced and vetted by the previous owner and mimics his writing style. But the buyer gains little advantage over other mimics from having bought the blog. In addition to selling advertising, amateur journalists can do public broadcasting-type "pledge drives." Blog donors may resemble contributors to nonprofits who would want some assurance that their donations would be used for the intended purpose—that is, to support the blog's particular views or specialty.

Unlike a typical large bureaucratic nonprofit, which may need to enlist state investigation and enforcement powers, the individual blogger's reputation might provide adequate incentives for quality and honesty. On the other hand, the donations may resemble commercial advertising to the extent that the donors are seeking a more tangible return, such as links to their blogs. This Chapter's analysis shows that amateur journalists have incentives that range widely across the commercial-noncommercial spectrum, and that these incentives are changing as new business opportunities become available. Even if blogging becomes more commercial, the supply side of blogging is likely to remain diverse. Some amateurs may be able to compete effectively with professional media.

Others may value their self-expression more highly and either refuse to sell advertising or carefully screen advertisers for compatibility with their content. All bloggers are likely to have some incentive and, via their "day" jobs, the ability to maintain a voice that differs from that of professionals.

Moreover, blogs are likely to continue to capitalize on the medium's inherently low startup costs by beginning modestly with no clear business objectives, and then adapting to changing circumstances, including the blog's popularity. This likelihood suggests that, though the business model is evolving, amateur and professional journalism are unlikely to merge.

Social Benefits: Blogging as Decentralized Knowledge

Blogs may have significant social benefits by enabling millions of people to contribute to the general store of knowledge in ways they could not do with higher costs of public access. The following subsections summarize these benefits.

- Exploiting Individual Expertise

Blogs provide a way to gather what F.A. Hayek referred to as individuals' "knowledge of the particular circumstances of time and place." Hayek viewed market prices as the mechanism for communicating this dispersed information. But blogs can make individuals' special information available to decision makers in a way that Hayek did not envision—without a price mechanism and able to inform nonmarket political decisions by government agents and voters. Blogs facilitate a new relationship between experts and the public. Bloggers can communicate their expertise directly to the public rather than simply by filling in quotes in articles basically shaped by mainstream journalists who are experts as writers but usually not in their subjects.

Moreover, blogs can focus on categories of specialty knowledge that would be too narrow for a conventional source. The expertise can be as small as the working conditions at a particular firm, users' experience with a particular product, or, as in the CBS News "Rathergate" incident, the capabilities of particular typewriters.

- Google as a Price Mechanism

The communication of information through blogs differs from the price mechanism that Hayek and Adam Smith emphasized. Blogs are deliberate expressions of opinion by individuals that can be aggregated technologically and used by voters and centralized decision makers. By contrast, markets provide a decentralized coordinating mechanism that operates without individuals' conscious intervention. People give this mechanism the information it needs not by expressing opinions deliberately, as with blogs, but unintentionally by trying to buy as low and sell as high as they can.

Blogs, however, also operate in part through a market-type mechanism. Search engines make blogs accessible in the Web's vastness.

A search on a popular subject might retrieve thousands of results, of which the researcher can read only a few. Google and other search engines solve this problem by ranking search results according to how many other web pages have linked the result.

This ranking resembles an unconscious market mechanism in which the "price" is links. Like buyers and sellers in the market, the linkers, though simply seeking to maximize their own welfare, unintentionally inform the market of the web posts that are most "valuable"—that is, most worthy of being ranked high in a search result.

- Bloggers as Benevolent Parasites

Blogs provide a benefit through their symbiotic relationship with conventional forms of mass communication. For example, a common blogging practice is "risking" articles in the professional media. As Internet FAQ Archives defines it, "risking" means [a] point-by-point refutation of a blog entry or... news story. A really stylish risking is witty, logical, sarcastic and ruthlessly factual.... Named after Robert Fiske, a British journalist who was a frequent (and deserving) early target of such treatment.

As this definition's reference to "ruthlessly factual" indicates, risking often refers to a detailed dissection of a work. This practice has significant ramifications for the application of copyright law.

Probably the most famous example of risking, aside from the exposure of the Fiske story, is bloggers' role in uncovering the CBS News fraud regarding the Texas Air National Guard service of President George W. Bush. Blogs' commentary role includes not only detailed "risking," but also posting on specific aspects of the subject work. This "parasitic" function of blogs suggests a possible long-term equilibrium in the relationship between amateur and professional journalists. Bloggers can be analogized to remora, a type of fish that cleans host fish such as sharks. Professional media sources, by acting as "sharks," help aggregate as well as present information. Major media sources like the New York Times are worthwhile targets for risking bloggers.

Professional media sources therefore may be more accurate than individual blogs not just because their own resources make them trustworthy, but also for the information their blog "following" provides. This outcome is comparable to the market efficiency function of securities analysts: because more widely traded stocks are followed by more analysts, their prices reflect more information, and so are more efficient, than less actively traded stocks. Blogs ironically may actually increase the value of at least some conventional media sources rather than just siphon audience share.

The "remora" function of blogs also might create a network effect that could affect competition among professional media sources. The largest conventional media sources may acquire extra value by attracting networks of bloggers. Some smaller organizations that do not attract networks, on the other hand, may be unable to compete effectively with either their larger rivals or low-cost bloggers.

A more skeptical view of blogs would question the "benevolence" of their parasitic action. Given the political antagonism among bloggers and between amateur and professional journalists, bloggers often may seem to be merely attacking rather than fleshing out information.

But such attacks can be useful in at least indicating the existence of another perspective. Also, if the attack contains misinformation, other bloggers more politically aligned with the original journalist can correct it through blog posts, comments, and trackbacks.

In other words, bloggers have their own "remora." Thus, even the most opinionated blogs have an information function. To be sure, opinionated blogs may be less useful than more objective blogs, other things being equal. But other things may not be equal because blogs' points of view may affect the supply. To the extent that self-expression is an important motivator of blogs, it might be seen as part of the "price" readers pay for the service. If blogs could somehow be made more objective, the remaining blogs might individually be more valuable, but we might have less aggregate information available.

- Interactivity

Web-only distribution enables blogs to be interactive with their readers through the comment and trackback features. Each entry can therefore generate a surrounding body of correcting and extending commentary and references. Professional media also are moving in this direction by offering blogs on their websites. However, professional media's potential for interactivity is limited by their need to prevent free web products from cannibalizing sales of print and fee-based web products. Amateur blogs do not usually have related products whose market they must protect.

Blogs might come to interact not only with each other, but also with professional journalists as part of their symbiotic "remora" relationship discussed earlier. Professional media can use their investigative resources to assemble stories that would be out of amateurs' reach. Amateur journalists can flesh out the story with additional information and points of view.

The challenge in promoting cooperation between professional and amateur journalists is that this cooperation requires some tradeoff of the strong property rights necessary to justify large investments in information against opportunities to leverage the value of the information by networking with amateurs. For example, professionals could promote collaboration with amateurs by disclosing their sources, analogous to the disclosure of code by the authors of open source software. The professional press might post transcripts of interviews on their websites, thereby enabling amateurs to offer alternative interpretations. They also might give up some ability to sell access to archives by keeping their stories live on their websites, while enhancing amateur researchers' ability to interact with their information.

- Lack of Professional Constraints or Biases

Although amateur journalists have been disparaged for the lack of "bricks-and-mortar" operations, these investments involve potential costs as well as benefits. On the benefit side, investments in hard assets can be viewed as a kind of "bond" in the sense that the assets' value depends on the firm's ability to sell its products, which in turn depends on the firm's reputation. A newspaper that becomes unreliable may, in effect, forfeit this bond. The firm therefore has an incentive to hire staff and develop internal norms that help ensure the accuracy of the product.

On the other hand, a potential cost of the bricks-and-mortar model is that the staff the firm hires to ensure quality and accuracy may seek to impose its own views both in what they write and the subjects they choose to cover or emphasize, even if these choices do not serve the organization's interest.

In other words, the professional media is subject to the agency costs, or conflict between nonowner agents and principals, that afflict all firms. For example, the controversial New York Times reporter Judith Miller described the "convent of The New York Times, a convent with its own theology and its own catechism." Professional journalists may have common biases because of similarities of training and predilection, as well as a desire to wield influence. Although surveys indicate that these biases reduce demand for professional journalism by consumers seeking greater accuracy, competition does not reduce the biases because agents of other professional news organizations share the same biases.

Moreover, media firms' costs of reducing journalists' discretion or otherwise monitoring them may exceed the benefits in terms of greater accuracy. Amateur journalists, therefore, may improve accuracy simply because they are amateurs and do not share professionals' biases.

This reality does not mean individual amateurs themselves are unbiased. Indeed they may be more biased and shrill than professionals, who at least are constrained by professional norms of objectivity. But amateur journalism's advantage is in providing many disparate views and a distinct alternative to professional journalism.

Whether amateur journalism as a whole is slanted toward the political right, no hierarchy filters out opposing views. Moreover, if amateur journalism is tilted right, this condition may be because left-leaning amateurs have, in general, less incentive to express themselves because their views already are appearing in professional media. This explanation would mesh with the notion of amateur journalism offering an alternative perspective.

Social Costs

Blogs may have social costs as well as social benefits. Like all speech, blogs can cause emotional harm, cause reputational damage, infringe property and privacy rights, and defraud. The particular problem with blogs is that they are not intermediated--they are simply individuals talking, amplified by the megaphone of the Web.

Regulation, however, also has potential social costs. Amateur journalists' private benefits discussed earlier are tenuous enough that even minimal regulation could significantly reduce the diversity and social benefits of blogs. Because individual bloggers do not internalize the social benefits of their work, the amount of amateur journalism may be socially suboptimal even in the absence of regulation. Moreover, markets and extralegal constraints can address many problems of blogs.

Finally, even if some regulation of amateur journalism is theoretically warranted, the regulation that is actually adopted may be inefficient because of the public choice considerations discussed. This Chapter will consider some categories of social costs and how regulation might balance the costs and benefits of regulating amateur journalism.

- Noise

The absence of "checks and balances" increases the dissemination of low-quality information, or "noise." Misinformation might cause misallocation of resources. Also, if readers cannot easily distinguish the good from the bad, readers may shun all blogs. This potential reaction suggests that even some amateur journalists might welcome blog regulation.

Amateur speech is not, however, necessarily less accurate than professional speech for lack of intermediation. First, the individual working in his pajamas that Jonathan Klein envisions can possibly produce high-quality reporting without internal monitors and fact-checkers. The Internet and Google now make a vast array of information easily available even to lone amateurs.

More importantly, many bloggers have an advantage as specialists in competing with the generalist journalists who work for conventional media. Journalists are generally trained mainly in getting facts and analysis from others who are either direct observers or experts.

In fields like law or finance that require special training, journalists often have to call on experts. But bloggers are themselves the experts—indeed, they may be the ones the professional journalists call for information. Unlike professional journalists, amateurs can focus on the stories they know rather than reporting on everything that is newsworthy.

Second, the relevant perspective from which to analyse regulation of blogging is not an individual offending blog, but the general set of blogs—either all blogs intended for general distribution, or blogs within particular communities or specialties. Thus, Richard Posner questions whether the risk of bad information is greater for blogs as a whole than for the professional media. Even if bloggers individually are not as accurate as a professional media source, they can be easily corrected by other blogs and by comments and trackbacks.

The accuracy difference between the professional media and blogs, then, might be viewed as the difference between "horizontal" checking by other bloggers and "vertical" checking within the hierarchy of the conventional media firm. But even this distinction blurs at the edges. The "remora" function of blogs discussed earlier adds a horizontal dimension to the professional media. Conversely, group blogs arguably add a vertical dimension to amateur journalism. Although uncoordinated horizontal checking may leave mistakes, widely followed blogs will tend to be corrected quickly and completely.

On the other hand, vertical checking by professional media may be constrained by biases that pervade a particular organization or profession, or by individuals who have important roles in the hierarchy.

For example, the desire to get an important story to the public, and the strong belief in the story and reporters by key people in the editorial process, may have contributed to CBS News' embarrassing failure to spot seemingly obvious problems in the "Rathergate" affair.

- Effect on Professional Journalists

Competition by amateurs also arguably might reduce responsible reporting by the professional media. Ben Bradlee would no longer have the luxury of insisting that Woodward and Bernstein carefully check their facts before going public with Watergate if he risked being "scooped" by amateurs. When "pajama bloggers" who need not answer to an editor can rush stories onto millions of computer screens, professionals might abandon their standards in order to compete.

This suggests that the investments necessary to produce high-quality news entail positive social externalities that a democratic society needs for its political well-being but that the market will not support given intense competition by zero-overhead bloggers.

Richard Posner responds that "when competition is intense, providers of a service are forced to give the consumer what he or she wants, not what they, as proud professionals, think the consumer should want, or more bluntly, what they want." In other words, journalists' demand for professionalism may be no more than any guild or carters effort to, as Adam Smith pointed out, keep wages artificially high and output artificially low.

This Chapter's analysis suggests that news organizations will be able to internalize the costs of high-quality news coverage in an environment of low-cost competitors—that is, a market for high-quality journalism will remain. The network aspect of amateur journalism's "remora" function suggests that the largest news organizations will have an advantage in a world in which professional and amateur journalists coexist.

In order to differentiate themselves, professional media would have stronger reasons than ever to provide a high-quality, well-researched product in order to offer some value over that which amateurs provide for free.

- Harmful True Information

The self-correcting characteristic of blogs does not mitigate the effect of harmful true information. Readers may reward rather than punish amateur journalists for disseminating copyrighted information or infringing privacy rights, and such information may be amplified rather than disparaged for its harmful characteristics. Even an obscure blogger can cause significant damage by placing harmful information in the public domain. Legal remedies may be necessary to constrain amateur journalists in these situations.

Amateur journalists, of course, are subject to general laws protecting privacy and property and restricting pornography. The question is whether the rise of blogs and amateur journalism requires special regulation. Special regulation perhaps is not necessary for amateurs as distinguished from professional journalists and media organizations. Although the professional media may be more subject to extralegal sanctions such as reputational penalties, it also may be less likely to be deterred by fines, damages, or the extralegal sanctions.

Regulation of amateur journalists thus requires identifying specific contexts in which:

- Existing legal and extralegal constraints are likely to be significantly less effective for amateur journalists than for professional journalists and other actors;
- Regulating amateurs does not present a risk of over-deterring socially beneficial conduct.

The test might be satisfied by conduct that clearly abuses property or privacy rights and yet is not disciplined by social norms or future dealings between the bloggers and the victims or victim class. For example, the blogger who allegedly revealed Apple trade secrets may have gained credibility and readers by revealing the secrets. On the other hand, regulating the conduct would not likely deter speech by ensnaring unsuspecting lawbreakers.

- Political and Social Discourse

Cass Sunstein has expressed a concern that the Internet may weaken general interest intermediaries and increase people's ability to "wall themselves off" from opinions they do not like. Indeed, a recent study showed that during the 2004 election conservative and liberal blogs tended to link more within their separate communities and focused on different news articles, topics, and political figures.

James D. Miller, responding to Sunstein, argues that the Internet has the potential to stimulate interaction because filters can encourage people to read specific material in journals that they generally disagree with. In other words, the Internet may decrease the costs both of accessing and filtering diverse viewpoints. The Internet's overall effect on political discourse therefore is unclear. Moreover, even if the Internet currently does have a "walling off" effect, regulation does not necessarily solve the problem in a way that prevents inhibition of efficient technological evolution.

Posner responds that "when competition is intense, providers of a service are forced to give the consumer what he or she wants, not what they, as proud professionals, think the consumer should want, or more bluntly, what they want." In other words, journalists' demand for professionalism may be no more than any guild or carters effort to, as Adam Smith pointed out, keep wages artificially high and output artificially low.

This Chapter's analysis suggests that news organizations will be able to internalize the costs of high-quality news coverage in an environment of low-cost competitors—that is, a market for high-quality journalism will remain. The network aspect of amateur journalism's "remora" function suggests that the largest news organizations will have an advantage in a world in which professional and amateur journalists coexist. In order to differentiate themselves, professional media would have stronger reasons than ever to provide a high-quality, well-researched product in order to offer some value over that which amateurs provide for free.

HARMFUL TRUE INFORMATION

The self-correcting characteristic of blogs does not mitigate the effect of harmful true information. Readers may reward rather than punish amateur journalists for disseminating copyrighted information or infringing privacy rights, and such information may be amplified rather than disparaged for its harmful characteristics. Even an obscure blogger can cause significant damage by placing harmful information in the public domain. Legal remedies may be necessary to constrain amateur journalists in these situations.

Amateur journalists, of course, are subject to general laws protecting privacy and property and restricting pornography. The question is whether the rise of blogs and amateur journalism requires special regulation. Special regulation perhaps is not necessary for amateurs as distinguished from professional journalists and media organizations. Although the professional media may be more subject to extralegal sanctions such as reputational penalties, it also may be less likely to be deterred by fines, damages, or the extralegal sanctions.

Regulation of amateur journalists thus requires identifying specific contexts in which:

- Existing legal and extralegal constraints are likely to be significantly less effective for amateur journalists than for professional journalists and other actors;
- Regulating amateurs does not present a risk of over-deterring socially beneficial conduct.

The test might be satisfied by conduct that clearly abuses property or privacy rights and yet is not disciplined by social norms or future dealings between the bloggers and the victims or victim class. For example, the blogger who allegedly revealed Apple trade secrets may have gained credibility and readers by revealing the secrets. On the other hand, regulating the conduct would not likely deter speech by ensnaring unsuspecting lawbreakers.

- Political and Social Discourse

Cass Sunstein has expressed a concern that the Internet may weaken general interest intermediaries and increase people's ability to "wall themselves off" from opinions they do not like. Indeed, a recent study showed that during the 2004 election conservative and liberal blogs tended to link more within their separate communities and focused on different news articles, topics, and political figures.

James D. Miller, responding to Sunstein, argues that the Internet has the potential to stimulate interaction because filters can encourage people to read specific material in journals that they generally disagree with. In other words, the Internet may decrease the costs both of accessing and filtering diverse viewpoints.

The Internet's overall effect on political discourse therefore is unclear. Moreover, even if the Internet currently does have a "walling off" effect, regulation does not necessarily solve the problem in a way that prevents inhibition of efficient technological evolution.

Alternatives to Regulation

Even if some amateur journalism is socially harmful and not amenable to self-correction, the need for legal regulation depends on the effectiveness of extralegal sanctions in controlling misconduct.

First, individual bloggers have strong reputational incentives to report carefully and truthfully. Although creating a blog is cheap, getting noticed may require bloggers to invest in developing a reputation that will cause others to link to them. They may spend significant time posting stories that gradually work their way up the Internet's attention span, finally being linked by major portal blogs.

Given low entry costs, many blogs will be competing for attention in every reporting niche. Accordingly, a few careless posts that erode the blogger's reputation for fairness and accuracy could abruptly drop the blog back into obscurity.

Second, bloggers can be constrained by informal conduct norms enforced by social disapprobation and psychological sanctions of shame or guilt and the desire for esteem. Norms have been described as social ordering arising outside the legal system. Because bloggers generally derive little direct financial reward from their activity, the reputational effects of norm violations can be significant. Law arguably can encourage the development of norms through its focal point, expressive, signaling, or similar effects. Developing norms that control amateur journalists' behaviour may not be easy. These journalists by definition comprise a vast group of millions of diverse people rather than a well-defined profession. It may be difficult to find a set of principles that amateur journalists generally can agree on and internalize as norms.

Moreover, the self-expression motives of amateur journalists suggest that they will tend to have libertarian views, or at least views incompatible with externally imposed order. The impulses that cause someone to value freedom of expression enough to publish to a small audience without direct compensation are also likely to make these writers resist external constraints. Bloggers' diversity and unruliness could make them especially resistant to efforts to impose norms through law that they have not otherwise internalized.

These considerations are especially relevant given the logistics of regulating the Internet. Individual states cannot easily impose their will on this international medium. U.S. federal law might have some effect, but its legitimacy in imposing norms is undermined by the public choice considerations discussed in the next subpart. Accordingly, the legal system may be unable to devise a coherent set of rules that would have the effect of establishing Internet norms.

Individuals might attempt to spur the development of extralegal norms by proposing informal codes of ethics. Given bloggers' diversity and libertarian tendencies, it is not surprising that they widely rebuked a New York Times writer who suggested that bloggers needed a code of ethics.

Even if it were feasible to develop norms for amateur journalists, it may not be desirable. An important social benefit of amateur journalists is that they are not subject to professional norms and constraints. In devising extralegal constraints, as with legal regulation, one must control the costs of amateur journalism in a way that does not sacrifice its benefits.

Examining an attempt to define a code of ethics indicates the relevant problems. A proposed "Bloggers' Code of Ethics" resembles a Boy Scout's laundry list of seemingly unobjectionable principles, including accuracy, honesty, "never" plagiarizing, respecting privacy and avoiding harm to subjects, and disclosing conflicts.

Some objectives, like honesty and accuracy, can be achieved through blogs' inherent capacity to self-correct. Others, like respecting subjects' privacy, are generally admirable, but also hint at the sort of self-indulgent, guild-like "professionalism" that Posner criticized. This might constrain amateur journalism's socially beneficial role in supplementing more constrained professionals.

Many of the remaining principles are not easily adapted to blogs. For example, amateurs who see themselves as spreading news and views rather than seeking academic or financial credit may see little reason not to plagiarize professionals. Those who take advertising and other compensation from sponsors with similar views may not be able to see the sort of clear conflict-of-interest line that can be applied to the supposedly neutral professional press. More fundamentally, the sort of standards that apply to the professional press may not be relevant to millions of bloggers publicizing their personal views and information. An attempt to apply such a standard to bloggers therefore may seem to be nothing more than an effort to limit the professionals' competition.

This may explain some of the negative reaction to a call for blogging ethics in the New York Times, particularly given the general political antipathy between bloggers and the professional media discussed.Although a single law or ethics code may not create blogging norms, some types of norms might arise in the same Hayekian way that blogs produce accurate information.

Amateurs can publish criticisms and alternative proposals, which can achieve ranking dominance in search engines, or individual proposals can evolve through comments and amendments, analogous to a wiki.

Given blogs' diversity, multiple codes likely will develop for particular categories, such as for academics and lawyers. Some specific rules might develop to suit blogs generally. Norms might develop against deleting or editing posts in a way that discourages discussion, or against blocking comments and trackbacks in a manner that defeats the interactivity benefits inherent in amateur journalism. Evolution likely will produce better-fitting rules than one-size-fits-all federal regulation, particularly at this early stage in the development of amateur journalism.

THE PUBLIC CHOICE OF BLOGGING

An analysis of efficient regulation of amateur journalism requires an understanding of the political forces that might subvert even the best-intentioned regulatory initiatives. In particular, any new type of business or technology threatens jobs and status that depend on existing businesses and technologies. The threat is obvious when millions of moonlighters can give away what the conventional media has been charging for, and without being subject to professional constraints.

James Miller has discussed three areas, in which blogs are particularly vulnerable to attack by incumbent professionals--campaign finance reform, libel law, and copyright. In each area, professional journalists can be expected to align politically against bloggers in order to protect their competitive advantage by lobbying for distinctions between "professional" journalists and "nonprofessional" bloggers.

Professional journalists also might argue for more liability under copyright and libel laws. Although such liability would apply to both professionals and amateurs, professionals are likely to have more legal and financial resources to defend themselves against infringement claims, and more intellectual property to protect. Professional journalists are likely to be able to out-lobby bloggers even if the latter are numerically a larger group. The professional media raises lobbying funds as a byproduct of its business: activities. Moreover, professional journalists are a particularly potent political force because they can lobby not only by financially supporting politicians who advocate for them, but also by directly molding public opinion. Indeed, the professional media frequently have portrayed bloggers in negative terms. For example, in addition to the famous "pajamas" quote, bloggers have been characterized as "partisan operatives whose agendas are as ideological as they come."

This characterization of bloggers as having a conservative political orientation obviously may be significant in encouraging Democrats to support limitations on blogs. This was evident in a vote on a proposed "Online Freedom of Speech Act" that would have excluded "communications over the Internet" from the definition of "public communication" in the Federal Election Campaign Act. The House was attempting to act prior to the release of final regulations that threatened to regulate Internet speech, including blogs. The measure needed a two-thirds vote to get accelerated consideration by the Senate but fell short because three-quarters of Democrats opposed it. Although Democrats might have been generally inclined to support a free-speech measure, liberal interest groups and a strong New York Times editorial opposed this one.

The interest group aspects of distinguishing amateur and professional journalism also apply to constitutional law. In particular, the depth of constitutional protection might depend on its breadth. Professional journalists thus stand to lose not only business, but also legal leverage, by the advent of the amateurs. As Frederick Schauer has pointed out, "[a] Supreme Court unwilling to distinguish among the lone pamphleteer, the blogger, and the full-time reporter for the New York Times is far less likely to grant special privileges to pamphleteers and bloggers than it is, as it has, to grant privileges to no one." In other words, legal privileges for journalists may be a zero-sum game--the broader the availability, the weaker the protection.

Several features of this activity should be emphasized. First, this Chapter applies to low-cost Internet postings rather than to print or more costly media. The ease of entry into amateur journalism implies a diversity and breadth of information and views that provides significant balance and accuracy at the aggregate level, even if individual actors may be careless or biased.

Second, the analysis concerns reporting or expression of opinions that is not the reporter's main income-producing activity. Amateur journalists typically have weaker incentives to engage in the activity than professionals, and therefore may be more easily deterred by regulation.

Third, amateur journalism involves one or more of several types of interactivity such as comments, links, and trackbacks, and is subject to the page-ranking mechanisms of modern search engines. Like the ease of entry, this provides self-correction, and therefore accuracy, at the aggregate level. Although blog features also can be adopted by professional journalists, they may be constrained by the need to protect investments in intellectual property.

Fourth, even if some regulation of blogs might theoretically be warranted, any laws that are actually adopted will be the product of interest group pressure. Professional journalists have a strong incentive to protect themselves against this powerful and emerging competition, and therefore to lobby against laws that relegate amateur journalists to a lower regulatory status. This counsels caution in proposing regulatory reforms of amateur journalism.

REGULATION OF AMATEUR JOURNALISM

This Part applies the above analysis to specific legal issues regarding amateur journalism. It focuses on the tradeoff between the social costs and benefits of regulation. On the one hand, amateur journalism raises concerns about lack of intermediation and market checks on harmful blogs. On the other hand, regulators should recognize the desirability of maintaining amateurs' easy access to the public sphere, the risk of overdeterrence because of amateurs' low-powered incentives, and the constraints inherent in bloggers' need to establish and maintain a reputation to gain attention on the Web.

The considerations discussed in this Part apply mainly when the regulatory concern is with the accuracy or balance of information. Given the attributes of amateur journalism discussed, extensive regulation may be both unnecessary and counter-productive because the proliferation and freedom of amateur journalists itself addresses inaccuracy and bias. Throughout this Part, the objective is not to recommend specific laws or approaches. That would require not only significantly more analysis than is possible in this overview, but also more detailed assumptions about the nature of amateur journalism than are warranted at this early stage.

Instead, this chapter recommends some considerations that should matter in addressing the legal issues amateur journalism raises based on the above general analysis of this activity.

APPLICATION OF SPECIAL PRESS PRIVILEGES

Professional journalists have a privilege under some state laws and, possibly, under the First Amendment, against being compelled in court to name sources. This privilege helps journalists to get information, and thereby bolsters the free press as a check on government abuse. The privilege was widely discussed in connection with a special prosecutor seeking testimony from reporters in his investigation of the leak of classified information that

Valerie Plame was a CIA agent. The question for present purposes is the extent to which amateur journalists should have any such privilege. This issue goes to the heart of the distinction between amateur and professional journalists. If amateurs are likely to contribute inaccurate or otherwise low-value speech, society should not encourage their activities by making it easier for them to get information.

On the other hand, if, as argued earlier, amateurs are subject to reputational and other sanctions and supplement the information and views of professional journalists, the law should encourage their activities by giving them privileges and protections similar to those of professional journalists.

The journalist's privilege directly implicates the public choice considerations discussed earlier. Extending the privilege to include amateurs would arguably weaken it as to both professionals and amateurs.

This applies both to constitutional arguments and to efforts to enact a federal journalist's privilege. Journalists' only political hope for an absolute privilege may be a bright line between amateurs and the professional media, even if the better policy result is a weaker privilege that extends to both categories. A leading case on this issue is Apple Computer, Inc. v. Doe 1, which denied a blogger a protective order that would have prevented him from having to disclose sources in a trade secret suit brought by Apple. The blogger claimed he was privileged as a journalist.

The court denied the motion, noting that "[d]efining what is a 'journalist' has become more complicated as the variety of media has expanded." It quoted a dictionary definition of "journalist" as "a writer who aims at a mass audience." The court, however, said it need not decide whether the blogger "fits the definition of a journalist, reporter, blogger, or anything else" because "there is no license conferred on anyone to violate valid criminal laws."

If the court had recognized a journalist's privilege under these facts, the movant may have been held entitled to its protection. The blogger described himself as having "co-founded the first dedicated Apple Power Book User Group... in the United States... has contributed articles to MacWEEK, MacWorld, MacAddict, MacPower(Japan)... [and] written chapters for The Macintosh Bible." Some elements of the definition quoted above suggest the need for a "mass" or "public" audience. The movant was certainly more than a casual contributor. But this case leaves the question whether the privilege should be available to someone who blogs only to express himself.

Spurred largely by the Plame controversy, Congress is considering a federal shield law, the Free Flow of Information Act, that would protect journalists from revealing sources except under designated circumstances.

The bill would apply to a person who, for financial gain or livelihood, is engaged in gathering, preparing, collecting, photographing, recording, writing, editing, reporting, or publishing news or information as a salaried employee of or independent contractor for a newspaper, news journal, news agency, book publisher, press association, wire service, radio or television station, network, magazine, Internet news service, or other professional medium or agency which has as 1 of its regular functions the processing and researching of news or information intended for dissemination to the public.

Congressmen have expressed reservations about applying the bill to bloggers. Senator John Cornyn said he doubted "whether the proposed shield law should apply to the 'Internet blogger who has a cell phone with a camera, and maybe a laptop computer, and can publish with equal ease as a journalist,'" and Senator Richard Lugar, the bill's primary sponsor, said "bloggers should 'probably not' be considered journalists." The most important question in deciding whether to apply the journalist's privilege to bloggers is whether bloggers should be deemed to serve an information function similar to that of journalists.

As stressed throughout this Chapter, although individual bloggers lack the checks and balances of journalists, amateur journalism as a whole is capable of self-correction that can produce equivalent accuracy. Moreover, the openness of blogs avoids the biases that can infect professional journalism.

On the other hand, these considerations might not support the extraordinary protection of shield laws and constitutional privileges. Indeed, they may cut the other way. As long as amateur journalism thrives, it may be unnecessary to offer privileges to individual bloggers. Indeed, even a professional journalist's privilege may be unnecessary in a world that includes bloggers.

Moreover, extending the journalist's privilege too broadly may involve the special danger of broadly disabling investigation of harmful or criminal behaviour. Thus, it may be necessary to ensure that the privilege is available only to those who are subject to strong professional norms and reputational sanctions, even if this distinction risks reinforcing professional biases.

Shield law politics also matters in evaluating potential legal approaches. Republicans, though apparently reluctant to protect them through a shield law, have urged strong protection of bloggers from the election laws. In the case of the election laws, the relevant speech may favour a particular viewpoint.

However, with respect to the shield laws no one can know who might be called on to provide information to prosecutors. This disparity of treatment indicates that the regulation of amateur journalists may be at least partly content-oriented rather than based on the method of speech. Whether this disparity raises First Amendment concerns, one should keep in mind these public choice considerations when considering how to approach legal regulation of amateur journalism.

These political and policy considerations suggest that the best result would be no federal law, leaving any protection to the laboratory of state law. Most states already have shield laws, which may or may not apply to blogs. National uniformity is unnecessary. The applicable state shield law can supply a default contractual term in dealings between the media and the source. A source who wants anonymity can go to journalists who work in a state with a strong state shield law.

Without federal statutory law or constitutional constraints, states can decide on their preferred tradeoffs between the accuracy costs of protecting sources and the increased information that results from protection. Because the Internet facilitates quick dissemination of news from any source, the national interest in whether a particular state has a shield law is minimal except to the extent that newspapers based in a particular jurisdiction have a special role in gathering and disseminating particular news.

A related question is whether amateur journalists are entitled to any extra constitutional protection afforded by the "Press Clause" of the First Amendment. Paul Horwitz argues for protecting blogs under an "institutional" approach to the First Amendment that asks whether blogs play a role in furthering democracy that is comparable to that of the "Fourth Estate" of professional journalism. Horwitz reasons that this approach calls for an examination of the norms and characteristics of blogging as an institution.

The courts might give bloggers an extra journalist-type level of constitutional protection only to the extent that they participate in the collective accuracy-producing process discussed earlier, as by enabling comments and trackbacks, and adhere to the evolving accuracy-related norms of blogging. This approach might, however, encourage the development of professional-type constraints on the activities of amateur journalists that reduce the benefits of amateur journalism in avoiding the professionals' biases.

This discussion is intended only to indicate considerations that should be brought to bear in regulating blogs--in this case, determining whether amateurs should have the same privileges as professional journalists. These considerations involve balancing the lack of constraints on individual blogs against the information function of blogs in the aggregate. The difficulty of arriving at the proper balance across the vast range of blogs, together with the politics of regulating amateur journalism, suggest the propriety of a state rather than federal solution to the problem.

Election Laws

Campaign finance and other election laws may implicate considerations closely related to accuracy of information in assuring presentation of a diversity of views.

Just as truth more likely emerges from many sources than from a single outlet, political decisions more likely reflect voters' preferences if voters and candidates can speak freely. Ability to speak, in turn, often depends on the ability to finance dissemination of one's views.

The application of the election laws to bloggers has been particularly controversial since the 2004 U.S. presidential election because of the perception that most bloggers supported the Republicans and affiliated causes.

Candidates might skirt campaign finance restrictions by coordinating with sympathetic bloggers. On the other hand, applying the election laws to millions of amateur journalists may require invasive regulation that could constrain amateurs' public access.

The Federal Election Commission (FEC) attempted to avoid the issue by broadly exempting Internet activities. These exemptions were invalidated in Shays v. FEC. FEC Commissioner Bradley Smith then elicited a strong reaction when he suggested that political bloggers may be subject to the McCain-Feingold campaign finance law.

The main issue here concerns the "media exemption" from the definition of "expenditure" in the Federal Election Campaign Act:

The Term "Expenditure" does not Include—

- Any news story, commentary, or editorial distributed through the facilities of any broadcasting station, newspaper, magazine, or other periodical publication....

Blogs may or may not be included in this definition depending on the emphasis on regularity in defining "periodical." Blogs raise at least three issues for regulation of campaign finance. First, political campaigns might coordinate with bloggers who link to campaign websites, thereby increasing the leverage of campaign expenditures. Second, corporations might establish and fund blogs and argue that the expenditures are excluded under the above provision.

Third, voters may not be able to determine when bloggers are paid for their opinions. Though this issue is potentially a problem in the professional media, it is harder to solve when readers must sort through millions of blogs.

One election law expert suggests that bloggers "should have to include on each blog page view a statement that the writing was paid for by the applicable candidate or committee."

As a policy matter, the election laws are supposed to address "corruption" of the political process by those with easy access to money. As a potential conduit of political money, blogs arguably are part of this problem. However, amateur journalists also can be viewed as part of the solution. When viewed on an aggregate rather than individual basis, the participation of many amateurs in political debate makes it harder for money to dominate.

From this standpoint, any regulation must not discourage the proliferation of true political blogs. Requiring disclosures or imposing other restrictions and sanctions easily could reduce both the number and the diversity of political bloggers. Most political bloggers are motivated by the desire to express themselves rather than to make money through advertising or by selling their expertise. They therefore generally may prefer not blogging to taking a significant risk of liability, paying for legal advice, or spending significant time complying with the law. Those who are not deterred may be a self-selected group with particularly strong views or links to campaigns. The market can solve some specific problems of coordination and bias even without regulation.

The large number of bloggers and low entry barriers to amateur journalism will guarantee that there are bloggers on all sides of political issues with significant self-expression incentives to expose cheaters. The risk of reputational harm may be enough to constrain the more influential bloggers, who also have the most reputation to lose, from damaging their credibility by maintaining excessive or secret connections with political campaigns.

These general considerations enable an evaluation of the FEC's recently proposed regulations of Internet activities, including blogging. An important issue the FEC grappled with is how the regulations should apply to corporate blogs. In general, little justification exists for restricting corporate contributions based on the need to constrain corporate "corruption" of the political process or agency costs within the firm.

Indeed, the real reason for regulating corporate campaign contributions is to protect corporations from "shakedowns." Blogs further complicate regulation of corporate campaign activities. Given the low-level incentives of many political bloggers, regulating" corporate" blogs could silence these voices and thereby give more power to, for example, large nonprofit groups that so far are unregulated.

The FEC's final rules indicate a recognition of these costs of regulating blogs. The rules clearly exempt Internet campaign activities that involve "uncompensated personal services," "regardless of who owns the equipment and services" that the individual uses. This broad exemption avoids several questions that were raised by proposed rules that turned on whether the blogger was working "independently" and on who owned the computer on which she worked.

As with the other issues discussed in this Part, this analysis is intended only to indicate the considerations relevant to regulating amateur journalism. In particular, with respect to the campaign finance laws, one must keep in mind that proliferation of blogs may be part of the solution to any supposed "corruption" rather than part of the problem.

Media Ownership Restrictions

FCC limits on media ownership are intended to prevent undue industry concentration and ensure a diversity of viewpoints in every market. The FCC recently tried to rationalize these rules, but ran into a roadblock in Prometheus Radio Project v. FCC.

Regulation of media ownership in local markets is questionable, particularly given the many specialized information sources now available on the Internet, including the rise of blogs.

As Judge Scirica, dissenting in Prometheus, noted: The FCC may want to reconsider how the Internet fits into the traditional concepts of measuring viewpoint diversity, especially the emphasis on local news. By nature, the Internet is uniform everywhere. Its content is not dependent on geographic or metropolitan boundaries. This fact should not undervalue this critical media as an important source for the dissemination of diverse information. In this respect, new modes to characterize diversity may be required. The Internet allows a dentist in Iraq to post a weblog with daily entries and photos from Baghdad for viewing anywhere in the world.

As with the campaign finance laws, blogs therefore can provide a solution to the perceived problem of big money corrupting public discourse, as long as they are not discouraged by excessive regulation.

Defamation Law

Amateur journalists, like other speakers, may be held liable for reputational injuries. The main question in this respect concerns the extent to which the First Amendment and laws protecting free speech insulate bloggers from liability and permit them to sue for defamation.

The most important case on many free speech issues relating to bloggers is Gertz v. Robert Welch, Inc., in which the Supreme Court held that states may permit defamation actions by a "private individual" based on negligence or other fault-based standards, whereas public officials or public figures must prove "actual malice." The Court reasoned:

Public officials and public figures usually enjoy significantly greater access to the channels of effective communication and hence have a more realistic opportunity to counteract false statements than private individuals normally enjoy. Private individuals are therefore more vulnerable to injury, and the state interest in protecting them is correspondingly greater.

An individual who decides to seek governmental office must accept certain necessary consequences of that involvement in public affairs. He runs the risk of closer public scrutiny than might otherwise be the case....

Those classed as public figures stand in a similar position For the most part those who attain this status have assumed roles of especial prominence in the affairs of society. Some occupy positions of such persuasive power and influence that they are deemed public figures for all purposes. More commonly, those classed as public figures have thrust themselves to the forefront of particular public controversies in order to influence the resolution of the issues involved. In either event, they invite attention and comment.

Amateur journalism may force rethinking of this distinction. For example, Gertz indicates that a blogger who is prominent among amateur journalists, even if not generally in society, would be deemed as a result of his blogging activities to have "thrust [himself] to the forefront" of a controversy. One who defamed the blogger would then be judged under the lax actual malice standard. Also, the blogger may be deemed to have "effective opportunities for rebuttal" through his blog.

Even amateurs arguably have access to a public forum to "counteract false statements" and have opened themselves up for attack by publicly posting comments. The availability of self-help was emphasized in the leading case on defamation specifically in the blogging context, Doe v. Cahill. The Delaware Supreme Court held that an Internet service provider need not disclose a blogger's identity in a defamation case, stressing the access for rebuttal discussed in Gertz: The internet provides a means of communication where a person wronged by statements of an anonymous poster can respond instantly, can respond to the allegedly defamatory statements on the same site or blog, and thus, can, almost contemporaneously, respond to the same audience that initially read the allegedly defamatory statements. The plaintiff can thereby easily correct any misstatements or falsehoods, respond to character attacks, and generally set the record straight.

This unique feature of internet communications allows a potential plaintiff ready access to mitigate the harm, if any, he has suffered to his reputation as a result of an anonymous defendant's allegedly defamatory statements made on an internet blog or in a chat room. Bloggers' public access, however, may be more apparent than real because it depends not just on being able to plug into the Internet, but also on the informal screening of Google and other search engines that enable readers to find the blog.

The courts might take blog rankings into account for purposes of determining public figure status and damages, or emphasize the blog's importance within a subcommunity that is relevant for reputation purposes. Additional questions remain concerning the extent to which amateur journalists are entitled to the same level of protection from defamation actions that professional journalists receive. The Press Clause of the First Amendment supports special treatment for the "press," but whether amateur journalists would qualify remains unclear.

Dun and Bradstreet, Inc. v. Greenmoss Builders, Inc. raised questions about a possible distinction between the journalists and other reporters that might be relevant to blogs. The Court held that a private individual could recover for defamation in a credit report, applying Gertz to a statement that was not a "matter of public concern." Justice White, concurring in the judgment, clarified that "the First Amendment gives no more protection to the press in defamation suits than it does to others exercising their freedom of speech." On the other hand, Justice Powell's plurality opinion noted that the speech here, like advertising, is hardy and unlikely to be deterred by incidental state regulation. It is solely motivated by the desire for profit, which, we have noted, is a force less likely to be deterred than others. Arguably, the reporting here was also more objectively verifiable than speech deserving of greater protection. In any case, the market provides a powerful incentive to a credit reporting agency to be accurate, since false credit reporting is of no use to creditors. Thus, any incremental "chilling" effect of libel suits would be of decreased significance.

This reasoning suggests that the Court might give a higher level of First Amendment protection to amateur than to professional journalists because the former have less robust self-expression motives for speaking. Distinguishing professional and amateur journalists for purposes of defamation actions may be particularly important in applying state statutes that provide protection from defamation lawsuits if the publisher retracts the allegedly defamatory statement.

For example, in Mathis v. Cannon, the Georgia Supreme Court applied the Georgia retraction statute to a posting on an Internet bulletin board. The statute covered a statement "in a regular issue of the newspaper or other publication." A lower-level Georgia court had held that the statute applied only to print media. The Cannon court noted that the legislature had amended the statute to substitute "other publication" for "magazine or periodical." The court held that a "distinction between media and nonmedia defendants... is difficult to apply and makes little sense when the speech is about matters of public concern" and "fails to accommodate changes in communications and the publishing industry due to the computer and the Internet."

The court also observed that a broad reading of the statute would avoid having to make difficult distinctions about covered publications "at a time when any individual with a computer can become a publisher." The court cited Justice White's concurring opinion in Dun and Bradstreet as to the inappropriateness of distinguishing among types of speakers. The court concluded that its ruling "strikes a balance in favour of 'uninhibited, robust, and wide-open' debate."

Although the above reasoning generally would support giving full protection to all Internet speakers, including bloggers, some of the court's reasoning applies specifically to the retraction context.

The court noted that punitive damages may be fairer against the media than against an individual, who may reach only a small audience and whose retraction would likely target the same small audience.

Finally, the extent of bloggers' liability for comments placed by others on their blogs is unclear. An advantage of blogs is interactivity, particularly blog posts' ability to evolve through comments and trackbacks.

Although professional journalism on the Internet has incorporated similar features, professionals' need to protect intellectual property rights might limit how much interactivity they can provide. Blogs' interactivity, however, may decline if amateurs are held liable for statements by others.

Bloggers and other journalists may have federal protection under section 230 of the Communications Decency Act against defamation liability for publishing material written by others. This provision has been held, for example, to protect America Online (AOL) from liability for statements by others it disseminates.

A blog author may be a "provider or user of an interactive computer service" under the Act who is insulated from liability for a comment on her blog on the ground that the comment is "information provided by another information content provider."

The Act defines an "interactive computer service" as any information service, system, or access software provider that provides or enables computer access by multiple users to a computer server, including specifically a service or system that provides access to the Internet and such systems operated or services offered by libraries or educational institutions.

A blog that enables comments might fall within this definition as an "information service" or, through the blogging front-end, "access software provider" equivalent to an Internet hosting service. In either case, the blog would be "provid[ing] or enabl[ing] computer access by multiple users to a computer server." If a blog is within the definition, the author would be insulated from liability irrespective of knowledge or notice of defamatory content or other facts.

The provision mainly has been applied to AOL-type internet service providers (ISPs) that provide a neutral medium. Broadening the application significantly beyond ISPs raises many questions about the law's potential breadth, and could make significant inroads on state defamation law.

On the other hand, broad application to websites that incorporate comments or postings from third parties arguably would comport with Congress's stated purpose "to preserve the vibrant and competitive free market that presently exists for the Internet and other interactive computer services." Congress clearly sought to prevent this medium from being strangled by the potential for open-ended liability. Imposing extensive responsibility for the accuracy of Internet posts could force firms like AOL, which serve millions of users, to sharply reduce the Internet's freedom. Bloggers who enable comments would not seem to face an equivalent mass-liability problem. But here again one must consider bloggers' low-level incentives.

Although bloggers derive enough value from self-expression to risk liability for their own statements, they may not want to take responsibility for others' statements. If bloggers are not protected, they thus might decline to take the liability risk of enabling comments. This outcome would reduce blogs' interactivity and perhaps even blogs' accuracy because comments enable corrections by disinterested readers. As with application to AOL, this would thwart the Internet's potential as a free and open market for information. A case applying section 230 to bloggers' liability for comments, DiMeo v. Max, is consistent with this analysis. The court dismissed a suit alleging that the plaintiff was defamed by comments written by others on defendant's website. The court held that the website fit the definition of an "interactive computer service." The court also held that defendant did not lose his protection by exercising editorial control over comments on his site because such a result "would deter the very behaviour that Congress sought to encourage."

The point here as elsewhere in this Chapter is not to draw definitive conclusions as to the extent of amateur journalists' liability, but to suggest the considerations that courts should bring to bear in adjudicating legal issues concerning amateur journalists.

Most importantly, courts should take into account the low-level incentives of amateur journalists, and therefore the significant potential deterrent effect of liability. They should also evaluate accuracy in light of the self-corrective and interactive nature of amateur journalism. Finally, courts should assess bloggers' ability to self-protect based on whether they are likely to be noticed and not simply on their access to the Web.

Professional Regulation

Blogs may be subject to regulation as professional practice or advice. Although the following discussion focuses on lawyer licensing, it is generally applicable to other professions, such as medicine or investment advice. Blogs on legal subjects raise potential issues as to whether they:

- Constitute unauthorized law practice by a nonlawyer;
- Might be unauthorized practice in a state other than where the lawyer is licensed;
- May be regulated as impermissible lawyer advertising.

The first two types of problems seem remote with respect to the sort of amateur journalism that is the focus of this Chapter. In the Internet context, the courts have defined legal advice for purposes of unauthorized practice of law as involving individualized legal services rather than generalized information such as self-help kits. This suggests that an answer to a specific legal query on a listserve might constitute practicing law, but a website that includes general legal discussions probably would not.

Even if courts extend unauthorized practice laws beyond individualized legal services, they should hesitate to cover general statements in lawyer blogs. This conclusion follows from the policies underlying lawyer licensing. The classic argument in favour of lawyer licensing is that the law should address information asymmetries between lay people and professionals in the rendition of professional services.

States accordingly prescribe standards as to who is qualified to give this advice, and regulate the conduct of those who are licensed to give it. Licensing standards are only rough proxies for the quality of legal services and might skeptically be viewed as the product of the lawyer's cartel, serving mainly to hinder access to legal services by low-income people. Even if some licensing laws are defensible, these laws should not be designed so as to deter speech that would alleviate information asymmetries in professional advice. Lawyer blogs can enable consumers of legal services to evaluate legal advice or inform them as to whether they need to see a lawyer.

To be sure, there is a danger that blogs might contain incorrect legal advice. This risk might be reduced by screening out those who do not have certain minimum professional credentials.

However, blogs are subject to correction by other blogs and by commentary. Moreover, applying licensing laws to blogs might lead to an adverse selection problem: practicing lawyers, whose blogs may be most valuable, are most likely to be deterred by the threat of unauthorized practice liability outside their home state, whereas nonlawyers, whose legal advice is least valuable, are least likely to be deterred by these laws. An alternative justification for lawyer licensing is to give lawyers the incentive to invest in the development of law by giving them a quasi-property right in the law of the state in which they are licensed. Applying licensing laws to blogs, however, is unnecessary to protect this investment.

Lawyer bloggers are mainly concerned with marketing their main business in the states where they are licensed, whereas nonlawyer bloggers' offhand legal-type statements are seriously unlikely to threaten lawyers' businesses.

An important aspect of applying professional licensing statutes to lawyer blogs concerns advertising restrictions. For example, Kentucky attempted to apply a rule charging fees for lawyer advertising to lawyer blogs. Whether or when blogs that do not directly advertise a lawyer or firm will be deemed to be advertising remains unclear.

As with the application of unauthorized practice laws to blogs, applying restrictions on professional advertising would be inconsistent with the analysis. Restrictions on lawyer advertising, like licensing laws in general, address laymen's inability to assess the quality of legal services. But enabling proliferation of blogs and comments, and the reputational constraints on bloggers, also can effectively address this asymmetry.

For example, a law firm's blog that discusses a legal issue in order to encourage readers to use the firm's services will expose the firm to commentary and refutation if its advice is erroneous. This exposure gives the firm an incentive to be careful about what it says.

As in the other legal areas discussed in this Part, the application of professional licensing rules to amateur journalism should take account of economics of blogging discussed in this Chapter. To the extent that licensing laws are intended to address information asymmetry, courts and regulators should consider blogs' aggregate information value and not just the potential inaccuracy of individual blogs.

Blogs as Commercial Speech

Regulation of blogs may involve significant First Amendment problems. For example, Kentucky's attempt to charge fees for lawyer advertising on blogs was criticized on this basis. The Supreme Court has applied the First Amendment in striking down overbroad regulation of attorney advertising, citing the information functions of these communications. For the reasons discussed earlier, this concern is particularly applicable to blogs.

The main First Amendment question regarding blogs is whether and under what circumstances they might be entitled only to the lower level of constitutional protection given "commercial speech." A blog might be "commercial" if it cross-promotes another business and thereby directly proposes commercial transactions, but not if it is primarily devoted to the author's personal opinions on politics and culture. The commercial speech doctrine provides little theoretical basis for drawing a line in marginal cases that have some commercial aspects. Indeed, the market for ideas arguably is constitutionally indistinguishable from other markets.

One feature of blogs ultimately may persuade the courts to take many of them out of the commercial speech category. Bloggers generally have low-powered reputational-type incentives rather than a strong profit motive, and therefore may be more deterred by regulation and the threat of penalties than conventional commercial speakers.

The Court's current distinction in Virginia State Board of Pharmacy v. Virginia Citizens Consumer Council, Inc. between commercial and noncommercial speech is based at least partly on the theory that profit-motivated speech is less likely to be chilled by regulation. This argument makes general economic sense.

However, it may not be useful in all cases, because many political speakers may have robust incentives, whereas many commercial speakers are agents who lack strong incentives to promote their firms' interests. But the chilling effect argument does apply generally to amateur journalists, who by definition lack strong economic incentives to speak and therefore may be easily deterred by regulation.

The fact that a blog carries advertising should not be enough to put it in the commercial speech category. Although the advertisements themselves are likely to be commercial speech, one who merely publishes the advertisements is not thereby proposing commercial transactions.

Applying the commercial speech doctrine to all publications that carry advertising, including most newspapers and magazines, would swallow most First Amendment protection. Indeed, the media's ability to get paid to support its activities is arguably itself an important First Amendment right.

Thus, Judge (now Justice) Alito held for the Third Circuit Court of Appeals that Pennsylvania's attempt to bar alcoholic beverages ads in school publications was unconstitutional, reasoning in part that "[i]f government were free to suppress disfavored speech by preventing potential speakers from being paid, there would not be much left of the First Amendment."

Whether the blog carries advertising, however, may affect its level of First Amendment protection apart from the commercial speech issue. The potential chilling effect of regulation may matter on its own rather than as a rationale for applying the commercial speech doctrine. The Court's plurality opinion in Dun and Bradstreet cited as a reason for applying the lower level of Gertz protection to a credit report the argument from Virginia State Board of Pharmacy that for-profit speech is less likely to be deterred.

The credit report did not itself propose a commercial transaction, but merely had a commercial incentive. Following this reasoning, the Court may hold in a marginal case that, other things being equal, a blogger who sells ads is less likely to be deterred by speech regulation than one who blogs without direct monetary reward.

Distinguishing blogs based solely on whether they carry ads, however, may not be a sufficiently nuanced way to assess bloggers' incentives. Even nonadvertising bloggers may reap financial rewards from cross-promoting their main businesses. Less directly, academic bloggers who do not have any "businesses" may receive tangible career rewards from blogging. Also, bloggers who are not currently selling ads may be exploring the market in preparation for doing so, or may eventually capitalize on their audience by selling their blogs. In general, the extent of constitutional protection of amateur journalism is a good example of how the regulation of blogs may depend on an understanding of the economics of blogging, particularly including bloggers' financial and nonfinancial incentives.

Fraud Liability

Misrepresentations on blogs may be subject to fraud liability, general consumer fraud statutes, or federal or state securities laws. The hybrid expressive/commercial nature of many blogs may raise reliance, materiality, and intent to defraud issues under these statutes. In other words, did the plaintiff, or would a reasonable person, rely on a statement casually made in a blog, and is it likely that the blogger intended to defraud?

As with the commercial speech issue, the blogger's incentives may matter. For example, a reader may assume that a blogger who sells advertisements or is cross-promoting her main business is more motivated, and therefore should be taken more seriously, than a blogger whose postings are intended solely for self-expression purposes. Even if a statement in an individual blog satisfies the usual tests for fraud, the interactive nature of amateur journalism may matter to the scope of liability.

A statement that is false in isolation may not be materially false, or may not have triggered reliance, given immediate correction through comments and trackbacks and by other blogs. Again, the technology and economics of blogs should determine the extent of regulation. As has been the case for the other issues this Part addresses, this analysis is not intended to state a definitive rule, but rather to indicate some relevant considerations.

Vicarious Liability

A blogger might be vicariously liable for a statement of a co-blogger on a group blog. In particular, a group blog may be a partnership unless the bloggers have explicitly selected some other form. This categorization means that partnership default rules would apply to the relationship, including partners' personal liability for their copartners' wrongful acts. Liability for blog posts on the partnership's behalf might extend to intentional torts such as defamation. Such liability is significant to the extent that it may deter bloggers who have relatively weak self-expression incentives.

The resolution of this issue may partly depend on whether the blog is a "business," which is part of the definition of partnership under the partnership laws. That issue, in turn, may depend on whether the blog carries advertisements. Bloggers who generate a little income stream to help cover expenses probably lack the sort of high-powered incentives to maximize revenues and minimize costs that induce conventional partners to monitor each other.

Instead they may recognize that they have strong self-expressive reasons for blogging and therefore hesitate to interfere with each other's activities. Thus, even if courts characterize some group blogs as partnerships for vicarious liability purposes, they might require more evidence of control and other partnership indicia to compensate for the weaker profit motive.

A group blog whose writers share revenue from advertisements and expenses might be viewed as a profit-sharing relationship that is at least presumptively a partnership. On the other hand, the blog might be considered only a loose association created solely for promotional reasons, analogous to sole-practitioner lawyers who share a receptionist and office space.

Even this situation may create a liability depending on how the relationship was represented to clients. But given blogs' novelty and evolving nature and the lack of a common understanding as to the relationship among co-bloggers, it may be difficult to determine how co-blogging relationships are "represented" to the public.

Group bloggers may argue that they had no interest in reviewing each other's posts and may even have a stated policy of not blocking posts they disagreed with. A court, however, might assume that the likely rationale for a group blog is to drive more readers toward each blogger's posts. This rationale requires some quality control, even if not in the strict hierarchical sense of a newspaper. If the blog also accepts advertising, it starts to look like a conventional profit-maximizing business. Courts therefore may deem group bloggers to have enough interest in co-bloggers' posts to have partner-like control. A group blog also might be an agency relationship, as when a separate firm hires the bloggers and acts as the principal. This is probably the case for "corporate" blogs that have a blog-type format but in which, unlike the amateurs on whom this chapter focuses, the bloggers are full-time employees. In this situation the employing firm is liable for the bloggers' acts in the scope of employment.

Liability is more ambiguous when a separate firm such as Gawker or Weblogs aggregates previously independent bloggers into a group blog. These writers may not regard themselves as colleagues with common interests and may simply want to maximize their joint advertising revenue. They therefore may be only a loose federation of independent writers who have hired a common agent to sell advertising, similar to the group of lawyers that hires a common receptionist and shares office space discussed above.

The network also might be considered a separate employer, in which case the bloggers probably would be independent contractors rather than "servants" for whose acts the employer would be liable. That classification depends on whether, instead of the employer supervising the details of the writer's work, the blogger "commits himself to providing a specified output, and the principal monitors the contractor's performance... by inspecting the contractually specified output to make sure it conforms to the specifications." This description seems to fit a blogger who agrees only to contribute a general type of commentary but does not submit to detailed monitoring.

The argument for agency in the latter scenario is that the blogging network or aggregator is analogous to a newspaper, with the writers analogous to reporters for whose acts the employer would be liable. Although the reporters resemble servant agents because they are employed and paid full-time rather than by the article, the problems inherent in a principal's supervising the work arguably are similar in both cases. From an economics standpoint, the partnership and agency issues arguably depend on whether a blogger should be deemed to be in a good position as owner to monitor his or her co-bloggers.

This general economic analysis of agency relationships, however, may not be appropriate in the context of blogging. The agency analysis assumes that the relevant monitoring occurs in the "vertical" or hierarchical relationship among the parties to the firm.

But as stressed throughout this Chapter, blogs are monitored by other blogs through such interactive mechanisms as comments and trackbacks. Courts should take this characteristic into account in determining whether group bloggers should be liable for inaccuracies in each other's posts.

The extent to which vicarious liability may deter blogging depends on how easily bloggers may avoid this liability. They, of course, could simply decline to take on co-bloggers. But group blogs may be useful in attracting more readers to the posts of all group members. Group bloggers also might attempt to avoid liability by contracting explicitly that their relationship is not a partnership. But courts may hold in favour of partnership despite such provisions in which other indicia of partnership are present.

The group may deal with the above ambiguities and reduce the risk that their personal assets will be exposed to liability by purchasing insurance. However, insurance may not protect them from all liability, including liability for intentional torts. The bloggers might incorporate or form some other type of limited liability business association--a limited liability company, limited partnership, or limited liability partnership. The quality of the liability shield depends on whether the bloggers have maintained the appropriate formalities and facts that would support veil-piercing, including separation of business and personal affairs.

Even if the bloggers successfully limit their liability to the firm's assets, they may incur other costs from forming a limited liability firm, such as triggering the application of inappropriate partnership-type default rules. Thus, the availability of limited liability is not a complete solution to the risk of vicarious liability.

In general, as throughout this Part, this discussion is not intended to reach definitive conclusions on the law of amateur journalism, but only to show the considerations that courts should bring to bear based on the economics and technology of blogging. Given the social value of blogs, the opportunities that blogs present for self-correction and informal filtering, and bloggers' relatively low-powered incentives, courts should be wary about creating broad vicarious liability for co-bloggers. Even if a blog is technically a "business," its moonlighting and self-expressive nature mean that it should not be treated as the sort of business for which partnership-type vicarious liability is appropriate. Also, application of vicarious liability may constrain governance, as by deterring some types of monitoring that courts might view as partner-like conduct.

Harmful but Accurate Speech

Regulation of blogs that is intended to protect against harms other than those involving inaccurate speech may present problems distinct from rules intended to ensure accuracy. Speech that is obscene or infringes privacy or property rights in information can be harmful without being false. Permitting more of this type of speech will not necessarily reduce social harm by correcting error. Also, the harm in these situations can be done by any blogger, not just one who has garnered special access through trustworthiness.

This reality suggests that, for some types of harm, courts and regulators should distinguish nonprofessional bloggers from professionals. To be sure, professional journalists, like amateurs, care more about forfeiting their reputations for accuracy, which is an important value for many readers, than they would about other types of harm, such as invasions of privacy or abuse of proprietary information. But professionals also must be concerned about their and their employers' reputations for respecting confidentiality and privacy in order to continue to have access to sources. Professionals and their employers thus have special incentives to protect their investments in information and to generally defend intellectual property rights.

Amateur journalists, by contrast, rely on commentary or on their own special sources of information. They are consumers, rather than producers, of the costliest and most valuable forms of intellectual property. Conversely, as discussed throughout this chapter, the costs of regulating amateur journalists may exceed those of regulating professionals.

Because of their weaker economic incentives, amateurs may be more easily deterred than professionals by sanctions for infringing property rights and other harmful speech. For example, a professional journalist could stifle criticism by amateurs by threatening to strictly enforce copyright against critics who excerpt or parody its work. Special issues are raised by the application of copyright and trademark law to amateur journalists. As discussed above, blogs can serve as "remora" in adding value to professional media stories by checking on their accuracy and completeness.

Yet links and references to professional media raise questions concerning violation of copyright law. Los Angeles Times v. Free Republic held that posting Los Angeles Times and Washington Post articles on websites constituted copyright infringement and was not protected as "fair use." This case illustrates the need to reach some accommodation with the professional press's property rights.

Although blogs may improve the health of the professional media, they also need the investigative reporting and other services that robust professional media provide. In other words, remora need sharks that are willing to invest in intellectual property. Professional media's incentive to invest depends on some legal protection from free-riding blogs.

A reasonable compromise may be possible. Rather than reproduce the full article, the blogger can simply link to the article, which is the accepted practice. The source thereby can control and charge for access to the actual article. To be sure, linking may not be equivalent to copying. In particular, a writer who wants to "risk" an article or photo may rind no substitute for reproducing the entire document in the blog. Moreover, some outlets, such as the Wall Street Journal, charge for access, even free registration can be burdensome (as by opening the registrant to spam), and there are some copyright constraints on linking.

Professional media can decide whether blogs' parasitic function is worth encouraging by making the source material freely available. If blogs add value, and controlling or charging for access to the original material reduces that added value, professional media has an incentive to allow free linking or pasting. Larger media sources may have strong incentives to obtain competitive advantage by becoming nodes for networks of blogs. Blogs and other websites that are motivated more by self-expression than commercial objectives may be willing to adopt Creative Commons licenses.

Some sites, however, may not adopt a formal policy. They may not be able to capitalize on the network advantages of blog commentary, or otherwise internalize the social benefits of making their material freely available. For these sites the private benefits of strict copyright protection may exceed the private costs.

This balance may leave a significant amount of intellectual property on the Web subject to the restrictions and uncertainties of copyright law. Because of their weaker profit incentives, amateur journalists may be reluctant to push the margins of copyright laws, particularly if they have substantial personal wealth and reputations to protect. This reluctance may significantly reduce the potential information advantages of blogs.

One possible solution is to raise the bar for default copyright protection. Alternatively, Congress might revise the fair use doctrine to better accommodate blogs, as by specifying that linking is not a violation unless the copyright owner clearly reserves linking rights. Either approach would place burdens on copyright owners to obtain strict protection. This condition would help ensure at least that this protection is reserved only for those owners who obtain the largest private benefits from protection.

As with the discussion of other legal issues in this Part, this analysis is intended to outline relevant considerations rather than to prescribe definitive rules. In particular, the interactivity of amateur journalism depends significantly on the ability to link and copy from other sources. This interactivity may require an accommodation of speech rights with protection of intellectual property. The relevant actors themselves may be able to work out the necessary rules. To the extent they cannot, the courts and Congress should do so, guided by the economics and technology of amateur journalism.

Blogs are a relatively new medium that could have significant ramifications for several areas of the law. In resolving these legal issues, it is important to consider the distinct technical and economic aspects of blogging. This Chapter is a modest beginning. It is important to keep in mind that the technology of the Internet and the Web in general and of blogs in particular is evolving rapidly. Amateur journalism may soon be very different from what it is today.

For example, authored blogs and authorless wikis might co-evolve into a hybrid that combines spontaneity and authorship. This potential development could have implications for the reputational bonding mechanisms emphasized in this chapter. Professional and amateur journalism might converge in ways that cannot now be predicted.

Thus, this Chapter can provide only a snapshot of amateur journalism's current phase of development. In order to be useful, an analysis of amateur journalism must focus on core principles that will continue to be relevant even if the technology changes.

The core of amateur journalism is open access and interactivity, in contrast to the more closed model of conventional bricks-and-mortar media firms. Open access has both benefits and risks that need to be taken into account in future regulation. In evaluating the risks, one must keep in mind that open access itself may serve as a self-corrective mechanism. Blogs, or whatever replaces them, therefore may be more an opportunity and a solution to the problems of bricks-and-mortar journalism than the problem Joel Klein's "pajamas" image suggests.

3

Op-Ed Journalism

To avoid the press in a lobbying campaign on a bill as major and potentially controversial as the ADA is a rarity, even a heresy. The press is central to the debate on policy issues. "When policy makers want to disseminate ideas about public issues, they hold press conferences, distribute press releases, leak information, and give speeches designed to receive press coverage," writes media scholar Martin Linsky.

"Even when they want to communicate only to other policymakers, they are very likely to do so through the press". In presidential election campaigns, the media play a central role in shaping political reality by the amount of coverage and prominence they give to specific issues.

Even events with life or death consequences may have little impact on the public unless the media put them high on their issue agenda. The 1984 famine in Ethiopia had been claiming lives for months with virtually no attention in the American press until a BBC film of the devastation was shown on NBC. The shocking images of dying mothers and their children made the famine a front-page story and moved Americans to a compassionate outpouring of donations for relief. To grab the attention of the media is almost always the first step toward changing public policy.

To that extent, public relations is a multi-billion dollar a year business in this country, supporting some 173,000 public relations professionals nationwide. Every corporation and every cause—from General Motors to the Tube Council of North America, representing the makers of toothpaste tubes and other similar containers—depends on the press to raise awareness of its issues.

The media have been particularly influential in battles for the passage of civil rights legislation to protect minorities. The 1964 Civil Rights Act passed after years of press coverage of events that stirred the conscience of a guilty nation to attempt to redress its history of separatism and racism.

The law was preceded by images of courageous Freedom Riders, marches, bus boycotts, lynchings, church bombings, peaceful protesters mauled by police dogs on the streets of Birmingham, and Martin Luther King, Jr., electrifying a crowd by delivering his "I Have a Dream" speech on the steps of the Lincoln Memorial. Disabled Americans got their civil rights protection without the same compelling imagery and absent the same sea-change in public attitudes. The media were of little use to the disability rights movement as it sought passage of the ADA, because journalists have been too slow to understand the new civil rights consciousness of disabled Americans.

As John Clogston, of Northern Illinois University, Douglas Biklen, of Syracuse University, Irving Kenneth Zola, of Brandeis University, and others have shown, press coverage of people with disabilities has tended to fall into one of two stereotypes. There is the sad, unlucky disabled person, in need of pity and charity. Or there is the plucky, courageous disabled person, celebrated for overcoming a disability and performing seemingly superhuman feats, whether holding a job or scaling a mountain. One is the image of Tiny Tim, the other that of the "super-crip."

In these stories, disabled people are grist for feature stories that usually focus on one person and his or her struggles to overcome a handicap. The overcoming is not connected to facing a societal barrier. The individual is not seen as taking part in any larger civil rights struggle or social movement of people with disabilities. The stereotypes of disabled people as either Tiny Tims or super-crips have slowed their progress toward full inclusion in American life. To be seen as a patient or in need of charity is to be thought incapable of the same life as others. To be lauded for superachievement is to suggest that a disabled person can turn our pity into respect only at the point of having accomplished some extraordinary feat.

Complicating the fight for the ADA was the fact that many people with disabilities had internalized these dominant messages and did not have a rights orientation. And some of the organizations most widely identified as representing disabled people relied on these very stereotypes to tug on heartstrings and get the charitable contributions to fund their organizations and their scientific research in search of cures.

Charitable groups like the Muscular Dystrophy Association still relied on telethons that played up sad stories of dying children, or inspirational stories, although many disabled people had come to find such telethons distasteful. Clearly, however, the self-definition of disabled people is changing rapidly. This has been spurred by two great consciousness-raising events of the disability rights movement: the Gallaudet student protest in 1988, and the fight for the ADA and its subsequent implementation from 1989 to 1992.

Even before those two events, a 1985 Harris survey found that 74 per cent of disabled Americans say they share a "common identity" with other disabled people and 45 per cent argue they are "a minority group in the same sense as is blacks and Hispanics". One can assume that these numbers would be significantly higher today in the wake of Gallaudet and the ADA. Anecdotal evidence, including the number of people who did not define themselves as activists but who are filing complaints over ADA violations, suggests that more disabled people are coming to see their issues in terms of rights. What made journalists of little relevance to ADA lobbyists is the fact that the press was one of the last institutions to catch on to disabled people's new rejection of old stereotypes. Among the first to catch on, however, were politicians, who quickly have come to recognize disabled people as a potent and activist group of constituents. That meant the disability lobbyists could avoid the long process of educating the public on its issues and take the case for disability civil rights directly to policymakers.

Not needing to make its case through the filter of the media, the ADA lobby in Washington put together a highly effective grass-roots campaign. Every member of Congress got a personal visit from a constituent with a compelling story to tell about civil rights discrimination.

Since disability hits nearly one in six people and cuts across class and racial lines, many key members of Congress understood the yearning for disability rights. Some key members had disabilities themselves, like Senate Minority Leader Robert Dole, who lost use of his right arm as a result of a World War II injury, and former Representative Tony Coehlo, who has epilepsy. The bill's original Senate sponsor, Connecticut Republican Lowell Weicker, has a son with Down's Syndrome. Iowa Democrat Tom Harkin, who took the lead when Weicker was defeated for re-election, has a deaf brother and a nephew who is a quadriplegic.

Senator Edward Kennedy, who led key negotiations with the White House, has a sister with retardation and a son who lost part of his leg to cancer. President George Bush, whose support for the bill was crucial, also understood disability: his son, Neil, has dyslexia, and the Bushes were told he would never be able to attend college (he did); and another son, Marvin, had a colostomy.

There were other reasons why the disability activists' strategy worked, in addition to having Congress and the President on their side. Business group opposition to a bill that would open companies up to a potential spate of lawsuits was surprisingly muted, especially when compared to the business community's vociferous fight against the 1964 Civil Rights Act.

This time, however, no business lobbyist wanted to look like a bigot fighting a civil rights bill, particularly one that seemed to be rushing to passage with strong bipartisan support from both lawmakers and the White House. More importantly, businesses had come to see disabled people as a new source of both labour and customers. The ADA would bring more of both.

Still, it was the personal connections that were most important to passage of the ADA. These allowed disability group lobbyists to avoid the media and to take their case directly to key players in the legislative and executive branches of government. However, in doing so neither the importance of the ADA nor the perspective of the disability rights movement was fully explained to all Americans.

The campaign for the ADA produced a law that would change society, but it had done little to build a foundation of understanding to make it easier to push for other, perhaps more controversial, disability policy initiatives in the future, and it left disabled people unprotected against a backlash when they tried to assert their newly-won rights under the ADA.

One way to describe news coverage of the ADA is to say that there was very little of it. The few stories that were published presented a mixed picture. New York Times early on ran an alarmist lead story on the front page, predicting "a wave of lawsuits" and reflecting business fears about the burdens of the bill.

A follow-up editorial asked whether Congress was offering a "blank check for the disabled". Publications like the New York Times and the Washington Post printed just a handful of stories on the bill as it moved through Congress, and, but for a few exceptions, ignored the broader disability rights movement.

Given the highly publicized struggle to pass the Civil Rights Act of 1964—and the fact that the ADA was the most extensive civil rights bill since then—the relatively little scrutiny afforded the ADA once again made clear that the disability rights movement has been a quiet, grass-roots rebellion. Yet, even without the aid of a knowledgeable press, the ADA passed.

There is, however, a danger in being a stealth movement. Disabled people have new civil rights protections, but society has little understanding of those protections or of why disabled people need them. Thus, as disabled people begin asserting these newly-won rights, clashes and misunderstanding are sure to follow.

There was little controversy when disabled people pushed for passage of the ADA, largely because the bill got little attention in the press and elsewhere. But as newly-empowered individuals exercise their rights, the fight moves from the closed halls of power in Washington to the realm of the public. The disability rights movement increasingly will be played out in streets, schools, workplaces, and the press.

Already there are signs of a backlash. Such reactions are common when groups assert minority rights, but in this case the process is exacerbated by a press that lacks the mindset or the history to understand the new thinking of disabled people.

As the employment title of the ADA went into effect, there were two bills in Congress to either limit the ADA or abolish it outright. Also, when disabled people demand the rights granted to them by the ADA and other civil rights laws, they are depicted in the press as a selfish minority with dubious claims.

A typical example was the press coverage of New York City's plan to set up public, outdoor toilets. The city's original proposal did not include any that were accessible for wheelchair users.

The ADA, as well as New York City law, was clear that such public accommodations must be accessible to wheelchair users. However, city officials complained that a toilet big enough for a wheelchair-user would take up too much space on a street corner.

Besides, officials argued, they would attract drug addicts looking for a place to inject themselves with needles, prostitutes seeking a place for illicit sex, and homeless people needing shelter to sleep. Press coverage of the controversy painted the dissenters as demanding a narrow right—one that would benefit just a small number of wheelchair users—over a common good that would benefit the vast majority of New Yorkers.

Most stories about the toilets presented them as a clever and welcome idea, and the complaints of wheelchair users, if mentioned, were of secondary importance. On the editorial pages, disabled people were presented as an unreasonable minority. One newspaper editorial chided the disability community, saying the issue was one of "weighing civil rights against common sense".

Another editorial, appearing in the New York Times after the four-month experiment with the toilets ended, declared them an "unqualified success" and that their continuation was threatened only by objections coming from disabled people that the separate units were discriminatory.

"But that objection ought not to obstruct the service for the whole city," the editorial continued. The "success" of the toilets "puts the burden on the disabled groups either to come up with a plausible alternative or accept the separate units". In each case, the editorial writers failed to see disabled people as having a legitimate claim to civil rights, but only as making a narrow, selfish claim that would ruin a good idea for everyone else.

To disabled people, the failure to make the toilets accessible was as outrageous as if the city had built toilets just for men, or put signs on them that said "Whites Only." The hope behind the ADA is that integration in workplaces, restaurants, parks, theaters, and government services will end others' impulses to offer pity or seek inspiration from disabled people, and that fears and misconceptions about disabled people will fade.

Will integration also make the media better understand the disability movement's claim to rights? There are signs that this is already happening. It is no longer easy, as it was for Clogston as recently as 1990, to separate reporting between the progressive and the traditional. More reporting now conveys disability as a rights issue, not just as a feature story.

Clogston has defined what made a story traditional or progressive. Traditional articles showed a disabled person as a medical or economic defective, the result of a disability. The newer, progressive model viewed a disabled person as limited by society, not by a physical or mental limitation. In this model, society either discriminates against, or is unable or unwilling to accommodate, a person with a disability.

Clogston found that 60 per cent of articles were traditional and only 13.2 per cent progressive. This author's survey of the 1991 clippings of general disability stories from the library files of U.S. News and World Report found the inverse proportion. Of 58 articles from 13 newspapers, 39 (67 per cent) fell into the progressive model, 10 (17 per cent) were traditional, and 9 (16 per cent) defied classification, including three that could be classified as "backlash" stories. These will be considered later.

Reporting is largely a reactive exercise, writing about events and how others present themselves. A journalist holds up a mirror to society. As more disabled people see their issues as ones involving rights, so will reporters.

Even if the disability movement has failed to do enough to educate reporters, journalists eventually will catch on, albeit slowly, by observing the new expressions of disability rights. This is confirmed in a study by Beth Haller, of Temple University, who looked at stories about deaf people in the Washington Post and the New York Times. Sixty-two per cent of stories before the Gallaudet student protest "reflected the traditional disability models," but "in the two years after the protest, the number of stories reflecting the traditional forms of presentation fell to 40 per cent." Haller, too, noted that on the whole there was little press coverage of deaf people, except for the spurt of stories in 1988 dealing specifically with Gallaudet. Otherwise, the number of stories in years following Gallaudet was roughly the same as the number of stories in the preceding two years.

While reporting at times describes the rights activism of disabled people, a strange phenomenon is on the rise in the wake of Gallaudet and the ADA. Some reporters now combine traditional stereotypes with the new talk of rights. The result is a peculiar hybrid, the "militant Tiny Tim" story. These are stories in which reporters tell a civil rights story, but use the negative imagery of Tiny Tims and super-crips, or they tell one of these traditional stories but dress it up with a little civil rights language.

Television seems slower than print journalism to give up the traditional disability images. Typical was a CBS Evening News "Eye on America" segment, broadcast on July 9, 1992, about a Massachusetts father and his son cycling across the country to gain attention for his son's cerebral palsy.

Anchorwoman Connie Chung introduced the piece with talk of how the new ADA was forcing the removal of physical barriers, and then noted, "Still, Americans with disabilities have to fight to overcome other barriers in people's minds." From that acknowledgment of the new rights thinking of disabled Americans, the story descended into more traditional stereotypes about disability.

The segment opened with a shot of the father pumping his bicycle across the California desert, pushing his son who is in a wheelchair-like seat attached to the front of the bike. "Dick Hoyt provides the arms and legs," says correspondent Meredith Vierra, "Rick, the inspiration that will keep them going." There is talk about how Rick has "lived inside a body that never worked." Vierra explains that she had reported on the Hoyts once before, and that the point of this piece was to see "how much has changed for Rick and the disabled over the last six years. We found a family still fighting. People may say they admire Rick, but it stops short of their pocketbooks. The Hoyts' trip was supposed to be financed through donations."

The idea that they had to finance the cross-country trek largely out of their own pockets is the only thing in the story that passes as a "barrier" against disabled people—never mind that there is nothing discriminatory about the public's failure to sponsor such a bike trip.

It is common in disability feature stories to find a trail of evidence that the disabled person defines his or her issues in terms of rights, but the journalist failed to catch on. In the CBS report, the father says, "I just think if people can see that Rick is being a productive human being with all the disabilities that he has that we're going to help out a lot of people."

Further, Vierra notes that the Hoyts have begun a foundation to help small businesses become accessible. However, the report told nothing of that business and ignored the important policy considerations of accessibility and removing barriers—who pays for it, whether it is worthwhile, or exactly what makes for accessibility—in order to conform to a journalistic cliche of celebrating a heroic disabled person.

A similar hybrid appeared in the Washington Post story about 27-year-old Jenny Langley, a quadriplegic who uses a ventilator as the result of an automobile accident. She was ready to leave an Atlanta rehabilitation centre, but needed accessible housing and personal assistance service or else faced being forced into an out-of-state nursing home.

The dilemma facing Langley was a typical civil rights story of a society that fails to provide for the basic needs of people who live with severe disabilities. However, the story, by freelance writer Remar Sutton, was done in the mawkish "overcome" model.

"First, you notice how pretty she is; then you think how nifty the bow tie around her neck is. And then you notice it's not a bow tie but the dressing around the hole in her throat," the reporter noted.

Later he explains how Langley needs help with quad coughs, described as an undignified treatment in which someone pounds on her chest several times a day. "If you're Jenny, you say thank you every time it's done," Sutton wrote. This story was a strange mixture of the typical feature treatment of a disabled person admirable for her courage (and in this cases her politeness). However, it also raised some of the important policy issues that disability rights activists have long claimed the press misses when it pursues a traditional feature story.

The article noted, for example, the fact that Langley could live independently, with an attendant, but was not given the opportunity. Yet, while the article hinted at the cost to society in wasted human potential—not to mention the issue of the indignity of a life of forced dependency—the author chose to stress Langley's courage.

This kind of reporting suggests that the disability community will have a hard time pushing for personal assistance services, the next big issue on the disability rights agenda. Disabled people see it as a right and a necessity for living independently.

There has been little reporting on the subject and, as is clear from the article on Langley, journalists have a hard time separating basic disability policy issues from traditional feature stories about disabled people. Since personal assistance service will require major expenditures by state and federal governments, whereas the ADA put the costs mainly on business, disabled people will need to find a way to explain the importance of such services.

Along with the hybrid stories is another new trend: the backlash story. This also suggests that there is a new, growing resistance to the disability rights agenda in social policy. There were three backlash articles in the random survey of stories from 1991. These articles looked at disability issues in terms of rights, but found the claim for rights to be wanting.

One was an August 25 story in the Philadelphia Inquirer reflecting the complaints of home builders that new barrier-free housing was not selling. "There are not as many disadvantaged persons who want barrier-free design elements as we were originally led to believe," complained a disgruntled builder.

The builders complained about the extra cost of making homes accessible. Nowhere in the article did the author note the benefits of universal design, that barrier-free houses in the suburbs may have little appeal to disabled people if local transportation is not accessible, or that disabled people often lack the financial wherewithal to buy a new house.

Most egregious of all, the story never mentioned that the entire housing industry was in a terrible slump. Instead, disabled people got blamed for not snapping up new, expensive homes in the midst of a recession. A story in the Baltimore Sun played up the fears of restaurant owners and others confused about their obligations to make their businesses accessible, and a story in the Washington Post argued that the local transit company's financial troubles "may deepen because of a new federal law requiring transit agencies to improve access to rail and bus systems by disabled people."

Nowhere did the article mention why accessible transit is important to people with disabilities. Nor did it seek out a spokesperson for a disability group who may have questioned the transit authority's claim that it would cost $28 million a year for Washington's system, already highly accessible, to come into compliance with the ADA.

Each of these backlash stories reflected, without challenge, the assertion of three interest groups—builders, restaurant owners, and transit authorities—that had fought against the ADA. None of the stories found a disability group spokesperson to respond. This is in part sloppy reporting, but the disability community is also to blame. Independent living centers and disability rights groups generally have done a poor job of making local reporters aware of them as resources on disability issues. One exception is Paraquad, in St. Louis, a good model of reaching out to the press, with a full-time public relations staffer and a newsletter that is sent to reporters and others.

Since the disability movement has been a stealth movement, reporters have little idea of where to go for a disability perspective. Reporters know of charity groups such as the March of Dimes or the ARC, but only go to them for help with stories on the specific disabilities they represent. The most consistent effort to reach out to reporters has come from groups like the National Easter Seal Society, to teach the media to use "correct" language when writing about people with disabilities.

Even groups like the Special Olympics give reporters who cover their events guidelines to proper language. There needs to be more active effort to educate reporters to the history and point-of-view of the disability movement.

One good first step toward this was a 1989 sourcebook for reporters, aimed primarily at journalism students, edited by Mary Johnson, editor of the Disability Rag. "Gripping personal sagas have been considered powerful writing," notes Johnson, arguing why journalists can benefit from dropping traditional ways of writing about disability.

"But issue stories can be more powerful. They can provide readers with information, they can involve people, they can change things". Johnson recently has received a grant from the National Institute on Disability and Rehabilitation Research to teach disability advocates how to communicate their issues to the press. There is one other way that disability activists can affect policy: with the same heart-tugging pity approach that these activists decry.

Many of the nation's 2,500 death-row inmates suffer from mental retardation. Writer and advocate Robert Perske estimates their number to include at least 10 per cent of all death-row inmates. Five states have now banned the death penalty for people with mental retardation, and similar legislation has been introduced in 21 more states.

Georgia, the first to implement such a ban in 1988, was the scene of a particularly disturbing execution of Jerome Bowden, convicted in the brutal killing of a 55-year-old woman. No physical or eyewitness evidence linked Bowden to the crime, but he signed a confession after a detective told him that signing it would help him out.

Like many people with retardation caught up in the criminal justice system, notes Perske, Bowden was eager to please authority figures and was confused by the legal process swirling around him.

As advocates Perske, James Ellis, and Ruth Luckasson have noted, this is a problem of police using heavy-handed tactics to force confessions out of easily-led people with retardation. However, defence attorneys, death penalty foes, and others sometimes infantize these people, to make broader criticism of the death penalty. "Like children, mentally retarded defendants don't have the ability to really appreciate what they are up to," one North Carolina defence attorney was quoted saying in an investigative series on the death penalty.

However, the series then devoted a sidebar to John Steinbeck's novel, Of Mice and Men, trotting out the big and powerful Lennie whose retardation made him unable to tell the difference between stroking a woman's hair and strangling her. This hoary image may help states pass bans on executing people with retardation, but it will set back efforts to get neighborhoods to welcome group homes and businesses to accept workers with retardation.

Even the disability rights movement is not above taking advantage of the public's need to see disabled people as brave and courageous. The one lasting image of the fight for the ADA was a "crawl up" of the steps of the West Front of the United States Capitol building.

The event came at the end of a 1990 march and rally for the ADA by ADAPT, or American Disabled for Accessible Public Transit (since renamed American Disabled for Attendant Programs Today, to reflect the policy fight for personal assistance services). ADAPT is the political action arm of the disability rights movement, a group of demonstrators who risk arrest in street actions that are designed to grab media attention.

ADAPT has a good record of getting attention from the local media when they arrive in a city and take over a government office building or disrupt the convention of the nursing home industry trade association, but they have received little national press attention, particularly when compared to ACT-UP, the AIDS activists who employ similar tactics to demand more urgent AIDS research.

This relative absence of press coverage may be due to a combination of the facts that the disability rights movement remains little understood, that there is great fear of AIDS as a disease that cannot be cured, and that there has been extensive public education of AIDS' devastating impact.

In Washington, in March of 1990, a few dozen ADAPT demonstrators left their wheelchairs and climbed up the marble steps of the Capitol, carrying a "disability declaration of independence" to give to lawmakers inside the Capitol. Some disability activists, including Mary Johnson, questioned this tugging on public sympathies.

The cameras, of course, zoomed in on 8-year-old Jennifer Keelan. A disabled child's struggle played to every media reflex. Even if the crawl up was a shameless play to old stereotypes, ADAPT knew what it was doing. The bizarre, but arresting, image of the crawl-up got the protest on the nightly news, albeit briefly. It is another sign of the dangers of being a stealth movement, that in order to get attention activists must play on the very misunderstandings they are trying to erase. Reporters have an unformed understanding of the new disability rights movement, but they are beginning to sense that it is important. Events like the "crawl up" only confuse their grasp on the issue.

The implementation of the ADA brings about a key period in disability social policy. Disabled people are arguing for government support, from personal assistance service programs to crucial enforcement of the ADA, but if reporters have only a limited understanding of the claims of disabled people, it becomes easier for the public and for editorial pages to question, dismiss, or even ridicule the demand for rights asserted by newly empowered disabled people.

It is easily assumed that an op-ed page, like an editorial page, is a regular feature of daily newspapers. However, not even journalism's most avid commercial list keepers can provide a list of op-ed editors or even newspapers with op-ed pages. The professional invisibility of the op-ed page and its editors is not readily explainable, unless there just aren't that many daily newspapers publishing such pages.

Of course the op-ed page should be a fairly important part of any newspaper. It encourages public discourse in an open forum of ideas that nurtures the community involvement so necessary to the effective functioning of government and democracy at all levels. Unlike a newspaper's signature editorial page where the discourse agenda is set by the editorial gatekeepers, the op-ed page is the one place in the paper where public discourse, through the mediation of a service editor, can emerge unfettered.

The evolution of the op-ed editors as a group distinct from their editorial page counterparts has occurred only in the last eight years with the establishment of the Association of Opinion Page Editors (AOPE). It wasn't until 1989 that the critical mass of op-ed editors had grown to an extent that they could consider a meeting as an entity separate from the National Conference of Editorial Writers (NCEW), whose membership is drawn from the editorial page editors and writers.

According to one of the AOPE's charter members and former president, Tom Peeling of the Palm Beach Post: In Philadelphia [1989], I watched a fledgling group try to define itself. In Minneapolis [1990], I saw it all come together as we met and passed bylaws that explained who we are and what our purpose is. When we met in West Palm Beach [1991], I saw the dedication of a small number of editors who had managed to talk their bosses into allowing them to make the trip despite tight economic times in the newspaper business; some even paid their own way. In San Francisco [1992] we attracted our largest group [to date]. From 1990 through 1991, submissions of the best op-ed pages for inclusion in AOPE's annual publication, hovered between

16 and 19. In 1992 that number increased to 29. Forty op-ed editors attended the 1993 annual meeting of AOPE in Chicago - the largest turnout in the group's five-year history. There the op-ed editors rejected the proposal of an NCEW representative for a joint annual meeting for fear that the op-ed editors would lose their autonomy to the much larger NCEW. This represented a milestone in the thinking of op-ed editors as they clearly defined their role and mission as totally distinct and separate from the editors of the signature editorial page or section. It remains to be seen whether this expansion indicates that op-ed pages are in a new growth phase or that professional self awareness among op-ed editors is on the rise.

The rapid emergence of the AOPE since 1989 and the vigorous courting by the much larger and established NCEW intent on merger, may indicate that op-ed journalism now challenges the importance and prestige of the editorial page in the minds of the readers. This could also be supported by the anecdotal evidence of readership surveys attesting to the popularity of op-ed pages.

But no data have been developed - either through the AOPE, list brokers or journalism scholars - to assess the extent to which op-ed pages have proliferated among American daily newspapers, the characteristics of papers with op-ed pages, and the general content of those pages.

While op-ed pages may have a long hidden history, they seemed to burst upon the editorial scene in 1970. The publication in 1990 by the New York Times of a 20-year anniversary retrospective of that paper's most prestigious or characteristic op-ed pieces underscored the prevalent but far-from-unanimous notion in editorial circles that the Times had formally invented what most observers consider a fairly widespread practice of publishing a right-hand opinion page opposite the official left-hand editorial page of a newspaper. It would take extensive archival research to verify such a claim, and much of that research in now defunct newspapers whose back issues, if preserved, may be consigned to storage rooms at libraries or universities when such institutions could be found to accept these often massive collections.

The Wall Street Journal, in a letter to the author, claims an op-ed tradition that goes back more than 100 years. A note from Baltimore op-ed writer Carl Pohlner says that he chanced upon such a page published in the now defunct Baltimore News-Post as long ago as 1946, and it included flee-lance whimsical essays of the type that Pohlner writes Kenneth Rystrom suggests the first op-ed page "may have been produced by the New York World in the late 1920s and early 1930s... heavily oriented toward the arts and culture." Rystrom notes that a book on newspaper editing published in 1942 "credited the Louisville Courier-Journal's editorial page and `page opposite editorial' or `op-ed' page with setting one of the outstanding examples in design for editorial pages".

Then why the fanfare and sensation that accompanied the Times' reincarnation of the op-ed page in 19707 The fact that one of America's most distinguished journalists, Harrison E. Salisbury, had put off retirement to accept the editorship heralded the importance of the new Op-Ed page. In his brief three-year tenure he turned the safe backwater of opinion journalism into a revolution (at least at the Times) that broke the exclusive hold of professional journalists on the most important level of political, social and cultural discourse in our then print-oriented society.

Salisbury, "whose capacity to project surprise and variety on the page set a high standard for his successors," structured a page that has not strayed far from its origins and continues to effect a subtle influence on other op-ed pages. Robert Semple, celebrating the page's 20th anniversary, wrote:

From the beginning there was a conscious effort to leave the relentless discussion of geopolitics with offbeat and sometimes whimsical essays.

Inevitably, the page - along with its distinctive illustrations - has reflected the major social, cultural and political debates of the day. The introduction of the Times op-ed page was followed in short order by the Washington Post, the Chicago Tribune, and the Los Angeles Times. Thus did the practice of including op-ed pages in newspapers finally take hold, thereby opening up the editorial and opinion pages of the nation's daily newspapers to a host of citizen writers, some representing special interests and some independent free-lancers.

This chapter reports the results of a survey of op-ed editors in order to develop a baseline profile of some papers with op-ed pages, the practices of their editors, and the contents of the pages. In the absence of any other published research on op-ed pages, other than a previous chapter drawn from this survey, this baseline data should be useful not only to future researchers but also to editors and publishers seeking to establish norms for the practice of op-ed journalism in their papers.

A survey was mailed to the Editorial Page Editor at the 1,650 daily newspapers on a list purchased from Editor and Publisher magazine. Since EandP could not identify newspapers with op-ed pages nor provide a list of op-ed editors, it was felt that most op-ed pages, where they existed, would either be edited by the editorial page editor or by an editor reporting to him or her. The survey was thus addressed with an up-front notation to pass on the survey to an op-ed editor if the page or section was assigned to someone else.

A portion of the survey covered the following areas:

- The characteristics of newspapers with op-ed pages.

In order to develop a common profile of the newspapers with op-ed pages, questions were asked about the paper's circulation, region, time of publication (morning or afternoon), and type (urban, suburban etc.). These then became the four variables used to examine the data. Also, the survey sought to find out how much space these papers devoted to op-ed pieces; that is, how often the pages appeared and how many pages are given to op-ed or perspective sections. Newspapers without op-ed pages were also asked to return the survey in order to develop comparison of op-ed and nonop-ed newspapers. There were also questions regarding circulation, header name, and number of years the newspaper has had an op-ed page.

- Practices of op-ed editors:

Editors were asked about their newspaper's policies for accepting pieces - such as desired length of the pieces, willingness to edit them, and payment policies. In addition, information was sought about the number of free-lance pieces received in an average week and the number printed. Issues concerning copyright and permissibility of simultaneous free-lance submissions to multiple markets were probed.

The results were analysed by five evenly divided circulation groups:

- *Group* 1:12,000 or below (21 per cent),
- *Group* 2:12,001-25,000 (20 per cent),
- *Group* 3:25,001-44,000 (20 per cent),
- *Group* 4:44,001-99,999 (20 per cent),
- *Group* 5:100,000 and up (19 per cent)

Respondents also defined themselves as: urban, suburban, metro, county, state, or national and whether they were morning or afternoon.

A total of 340 daily newspapers returned the survey, for a response rate of about 21 per cent. Of those returning the survey, 159 respondents (47 per cent) reported an op-ed page, while 53 per cent reported not having such a page. The 159 papers answering in the affirmative are termed respondents.

The average circulation of the 159 respondents is 92,457. The much lower median circulation of 37,000 reflects the presence of a few national newspapers in the highest circulation group and is much closer to the national average circulation of all dailies in the United States.

Based on independently published figures, the average circulation of the responding newspapers without op-ed pages is 16,750. The comparison of circulation data reveals that papers under 44,000 circulation are less likely, by a significant margin, to have op-ed pages.

Only 18.6 per cent of the respondents (n=113) reported that their pages were at least 20 years old, the time period coinciding with the introduction of the Times op-ed page. The average age of the op-ed pages was 13 years, with about half being older than 10 years and half founded since 1981. Most (81.4 per cent) of those responding to the date-of-origin question began publishing their op-ed pages after the introduction of the Times' version. The profile of the respondents (n=159) shows that they are rather evenly distributed among four broad geographic regions. The larger circulation dailies were more likely to have op-ed pages than the smaller circulation papers. The respondents overall were 59 per cent a.m.'s and 41 per cent p.m.'s.

There were no significant variances when the data were run against the frequency of publication variable, except that the larger papers published their op-ed sections or pages more frequently - usually weekdays plus weekends. About half the respondents published their op-ed pages daily, while about one-third reported an op-ed page on Sundays or weekends only.

A significant minority published their pages only on weekdays. About 80 per cent of the respondents (n=155) reported that op-ed pages did indeed sit "opposite the editorial page" (76.8 per cent to the right and 5.2 per cent to the left). Of the remaining newspapers, 11.8 per cent of the respondents include the op-ed function on the editorial page, 3.7 per cent have a four-page pullout section, and 2.4 per cent have a non-facing page preceding the editorial page.

There were 24 different headers on the op-ed page. The most common headers were Opinion (33.6 per cent), Commentary (11.9 per cent), Op-Ed (9.8 per cent), Viewpoints (7 per cent), Forum (4.9 per cent), a miscellany of titles (18.9 per cent), and no title (13.9 per cent).

According to previously reported survey results, "almost all the op-ed pages (87.2 per cent) include syndicated columns, and 75 per cent also include staff-written pieces. In addition, more than one-third of the respondents reported that advertisements were printed on the opinion page."

Only 37.5 per cent of the papers accepting op-ed advertisements limited the size of such advertisements (with a half-page maximum), and a scant 9 per cent have content guidelines for op-ed page ads. Of the pages accepting ads, 19.6 per cent indicated that there were no limitations in size or content.

Despite heavy use of syndicated columns and staff-written pieces, 78.2 per cent of the respondents accept free-lance submissions. The preferred number of words for free-lance pieces ranged from 100 to 2,000 words, with 47.6 per cent responding (n=124) that 600 to 750 words was the preferred length, 33.8 per cent preferred more than 750 words, and 18.6 per cent 100 to 500 words. Only 25 per cent of the respondents (n=124) pay for unsolicited free-lance pieces. The majority of the paying papers fall into these categories: $100 per piece (18.8 per cent), $75 per piece (16.6 per cent), $35 per piece (12.5 per cent) and $25 per piece (18.8 per cent).

Since daily newspapers generally are staff written, many editors have limited experience in dealing with outside contributors.

And given the extent to which op-ed editors depend on good free-lance submissions, the terms of that relationship would seem to be fairly important. The survey reveals no consensus regarding copyright ownership policy.

For instance, 51.1 per cent of the editors have no policy regarding ownership of the copyright on a free-lance piece, while 29.3 per cent of the papers reserve the copyright for themselves, and 19 per cent purchase a piece for one-time use only, leaving copyright ownership to the writer.

The practice of papers reserving is partially accounted for by the fact that 23.7 per cent of the respondents make free-lance pieces available to other papers through a news service or chain arrangement. All the papers differ substantially regarding policies on multiple submissions. Most papers (85 per cent) will permit free-lancers to submit pieces simultaneously to other papers outside the readership area, but 36 per cent will permit simultaneous submission in an overlapping market.

The permission to submit to an overlapping market doubles to 73 per cent if it is post publication; in other words, most editors want first publication rights within their circulation area. The expectation that the respondents would far outnumber those dailies without op-ed pages did not materialize. This can be attributed to the fact that small dailies, under 100,000 circulation, with fewer economic resources and less cosmopolitan readership dominate the publishing landscape. This also accounts for the fact that the larger papers are disproportionately represented among the respondents because they are more likely to afford op-ed functions and have the readership that practically requires it, especially in multi-newspaper competitive markets. Since it is the smaller paper that usually does not have an op-ed page, economic and competitive (one-paper market) factors must loom large: editor's salary, fees for syndicated and free-lance pieces, and production costs associated with an extra page.

This conclusion triangulates neatly with the fact that 56 per cent of the respondents are morning newspapers, though there are 35 per cent more p.m. newspapers nationally than a.m.. Since mornings generally tend to have larger circulations than afternoons, factors of size, budget and competition can be assumed to be actively involved. Smaller dailies were well represented among the respondents. This might be due to the greater motivation of papers with op-ed pages to return the survey.

If all the respondents paid for free-lance pieces at the same rate as the average, this small group alone would be generating $800,000 a year in freelance fees. In an ideal world, one in which each of the 1,650 dailies on the survey mailing list published at least one unsolicited op-ed piece a day, the newspaper industry would need to be spending about $5.8 million a year on free-lance pieces.

That would break down to an average of $3,500 per newspaper per year or $68 per week. This amounts to an investment of about eight cents per reader per year in a section that consistently scores high in readership surveys. These are not very stressful numbers compared to what is now probably being spent for syndications.

That the New York Times did not invent op-ed journalism is evident from the 18.6 per cent of the respondents whose pages either pre-dated or coincided with the Times' 1970 inaugural issue.

Even the literal explosion of op-ed pages after that date cannot be attributed solely to the impact of the Times' page and its star-quality editor, though the influence of the Times on journalistic practice and national policy was pervasive and unchallenged before Watergate and the emergence of the Washington Post as a national newspaper. The Vietnam era was domestically contentious, and the need for coherent public discourse was never greater. Op-ed journalism was a response for its times, stimulated largely by a general disaffection with the establishment. The Times' mission was both public and self-serving:

As an editorial explained, Op-Ed would provide a forum for political, social and personal expression by writers with "no institutional connection with the Times" - views that would "very frequently be divergent from our own."... During the 1960's John B. Oakes, then editorial page editor, argued that the paper needed to make room for outside articles... that would provoke robust discussion.... [T]he publisher, Arthur Ochs Sulzburger... had powerful reasons for wanting a new forum - chiefly a gut feeling that the Times would honour its traditions and better serve its readers by welcoming a variety of views providing doctrinal counterpoints to the liberalism of the paper's editorial columns and its columnists.

And this remains op-ed journalism's dominant philosophy, as executed by first editor Salisbury, whose "concept of the page, a free-flowing marketplace of ideas, became the prototype for most other op-ed pages and continues to serve as a model even today." Thus the Times' contribution to op-ed journalism can be described as more substantive than chronological.

Despite the limited number of op-ed outlets and their internal restrictions, there is a surprisingly lively and large group of free-lancers vying to be heard - this despite low or no pay, chaotic copyright conditions, and a general bias toward well-known contributors. The resulting frustration could greatly impact the quality and number of free-lance submissions, thereby affecting the tone and mission of the op-ed page.

When this survey was begun, expectations were high that after a quarter century of highly visible op-ed pages in national newspapers, the op-ed phenomenon would be widespread.

The results, later confirmed by a commercial publisher seeking to sell a directory of op-ed editors, revealed not more than 12 per cent of American dailies with op-ed pages. The purpose of this survey and the value of this baseline data is linked to the emerging phenomenon of public journalism and its community connectedness. The study is important to publishers, editors and academics - but for differing reasons.

Before looking beyond the newsroom to community involvement, publishers need to consider whether their newspapers are fully invested in the editorial means already at their disposal to meet these new objectives. The core business of the newspaper - information, analysis and opinion - must be fully engaged before turning to other initiatives to solve newspapers' public relations and marketing problems. The AOPE needs to promulgate professional standards for the practice of op-ed journalism, including a clear articulation of the page's mission and function. Not only do the editors need to consider ethical practices in dealing with free-lancers (e.g., extra pay when an op-ed submission is moved on a regional or chain wire), but they also would benefit by establishing a professional identity within the field in order to attract top journalists to their ranks.

And finally, academics need to pay detailed attention to every aspect of newspaper journalism if they are to provide a context for survival in a changing media environment. Every aspect of newspaper journalism - such as travel, reviews (cinema, theater, music, art, etc.), real estate, commerce, health and science to name a few - begs for closer scrutiny. It is a disservice to the field that op-ed journalism has gone unexamined for so long. The emergence of the internet and its on-line opportunities should not deflect publishers, editors and academics from the basics of newspaper journalism. Newspapers were losing circulation and going out of business long before the emergence of interactive media. A flawed or irrelevant product in print cannot achieve excellence or relevancy simply by going digital.

The temptation for many newspapers will be to consider their public obligation fulfilled by creating electronic forums in which readers post their opinions and comments in an untended free-for-all. No one can be heard over the din. It takes a well-run op-ed page, with a professional gatekeeper, to focus the citizenry's attention on issues confronting a community.

4

Media Discourse and Serious vs. Tabloid Journalism

In addition to the particular studies cited above, the works of Bird, Jensen, Pauly, and Eason contribute to our theoretical framework for interpreting the mainstream news media's handling of the three high-profile events studied here. This framework views communication as a symbolic social practice and media content as the negotiated outcome of the social practices of its producers and the public.

Bird writes about supermarket tabloids as cultural phenomena, existing "alongside and because of other cultural phenomena" rather than merely as disconnected parts. She stresses the importance of considering intertextuality, or the relationship of one media product to other media and oral traditions, when studying the role of a media product (in her case, tabloids) in people's lives.

Bird argues that the writer, the reader, and the content itself contribute to "the cultural phenomenon of the tabloid", and she counters criticism of tabloid journalism by "serious" journalists with evidence of the close connection between "serious" and tabloid journalism, both past and present.

The connections to be made with our study are several. First, we must consider the cultural phenomenon we are examining, the assignment of blame in newspaper journalism to elements of popular media, in context with other cultural phenomena. If popular media are being portrayed in a negative light in print news media and the reader is a fan of popular media, a complex intertextual scenario may transpire. How audience members read news coverage that places responsibility for social ills on popular media may certainly be mitigated by audience members' own relationships with popular media.

Also relevant to our study is the relationship between "serious" journalism and tabloid journalism. In our study, we expect tabloid journalism will be directly implicated in both the "Jenny Jones" and the Princess Diana cases. In the Columbine case, we expect that the popular, entertainment-based media (video/computer games, movies, television shows, recorded music) will be implicated in press coverage. Central to our discussion of the treatment of these entities by journalists employed at major newspapers is the apparent division between the popular and the "elite" being drawn by the "serious" journalists in non-tabloid publications.

We argue that in order to point the finger of blame at media in general but deflect blame from one's own media outlet, this delineation is drawn. Yet, as Bird suggests, the distinction between "serious" and popular media is not one of opposite sides of a polemic but rather of blurry points on a continuum.

Jensen analyses decades of discourse about ill effects associated with media, although she examines scholarly arguments made by media critics whereas we examine news articles appearing in major newspapers. Jensen argues that when critics rail against the powers and persuasions of media, the underlying assumptions and beliefs they are advancing are fundamentally complaints about modernity or what modern times have wrought.

She does not attempt to determine whether there are unfavorable influences of the media on society or on individuals but rather she analyses the discussion or discourse surrounding that topic. We adopt the same stance in our study in that we do not attempt to determine whether the popular media discussed in newspaper coverage of these three events are to blame for the three tragedies. Rather, we examine the process by which they were blamed, in discourse located in newspaper coverage of the events.

Jensen's argument about modernity can be applied to our study. It is possible that though media criticism is easier to articulate as a cause for these tragic events, perhaps truer culprits are modern issues and circumstances.

Among these are an emphasis on commercial interests (e.g., ratings for Jenny Jones, money for the photos of Princess Diana, sales or ratings for the movies, music and video games mentioned in coverage of the Columbine shootings) or the alienation and disconnection experienced by many in contemporary life (e.g., the ostracism of the Columbine perpetrators, the claims of humiliation for the Jenny Jones assailant, the identification with and adoration of Princess Diana).

Jensen presents the key media criticism arguments advanced by Macdonald, that media and mass culture jeopardize the presence of high art; Boorstin, that "pseudo events" created by the media and presented to audiences as fact obscure the truth; Ewen, that consumer culture promotes an ideology of consumption that functions as an agent of social control; and Postman, that television has led to the transformation of serious and important aspects of public affairs into entertainment, thereby robbing audiences of information they need to conduct themselves as citizens.

Jensen identifies a common element in these criticisms: each suggests media change us, as audience members, by offering something more appealing or easier to make sense of compared to those things that would be better for us. Implicit in this criticism are the beliefs that there is consensus regarding what is good for society and that ordinary citizens themselves cannot be trusted to know what that may be.

However, in media criticism the blame is often not directly placed on the audience for choosing lazy or flashy options; instead blame is placed on the media for duping the audience into doing so by presenting no better options.

These notions about audience preference and this sense of protectionism are central to our study. The angles chosen, words used, and sources employed in reporting about these events (as part of the social process of news gathering) may reveal a similar "elite" protectionism and unflattering belief about the nature of audience preferences and desires. The news coverage may imply that members of the news media know what is best in order to protect the masses and to sustain social order.

By assigning responsibility to popular media for these three tragedies, "serious" journalists can adopt a prescriptive stance toward improving social conditions by leading audiences away from the ostensibly harmful and salacious content in the popular media to which they are presumably drawn.

Jensen discusses the moral element in the comparison of tabloid journalism with "serious" journalism, with the distinction drawn between the two indicating "a moral tension between self-indulgence and self-denial". The loyalty of tabloid journalists to audience interests and therefore profit making is contrasted in media criticism to the loyalty of "serious" journalists to "higher" processes of rationality and the virtues of high culture.

The distinction is made more obvious in the aspect of media-influence discourse that refers to the "lowest common denominator" presumably appealed to by certain types of media content such as tabloid journalism or popular media. A particular view of audiences as being ill equipped for reason and inevitably drawn to more "shallow symbolic forms" underlies this commonly used phrase.

This is central to our discussion in that implicit in the criticism of popular media by elite news media is a sense of shamefulness associated with "pandering" to "base" human instincts toward violence (Columbine, Jenny Jones), intrusivcness (Jenny Jones, Princess Diana), and sex (Jenny Jones). An essay by Pauly about media mogul Rupert Murdoch in Carey's Media, Myths, and Narratives also informs this discussion of "elite" and "non-elite" media.

Murdoch was criticized for his use of "promotional journalism" and accused of devaluing journalistic ideals by not "honoring the stylistic conventions that journalists used to defend the social importance of their occupation". Pauly discusses the defensive strategy of distinguishing between information and entertainment as a primary means of defining "elite" and "non-elite" media. Yet, he argues that this is an artificial construction since news content is increasingly presented in a manner and in a context that seeks to entertain: Because mass-circulation dailies comprise vast and varied symbolic materials, different groups can argue that the 'essential' part is the one that they most enjoy or that sustains their sense of identification. Thus the professional journalist emphasizes the investigative role of the newspaper out of proportion to the actual number of stories undertaken.

In other words, the investigative, purely informational, "factual" content in a daily newspaper is a small portion of the whole, but is magnified in importance by those with a vested interest in arguing the difference between "serious" and tabloid journalism. This argument is at the centre of our study, which suggests that in order to blame some aspects of media and popular culture, newspaper journalists must imply that this content is fundamentally different (and comparatively "worse") than what they transmit to audiences.

The alleged dichotomy between "what audience members want" and "what audience members need" is also raised in Eason's essay in Carey's Media, Myths, and Narratives, in which Eason discusses the controversy surrounding the fabricated elements in Janet Cooke's award-winning news story, "Jimmy's World." Eason argues that journalism has experienced an evolution away from the repertorial function of transmitting facts and more toward the creation of "reality " with the words and elements of a story chosen by journalists.

We argue similarly that the journalists in the news stories we reviewed about these three high-profile tragedies create a reality in which popular media and popular-culture products bear responsibility for the tragedies. Although the journalists whose stories we review presumably did not fabricate any information they conveyed, they did choose to highlight certain "facts" that appear to have made their stories more marketable to a large audience while downplaying other "facts" that may have been deemed of less interest to readers.

FACTORS AFFECTING MEDIA COVERAGE

A somewhat different though complementary view of the phenomenon of popular-culture culpability is seen from the perspective of Shoemaker and Reese. Their approach examines how media content is influenced by factors in the context in which it is created.

Though one could view their theoretical perspective as examining media content as shaped by external social processes in a unidirectional (external forces lead to media content) manner, we argue that their theory can be expanded to examine the interrelated, multidirectional, dynamic relations between all elements-content, producers, public.

In Mediating the Message, Shoemaker and Reese identify five major spheres of influence on media content, from the most microscopic to the most macroscopic. We use these labels to identify sources of influence on the producers of news content as well as on the content itself. Though the labels are presented individually, we argue for their overlapping, multidirectional relationship with content as journalists go about the social practice of determining how to cover "the news." We introduce the levels of influence here briefly and will then apply them to each of the three events examined in this chapter.

The most microscopic level of influence on media content is the individual level, that is, the influence exerted by the individual reporter or columnist, the copy editor, and the editor-each person who has a hand in creating the news content. This can include deciding what constitutes news, selecting the angle of the story, writing the story, and editing it. Some of the factors that influence content decisions at the individual level are personal feelings, tastes and preferences, values, opinions, and the professional backgrounds and training of those directly involved in content decisions.

The media routines level focuses on the routines, or standard procedures, for gathering and disseminating news. Among the influences found at this level are news values-those characteristics that make an event newsworthy, such as deviance from the norm, sensationalism, prominence, proximity, timeliness, conflict or controversy, human interest, and impact on audience members or society as a whole.

Other media routines include objectivity, the five "Ws" (answering who, what, when, where, and why in every report), pack journalism, competition, reliance on other media for information or for whole stories, localism (getting the local angle on a story that takes place far away), simplicity (offering pat "answers" because complex situations are hard to explain and hard for readers to understand quickly), and over-reliance on a handful of sources.

The next level of influence, moving toward a more macroscopic perspective, is the organizational level. Analysis at the organizational level focuses on the impact of policies, managers, and owners of the organization in which the media content is produced. It is difficult to discuss influences at this level, as we do not know what went on in each newsroom during coverage of these three events. However, the opinions of upper management or concerns of those in the circulation or advertising-sales departments can influence coverage, as can organizational policies such as the degree of autonomy allowed to each reporter.

The extramedia level has to do with elements and factors outside of the media organizations themselves, such as news sources, advertisers, government, interest groups, and the audience. This level includes actual, direct influences as well as the influence that news media personnel's perceptions of what these entities might do or how they might feel that also shape content. While influence of advertisers might weigh against extensive blaming of popular culture in news coverage, for example, pressure from some interest groups and activists, as well as governmental concern, could weigh toward the pursuit of this angle.

In terms of perceptions of audience preferences, some journalists may believe that audiences want to see and read about violence, sensationalism, scandal, and the lives of celebrities. This perception could have a profound impact, because giving the audiences "what they want" will presumably sell newspapers and space to advertisers. Thus, angles that have popular appeal may be advanced while more esoteric or abstract angles, such as the notion that society in general is responsible or that a complex nexus of forces are at fault, may take a back seat.

The notion of audience preference is also a cultural one. de Mooij argues the one such preference that is culturally bound is America's adherence to a cause-and-effect paradigm. She argues that it is a cultural norm in the United States to expect to have a logical explanation for any given event and that any event has concrete and measurable answers to the question of what caused it.

Journalists, if following this cultural norm or if presuming audiences follow it, may provide a concrete explanation rather than leave the tragedies unexplained. Subscribing to this cause-and-effect paradigm can be viewed as an individual influence on the part of reporters and editors, an extramedia influence that takes the shape of conceptions about audience preferences, or an ideological influence that entails broad-based cultural and societal beliefs.

The ideological level includes the influences that broad systems of beliefs and values have on the news-gathering process. Among the factors at play here are notions of "elite" and "popular" media, representations that define "mainstream" and "deviant" content, and the concept of hegemony. The latter suggests that entities enjoying political and economic power in existing societal structure will act in the interest of thwarting social change in order to protect their dominant status. We predict that these three case studies will show the use of defensive strategies when other media are, indeed, blamed.

Through the use of labels such as "tabloid," "paparazzi," and "trash TV" to draw theoretically distinct lines, journalists may construct readings of their own stories as the dominant discourse and those of "tabloid" media and "trash TV" as deviant. A subtext exists in this type of criticism that suggests a need to save people from their own tastes in media and popular culture. This is similar to the points raised by Bird and Jensen above, and is the central theoretical element of the study at hand.

de Mooij's suggestion that as part of American culture, we-as members of society-need someone or something to blame whenever there is a tragedy, also has implications for hegemony and social order. In order for members of society to feel secure about the world around them, there has to be a rational cause, with a clearly identifiable source of blame, for each event. Thus, it is much more satisfying to place blame on a specific, tangible targetin this case, the non-elite media-rather than advancing the more unsettling notion that something is amiss in society at large.

The first case study involves the death of Princess Diana of Wales and the automobile accident that took her life and the lives of Dodi al Fayed and Henri Paul on August 31,1997. The accident occurred shortly after midnight in Paris when the Mercedes Benz in which the princess and her friend were travelling crashed in a tunnel near the Seine River. Dodi al Fayed and Henri Paul, the driver, were found dead at the scene. The princess died a few hours later of injuries she sustained in the crash.

The event was reported in newspapers around the world. The larger U.S. and U.K. newspapers gave extensive coverage to the event in the days following the crash. For example, on the first day of coverage The London Observer ran 28 articles, The New York Daily News ran 10 articles, and The Atlanta Journal and Constitution ran four articles.

This case study is based on analysis of those articles and others that were published in English-language newspapers from the day of the crash, August 31, 1997, through the day of Diana's funeral, September 6, 1997, when the focus of coverage shifted from the accident to the funeral. The articles were retrieved from the General News archive of LEXIS-NEXIS Academic Universe. In all, 507 stories were reviewed for relevant content, and those with relevant content were studied more closely.

Often, the first news reports of a tragic and unexpected event will present only the basic facts of the story, answering the fundamental journalistic questions of who was involved, what happened, when it happened, and where it happened, without speculation as to the causes of the event. It usually takes another day or more for the "how" and "why" questions to be answered.

However, this was not the case in the early reporting on Princess Diana's death. Answers to the "how" and "why" questions were included in the initial reports of the event because tabloid-press photographers were said to have been chasing the princess's car at the time of the accident.

Approximately 11 photographers, sources said, some on motorcycles and others in a car, set out after Diana and Dodi's Mercedes when it left the Ritz hotel in Paris. The photographers were apparently trying to get pictures that would confirm rumors of a romance between Diana and Dodi.

Several sources in the earliest stories claimed that the photographers caused the accident. Among them were Paris police, unspecified police, French journalists (their sources unnamed), a photographer for a London paper, Agence-France Presse (the French news agency), and British reporters.

No eyewitnesses to the crash were quoted in the early coverage-in other words, no source knew for certain that the photographers had actually caused the accident (and some sources even claimed that the car had lost the photographers). In spite of this, the idea that the photographers caused the accident became a part of every story reporting the facts of the event.

The Boston Heraldbegan an article by Joseph Mallia (Aug. 31,1997) with "Princess Diana and her companion Dodi Fayed were killed in a high-speed car crash early today in a tunnel near the Seine River in Paris, as their Mercedes was being pursued by photographers."

The Hindu of India began a story (no byline, Aug. 31) with "Britain's Princess Diana and her millionaire companion, Dodi El-Fayed, were killed in a car crash early on Sunday while being chased by photographers on motorcycles in a road tunnel in the French capital Paris." The third paragraph of an Associated Press story that ran in The Buffalo News on August 31 read "The crash happened shortly after midnight in a tunnel along the Seine River at the Pont de l'Aima bridge. It came as paparazzi-the commercial photographers who constantly tailed Dianafollowed her car, police said."

During the week after the fatal crash, when coverage of the event was at its most intense, nearly every article contained at least one source who blamed the producers of popular culture for Diana's death. Among these were family members and family representatives, dignitaries, ordinary citizens, and journalists themselves.

Other sources who blamed "the paparazzi," "the press," "the media," or "the tabloids" (sometimes including tabloid-style television shows) were an Arizona talk-radio host and many of his callers, Britons living in the United States (usually interviewed in pubs), un-named TV commentators, and David Perel, executive editor of the American tabloid The National Enquirer. Perel was quoted in several newspapers as saying that reckless action by the paparazzi probably caused the accident.

Some family members of the crash victims extended the blame to all photographers who pursue celebrities for photos to be printed in tabloid newspapers. Ellen Tumposky and Mike Claffey of The New York Daily News (Aug. 31) reported "The dead Egyptian playboy's father, Mohammed Al-Fayed, blamed the tragedy on the paparazzi, who were being held for questioning by Paris police. There is no doubt in Mr. Al-Fayed's mind that this tragedy would not have occurred but for the press photographers who have dogged and pursued Mr. Fayed and the princess for weeks,' a spokesman for the Egyptian billionaire said."

The Houston Chronicle (byline Houston Chronicle News Services, Aug. 31) reported "(Michael Gibbons), a spokesman for Buckingham Palace, noting that the incident occurred while the couple were being chased by photographers, said it was 'an accident waiting to happen.'... he repeated the palace's anger at the actions of photographers who pursue the royal family around the world." Other family members blamed not only tabloid-press photographers but also the editors and publishers of gossipy tabloid publications. The London Observer was one of the first to report a scathing statement from Diana's brother.

"This is not a time for recriminations," said Earl Spencer, "but I would say that I always believed the press would kill her in the end. But not even I could imagine that they would take such a direct hand in her death as seems to be the case. It would appear that every proprietor and editor of every publication that has paid for intrusive and exploitative photographs of her, encouraging greedy and ruthless individuals to risk everything in pursuit of Diana's image, have blood on their hands today."

None of the first-day stories reporting the reactions of world leaders and diplomats (such as President Clinton, the Singapore government, and the Pope) contained quotes that blamed popular culture. However, on the second day of coverage, several French government officials made statements blaming the paparazzi, as reported in The Hindu (by Vaiju Naravane, Sept. 1).

The president of the French Parliament, the former prime minister, Mr. Laurent Fabius... said that death precipitated by paparazzi proves that "photos, words and attitudes can also, in a certain sense, kill. These people must now face their responsibility."...The government's spokeswoman, Ms. Catherine Trautmann, who is also France's Culture Minister, was more vehement in her denunciation of the paparazzi. Princess Diana was the victim of the stubbornness of the press, she declared.

"The singlemindedness of the press had increased dramatically these past weeks... The circumstances of her death have thrown up questions about the functioning of this profession and above all of our society," Ms. Trautmann added. Among the stories that reported the reactions of ordinary citizens, most contained at least one source who blamed either the paparazzi who pursued the Mercedes or the press in general. Most of these "average-citizen" sources did not distinguish between the popular press and the elite press or their producers, nor did the reporters attempt to make any distinction for the sources. The blame laid by these sources was among the most vitriolic. The New York Daily News (article by Barbara Ross, Aug. 31) reported:

Britons in New York mixed their grief at Princess Diana's death with criticism of the press for its relentless pursuit of her.... Beverly Dorking, 25, of Leeds in northern England, said, "...she's been dogged and hounded by the media. They've been in her face since she was 19, and now they've taken away the world's most popular woman." Nicola Shigley, 24, of northern England, predicted a backlash against the media. She accused the media of spending "the last 10 years trying to put the woman to an end."

The San Diego Union-Tribune (article by Lillian Salazar Leopold, Aug. 31) reported '"The press has a lot to answer for,' said Mary Simpson, also of Liverpool. 'They hounded her to death. Literally, now.'"

The Seattle Times (article by Chris Solomon, Aug. 31) reported "Mitch Lease, 23...reflected bitterly on the circumstances of her death, a chase by photographers. I think the media should have given her a break a long time ago, and now they've killed her.'"

The London Observer (article by Roy Greenslade, Aug. 31) reported "In one bitter outburst on BBC TV, a woman demanded that a reporter and his cameraman slop filmmg. 'You've done this Io her,' she screamed. 'You're to blame. The media, the papers, all of you.'" Some articles blamed popular culture by quoting other publications and thereby demonstrating what seemed to be a world-wide consensus as to who was to blame for the tragedy. A London Observer article (byline: "foreign staff," Aug. 31) read:

The French newspaper Liberation gave over its whole front page to a picture of (Diana) with the headline, "One photo too many. "... Italy's La Stampa took up the same theme, stating tersely: "Dead for a photo".... Hong Kong newspapers agonised over their own home-grown paparazzi, with the Oriental Daily News recalling that a local pop singer, Leslie Cheung, had crashed his Porsche while being pursued by photographers.

It branded paparazzi as "criminals of a thousand years." The Daily Star, a Bangładesh newspaper, said that "Western press and society will need to embark on a long search of their souls to come to terms with the sense of guilt Diana's death must generate."

Alongside the just-the-facts stories and reaction stories were articles focused primarily on the causes of the accident. Many of these stories found some aspect of popular culture (either the photographers who chased Diana's car that night, tabloid-press photographers in general, tabloid newspapers, the editors and publishers of tabloid newspapers, or any member of the press who had purchased paparazzi photos) to be at fault. The tone of these articles was often angry and disgusted.

Earl Spencer's statement was used in several of these stories as a starting point for further discussion of the role of the paparazzi in Diana's death. Dave Walker, writing for TAe Arizona Republic (Sept. 1), began such a story by asking "Do the media have blood on their hands for the death of Princess Diana? That's what her brother, Earl Spencer, suggested in the aftermath of the car wreck..."

Walker went on to cite several sources who agreed with Spencer, including Dodi's father, Mohamed al Fayed, unnamed network television commentators, and Phoenix-area talk-radio host Charles Goyette, whom Walker quoted: '"The media are clearly to blame,' said Goyette, summing up the majority opinion among his callers. 'The consumers of this trash don't have the culpability, the media do.'"

An article in The Glasgow Herald (by Catherine Macleod, Sept. 1) quoted a source who followed Spencer's lead and blamed all the producers of tabloid newspapers: "...the Prince of Wales's biographer Jonathan Dimbleby said: 'It isn't only the reporters and photographers, it's those who hired them.' He added: 'It's the editors and proprietors who too often, offer glossy excuses about the public interest who need now to examine their consciences.'"

Some of the stories that discussed causes were actually editorials expressing the views of the writer or writers. For example, The London Observer (no by-line, Aug. 31) expressed the following opinion: "Anyone in the British Press who has bought and used the pictures snatched by paparazzi on so many previous utterly private occasions helped ensure that the ravening pack would be on the trail on Saturday night." Some of these articles were written in a narrative stylo, retelling the facts of the story dramatically while characterizing the photographers as degenerates. For example, Michael Daly of The New York Daily News (Aug. 31) wrote:

No matter how fast her car sped through the Paris night, the paparazzi on the motorbikes were sure to stay right behind her, for she was with the man said to be her lover.... The following Sunday, she was swarmed by those only interested in violating her private life.... They were still after the couple when she arrived in France.

The hounds kept baying, right up to early this morning, when motorcycles sped after Diana's car along the Seine. Her pursuers were right out of the 1961 movie "La Dolce Vita," in which a photographer named Paparazzo chases his prey on a motorscooter.... They chased the biggest score ever right to her death. The frenzy that began with "The Kiss" ended in two children being left without their mother.

Similarly, Luke Harding, Owen Bowcott, John Hooper, Paul Webster, Alex Bellos, Stephen Bates, and Chris Mihill of The London Observer (Aug. 31) wrote:

Even before Princess Diana and Dodi Fayed had strolled through the baroque central corridor of the Ritz hotel in Paris...the paparazzi were lurking in wait.... (Diana and Dodi's) presence was common knowledge among the small, ruthless, multilingual band of photographers who pursue her, very lucratively, for a living.... Around 7 p.m. on Saturday Diana left the Ritz in a chauffeur-driven car to do some shopping in the Champs Elysee. The press pack were, reportedly, in close pursuit....

Quite a few stories blamed "the press" in general or "the media" in general, not distinguishing the mainstream press from the tabloid press.

Among these were stories reporting that Diana herself had condemned the practices of the British press in an interview published in a French newspaper the week before the accident. J. Frank Lynch of The Atlanta Journal and Constitution (Aug. 31) reported "In Great Britain, 'the press is ferocious," Diana said in the article in the French daily Le Monde. 'It forgives nothing and is only hunting down mistakes. Each act is twisted; each gesture is criticized.'"

A number of stories about the causes of Diana's death divided the blame among several culprits. One of these culprits was Henri Paul, the driver of the Mercedes. On the first day of coverage, many articles noted that Paul had been driving at a speed well above the limit and that he lost control of the car, thus implying that the accident was at least partly his fault.

When the news of Paul's very high blood-alcohol level (which was more than three times the French legal limit) was released on day two, he became the target of finger-pointing in many more articles. However, none of the stories that blamed Paul let the producers of popular culture off the hook completely. An editorial in The Arizona Republic (no byline, Sept. 3) argued:

The swift and reckless rush to judgment, the desire to fix certain blame for the death of Diana, is also destructive and promises to leave victims. Misplaced blame might mask sorrow's pain, but it does not heal.

Diana Spencer, queen of celebrity, died from the impaired judgment of millions. We'll name a few. The paparazzi, a subset of photojournalists identified first and perhaps forever as the villains who ended the strange, fairy-tale existence of a lovely young woman, continue to receive disproportionate blame. Seven photographers face some type of charges related to the fatal crash.... So what of the judgment of those editors and publishers who buy sleaze and resell it under some loose definition of news? Impaired?

Morally warped? Yes.... And, so whal of the judgment of millions of readers who purchase the product now blamed for the death of a princess? Impaired? Warped? Yes.... However, in this tragedy, the person whose impaired judgment seems most responsible for the death of Princess Diana, is the man behind the wheel of the car carrying her and her boyfriend....

One of the few articles to seriously consider the culpability of Henri Paul was published by The Boston Globe (Sept. 1). (This story also contained several sources who blamed the paparazzi at the scene and the press in general.) Author Peter S. Canellos wrote:

Ralph Whitehead, a journalism professor at the University of Massachusetts, said all the hand-wringing over the misdeeds of media is "a momentary hysteria."

Unless proof emerges that paparazzi on motorcycles actually interfered with the progress of Diana's car, responsibility for the accident should rest with the driver, he said. The Mercedes limousine was traveling faster than 60 miles per hour-perhaps much faster-in a tunnel where the speed limit is 30, police said. The princess and her companion, Dodi Fayed, did not appear to be wearing seatbelts.

"What would Diana and the rest of the people in the car have lost if they'd been overtaken by photographers?" Whitehead said. "If you're a celebrity, you have a right to regard the paparazzi as a pain in the neck. But it's not the right response to put your life in jeopardy by speeding away."

For a few days, there was a bit of a tug of war between those sources representing the photographers (primarily their lawyers) and those representing the driver (the Fayed family and Paul's co-workers). Some of the stories printed on days two through seven offered opinions as to which party deserved more blame, while others blamed Western society as a whole for its fascination with celebrities.

In an article called "Time Has Come to Point Finger in Right Direction," Steve Wilson of The Arizona Republic (Sept. 3) wrote "I would like to interrupt all the finger-pointing in Princess Diana's death-do the paparazzi or the drunken driver deserve the most blame?-for this important message: It's the culture, stupid. Or more precisely, it's the stupid, celebrity-obsessed culture."

When the playwright Arnold Wesker spent several months at the offices of the *Sunday Times,* gathering background material for his drama *The Journalists,* he decided to produce an account of his observations. The resulting slim volume caused such offence to some of those he observed that its publication was held up for five years. This was his conclusion:

The journalist knows his world is among the least perfect of all imperfect worlds. Most are raring to get out and write books-the best of them do, frustrated by small canvases and the butterfly life of their hard earned thoughts and words. Wesker was not, suffice to say, overly impressed by what he found. Indeed, his book conveys a sense of bemusement that grown men (as national newspaper journalists in the main then were) could want to subject themselves to such demeaning work. More than a quarter of a century later, many people outside the media seem still to share that view. The industry has changed out of all recognition: relatively large numbers of journalists at all levels are women and not a few are black; and technological advance, long delayed while the trade unions remained strong, has transformed the job.

Yet the popular image of journalism appears often to remain that of the unscrupulous, dog-eat-dog press of 1920s Chicago, immortalised on stage and screen in *The Front Page.* There is undoubtedly a fear of the media, but above all there is a lack of understanding. And nowhere is that lack more evident than in the world of social policy.

NO TABLETS OF STONE

Probably the single most common misconception about what I do is that I do it to edict, or that it is at least pre-determined according to policy positions and protocols. One assumption is that my editor decrees which stories are to be covered, how they should be treated and what editorial line is to be taken.

Alternatively, because of the *Guardian's* liberal image, other people assume such matters are thrashed out in policy discussions involving me and other colleagues. Either way, there is a widespread belief that I approach the working week with a shopping list of news and feature issues to be written about, and with detailed briefing on the angle to take on each.

The reality is that papers are much more chaotic operations than their readers ever imagine. While it would be wrong to say there is no top-down editorial diktat, the great bulk of day-to-day decisions about coverage are taken by individual writers or desk editors without reference to colleagues, let alone the editor.

There are two circumstances in which the editor will insist on something being reported. One is when the paper is running a campaign on a particular issue, as with the *Independent's* focus in the mid-1990s on the emerging pattern of abuse of children and young people in residential care over the previous thirty years. To sustain the momentum of such a campaign, developments which ordinarily might not meet the criteria for publication will be carried in what is, in effect, reserved editorial space.

The other circumstance is what is known as an 'editor's must', a term laden with significance and with implied adverse consequences should expectations not be fulfilled. As the words suggest, they refer to a story that must be carried, no matter what. This can range from a pet hobbyhorse to something the editor half heard on the radio that morning.

For many years, one national paper would regularly carry reports of the most obscure issues to do with sailing on the River Crouch in Essex. More common is an elliptical reference by the editor, of a deputy, to an 'interesting' issue. This will be taken by their lieutenants as a clear instruction to ensure the said issue is covered fully in the next edition.

By and large, though, journalists take on-the-run decisions about what to cover, and what not, on the basis not of any written or even verbal orders or guidelines but according to an almost intuitive sense of what is important and what fits the bill for the paper in question. For the *Guardian,* with its particular constituency, this means a greater-than-average interest (though not as great as people often think) in social policy issues. For the *Daily Mail,* with its well-known stance on 'traditional' family values, this means a bigger appetite for stories about marriage, divorce and abortion.

This is not to say that the process of putting together a paper-or, for that matter, a TV or radio programme-is without structure. On a national paper, the day begins with an editorial conference at which desk editors representing the various departments of news and features review that morning's product, assess the efforts of the competition and, usually, pat themselves on the back for a job well done.

The conference then turns to the next day's issue, with each department-essentially home news, foreign, features, city and sport-outlining the events and issues they plan to cover.

At this stage, the listing may simply be, 'Home Office press conference on crime figures', or it may be a more detailed, 'Crime up: Home Secretary to announce new measures'. (With the modern trend of pre-briefing, rare indeed is the announcement not already trailed in the press by government spin doctors.) And listing at this point does not necessarily mean that the proposed article will end up in print.

News and features lists change as the day goes on and plans can be torn up and rewritten well into the evening. Indeed, when the first editions of the dailies become available after 10 p.m.-there is a swap system among the main titles-good stories in the rivals are picked out, checked for veracity and written up for later editions. What is read in the first version of the paper in Cornwall and Scotland can, therefore, differ considerably from what is read in later versions in London.

Setting the Leader Line

While the morning meeting is the main planning forum, there are further, though smaller, editorial conferences as the day wear on and the pace of the operation picks up. These include a leader conference at which the senior journalists who write the editorial comments-usually not, contrary to popular belief, the editor-decide which issues to tackle.

They may discuss what line to take, although much again is left to the individual's assumptions about the paper's values. Exceptionally, there may be a general debate among the staff about a leader line-on the merits of the Gulf War, for example-but the usual pattern is for the leader writer to discuss the issues with the relevant specialist correspondent.

As with so much else to do with the media, those on the outside, looking in, tend to overestimate the sophistication of what is a fairly crude process.

In an analysis of the *Guardian*'s coverage of alleged ritual child abuse in Rochdale in 1990, Meryl Aldridge has remarked upon the fluctuating leader line: here supportive of social services, there critical in a 'very un-*Guardian*-like way. She concludes that the position the paper eventually arrived at, supporting the families involved against social services, may have had a historical basis: Yet over Rochdale, after an initial struggle, the paper leapt to the parents' defence, ditching the concerns of its stereotype readership. One possible explanation of this apparent paradox is the newspaper's roots, as the *Manchester Guardian,* in the northwest. As a result, over Rochdale, it reacted more like a local paper than a liberal national broadsheet.

The prosaic truth is that the varying leader line through the saga reflected the differing views of two leader writers. The apparent supremacy of one position in such situations results less from informal, intellectual debate, more from practical considerations such as one party going on leave.

Where News Comes from

Whereas general reporters are assigned to stories chosen by a news editor, specialists typically propose stories to the news desk. Whether proposals are taken up depends on the individual news editor's view and the number of story ideas already on the newslist.

Most days, I will put forward two or three ideas in the expectation of being asked to write one or two, of which one may get into the paper. I rely heavily, indeed too heavily, for story ideas on institutional sources.

That means Whitehall, leading professional associations and, increasingly under the contract culture, voluntary groups. Pressure not to miss a government announcement is an enormous incentive to do the job from your desk, and a corresponding disincentive to take time out to see social policy in practice. People are often surprised, and by implication disappointed, at how little I see on the ground of what I write about in the abstract. It is a failing I readily admit to, though I like to think I witness more practice than do most of my peers. Other sources of material are the 'trade' press, the specialist weeklies or monthlies, and tip-offs from readers. The Thatcher/Major years, when there was a clampdown on the passing of information by public servants to the media, undoubtedly slowed the flow of tips and certainly that of confidential documents.

It was on charges of breach of confidentiality that one of my best sources, nurse Graham Pink, was eventually disciplined by NHS managers in Stockport-though not, thankfully, before his powerful testimony of hospital elderly care had already had a profound impact on public and political opinion.

The Labour government elected in 1997 promised protection for whistle-blowers, as in fairness had the Major administration. But experience of the first years of Labour rule suggested that public sector workers were, if anything, even less likely to pass information than they had been under the Conservatives. This obviously had some political basis, in that sources have very often been trade union activists who would at least have been giving Labour the benefit of the doubt, but it also suggested that there was to be no return to the days of brown paper envelopes arriving at newspaper offices by the sackful.

Working as a Specialist

As a specialist, my job is to patrol the areas for which I am responsible. I am there to make sure that the paper does not miss stories that appear elsewhere, to produce exclusive stories of our own and to provide interpretation of, and sometimes informed comment on, emerging issues.

I also see my role in part as acting as a bridge between the paper and the interest groups, professional and user, on my patch. In this respect, the trick is to be and remain a perfectly balanced bridge, leaning in particular not too far towards the 'client group', for want of a better term.

The most heinous crime a specialist can commit is to go native, to become too closely identified with their professional sources.

This is not generally a question of corruption, certainly not in social policy, but it can over time become easy to adopt professional perspectives on issues such as resource constraints-i.e. there is never enough-than to question the use of resources already available.

One information source that never dries up, sadly, is the constant stream of people dissatisfied, and very often angry, with the treatment they have received from public services. Indeed, the growth of a more consumerist attitude towards such services, in contrast to the gratitude of the '1945 generation' at having any services at all, seems to be fuelling dissatisfaction. I receive calls and letters every day, almost without fail, from people who feel at their wits' end with social security, the Child Support Agency, the NHS and, most often, social services. The most distressing approaches are those from parents who believe their children have unjustifiably been taken into care. Rarely can such complaints be explored, not least because of social services' reluctance to discuss them on grounds of client confidentiality. But it is difficult to find the time to look into any grievance.

Contrary to widespread supposition, specialists in the press are very much one-person shows: there is no research backup and rarely any designated understudy on the general reporting staff. It would be quite possible to spend all the time pursuing readers' problems. In order to do the job, you end up pursuing almost none.

The good Story

What makes a good story? It seems to be to the eternal bafflement of social policy professionals that good practice does not win headlines; that journalists are not falling over themselves to report, 'Child saved from abuse' or 'Patient treated successfully'.

Social services journalist Anne Fry has it about right, 'A good story-contrary to popular social work belief-is not about some worthy policy development, practice initiative or social services personality. It is about raw emotion, disagreement between professionals and, best of all, culpability'.

This came to a head, not for the first time and surely not for the last, in coverage of the early joint reviews of social services departments by the Audit Commission and the Social Services Inspectorate. While many of the first thirty review reports were positive, media attention focused on a handful that were critical, notably those on Sefton, Barking and Dagenham, Sheffield and Coventry. Social services leaders were angered by the imbalance and, at the 1998 social services conference, Rita Stringfellow, chair of the Local Government Association's social affairs and health committee, publicly criticised the 'unhelpful' language being used by this writer and, indeed, by the newly-appointed chief inspector of social services, Denise Platt.

Government ministers sought to blame the media for dwelling on the few negative reports, and ignoring the rest, but the fact was that the Whitehall publicity machine had deliberately played up the negative joint review reports in order to portray the Labour administration as tough on poor social work. If there was a media conspiracy, the politicians were very much party to it.

Culpability is very much top of the media agenda: witness the (usually frustrated) demands for at least one head to roll on publication of every inquiry report into a so-called 'care-in-the-community killing'.

But other factors can serve to raise the level of interest in stories. Research for the Department of Health on communication and the risks to public health has identified ten 'media triggers' likely to make a story about a health risk a major one.

They are:

- Questions of blame
- Alleged secrets and attempted cover-ups
- Human interest through identifiable heroes, villains, dupes, etc. (as well as victims)
- Links with existing high-profile issues or personalities
- Conflict (between experts and/or between experts and the public)
- Signal value: the story as a portent of further ills ('What next?')
- Many people exposed to the risk, even if at low levels ('It could be you!')
- Strong visual impact
- Sex and/or crime
- Snowballing of reportage: the fact that something is a major story is often itself a story, and this becomes self-fuelling as media compete for coverage.

Most of these factors can be said to have general application. But in the field of social policy, I would add an eleventh trigger: that the story has development potential, that it can be turned into something more than the sums of its present parts.

One of the most hilarious, but at the same time cautionary, accounts of this has been written by sociologist Robert Burgess, now Vice-Chancellor at Leicester University. He had been awarded a research grant to lead a study of children's knowledge of nutrition, as part of the Economic and Social Research Council's Nation's Diet initiative.

The first media treatment of this, in a regional daily paper, was fairly accurate. But as the story was picked up, sequentially, by news agencies and other papers, it became increasingly distorted into a shape more to the media's liking. In the end, the *Sun* reported: Din-dins prof hunts chip kids. A professor is to share bags of chips with kids for two years-to find out why they prefer junk food to school dinners. Sociologist Robert Burgess, dubbed Doctor Din-Dins, will visit schools around the country and follow children on lunchtime trips. In a similar vein, though mercifully less extreme, much of the media went into overdrive in December 1997 about the threat to the great British doorstep. This was supposedly posed by amendments to the building regulations to make homes wheelchair accessible.

'Hilda Ogden would be tearing out her curlers-they're planning to do away with the great British doorstep, ' lamented the *Daily Mail*.

The fact that the change would apply only to new properties was played down; that it was part of a bigger package to improve general accessibility and was supported by organisations including the Chartered Institute of Housing, the Royal Institute of British Architects and the Consumers' Association, was scarcely mentioned at all. The converse of this compulsion to push stories beyond their natural limits is to be found in media coverage of the voluntary sector. Here is a burgeoning, £13 billion-slice of the economy, employing almost 500,000 paid staff and at least 3 million volunteers, delivering a fast-growing wedge of public services. Yet it is as if the media do not want the sector to have grown up.

Coverage remains very much stuck in a 1950s charity time warp of good-cause fundraising, lifeboats, guide dogs and helping sick children. Even on the broadsheet national papers, there is a clear antipathy to stories that treat the leading charities as the big businesses they now are. But stories exposing the 'fat-cat' salaries of charity bosses, earning in excess of £65,000 a year for running multi-million-pound operations, are lapped up.

As a specialist correspondent, the challenge is to survive within this environment, observing the unwritten rules about what is a good story and demonstrating obeisance to some of the (least objectionable) prejudices, while keeping faith with your constituency. The tension implicit in this can be very great. It has been with increasingly heavy heart over recent years that I have approached the task of covering inquiry reports on care-in-the-community homicides. On one hand, it has been clear that the reports have been revealing fewer and fewer insights into the underlying problems and have been contributing to a grossly distorted picture of mental health care.

On the other hand, when the rest of the media are carrying the reports in full and gruesome detail, it is simply not an option to argue for no coverage. The compromise is to try to present the issues in as restrained and balanced a way as possible.

This is not to say that, by doing so, you are seeking to protect your professional contacts. Of course it is true that specialists rely on their contacts and cannot afford to risk being cut off by betraying confidence or reporting in an overly hostile manner. But it is impossible to avoid reporting critically, when justified, and experience suggests that most social policy professionals take a mature view of this.

Over the past ten years, I could count on the fingers of one hand the number who have reacted so adversely to something I have written that further working relations have been damaged.

Playing the System

One of the lasting impressions of specialising in this field is how poor the social policy world appears to be at shaping the media agenda. If you remain purely reactive, as too many seem to, coverage tends to be framed by the trigger factors: blame, cover-up and so on. 'But you never print the good news!' comes the protest. And it is undeniably true, as discussed above, that you will never find a paper clearing page one for a graphic account of the successful rehabilitation of a young offender.

But that is not to say that the promotion of positive images is a lost cause. For all the media bias against social workers, and there undoubtedly is such bias, the profession has in recent years been pleasantly surprised to find itself praised for its counselling and other work in the aftermath of civil disasters. Skilful, proactive handling of the media has even been known to turn near-catastrophe (in every sense) into a veritable public relations triumph, as in the case of the abduction and return of baby Abbie Humphries from the Queen's Medical Centre, Nottingham, in 1994.

So what kind of news and feature ideas am I looking for? The essential answer is anything which offers robust evidence, quantitative or qualitative, of the functioning of both society and the controls upon it. Social welfare agencies are sitting on a wealth of this kind of information, but very rarely do they seek to make use of it. Whitehall has recently woken up to this, beginning quite aggressively to market the social data series held by the Office for National Statistics.

One result has been a much higher media profile for the various official surveys and one-off reports based upon them. While it would be absurd to suggest that a voluntary organisation could match the number-crunching of the Government's statistical arm, even the smallest charity is likely to have sound empirical evidence of the social issues it works with.

Put into the public domain in the right way and at the right time, for timing is a great deal in successful use of the media, such evidence could be invaluable. As regards promotion of good practice, the *Guardian* is unique among national papers in having a weekly supplement, *Society,* devoted to social policy in the broadest sense. Yet, with honourable exceptions such as the Joseph Rowntree Foundation, it is remarkable how few organisations seek to have their work highlighted in this way.

This may reflect fear of being 'stitched-up' by the press, of being drawn on to territory you do not wish to discuss and of saying things you do not mean to say, but I believe the professional magazines encounter a similar reticence. In stark contrast to the private sector, where even the smallest advance of process is trumpeted abroad, those in the public service seem diffident to a fault.

Problems of Client Confidentiality

There is, however, understandable caution about publicity when it might involve identifying service clients. This is one of the principal causes of strain between the media and social policy practitioners. Papers, just as much as TV and radio, are these days looking to personalise policy stories.

If you approach the news desk with a proposal to cover a research report, the first question will be, 'Are there any case studies?' Very often, availability of a case study will be the difference between the paper carrying a substantial article on a report or survey, and carrying nothing at all.

The problem of client confidentiality is clearly greater in some spheres than others. It is perfectly reasonable that people with mental health problems, for example, may be reluctant to be profiled in the press or interviewed by electronic media. But too many social welfare organisations assume automatically that none of their clients would want to be identified. Too often, no effort is made to find case studies or negotiate conditions by which their anonymity could be preserved. While news and features editors naturally prefer people to be named, and indeed pictured, when push comes to shove there is always room for pseudonyms and pictures in silhouette.

Some of the more media-wise charities have absorbed this lesson to good effect: it would be unthinkable of the NSPCC, for one, to issue a report without having lined up a selection of families and/or workers prepared to talk about their relevant experiences.

Even MIND, the mental health charity, is now invariably able to find service-users willing to speak to reporters on one basis or another. Statutory service-providers remain way behind on this, however, and very often refuse even to ask clients about the possibility of co-operating with the media. If they did, they might very well be surprised by the response.

Missing the Trick

Unfortunately, it is not just in terms of failure to help personalise issues that many social welfare organisations are missing a media trick. The bulk of my daily postbag goes straight into the wastebin, very often unread beyond the first couple of lines, because it is hopelessly irrelevant to the interests of a national paper. I receive astounding numbers of press releases about openings of day centres and health units, launches of training packs and Web sites, sponsored events and cheque presentations (complete with cheesy photographs), even though there is not a shred of evidence that my paper ever carries such things.

Many, depressingly, come from public relations consultants doubtless charging fat fees for their special expertise in accessing the media. I also receive considerable numbers of press statements written in jargon impenetrable even to me, let alone the general public, or put together in such an unappealing way that you might conclude there was some intent to discourage interest. This is the opening paragraph of a press release on a revolution in training for the 2 million people working in health and social care:

The two National Training Organisations (NTOs) which are being established for the Personal Social Services and Health Care sectors will work together on key projects and initiatives. The two NTOs, whilst covering distinct areas, also have a range of shared issues and concerns which will benefit from joint working.

This, similarly, is the opening of a press statement on a prestigious international conference of experts on mental illness among older people. It shows all the signs of having been written by a committee. Today...experts in the care of the elderly discussed the enormous challenges which face both the developed and developing worlds in coping with the serious mental health problems of aging populations. They paid particular attention to the burden of dementia, the illness most devastating to the individual, distressing to the care-giver and demanding of society, which is estimated to affect some 22 million people worldwide.

It is vitally important to put in the first paragraph the main hook to lure journalists who will scan only a few lines. This is the opening of a press release from a leading insurance company:

XXX have surveyed more than 1,000 customers on the issue of effective eyesight and discovered that nearly nine out of ten of those questioned feel that motorists should have their vision tested more regularly for road safety purposes. Hardly very surprising, you might think. Nine paragraphs later, at the very end, the company spokesman is quoted, 'In our survey, nearly one in five of our over-50 customers felt they knew someone whose eyesight was poor enough to cause a danger to other road users, yet that person continued to drive.'

Many organisations fail to realise that the chances of getting something into the papers are much improved if the material relates to something of current debate. At the same time, there is a general lack of appreciation that, while papers can and do make last-minute changes to cover an emerging issue, most features are planned a week or two in advance. Almost weekly I am asked on a Monday if I can get something into *Guardian (Society)* forty-eight hours later.

The short answer is no. The overriding problem I encounter, however, is a simple failure on people's part to read the paper: to look at what is carried, and what is not, and to tailor submissions accordingly. It may seem blindingly obvious, but it very often appears to be beyond even the most pricey public relations agency.

Worrying Trends

Anybody reading the press closely for the past few years must have been struck by the changes that have taken place. Certainly any direct comparison of a broadsheet paper with an issue of the same title a decade ago is arresting. There are fewer stories, fewer words to the page and the overall content is a lighter, frothier mix. Pages are dominated by packages of words and pictures: a main article, though typically no longer than 600 words, together with a large photograph and usually a box or panel giving bullet points or a list of related facts (as in, 'Six other unhappy lottery winners' or 'Ten more celebrity alcoholics').

There is a new emphasis on the arts and a seemingly insatiable, if somewhat incestuous, appetite for stories about the media. Above all, there is a concentration on 'lifestyle' and consumer issues. This trend, which some have called 'dumbing-down', has extended also to television and radio. It has made it increasingly difficult to win editorial space and airtime for policy matters, especially if they cannot be presented in terms that the media can easily assimilate. Some issues of considerable importance have gone almost wholly unreported in the media because of this. The Labour government's reforms of the NHS in 1999, for example, have simply been ignored by most papers and electronic media because of their complexity.

As most people, and most news desks for that matter, never understood the Conservatives' NHS internal market system, it was argued, it mattered little if Labour's further change-introduction of primary care groups and trusts-therefore went unexplained and unexplored. This carries all kinds of dangers, however. The lesson of the fiasco of the Child Support Agency in the early 1990s was that when the political process fails, producing unworkable legislation, and the media in turn fail to exercise proper scrutiny, the outcome is disastrous for society. Thus, too, the media excused themselves on grounds of the complexity of the issue. It is all very well devoting double-page feature spreads to searing questions of the day such as, 'Should men wear shorts?', but there are wider responsibilities to bear in mind. The other important trend in recent coverage of social policy has been the rise of the spin doctor. The 1997 Labour government did not invent the black art, contrary to popular belief, but it certainly put it into practice with enthusiasm and ruthlessness.

The significance is twofold. First, the rigorous briefing of favoured journalists ahead of a government policy announcement means that the 'line' is firmly established before any detail officially emerges. Should the details then fail to support that line, or suggest another, it is very difficult to swim against the tide. It is doubly difficult for TV journalists who, very often, have been tipped the wink to prepare background filming to support the line being briefed. With that film in the can, they are pretty much locked on to the line. And with TV following the line, it becomes even more unlikely that individual newspaper journalists will be able to argue for anything different.

The influence of TV cannot be overestimated: it is not unknown for national papers to turn upside down their take on a story to fall in step with the BBC early evening bulletin. The second significance of spin doctors is that they dislike specialist correspondents. We know too much. Much the preferred conduit for briefings is the parliamentary lobby, where what is said is not only unattributable, but supposedly never uttered, and where political journalists will generally take at face value what they are told.

Ministers can in this way launch crackdown after crackdown, fly policy kite after kite, without ever being challenged too closely on detail, cost, or indeed whether they have already said as much, or something wholly contradictory, some time previously. Since the change of government, the number of opportunities for specialists to quiz ministers at press conferences or other events has fallen sharply. Access to departmental officials has also been curtailed. Again, the trend cannot be a healthy one for proper scrutiny of policy making, for the overall working of checks and balances.

5

Media Reporters and Media Critics

News media-newspapers, magazines, broadcast journalism, and websites with journalistic content-usually start worrying about ethics only in times of crisis, says French scholar of mass communication Claude-Jean Bertrand.

In fact, codes of ethics, ombudsmen, press councils, and journalism reviews have been created during times of great social disaffection and "increasingly angry disillusionment" among the public about the news media, when people have "a growing sense of being baffled and misled," as Walter Lippmann once put it. For example, the first code of ethics for journalists was created in 1923, shortly after World War I, following criticism about the influence of political propaganda and the advertising industry on news media content.

Ombudsmen, press councils, and local journalism reviews, meanwhile, flourished in the United States during the social upheavals of the late 1960s and early 1970s. They all can be called instruments of media self-regulation because ombudsmen and authors of journalism reviews and of codes of ethics, as well as members of press councils, are generally media professionals who engage in monitoring, investigating, and analyzing developments in journalism and in the media business.

As such, they expose mistakes, point toward potentially harmful developments, and encourage attention to ethics among journalists. Bertrand describes press councils, codes of ethics, journalism reviews, ombudsmen, and some nongovernmental institutions concerned with media issues as "media accountability systems," defined as "any non-State means of making media responsible towards the public." Since the State should not participate in monitoring the news media, "except by delivering the threats that media often need to start the process of selfregulation," Bertrand urges media owners, media professionals, and media consumers to hold the news media accountable.

But then, because media consumers often prove too "apathetic or unorganized," Bertrand emphasizes the importance of self-regulation by media owners and media professionals, who are asked not only to hold politics, business, and other systems of society accountable, but also to inquire if media professionals fulfill their primary responsibility, which is "to provide a good public service."

The goal of media accountability systems is thus to "improve the services of the media to the public; restore the prestige of media in the eyes of the population; diversely protect freedom of speech and press; obtain, for the profession, the autonomy that it needs to play its part in the expansion of democracy and the betterment of the fate of mankind."

To reinforce media accountability by means of media self-regulation, media professionals are limited to "moral pressure." "But their action can be reinforced by the authority of media executives or persisting legal obligations," adds Bertrand. In addition to the "systems" mentioned before, Bertrand includes "media reporting" and "media criticism" in his list of media accountability systems. He emphasizes that specialized journalists should monitor the news media and write critically about them for a mass audience.

Since the news media "have become one of the nervous systems in the social body, the public needs to be informed about them. Some journalists must specialize in that field so as to cover its news well and investigate uncompromisingly." But Bertrand says: "With exceptions (usually due to ideological animus or business rivalry), media do not criticize each other: blind eyes are turned on the failings of colleagues.

Self-criticism is almost unknown.... In this profession, as in others, solidarity sometimes verges on collusion." Although written more than fifty years later, his conclusion recalls the 1947 Hutchins Commission's critique, issued after its inquiry into the social responsibility of the U.S. media: "We recommend that the members of the press engage in vigorous mutual criticism. Professional standards are not likely to be achieved as long as the mistakes and errors, the frauds and crimes, committed by units of the press are passed over in silence by other members of the profession."

Bertrand's accusation about a lack of media criticism is no longer valid. Since the mid-1990s, there has been "an absolute explosion of the genre" of media reporting and media criticism in the United States. Leading newspapers like the New York Times, the Washington Post, and the Boston Globe now regularly report about developments in journalism and the media business, as do magazines like Time and The New Yorker.

Howard Kurtz of the Washington Post, David Shaw of the Los Angeles Times, Felicity Barringer of the New York Times, and Cynthia Cotts of the Village Voice have become well-known for covering the news media. They call their relatively new beat the "media beat" and describe themselves as "media reporters," "media writers," "media critics," or "media columnists," while they speak about their journalistic work as "media reporting" or "media criticism."

Today, media issues are also discussed in the broadcast media like CNN's "Reliable Sources," the National Public Radio's weekly "On the Media," and productions with a regional focus, such as "Beat the Press" in the Boston area. Finally, many online media have been established for such critiques.

Among them are media consumers' sites like Mediachannel.org and Websites for media professionals, such as Jim Romenesko's MediaNews, now part of the Poynter Institute's Website. In a special edition of the Columbia Journalism Review describing the booming media beat in March 2000, James Boylan concluded: "At the turn of the century, media critics are blossoming like spring."

It could be argued that the impetus for this increase in media reporting and media criticism has again been a growing public discontent with the news media. For example, the excessive reporting about the O.J. Simpson case and about the affair involving former President Bill Clinton and White House intern Monica Lewinsky stirred intense criticism.

The news media might have reacted by monitoring each other more intensely; at least, many of the "media scandals" discussed in the late 1990s have been investigated and publicized by the news media themselves. For example, the Boston Phoenix was involved in exposing Mike Barnicle's and Patricia Smith's plagiarism and invention of quotes in the Boston Globe.

When the Los Angeles Times entered a profit-sharing agreement with one of the subjects of its reporting, the sports centre "Staples Arena," the paper was caught by one of its local competitors-and the L.A. Times reacted with the publication of an in-depth, selfcritical report about its own failure.19 Similarly, the Ncii' York Times published long, self-critical pieces recently after reporter Jayson Blair was discovered to have fabricated quotes and interviews. Obviously, not all "mistakes and errors" have been "passed over in silence."

Media economics also helps explain the increase in media reporting. The last decade was marked by numerous big-time media mergers involving, for example, CBS and Viacom, or AOL and Time Warner, and by a boom in the media business due to new media technologies like cable and satellite television and the Internet. Finally, media professionals themselves have increasingly become a topic in the news media. Jonathan Yardley already laments: "The good intentions... have gone seriously awry. The laudable idea that the press should police itself in the best way it knows how-by covering itself with the same objectivity and thoroughness it tries to bring to all other subjects-has been twisted, and diminished into just another variation on the culture of narcissism, celebrity and gossip."

While many more media professionals now write and comment on the media, little research has been done so far on media reporting and media criticism as a media accountability system. The bulk of academic literature available deals with the history of media reporting and media criticism, or with single high-profile media critics. Half a dozen content analyses examine how the news media covered the news media's work with reference to specific events, such as a war or political campaigns. Merger and acquisition activities have also been studied. Pieper and Hughes found that Time and CNN generally restricted their coverage of the merger of their parent companies to the business aspects of the transaction, i.e., the consequences for the stock market. They left it to competitors like the Washington Post and The Nation to question the consequences of the deal for the independence of the newsrooms at Time and CNN.

Similarly, Turow found allusions to "self-censorship" in the newsroom of Time with regard to the company's business strategies. Robinson's 1983 content analysis of articles on media issues in leading newspapers found that most news media, with the exception of the Washington Post, shied away from criticizing themselves. Instead, print media emphasized the problems of the broadcast media, while national organizations covered the local media. Northington, having surveyed two dozen journalists on how they reacted to being criticized in trade magazines like the Columbia Journalism Review, found that journalists generally did not change their professional behaviour.

The media reporters and media critics specifically have not been studied so far, but ombudsmen have been surveyed several times. Research indicates that the ombudsmen's interest in remaining on good terms with their peers and the news organization can interfere with their potential as instruments of self-regulation. Also missing in the context of media reporting and media criticism are studies about media owners and media managers as well as media consumers-if and how they follow the "media beat," and what they make of the information they receive there.

This exploratory study of leading media reporters and media critics in the United States involved interviewing media reporters and media critics about three key issues:

- How do these journalists cover peers and employers; are "blind eyes" still turned on the failings of colleagues and bosses?
- Do they address a general audience, an "insider audience" of media professionals, or both?
- To what extent do they regard media reporting and media criticism as a media accountability system?

The total number of media reporters and media critics in the United States is small. A comprehensive list on the website MediaNews names 32 "media people" (media reporters and media critics) and 37 media critics from "alternative weeklies." For this study, 30 media reporters and media critics were selected.

This sample included:

- Journalists presumed to have widest reach within the peer group, because their papers or magazines are most widely read by other journalists, according to Weaver and Wilhoit;
- Journalists who have been proven "innovators" in the field of media

reporting and media criticism: for example, the media critic from the Village Voice, which was a pioneer in media criticism in the 1970s; Jim Romenesko, whose website Media News has been ground-breaking in providing online articles on media issues; and one of the editors of the now-defunct Brill's Content, which sought to pioneer as a "media consumers' magazine."

In addition, journalists from the Columbia Journalism Review (CJR) and the American Journalism Review (AJR) were interviewed because, in contrast to the other interviewees, they explicitly address an insider audience with their trade magazines.

From the sample of 30, 21 journalists agreed to be interviewed in person. None of the full-time TV and radio media reporters responded or agreed to participate in the study. The interviews took place in the United States in November and December 1999.

The average length of the interviews was 50 to 60 minutes, with the longest one taking about two hours. The tapes were later transcribed by the author. Nine interviewees described themselves as "media writers" or "media reporters," with the task of objective reporting about the content of the news media and the development of the media industry.

They will henceforth be referred to, for the sake of brevity, as "media reporters." For example, Felicity Barringer, of the New York Times, described herself as "a media reporter." "That involves covering journalism, the business, and lots of other things, but I abhor commenting on my colleagues and my profession. I just describe what they do.... What's happening with corporate earnings and mergers... what's happening in the coverage of a major news event...." Twelve interviewees emphasized their critical approach by describing themselves as "media critics" or "media columnists." They will be described as "media critics." They said their task was to comment on the content of the news media and the structure of the media industry; they offered "critiques" or "opinions," or provided "checks and balances" on the news media, as the New Yorker's Ken Auletta put it.

However, no clear-cut distinction between the two role models has yet emerged in this nascent beat. For example, at one point media reporter Mark jurkowitz also referred to himself as a "media critic."

All but 2 interviewees covered or criticized the news media full-time. Of the 21 journalists, 17 wrote for leading newspapers, magazines, and online publications, and could therefore potentially reach large audiences. Two interviewees, Mark jurkowitz and Geneva Overholser, reported having worked as ombudsmen for some years, but both had stopped doing that long before the interviews took place.

Findings

Peers and Employers as the Subject of Media Reporting and Media Criticism. As discussed earlier, the work and the decision-making processes of journalists have become a more frequent subject in the U.S. news media in the last decade. Many media professionals react to the public criticism with high sensitivity, according to most interviewees.

For example, Howard Kurtz of the Washington Post said "you inevitably anger and alienate many people in the business who would otherwise be your friends. People are wary around you, even in your own newsroom...." Dan Post said that as the San Francisco Chronicle media critic he would face "a lot of scrutiny" by the fellow journalists who followed his columns. "So you have got to make sure that you got it right."

Establishing a professional distance from peers was described as being difficult by the interviewees, because they already knew many of the people they write about. This was very different from covering a foreign country, for example, or a government agency. "You've been through a lot of what they've been through," said Felicity Barringer, the New York Times media reporter.

Dan Kennedy, the Boston Phoenix media critic, stated that it took him "an awful long time really getting comfortable and confident in going after other journalists. I know how difficult the job can be.

Sometimes you are going after people who are more accomplished than you are. But then you have to step back and think, gee, if a movie critic just trashes a Stanley Kubrick film, that doesn't mean that the critic thinks he should be a better director than Stanley Kubrick. I have to put myself in the same slot." Many interviewees indicated that they felt a responsibility for the consequences of their writing. Cynthia Cotts of the Village Voice expressed sympathy for the use of anonymous sources on the media beat because "simply to be suspected of being a source for someone like me could jeopardize that person's job." Likewise, freelance journalists who she criticized had to fear for their livelihood afterwards, which made her more cautious when criticizing their work.

Similarly, Mark Jurkowitz was aware of his influence on peers and other media organizations, and was cautious to criticize small publications, for example. On the other hand, Cynthia Cotts described "puff pieces that media journalists do, including me." She explained that writing only critical pieces "diminishes the chance of anyone ever talking to me."

Many interviewees identified strongly with fellow journalists. David Shaw, the Los Angeles Times media reporter, said: "Actions that I might have previously regarded as a result of some carefully calculated decision, or perhaps even a conspiracy... are very often a product of ignorance and stupidity and inefficiency...." Like most other interviewees, Ken Auletta was convinced that mistakes made by journalists were often a result of the high business pressure in today's media companies, led increasingly by managers unfamiliar with journalism. Covering one's own employer was likewise described as a challenge, since "you are certainly aware of your relatives."

However, all interviewees stressed their efforts to avoid the impression that "you're trying to further the interest of your own newspaper or company that owns your newspaper."

Howard Kurtz always disclosed his affiliations, and said he would make an effort to be tougher on CNN as well as the Post, because of his connection there. David Shaw said that he would sell the Los Angeles Times shares he regularly received as soon as possible. On the other hand, the interviewees also reported that although they were "inside the building," they were treated no differently by their own employers than any other reporter.

Mark Jurkowitz recalled covering the scandals involving his colleagues at the Boston Globe, Mike Barnicle and Patricia Smith: "You are hoping that your own publisher will talk to you, which sometimes he didn't.... I got the same press releases...." Dan Post's experience covering the sale of the San Francisco Chronicle was similar. Still, these journalists conceded that their employers' business interests might influence the way they covered the problem of media concentration. All regarded media concentration as dangerous for journalism. Nonetheless, journalists from smaller publications who were not part of a large media conglomerate, like the Village Voice, the Boston Phoenix, the former Brill's Content, and the trade magazines AJR and CJR, seemed more eager to tackle the issue of ownership and its consequences.

They also complained about the quality of media reporting in the major news media: "It is always the business implications-what does this mean for stockholders.... It's never, what is this going to do with the diversity of opinion...." Meanwhile, media reporters from large newspapers like the New York Times and the Boston Globe doubted that media concentration would be a number-one topic for their audiences. Mark Jurkowitz said that since "the public has never really cared about this issue," writing about the stories that do not get covered was difficult: "You are trying to prove the negative." He added: "My problem with it is, I just don't see how you turn back the clock any more.... Everything's been deregulated."

In sum, the interviews indicate a high degree of peer orientation. The media reporters and media critics considered the implications of their work on fellow journalists arguably more than they might when they covered politicians or businesspeople, with whom they did not share a professional background. This does not necessarily imply that they are softer on media professionals. The harsh reactions of media professionals to Howard Kurtz, for example, indicate that he is hard-hitting.

And the account the interviewees offered about how they strove to cover their own employers as objectively as possible can be taken as proof that they seek to achieve impartiality even under difficult circumstances. On the other hand, only a few interviewees were as frank as Cynthia Cotts, who even admitted to writing "puff pieces." And many interviewees conceded to producing "too little coverage of the commercial interests of our bosses and the subtle pressures that that imposes on journalism," because these journalists apparently assumed that this would interfere with the business interests of their employers.

Additional research will be needed to determine whether journalists apply the same ethical standards to members of the Fourth Estate as they do to representatives of other social groups. Media Users and Media Professionals as Target Groups of Media Reporting and Media Criticism. Of course, the journalists from AJR and CJR focused on a professional audience. But many interviewees adhered to Bertrand's thesis about a relatively passive general audience. The majority of both media critics and media reporters doubted the public's interest in media reporting and media criticism, generally because they received little feedback from the popular audience, and a lot of feedback from insiders. Tim Jones, for example, was firmly convinced that the majority of his Chicago Tribune readers were "more interested in complaining about the media than reading about and understanding the media."

Few of the interviewees reported a high degree of feedback from the general audience. One exception was Howard Kurtz: "Those who think that my primary readers are simply other journalists... totally misconstrue how interested the general public is in media coverage and media criticism." Mark Jurkowitz said he wanted to "train" the media users to skepticism towards the news media by "treating it like a consumer beat in some ways." Slate's Scott Shuger, who also reported considerable feedback from lay users, described his goal: "Readers should ask themselves: Whose interests are being served by this story told in this way and whose are being left out?"

The varying degrees of response from the general audience may result from different ways of covering media issues. Several interviewees said they could attract larger audiences among media professionals with insider stories about media celebrities. Sean Elder, former Salon media critic, gave an example: "Tina Brown: Just mentioning her name-always gets hits.... Things that are considered a little more fringe, like... supermarket tabloids... don't get that much interest."

While few interviewees admitted explicitly that they pander to media professionals, quite a few seemed to do it-and a glimpse onto MediaNews confirms that much "media gossip" is published in the news media every day. Mark Jurkowitz commented: "A lot of the media writing is inside baseball. It's about us, it's for us, it's gossip about our industry." He added: "The public is... interested. But if you only talk about your own industry gossip, they are not going to be interested."

Those who exploit their peers' craving for gossip without regard to the interest of the general public usually get away with it, since media reporters and media critics seldom go after other media reporters and media critics. It could even be assumed that "media gossip" and "insider reporting" is encouraged by some news medi a executives, if one considers Dan Post's account of how his own column was created: "I think that is also part of the idea behind having that type of a column in the paper, to be perfectly candid.... By writing about the media, it is sort of a way to get other media reading your paper. It helps the newspaper's reputation...."

In sum, the majority of the interviewees received more feedback from media professionals. This apparently tempts many media reporters and media critics to pander to their professional audience by providing insider news. Those who strove to choose topics relevant and understandable for a popular audience also reported substantial feedback from average media consumers. It could be argued that media reporters and media critics need to watch each other more closely to make sure that their peer orientation does not result in more and more "inside baseball."

MEDIA REPORTING AND MEDIA CRITICISM AS A MEDIA ACCOUNTABILITY SYSTEM

The central goals of media accountability systems, Bertrand said, are improving the news media's service to the public, restoring the news media's prestige among the public, and preserving its autonomy from state interference. Do the interviewees use "moral pressure" to further these goals? While most interviewees said they had an impact on peers, many said they doubted they have any influence on the media owners and media managers, or the media business in general.

Few interviewees were fully confident that they could help improve the news media's service to the public by holding the media accountable. Those who believed they had influence were the best-known and most respected media reporters and media critics in the United States. For example, The New Yorker's Ken Auletta said he wanted to "educate" corporate leaders to be more sensitive toward ethical matters.

The Washington Post's Howard Kurtz stated that the "essence" of his job was "to hold journalists and news organizations accountable." He added that he had often been described by other editors and reporters as having had "a bit of an impact." "A former editor of Newsweek once wrote a memo to his staff on ethical matters, and included a line, saying: Don't do anything that you wouldn't want to see in Howard Kurtz's column.... I have certainly seen instances where media outlets have changed policies, at least in part, because of something that I have written, apologized for stories that turned out to be wrong, for example."

Meanwhile, many of the younger interviewees-even those who were aware of their immediate impact on peers-considered their influence on the improvement of the news media to be limited, and took an explicitly humble approach. They wanted to be reporters, not "reformers," and could only "sometimes" help serve readers. Sean Elder, from Salon, wanted to keep "people honest," but added that he had "a little more sympathy for the point of view of the editors, who're just trying to keep their jobs and sell something." Eric Alterman, of The Nation, was convinced that "the media is large and so amorphous" that "they can absorb any criticism you make." He said that there had never been a more important time to be a media critic-but that he would not kid himself that it made a whole lot of difference. Geneva Overholser saw too much media gossip instead of thoughtful media criticism. Therefore, she asked, "[W]hat difference does it make?"

Only the two journalists from the trade magazines emphasized that they also wanted to help restore the media's prestige, at least among colleagues, by trying to "write about examples of things we've done well," as Alicia Shepard from the AJR put it. And Mike Hoyt from the CJR said that "not enough attention is given to the positive side of what journalists do."

Also, David Shaw of the Los Angeles Times, a veteran on the media beat, was the only interviewee to mention the danger of state interference when he said that media reporting and media criticism was "better than nothing. We don't have anything else. I certainly don't want any kind of government regulation." Meanwhile, the professional spectators of the news media interviewed here apparently did not regard media freedom as endangered, since almost none mentioned the danger of state interference.

In sum, media reporters and media critics disagreed about the purpose of media criticism and media reporting. A minority of journalists considered themselves "advocates" of the public and adopted a "missionary approach" to their work. Among this faction were the few well-known media reporters and media critics, who were confident that they could improve the news media's service to the public by holding journalists accountable.

The two journalists from the trade magazines who saw themselves also as "ambassadors" of their profession were another exception. Many of the younger journalists emphasized that while they wanted to inform readers about the news media and teach them to analyse the media, they did not want, nor did they think themselves able, to change or even improve the news media in general, or restore their prestige.

Many long-time prejudices about a "conspiracy of silence" among media professionals can no longer be considered valid. The journalists on the still-young media beat generally strove to cover the news media, its structure, and even their own employers comprehensively and impartially. They said that as media reporters and media critics, they could have an impact on their peers who have lost jobs or were confronted with changed newsroom policies, for example, after having been criticized by them. This suggests that media reporters and media critics have a considerable potential as instruments of media self-regulation. This potential, however, is not yet fully exploited.

Many media reporters and media critics still appeared to be more reluctant to go after fellow journalists, as well as media managers and media owners, than after politicians or businesspeople, for example. The apparent reason for their cautiousness is their dependency on other media professionals as sources, colleagues, and employers. Media professionals are also the most important target group for their writing, since many media reporters and media critics lamented a lack of feedback from the popular audience.

And in fact, the expansion of the media beat went along with an increase in "media gossip" in the news media. Media reporters and media critics might need to be reminded at times that their prime duty should be service to the public, and not their peers. That said, media reporting and media criticism in the news media have emerged from the media boom of the 1990s as a promising media accountability system in the United States. Once the media beat is even more established in the news media, media reporters and media critics might also become more confident in their "watchdog roles."

6

The Media Mainstream

The 1991 debut of the "Womanews" section in the Chicago Tribune sparked a nationwide reintroduction of women's pages that caught on as rapidly as the move to kill them had 2 decades earlier.

If not as long-lived as the earlier opposing movement, this move proved at least as controversial. Through textual analysis of the section's editorial voice, this research attempts to determine how "Womanews" positioned itself for such immediate popularity and potential for success.

This study listens to "Her Say," the editorial voice of "Womanews," during the section's launch to determine how its call promoted a women's culture and what it promised for readers as well as industry.

In determining the significance of this call, this study employs a cultural feminist theoretical perspective, one that has not often been used in media studies. From this perspective, this research seeks to define examples of cultural feminist practice. The method has been to define key issues in the editorials and from them to determine themes and the metathematic considerations that structure the discourse as cultural feminist as well as tie it to the conventions of the news industry.

With these issues, themes, and metathemes not expected to be mutually exclusive but interwoven, this qualitative study attempts to analyse the call that launched this section without losing the richness of its discourse. "Womanews" premiered on Sunday, April 28, 1991, in the Chicago Tribune. Providing a space for women, the section profiled women, highlighted women's accomplishments, and examined family and societal relationships.

With women writing most of its articles, the section incorporated columnists from around the nation as well as writers from other media in addition to Tribune staffers. Each week, the section ran articles on pages designated by topic. The "News and Opinion" page ran what can be viewed as the section's editorial, "Her Say."

"Womanews" was a newspaper within the newspaper. The section front had the look and feel of a newspaper front, complete with sky boxes. Averaging 14 pages from the start, the section was thick with its news/advertising mix, each week running regular pages including "Family Matters,"

"Helping Hands," and "Health and Well Being." The completeness of the presentation of this section signaled by its newspaper-within-a-newspaper structure offered women what appeared to be a fully formed culture of their own, a women's culture within the male-defined mainstream.

This structuring differentiated the section from the complementary nature of women's pages as they had appeared in newspapers until the 1970s, and in so doing it offered advertisers the prepackaged women's audience that they had been missing for the intervening decades. "Womanews" also differed from the earlier women's pages with its content and how it approached that content. The fact that "Womanews" carried news impressed at least one scholar, who commented, "This fact alone separates 'Womanews' from traditional women's pages...". Editorials are the bedrock of a newspaper, and "Womanews" showcased its opinion on the "News and Opinion" page with the "Her Say" column as its lead article. This study points out how "Her Say" provided a collective feminist editorial voice that defined female values for this groundbreaking section, constructed a women-centered ideology that drew immediate interest, and made a call compelling enough to propagate women's sections across the country.

In its consideration of topics, from pregnancy to violence against women, "Her Say" differentiated women from men, extolling the virtues of being female and drawing similarities among women regardless of their feminist leanings. "Her Say" resurrected earlier notions of femininity, bringing the more traditional definitions to the forefront in order to refit them for contemporary women.

WOMEN'S PAGES TO "WOMANEWS"

Although by the 1960s some women editors were making inroads in modernizing the traditional women's pages, the industry was slow to take advantage of such progress. Instead, by the mid-1970s, newspapers had transformed their women's pages into lifestyle sections, prompted by the influx of women and driven by the notion that it was time to incorporate women - as writers, readers, and subjects - more fully into the newspaper as a whole. But these moves at integration backfired, and women's newspaper readership began a precipitous decline.

"The continuing use of media and the concomitant call for reform of their employment practices," one researcher stated in retrospect, "indicated an ultimate faith in mass media as agents of change in the nation. Not sufficiently recognized were the limitations of mass media imposed by the craft tradition of news, nor the undergirding benefit mass media receive from support of the status quo". Although progress was made, women were left unequal and without a home.

Nancy Woodhull, as president of Gannett News Service and New Media, said, "We may have thrown the baby out with the bath water when we stopped women's sections 25 years ago". Even the highly touted lifestyle sections were not improving coverage of women. Without a section of its own, discussion of women's issues ebbed in newspapers. The papers reasserted their "male personalities." No longer finding newspapers relevant to their lives, women were moving to other media. Although the loss of women readers was further crippling a struggling newspaper industry, the industry did not seem willing or able to include women in meaningful ways. Two decades later, examples of incorporation stood out as exceptions.

Desperate by the late 1980s, newspapers began to turn an ear toward advertisers, who were demanding targeted markets to compete with specialized media. "The trend toward 'sectionalization' is not new but has accelerated dramatically in recent years". Recognizing that many women readers who had left newspapers had gravitated toward magazines, which offered advertisers niche marketing, a few in the newspaper industry began efforts in that direction, in particular two feminists.

Associate Editor Colleen Dishon, who had helped kill the Chicago Tribune's women's pages, became instrumental in the move toward reincorporating women. She returned to the paper and began a magazine-like section within the lifestyle pages called "TempoWoman", the forerunner of "Womanews." Working with Dishon, Woodhull chaired the American Society of Newspaper Editors committee that created the women's section prototype. Focus groups evaluated this prototype section for ASNE in 1989 and 1990.

After being brought forward at the 1990 conference, it debuted as "Womanews" the following year in the Chicago Tribune, replacing the Sunday "TempoWoman." Dishon said, "The idea was to use stories from everywhere to show ordinary women having an impact on their world". With "Her Say" as its envoy, "Womanews" piloted a reintroduction of women's sections. A potential powerbase for women, such sections would have to be established and maintained by women themselves in order to give voice to the power such an enterprise could command. A recent study showed that the "Womanews" section exhibited characteristics of women's media, which historically have been located outside mainstream media.

"Womanews" was introduced during a widening of the gender gap in readership nationwide. According to Newspaper Association of America figures, women readers, particularly younger women, were leaving the fold in increasing numbers. Perhaps predictable by such visible industry trends, the launch of "Womanews" nonetheless proved controversial among editors and researchers. "Womanews" reignited the debate over sex-segregated sections, particularly as women's sections were rapidly introduced in newspapers across the nation in the wake of its launch.

Although the Chicago Tribune quietly added "Womanews," as a section one Sunday in April, the section did not go unnoticed in industry. For example, less than a year later the Cleveland Plain Dealer introduced its own

"EveryWoman" with a splash. Modeled on "Womanews," it would not be "the same old '50s women's stuff coming around again in a new form". Eighteen years after it had ceased priblication of women's pages, the Cleveland paper promised that its reintroduced women's section would be relevant, readable, and as audience interactive as possible.

In New York, the launch of the tabloid Her New York was met with questions. Betsy Carter, editor of New York Woman, which had folded, said, "I think from a marketing point of view it's actually brilliant.... But the larger question? I'm just not sure women roally need a special newspaper. If you announced a newspaper for men, there'd be a terrible reaction".

Estimating that, by 1993, about 40 women's sections had already been introduced around the country, Woodhull cautioned, "I don't think women's sections are the end-all. We also need to mainstream women. You have to be really careful that the result isn't ghettoizing women". Woodhull resurrected the term "ghettoizing" from the late 1960s, when the movement against sex-segregated sections had begun to rumble through the industry.

SECOND WAVE FEMINIST THEORIES

The culture of the late 1960s and early 1970s gave rise to a second wave of feminisms in the United States, with liberal feminism striking mainstream chords in the newsroom, society, and academe. Relying on legislative and other institutional adjustments to enforce and ensure that the basic demand was met, liberal feminism sought equality of opportunity for women. Liberal feminist logic reasoned that if women achieved political and economic equality they could achieve autonomy in society. Observing that it is easier to accommodate women through media content and policy changes within institutions than it would be to radically change the socio-economic system, Rakow noted that liberal feminism does not challenge the underpinnings of social institutions.

Largely because of this lack of institutional overhaul, by the 1990s, some were questioning whether liberal feminism had enabled women to make actual gains. Creedon noted, "Though feminist challenges in the name of equal opportunity have brought new responses from government and industry, all in all they have brought about little substantive change because the basic issue - the gendered nature of the system - is never addressed".

With more women in the university as well as in the newsroom, feminist media research surged in the 1970s, relying on liberal feminism to guide the majority of the studies. "Sex role stereotypes, prescriptions of sex-appropriate behaviour, appearance, interests, skills and self perceptions are at the core of liberal feminist media analyses". The bulk of 1970s and early 1980s feminist media studies examined images of women.

As Zoonen stated, "Initially the new themes that feminist media scholars added to the agenda of communication research were the stereotypical images of women in the media and the effects of these images on the audience". Steeves pointed out that while liberal feminist theory provided the dominant perspective for this initial body of latter 20th-century media research, it was a perspective more often assumed than articulated.

While it did widen research parameters and news purviews to include women, through its ideological link with liberal democratic philosophy liberal feminism tended to reproduce the elitism, oversights, and values of the larger culture and its media. The snug fit between theory and subject matter masked the problem of liberal feminist theory's ability to fully critique women's representation in the media.

Although it was the feminist theory most compatible with American culture and its media because of their shared liberal democratic heritage, liberal feminism was nevertheless not the only feminist approach that resurfaced during the second wave. Differences among the feminist perspectives, however, were not always clearly defined in the research.

Zoonen cited difficulty in classifying feminist media studies because "feminist theory and practice is often rather eclectic, incorporating elements from different ideologies as circumstances and issues necessitate". Radical feminist Freeman stated that differences in approaches among various feminists "reflected their past experiences more than their understanding of what feminism meant".

Despite this lack of theoretical articulation in the research, Rakow noted that "feminists did manage in the 1970s to publish works that reverberated with the feminist activism of the day, drawing attention to stereotypes and discrimination in communication contexts...".

In the 1980s, feminist media theory came of age with self-reflexive assessments of the field and critical compilations of earlier studies. Feminist media scholars contextualized the early body of research that relied on liberal feminist theory by incorporating other feminist perspectives. Carter, Branston, and Allan defined their overview of feminist media research in terms of "eight interrelated problematics" - ownership and control, employment, professional identity, news sources, representation, narrative forms and practices, feminization and sexualization, and news audiences.

In a historiographie approach, Kitch noted that the scholarship on women's images in American media displayed a sophisticated evolution from 1970s analyses of stereotypes to 1990s considerations of images as polysemetic texts. While observing this evolutionary quality, she also proposed that the stages of feminist research overlapped, coexisting to critique and enrich the field.

Noting the significance of the field's interdisciplinary nature, communication theorist Rakow commented on the maturity of the research by the 1990s, "In media studies, feminist scholars have moved past initial work on women's images in content and women's employment in industries to more complex questions that make it impossible to separate study of the media from all other communication contexts". But Cirksena worried that the research of the intervening decade had not kept pace with the 1970s: "Gender, as a germane question in mass communication research, has failed to engage either mainstream America or critical theorists. Nor has a significant body of theory and research built on those early studies, however marginalized, developed".

In an attempt to track the shift away from the "flurry of activity in the late sixties and early seventies on how women were portrayed in media, "Dervin stated, "Now much feminist literature is looking at women in their own terms. Giving voice to women is the most audible goal of feminist scholarship at this juncture".

Baehr questioned whether that flurry of feminist media research had been merely a "commercial break" in business as usual. Cirksena echoed that skepticism; while acknowledging that feminist media studies in the 1970s did "affect the field of communication research," she observed that by the end of the 1980s "feminist perspectives have yet to make any significant impact". In their study of news, Brown and Gardetto urged that cultural critical studies as well as the empirical research on women's representation begun in the 1970s be built upon "to clarify if and how actual women are caught in a web of ideological frameworks that fail to capture the particular woman's seemingly incongruous subject positions or that seek to place her firmly as 'woman' rather than as 'person'".

During the 1970s, one of the feminist theories that reemerged alongside liberal and other second wave feminisms was cultural feminism. Freeman defined the emergence of latter 20th-century cultural feminism as "an attempt to identify and extol what women had in common, to put substance on the concept of sisterhood. It became a celebration of all things female without concern for whether these things came from hormones, socialization, or social status. As had happened earlier in the prior woman movement, difference between the sexes was elevated to a primary principle, with female characteristics claiming the moral edge".

Contrasting cultural feminist work against the earlier media studies that had been driven by liberal feminism, Fenton noted the major import of this separatist strain of feminism by locating it among post-modern approaches. Based on discussion of sex differonce that transpired largely outside U.S.-based feminist media research, Fenton defined what difference meant to feminist media studies through what she termed a "paradoxical universalism," or "use of the concept of universalism... hand-in-hand with its deconstruction", in this way acknowledging a universalism while exposing its patriarchal construction. She defined the task for feminist media analysis as one that recognized media convergence while at the same time valued the audiences' everyday interactions with the media.

Feminist theorists such as Donovan have noted that late-20th-century cultural feminism had its roots in 19th-century women's moral reform.3 In that movement, white upper-middle-class Protestant women attempted to make society aware of the evils that plagued women, from rape and incest to harassment and discrimination.

These evangelical women worked by banding together in auxiliary religious groups to rescue women from houses of prostitution and train them for legitimate employment. To further awareness of the problems women faced, the national society, the American Female Moral Reform Society, circulated its long-running publication, the Advocate.

This society trained former prostitutes to typeset, print, and mail the Advocate, an effort so successful that by 1861 the publication was produced entirely by women. Journalism historian Henry noted that the Advocate was an excellent example of "the journalism produced by the women who lived and believed most fervently in the values" of women's culture, in which they "developed shared female-identified values, rituals, relationships, and modes of communication that were sources of satisfaction and strength".

Despite an inherent conservativism that placed value on women from within the bounds of patriarchy, cultural feminism was, by the mid-1980s, often equated with latter-day radical feminism, which had gone through a number of permutations since the late 1960s. Echols traced a development from radical feminism to cultural feminism based on the idea that cultural feminism "equates women's liberation with the nurturance of a female counter culture which is hoped will supersede the dominant culture".

However, she admitted that identifying cultural feminism as an evolution of radical feminism was flawed because of the basic "theoretical incompatibility". In contrast to radical feminism, which advocates a separate women's culture that functions outside patriarchy, cultural feminists create a women's culture within patriarchy.

They bring women together to assume a conservative agenda, an ostensibly non-threatening move that facilitates creation of a space for women that often goes unnoticed by the dominant culture. Relying on legal theorist Robin West, Tong pointed out that a fundamental difference between cultural feminists and the type of feminist she defined as radical-cultural was that the radical feminists viewed women's difference as a type of curse, while cultural feminists tended to view women's essential condition as a blessing.

"Valorizing the traits and behaviors traditionally associated with women, cultural feminists praise women's capacities for sharing, nurturing, giving, sympathizing, empathizing, and especially, connection. They believe that the fact women menstruate, gestate, and lactate gives women a unique perspective on the meaning of human connection".

Cirksena and Cuklanz noted that cultural feminism's association with the body, both direct and symbolic, "has been criticized for its tendency toward abstraction and inaccessibility". Yet, they predicted, "Cultural feminist work in communication studies will most likely continue to elaborate the processes through which the symbolic realm has constructed and made real certain ways of understanding and thinking about gender".

Cultural feminists seek to create a women's culture within patriarchy so that a separate set of female-identified values and practices can be nurtured. Equating women positively with culturally defined female traits, "cultural feminists wish to establish a female standard of sexuality" within this women-centered culture. Cultural feminist theory does not question femininity or its positioning in opposition to masculinity.

Infact, Echols observed that cultural feminism was "committed to preserving rather than challenging gender differences". Alcoff further noted that cultural feminist theory was "grounded securely and unambiguously on the concept of the essential female". The ideology of cultural feminism is based in essentialist notions of sex difference and put forward in the cultural context of gender description. Recognizing that patriarchy has described femininity in negative and restrictive terms in order to define masculinity as normative, cultural feminists reclaim the terms for femaleness in order to imbue them with women-defined positive meaning.

"By equating feminism with the so-called reassertion of a female identity and culture," Echols observed, "cultural feminism seems to promise an immediate solution to women's powerlessness in the culture at large". Despite the debates this theory has engendered among feminists, its perspective has drawn together diverse feminists and has enabled them to take action.

Citing activism such as that found in the anti-pornography movement, Echols acknowledged that "cultural feminism has succeeded in mobilizing feminists regardless of sexual preference, however fragile the alliance". Freeman noted that the stance and concerns of cultural feminism "were structuring the major debates" by the mid-1980s. "New issues, such as male violence, pornography, sexual desire, divorce, and surrogacy, were often argued as conflicts over the importance of equality versus difference".

Having sex difference as its defining characteristic creates limitations for cultural feminism on both the theoretical and the practical levels. While it could draw women together by putting "substance on sisterhood," cultural feminism's uncritical assumption of sex difference also collapsed critical differences among women.

Feminists who have produced women's culture have traditionally held cultural privilege; therefore, the tendency has been for cultural feminists to reproduce their own white, upper-middle-class culture, with adherence to their values a prerequisite for participation. Given these characteristics, the women's culture is not perceived as a threat by the dominant male culture, which indeed may lend it implicit support. In the case of commercial media in the latter 20th century, this support took on a literal, and conservative, dimension in the form of underwriting by mainstream advertisers. The male-female dichotomy could operate on a number of levels to mask and inhibit the very reform cultural feminism envisioned. Gathering women to talk, reexamine sexuality, and redefine cultural values is empowering; however, actualized through cultural feminism such a strategy is more subversive than openly radical, since the women's culture is dependent on male culture.

In the conservative climate prevalent in America at the outset of the 1990s, which included a backlash against women's gains, hope for success in introducing a women's section would rest on a good match between the section's orientation and the cultural context, such as a conservative feminist approach generated by knowledgeable and influential media women.

A liberal feminist push for women's equality in the 1990s would not have necessarily interested advertisers or taken hold in the industry. On the other hand, a return to traditional women's pages would not have been able to capture either a female audience that had made some tangible progress in the wake of the modern women's movement or women, particularly younger women, who were convinced that equality had already been secured.

"Her Say" was at the helm of the women's section that opened the floodgate for a surge of new women's pages across the nation in the 1990s.

However, this immediate popularity of "Womanews" lent an overarching ambiguity and a feminist skepticism to its reception among news workers and media researchers. Whitt cited caution, "One thing is sure: With the advent of 'Womanews,' the Chicago Tribune is making history. Less certain is whether the decision breaks new ground or rebuilds old fences".

This study was undertaken as an exploration of the editorial voice of "Womanews" to uncover the strength and the power of a call that rallied women - editors and readers alike - and seemed to hold the potential to revitalize an industry. "Her Say" provided the editorial voice of this women's newspaper-within-a-newspaper that heralded a new and important place for women. The research employs a thematic analysis to determine the significance of the "Her Say" discourse and its positioning of "Womanews." An examination of the guiding voice in the start-up of "Womanews" is essential to defining the character of and to identifying the approach of this section that initiated a nationwide reintroduction of women's pages.

"Womanews" was launched as a weekly section April 28, 1991. "Her Say" ran in all but two issues of the section that year. All 34 "Her Say" columns published during the 1991 launch - April 28, 1991, through December 29, 1991 were examined to discover the key issues that were being discussed. Themes and metathemes were drawn from the development of the interrelated issues.

Since, from its inception, "Womanews" was a separate section of designated women's reading, cultural feminism was chosen as a theoretical perspective appropriate to guiding an analysis of the issues in "Her Say" and tracing the thematic development. Freeman's observation that by the mid-1980s cultural feminism was addressing new issues - male violence, pornography, sexual desire, divorce, and surrogacy - provided this investigation a ready template for its analysis.

Her further observation that cultural feminism structured these major debates along the lines of equality versus difference prompted the researcher to seek evidence of metathematic treatment of difference. Despite their industry repositioning to adjust for an increasingly competitive media marketplace, newspapers retained many traditional news values. In order to survive, this modern revival of the newspaper convention of the woman's page would need to make some familiar industry appeals. Therefore, this research, in addition, sought evidence of metathematic considerations that would align this section with traditional news values.

"Her Say" as editorial voice

Headlining the "News and Opinion" page, "Her Say" can be seen as an editorial through its placement and its function, appearing double-wide at the top of the page and providing authoritative views on women's issues supported by arguments and evidence. The column, however, differentiated itself from traditional editorials by its writing and its representation. The opinion of each "Her Say" piece stretched beyond the personal politics of the writer and gave voice to a larger population, but the editorial "we" was absent. It was not staff written like the typical newspaper editorial.

"Her Say" was instead written by women outside the "Womanews" and Tribune staff, so the voices that launched the section emanated from the larger women's community outside the newspaper and did not ostensibly represent the publication's views. To further this nontraditional journalistic strategy, this column avoided the appearance of typical editorial anonymity by giving a face to the writings. Each week the writer's signature, mug shot, and biographical blurb ran beneath her column.

To navigate this section through the mainstream of a culture that had taken a conservative turn, "Her Say" would need to speak to women without being outspoken. It would need to be strong without seeming strident, feminine without being weak. A section labeled "Womanews" would not be a magnet for male readers. If this conservative approach to feminism were successful, it could attract advertisers without attracting unnecessary male attention, and the section could gather a sisterhood of readers without being perceived as a disruption of the gendered social order.

"Her Say" of April 28, 1991, heralded the section by relying on a quintessential sex difference - pregnancy - situating that essential women's issue in the contemporary context of the workplace, which it defined as a male-dominated space. Equating the female-male dichotomy with private and public "spheres", "Her Say" voiced an identification among women, who were shown to be still out-of-sync with the dominant male culture.

Over the course of the rest of the year, the column spoke to women about their roles and responsibilities as mothers, as victims of violence, and as consumers of media. A diverse group of women gave voice to the commonalities of womanhood for the "Her Say" columns of "Womanews." Instead of drawing on the ranks of an in-house editorial board, staffers called upon celebrities, experts, and local freelance writers to pen the column each week.

While most of the writers were white women, women of colour wrote several of the columns. With some authors writing more than one column during the 1991 launch, 29 of the 34 columns were written by white Western women; 1 column was written by a Russian scholar; and 4 of the columns were written by African- and Native-American women.

"Her Say" writers were generally drawn from the professional class, with academics, lawyers, and doctors represented; working-class women were included, but to a lesser extent. Well-known broadcaster Marlene Sanders wrote about the grudging acceptance of pregnancy in the broadcast newsroom. Popular author Sara Paretsky warned women that their patronage of media violence helped sanction real violence against women. Actor Shari Belafonte faulted Hollywood for not keeping up with the times, noting its lack of portrayal of interracial couples and friendships. In addition to celebrities, "Her Say" relied on specialists.

For example, psychologists wrote on motherhood without marriage, and on rape. Traditional women's page treatment of advice columns, however, was avoided by these experts. The columns were more activist oriented than authoritative. Even a column by a medical doctor, a traditional stronghold of women's page advice, encouraged women to be critical of health information in general circulation media and to refer to more specialized materials when they needed medical information.

Throughout the year, columns by free lance writers, particularly those with a Chicago affiliation, were integrated among the writings of celebrities and specialists to explore cultural issues that confronted women on a daily basis, from the fear of rape to the propagation of sexual myths, feminist stereotypes, and ideal images of women. Anchoring their discussions in the nature of parenting, marriage, and workforce labour, this diverse cast of non-staffers discussed myriad aspects of the value of women in society.

MOTHERHOOD, MEDIA, AND MALE VIOLENCE

The proverbial baby thrown out with the bath water was reborn in "Womanews." In its debut devoted to pregnancy, "Her Say" established the bonds of female connectedness that the section title implied. Sanders cast the workplace as male, with women as outsiders who were discriminated against because of their, albeit beneficial, biology. As she voiced concern over the discriminatory treatment of pregnant television anchors, she wondered whether times were changing. If a woman were to become pregnant in what Sanders characterized as the fiercely competitive business of media, her only chance of not being considered a liability would be if she were considered a star. A star herself, Sanders was hopeful that soon celebrity status would not be required for women to avoid job discrimination.

Women having children later in life, with some leaving prominent careers for the homefront, provided ample demographic incentive for pursuing discussion of multifaceted aspects of motherhood. A Chicago writer took issue with those "who monitor an expectant woman's habits to protect her unborn child." She pointed out the hypocrisy of those "pregnancy police" and lamented, "The basic problem here is that we no longer seem to believe that Mother knows best".

In another column, this writer expanded her aphorism of a mother's omniscience to include abortion. Sharing her realizations while she prepared herself to have an abortion, she identified with women who had to make that decision. This column approached women's reproductive rights through a sensitivity to sisterhood, not a liberal feminist appeal for legislated equality. Key, though, in her presentation of this issue was that she was choosing an abortion to forestall an inevitable miscarriage.

Taking this shortcut to empathy, she made it clear to the readers that she wanted the baby. Hers was framed as the selfless decision of a good mother. The fetus would die regardless. Shifting the concept of choice from a liberal to this more conservative positioning was necessary in order to extract the issue from the politics of legislative control and situate the agenda of reproductive rights back under women's control by legitimizing her decision-making abilities as a mother.

To strengthen the author's positioning, her biographical blurb for this particular column strategically identified her as the mother of an 11-year-old. Locating choice firmly within the context of a women's culture allowed abortion to be addressed by constructing women, in their potential as mothers, as capable of making the decisions that had been transferred into male-based legislative and political institutions.

Adoption was also retrieved from the top shelf of male-defined public discourse and politically repositioned, not as a panacea for abortion but as an argument against what was viewed as a national obsession with having biological offspring. Freelance writer Weldon established another shortcut to reader empathy in this anti-surrogacy argument by stating that she was told she could never have children.

Her longing, she reasoned, "did not mean that the children I hoped to cradle would have to be biologically my own. Or that... one of my sisters would have to carry the child for me and become the mother of her own niece or nephew." She wondered whether the many medical options available to women who could not conceive were muddying the very definition of motherhood, particularly in situations she saw as incestuous, such as grandmothers bearing their own grandchildren. "The lines of responsibility and parentage are crossed and crisscrossed," she worried.

"That creates myriad emotional and legal complications that can only be confusing to the child they wore supposed to help". She did not view adoption as having such complications. "Put simply, there are too many parents who insist on having their own children, no matter what, while there are still too many children whom no one will have. And there are too many questions not easily answered.... ow can motherhood be defined, if not in the most simplistic sense as the woman who bore the child?" She established personal circumstances to position her appropriately to pursue this conservative line of argument.

The empathetic bond she established weighed in favour of her response to a situation with which many readers could identify: She could not have children. However, later in the article she pulled the emotional carpet out from under the reader when she revealed that hormonal drug therapy and two sons later she "was lucky".

This undercutting reaffirmed an ideal of biological motherhood while allowing the author to voice pro-adoption arguments that railed against medical advances that, when framed as expensive, experimental, and unnatural, strained the traditional bounds of motherhood. "Her Say" was reclaiming the right to define motherhood, which, in terms of surrogacy, had been handed off to the male-based medical establishment.

Another author yearned for a golden age as she wondered if the "now" trend in motherhood she observed, "choosing motherhood without marriage," was good for "the future of the family." This clinical psychologist pondered: "Whether that fatherlessness will harm the child is a critical question. As a psychologist, I'm convinced that the ideal way to raise a child is with a mother and father in love in an intact family".

Her female authority in affairs of the family, bolstered by her membership in the professional community, lent a solid upper-middle-class view to describing heterosexual normative gender roles. "Her Say" was defining acceptable boundaries for the women's sphere of the 1990s by barkening back to a nostalgic 1950s ideal in order to bring forward a reaffirmation of marriage and the middle-class institution of a nuclear family in which motherhood had a place, a home, and power.

Arguing that a mother's role was both learned and inherent, freelancer Weldon debunked the Mr. Mom myth circulating in popular culture. "Mothering is instinctual. It is a process of learning and adaptation and survival that metamorphoses a woman into a mother." While defining fatherhood as "more than just a man with children," she clearly demarcated the roles of father and mother in biological as well as cultural terms. "A father is not a mother. They are not the same brand of parent." While she admitted her own father was a good father, "my mother mothered me. Like yin and yang, their roles were different". The mother was being mythologized in modern terms by women who ventured beyond the homefront, and, battle-weary but savvy, returned. A column by a self-proclaimed full-time mom, who was nevertheless identified as a former news director, examined how professionals who chose to stay home wrestled to define their worth in this new role of motherhood.

Through the frustration brought on by having to fill out the line "occupation" on a form, the author had an epiphany that showed her the importance of the connections to the mothers in her life - her own mother as well as her friends she could not identify with while she was working outside the home because they had children. She took a vow of sisterhood based on the revelation of the mother-daughter bond. "I called my mother and my friend with the four children. I owed them both an apology. A big one". This mea culpa would allow her back into the sisterhood gathered at the domestic hearth. For too long, she had allowed herself to accept the (mis)representation of women in the home. The apology would be for her having chosen a solidarity with men in the workplace that had garnered her prestige at the expense of her full participation in the domestic role.

While establishing motherhood as being within the institution of marriage, and marriage a microcosm of patriarchal society, the column did open the discussion of marriage to include interracial relationships. A white writer posited that many potentially revealing questions went unasked when the press ignored the fact that U.S. Supreme Court nominee Clarence Thomas had an interracial marriage. She observed that the press overlooked an "important chance to gain some insight into his character."

A justice for life, Thomas's decision making could have a profound impact on women and the nation. She pondered his reasons for not deciding on "the safe route," instead marrying a woman of another race: "Deep down, is he running away from his past? Is he a closet rebel in Republican clothing? Or is he colorblind in a private way that his society may never be?" Belafonte spoke personally to the issue with, "My husband and I are an interracial couple." In her media critique, she observed that when interracial marriage was depicted at all, it was often stereotyped. She wondered whether an interracial couple could be portrayed "without making an issue of race".

A sociologist described her exclusion by white society as exemplified through her use of media: "I'd watch television and pick up magazines hoping to see someone who looked like me being called beautiful. I saw myself there briefly in the late '60s, but then things returned to 'normal,' and that 'normal'... didn't include me. The harder I looked, the more invisible/ugly I became." This writer did not idealize the pre-Civil Rights 1950s, but she did long for the hope and pride that the 1960s brought to African Americans. "We need to go back to a time when we said out loud that we were black and proud, a time when we discovered that big noses were beautiful and nappy hair glorious." Shifting the responsibility from media to mothers, she couched her quest for racial recognition in a mother's tongue: "We must teach our children that their uniqueness is to be praised. We must do that by praising them ourselves". Whereas earlier feminist media observations by white women about the representation of white women had opened the dialogue on media portrayal, this 1990s discussion was inclusive of race. Incorporation of multicultural dialogue in the establishment of this women's culture meant that race would have less leverage as a divisive tool than it had had in the earlier women's movements.

The column discussed physical attributes that were at odds with the male-manufactured cultural ideal, such as questioning how weight gain by female celebrities could routinely be considered newsworthy.

Through a range of voices, the column reconsidered women's imagery, casting the cultural ideal into a less central role. In devaluing the male-constructed ideal, writers diffused competition among women, forging bonds that connected them across such superficial divisions.

Writers pointed to the need to correct for male-defined media images that kept women divided and defined women's worth, including newsworthiness, by a narrow physical standard of measure. They discussed the debilitating effects of the negative media images of feminists and the need for feminist voices in the media to counteract the dominant images of women.

Speaking to the fact that a generation had been reared on pervasive media stereotyping, a 20-something feminist noted that "the stereotype is all we know about feminism". In the lingo of the road movie genre, one writer discussed a contemporary film that resisted stereotyping women, " [S]creenwriter Callie Khouri is exposing sexual myths faster than Louise's convertible eats up the miles on those backcountry roads".

The movie, Thelma and Louise, had burst onto the scene "like a bolt of lightning illuminating the dangerous complacency of the feminist landscape and the appalling lack of worthy roles for women on the silver screen." The two-dimensional nature of the typical women's media images was revealed by contrast with the complexity of the film's lead characters. "We realise Thelma and Louise are so richly layered that we are just beginning to know who they are, what they feel and how they think". Thelma and Louise was a feminist story for the big screen that made it to the big time.

The mainstream success of this feminist-movieturned-blockbuster ensured that its characters, its images, its story, and its voice became part of the cultural dialogue on gender and gender representation in the media. Because the movie employed the star system and grafted its narrative onto the enormously popular male genre, the "buddy movie," the film had enough mainstream trappings that its feminist voice was not marginalized. The story was told at the community multiplex and reviewed in the daily papers. Its success ensured that it could not be treated as an inessential alternative that could be ignored. Viewers were confronted with complexities of character as they watched the protagonists become outlaws by virtue of their sex-role transgressions.

The movie Thelma and Louise allowed its title characters to explore complex, powerful roles. But its message was blunt - women could not claim male power in society and live. Also emblematic of its time, "Womanews" displayed a wariness of male power and the consequences of questioning its control; therefore, "Her Say" guided the section along a conservative tack. It encouraged women to explore their own contradictions and complexities as traits of being female, by creating for them a mediated space within but apart from the men's surrounding territory.

In 1991, the issue of violence against women took on particular timeliness with the news headlining Senate confirmation hearings of Clarence Thomas that dealt with accusations of sexual harassment and the trial of William Kennedy Smith on charges of rape. A regular contributor observed how the confirmation hearings of Thomas revealed the Senate as an exclusionary all-male club.

Another "Her Say" writer, academic Deborah Tannen, noted that men do not understand sexual harassment because of their privileged position in culture. Paretsky (1991) warned that women participated in their own oppression by accepting violence against women as entertainment, and a sociologist noted that psychological thrillers were purely expressions of violence toward women. A former news director pointed out that television sweeps weeks were a time to programme women as victims, both literally as the networks scheduled show after show with this theme and sociologically as women viewers learned their cultural role through this saturation.

"Her Say" used discussion of violence to differentiate women from men by exploring how even the threat of violence had a defining influence on women's daily lives and life decisions. One writer found a way of confuting essential sex difference. She carried a gun. "Every night, before I leave the office, I clip the gun to my belt in plain sight and say with it what a man can say simply with his presence: Don't mess with me".

The implication was that without the gun she was just another woman, and a potential victim. Victimization was equated with being female and living in America. Columns explored many levels of victimization to reveal male violence as a prime shaper of the culture. A Massachusetts freelancer examined rape as chilling social control, with the fear of rape as a threat that effectively constructed women as the vulnerable, weaker sex. "I can't help wondering which of my friends will be next, or when it will be my turn". In an analysis of what she termed a second rape by society, a psychologist noted how women have been made powerless by being further stigmatized by silence.

"Women have instinctively known deep down that they had better think twice about reporting rape." Despite the verdict in favour of Smith, she urged,

"It would be my hope that the handling of the Smith case will make people aware of something that is very wrong in the fabric of our society. People need to examine the very harmful and illogical myths about rape." While accepting basic sex differentiation as normative, she questioned the dangerous imbalance in the social definitions of gender.

This psychologist called for a reconceptualization of gender categories and the values culture assigns them. "Particularly we need changes in how we conceptualize 'masculinity' as synonymous with violent aggression and domination and 'femininity' as synonymous with masochism and shame".

Relying on violence as a defining factor, "Her Say" constructed culture as male. Equating masculinity with violence, "Her Say" was making a call for a redefinition of culture that could awaken women to the need for essential cultural reform. What emerged from these women's discussions of their intrinsic benefit to society was women's confined position.

In culture, women had no real choice. They were victims by virtue of their sex difference, with dominant culture keeping power from them by its reliance on violence. The disconsonance of the recognition of women's -worth versus their exclusion allowed a gap in this constructed reality, through which could be glimpsed a vision of a reformed culture in which women were no longer constrained to the role of victim. Another psychologist used the Smith trial as an occasion to examine sex-role difference in what she defined as the Kennedy family code: "Men are revered - destined to be great - so they are to be indulged. They can carouse together, pick up women and expect sex. The women's first duty is to family and home." Part of the code for women was "steadfastly defending their men, discrediting their attackers".

But she noted that the Kennedy women's self-denial had personal costs as well as "producing men with severe intimacy problems and contempt for women." Selfless support may have created a few prominent public men, but she estimated the personal and social costs as too high. This psychologist called for a reevaluation of gender through adjustments within the traditional marital relationship. She gave wives permission to be selfish in their marriage partnership, but she gave it a selfless frame: It was good for their husbands.

And in keeping with the theme of sisterhood, readers were asked not to vilify the "other woman," with statistics that showed that over half of them would face the situation of a husband's infidelity.

Without devaluing the homefront, this writer used the women's side of this "Kennedy code" to expose the misogyny of marriage embodied in its two most sacred tenets selflessness to satisfy the husband and solidarity with the husband against other women. In debunking marriage attributes that forced women to devalue themselves and to channel that self-hatred against other women, this psychologist called for women to respect themselves.

In highlighting the dysfunctional nature of the marriage contract by noting that over half the male partners break it, she justified redirecting married women's selflessness to themselves and other women instead of first and foremost to their husbands.

By rewriting the marriage contract without the elite underpinnings implied by the emulation of a prominent family's gender code, women would be taking on the responsibility and enjoying the freedom of defining themselves as opposed to allowing themselves to be victimized by unconsciously adopting a model that performed the hegemonic function of maintaining the gendered power balance. The radical potential of such a strategy that recast a gender-based institution was veiled by its conservative veneer: By taking such responsibility, women would be saving traditional marriage.

By redirecting selflessness into a bond with other women and revaluing themselves, women would have a salving effect on the unidirectional contract and enable marriage to be a partnership well positioned to continue the cultural reform fomenting in the women's culture.

Women's Worth

The bedroom was key to redefining sexuality. Through nostalgic appeals to a gendered cultural tradition, "Her Say" columns endeavored to take readers back into the pre-liberal feminist bedroom as a starting point for a reexamination of sexuality. A psychologist wrote that erotica might light the marriage flame, but she warned that it might also burn the house down. "The once 'good girl,' who reserved sex for the privacy of the bedroom and protested if her man viewed 'dirty' movies is now viewing, or making them herself.... [I]n this age of AIDS and renewed desires for monogamy, she's finding video sex to be safe sex".

Using the 1960s as an analogy of cultural adolescence, this psychologist noted that the "good girl" had grown up. "She's come of age, sexually. Now more financially and emotionally independent, she has let the message of the sexual revolution sink in: Give yourself permission, drop inhibitions and fears, appreciate your body, experiment with your sexuality." But this writer noted that so-called safe sex held a false sense of security, warning that the use of pornography could lead to psychological problems "masking as liberation."

Couched in a conservative appeal to womanly virtue, she gave women permission to take one more step, and that step, perhaps more radical than all liberal license combined, was to set aside male standards of sexual desire. Men had defined sexual pleasure in pornographic terms, and women acquiesced to potentially victimizing definitions of sex by their participation. She called into question male prowess as she asked women to discuss among themselves what pleased them instead of blindly adopting male fantasies as synonymous with their own sexual desire. Casting her argument in the context of a pre-liboration ideal, this psychologist put the onus on women to set a standard "based on their moral and religious convictions.... Talking together about what they like and object to about erotic entertainment can give women valuable insight into their feelings about their bodies, sexuality, and relationships". Despite a reliance on the liberalizing that had enabled women to be "more financially and emotionally independent," her rejection of mainstream women's liberation as flawed brought forward the notion that women were different, not equal.

To begin the discussion anew, the column situated readers in the time before liberal feminism had become a part of the mainstream apology for anti-woman media. Nevertheless, the appeal attempted to build on the knowledge and freedom that had been fostered by liberal feminist opportunities by asking the women to bring their experience back to a time of cultural innocence in order to engage in informed discussions. The need for a strategy different from a liberal feminist approach had been evidenced by the impasse liberal feminism had reached in some of the major debates on issues such as pornography, which had signaled liberal feminism's inevitable collusion with dominant ideology: "[T]here are many feminists who think...that pornography is anti-woman speech which unfortunately deserves constitutional protection".

Since liberal feminism had succumbed to its liberal democratic philosophic heritage, in order to build on the independence women now enjoyed, this new appeal took readers to an idyllic pre-liberation bedroom before the "bad girl" had been reclaimed as culturally cool across popular media. Pornography itself had become so equated with freedom and individuality that its use was recognized as a birthright, rite of passage, and a defining characteristic of the healthy American male.

"Her Say" urged women to revisit the issues of values, standards, and sexual pleasure by talking among themselves in order to arrive at a new definition of sexuality and bring it back to their conjugal bedroom. Women were then expected to take the sex relationship beyond the bedroom. From the first column, with Sanders's discussion of pregnancy set in the broadcast newsroom, it was clear that discussion of women in the workplace was of signal importance to defining women's worth. That women worked, often outside the home, meant that they would be asked to carry their sexual standard of worth beyond the household.

The executive director of a national women's research centre wrote in her column that although nearly half of the U.S. workforce was female the value of women to the larger society was overlooked. Citing a reliance on cultural myths as the culprit, she pointed to the ramifications.

"What employers often fail to realise is that many issues such as child care, parental leave policies, more flexible working hours and pay equity are of great concern not only to women but also to the national economy as a whole". The column did not rely on the voices of working-class women, but it did address their plight through a national overview of working conditions. That, by the 1990s, women were not taken seriously in the paid workforce pointed out their second-class status in society and necessitated their banding together to demonstrate their worth along with their needs.

The president of the Women's Bar Association of Illinois did not mince words in her column: "The wall women find themselves up against is grounded in a fundamentally middle-class and sexist foundation. Put succinctly, women in 'traditional' jobs, such as secretaries and teachers, are perceived to be filling positions that are secondary to 'traditional' men's jobs, such as businessmen and doctors.... [T]he barriers that keep women from achieving pay equity, recognition of the service women provide their employers and access to higher paying jobs must be destroyed".

In a focus on professional women, the president-elect of the Chicago Bar Association wrote that she had a good news-bad news answer about whether women lawyers had a glass ceiling. "The bad news is that we do. The good news is that it's getting higher and that the glass is no longer shatterproof". Guided by its liberal feminist voices in the cultural mainstream, the women's movement had enabled steps toward equality in the workforce, but by the 1990s women still found obstacles. "Her Say" brought a different approach. Since women could not rely on men or maledominated institutions to recognize or reward their labour, they would have to do it themselves, as women.

DIFFERENCE AND MIDDLE-CLASS CONSTRUCTION OF GENDER

The dialectic of sex difference operationalized in the section worked to utilize as well as to dismantle the constructed nature of gender imposed by the patriarchy. "Womanews" made sex separation a physical characteristic of this women's paper-within-the-paper as well as an ideological construct, the terms of which were being framed in "Her Say" during the start-up. Within the newspaper but separated into its own section, "Womanews" cultivated an essential femininity to make a more inclusive appeal to women than liberal feminism had been able to do earlier, encouraging women to cloister themselves in order to redefine their own female nature and to find its power.

"Her Say" often revealed a level of conscious reconstruction in its musings on the attempts over the past decades to bring women into the male sphere. Authors often employed nostalgia in order to revisit a time before parameters of sex difference became obscured by liberal feminism's assumption of cross-gendered monikers of equality. Instead of presuming gender equality, this feminist strategy started from a point of male-female difference to make connections among women. A liberal feminist drive for equality in the late 1960s and early 1970s had brought women out of the "ghetto" of the women's pages with the intent that they would be fully integrated into the newspaper. Although that move did provide women some autonomy and top-down equality, this push may have been premature, as was indicated by the dramatic loss of women readers. However, the extent of women's progress that that era brought to the newspaper has only recently begun to be fully assessed.

The financial independence that liberal feminism had acknowledged as essential for autonomy had been actualized to a certain extent across the culture. It allowed women to seek a space of their own, and the means for the new section to thrive, as this separation worked to bring in advertising dollars.

The launch of "Womanews" created a space for women and their discussions within a still male-dominated media mainstream. It took controversial issues including adoption, abortion, and surrogacy, as well as sexual desire, porno-graphy, and rape, and reworked them from a women's perspective of difference in a controlled public forum. "Her Say" heralded the emergence of a women's section for the 1990s as one that conducted the discussion of women's issues and women's place as a dialogue structured by difference vis-a-vis men, not one of presumptive equality.

Shaping an Everywoman appeal, "Her Say" advanced a cultural feminist agenda that relied on sex difference to acknowledge that by the very nature of their difference from men, in culture women were victims. Asserting the importance of women and a female system of values relied on contrast with masculinity to complete the social contract. "Her Say" established its authority by differentiating itself from the dominant male voice and basing its legitimacy on the mother's tongue. But inherent in using female-male difference as the foundation for a mediated construction of gender was the difficulty of incorporating those who transgressed this dichotomy.

The marriage contract was privileged in order to legitimize this complementary construction of difference; therefore, the issue of divorce, one of the major institutional tools for women's independence, was not addressed in these early "Her Say" columns. In addition, because of the centrality of the malefemale dichotomy in this social construction, inclusion of sexual orientation other than heterosexual could not be part of the ideological setup of this section. None of the 1991 "Her Say" writers was identified as lesbian. In fact, marginalization of sexual orientation was used to strengthen a heterosexual agenda. For example, in speaking out against single motherhood, psychologist Kuriansky did not want readers to think hers a marginal concern, so she stated reassuringly, "Some are lesbians, but the majority are heterosexual".

Based on sex difference, with marriage as the defining relationship, the formation of this women's alliance was so "fragile" that it did not initially allow for articulated inclusion along the lines of sexual orientation. However, the section's premise of sisterhood held the promise that once this women's section became established it might better incorporate women of other sexual orientation. Whitt made the observation about a 1994 section front that showed women who were "black, Asian, Latino, native American and European-American. They aren't necessarily heterosexual".

Men were implicitly present as the presumptive complement to the female, their presence fortified by the occasional mention. "Her Say" did not give men a central role, but it gave a nod to how men might benefit by the women's issue under consideration. For example, Sanders noted that a "more human set of rules would help our male workaholic colleagues, too". Recognition was also given to the work of men who had begun to redefine masculinity without the requisite violence.

"In California and elsewhere, the seedling 'men's movement' examining the concepts of masculinity is a start". What the acknowledgment ofthat start implied was that as "Her Say" encouraged women to redefine their sexuality it would next be incumbent upon men to redefine masculinity. But such reconsideration would necessitate that men respond to a femininity redefined by women themselves. In making the call to women, "Her Say" also implicitly voiced the dynamics of the next stage, the complementary masculine transformation necessary to achieve the cultural feminist vision of a society in which women were valued as women.

In (re)separating the spheres by sex, "Her Say" did not absolve women from responsibility - quite the contrary. Shifting from a liberal feminist reliance on legislative action, this forum propounded that women were again responsible for themselves as well as pregnancy, children, and the essential relationships that had been abdicated to male institutions.

Assumption of these responsibilities meant reclamation of traditional female decisions from cultural institutions in which it had been presumed women would have developed a voice. Women taking on and recognizing the importance of these decisions was necessary in order for them to construct a domain for American women in the 1990s, which could provide a separation conducive to sparking the discussions that would act as a catalyst for cultural reform. One writer stated, "Somewhere, some people got the idea that women are selfish, stupid creatures who can't assess risks and take responsibility for themselves and their unborn children. Somewhere we decided to throw off our own responsibility to provide a safe, secure society in which children can flourish".

Admitting their difference from men and the cultural imbalance of that relationship meant that the hope of tipping the balance of power lay in women using this acknowledged difference to redefine themselves and their worth as women. "Her Say" began anew a dialogue of women's power and responsibility, as defined by women themselves. Women were regrouping in order to make another attempt at cultural inclusion. This time, two decades after the foiled push for equality at the newspaper and beyond, their approach was through a recognition of difference. In cultural feminist terms, this regrouping of women was essential to attaining cultural reform. First women had to gather together, find value in themselves, and define their own worth in terms comprehensible to society. Women could then enable society to see the value of women and begin enacting change on the cultural level. "Her Say" tapped women who held the most cultural sway to guide the reform. Mothers have traditionally been recognized both biologically and culturally as holding a legitimizing power in the home.

In addition, professional women, as power brokers outside the home, were relied on to share their expertise with the women's community. Professional women who were mothers were called on as leaders for this movement that asked women to redefine sexuality, sex roles, women's place in society, and ultimately the culture itself. These were the voices that led the discussion, bringing to this newspaper home their expertise and authority, along with their willingness to embrace a limited notion of sisterhood and their strategies for women's empowerment.

The "Her Say" reclamation of motherhood - through discussion of pregnancy, adoption, abortion, and surrogacy - along with its perspectives on marriage, media imagery, male violence, and the thematic development of women's worth built upon two metathematic considerations - a dialectic of difference and a middle-class construction of gender. Prominently showcasing the section's values through the voices of the professional class, "Her Say" constructed gender along the lines of middle-class values. Women identified as stay-at-home moms were doing so by choice.

None of the "Her Say" authors was identified as holding occupations such as "waitress" or "secretary." Workforce inequities were given voice through high-profile, college-educated women.

A middle-class construction of gender may be most clearly revealed in the column's handling of a piece by a woman who ran a strip club. The woman noted that nude dancing was "most certainly a form of artistic expression. And it is unconstitutional to stop a free expression of artistic form." Such indignation aligning her with liberal feminist values and economics aligning her with middle-class status, she took her stand: "Women should have the liberty to view this type of entertainment or to be nude dancers if they wish.... I, as a woman, am offended if they're going to try to tell me what I can or cannot do".

Use of her as a "Her Say" columnist can be seen as an instance of folding liberal feminist ideology into a cultural feminist alliance. At the same time it manifested an acceptance of women who were not of traditional middle-class background or employment considerations into the f"Her Say" employed the frame of difference that Freeman identified with cultural feminism in the mid-1980s, using this dialectic tension in a metathematic development of the topics of male violence, pornography, sexual desire, and surrogacy.

One topic Freeman cited, divorce, was not directly pursued in "Her Say." It was, however, addressed by implication through discussions of the consequences of women leaving their men, for example, in the ultimate fate of the film characters "Thelma" and "Louise."

"Her Say" moved the discourse into the cultural feminist perspective from the mid-1980s transition that structured debates along the lines of equality versus difference to more fully adopting a dialectic of difference.

The launch of this feminist standpoint privileged the marital relationship, albeit as one that women needed to redefine, in order to adhere to a conservative middle-class ideal. This essential relationship with the male mirrored women's sex-differentiated role and place in society. In a hegemonic: cultural feminist approach, "Her Say" demonstrated how women could function within this male-dominated relationship. Differentiation was made tangible at the level of having their own section within the newspaper, which told women that they were real, different, and worthy.

Providing an acculturation function in its reflection of the widening American middle class, the section's editorial discourse absorbed and redefined female values of a working class that found itself identifying economically with the middle class.

While further research may show whether this level of elite discourse characterizes the tone and article mix of the section overall as it progressed through the 1990s, it is fair to question whether the editorial voice of "Her Say" contributed to what researchers such as Ehrenreich have termed the disappearance of average working people from American media. The initiation of cultural feminist action has in the past relied on the commitment of privileged women to create a women's culture. Professional women provided the key to unlocking a cultural feminist vision of reform that included women's lives outside the home as well as in the home, an omission that had left liberal feminism open to criticism.

Linking professionals with mothers, "Her Say" provided a recognition of the home as powerbase. Mainstream media positioning of "Womanews" legitimized women working with other women. In creating these alliances, "Her Say" warned professionals, imploring them to guard against the seduction of collusion with the male vanguard and to instead take their positions as loaders in defining women's worth.

Calling together women was a potentially empowering strategy, with awareness of difference as its first stage. To enable readers to see how women's place was subordinate, inessential, and even dangerous, "Her Say" used sex difference. From a cultural feminist perspective, the inescapable implication is that women are essential for any definition men can construct of themselves. But the fact that this women's medium was ensconced in the dominant media made real the threat that women's power could diffuse into the male-dominated mainstream.

The temptation of pre-packaged commodification of women could easily work against any meaningful redefinition of news and cultural values relevant to women prior to group action or cultural transformation. Perhaps one function served by the undercutting that several columnists employed as short cuts to reader empathy - such as the author who had been "lucky" enough to have children so that she did not have to heed her own anti-surrogacy argument - was to warn the reader against becoming passive or complacent or putting her entire trust in patriarchal institutions.

While "Her Say" heralded "Womanews" as a safe space, through such devices it reminded readers that there is no safe space. Mindful that this space was located within patriarchal constraints, women should maintain their vigilance. The setup of the section told women that their essential womanhood was the key to what it defined as the primary relationship, the relationship with the male. Operating on the symbolic level of media, "Her Say" spearheaded the call of "Womanews" that reaffirmed women's worth in order for women to interact with men from a position of power, and then, strengthened, face the inevitable - daily life as a woman in a man's culture.

Whether the decision deals with abortion, surrogacy, the workplace, or violence, it is made within a cultural context that limits women's range of choices. "Her Say" demonstrated that these decisions can and must be made by women themselves as it reclaimed each piece of womanhood by revisiting each "women's issue" that had lain dormant or had been dismantled. In reclaiming women's issues from cultural institutions, "Her Say" argued that women could recognize their choices.

Editor Dishon saw herself continuing what she described as the Tribune's tradition of going after women readers. She explained, "We do have an opportunity to have it all, but we need to appreciate how hard that is. There is a price to be paid. Sharing that philosophy empowers us to make decisions. Then, it's all a matter of choices". Calling on women to do it all conjured the 1980s Superwoman stereotype, but with choice as the key.

Women had the responsibility to make choices, and in order to do so they had to have access to information and the power to implement those choices. With choice added to the Superwoman mix, what emerged was a myth for the 1990s - that of a prodigal daughter. The working daughter, having prostituted herself to male cultural ideals that devalue women, apologizes to her mother and is welcomed back to the hearth. In choosing to rejoin the women, she also brings with her valuable knowledge of cultural workings.

As appealing as "Womanews" was to a cross-section of readers, and as widely as the practice was implemented at newspapers throughout the country, "Womanews" did not prove to be the industry's immediate salvation. In an increasingly competitive media marketplace, newspapers did not make a miraculous comeback; women readers did not flock back to the newspaper.

Studies, such as an overview of media use in the latter 1990s, showed a continued decline in female as well as male newspaper readers.

Women's sections, begun so enthusiastically in the early 1990s, were fading from the national landscape 10 years later. By the close of the decade, for example, Tuesdays in Cleveland no longer brought the "EveryWoman" section; "Womanews" itself was no longer circulated on Sundays or in the Tribune's national edition.

The stage of a cultural transformation that turns on a reevaluation by those holding power based on self-definitions generated by the traditionally marginalized is often the point at which the cultural feminist vision has stalled. At newspapers, readers had to be wooed from now-established media habits. A decade under such circumstances would hardly seem time enough to effect essential cultural change. Perhaps, in reference to Woodhull's observation that creating a space for women was a temporary and transitional step, by the end of the decade women no longer needed a separate space.

The call of "Her Say" was quickly heeded, but in the boom-bust dynamic of the new women's sections was embedded an industry imperative to get on with the business of redefining news.

Spearheadedby "Her Say," "Womanews" symbolized the start of an end-of-the-century movement to engage women by creating cultural feminist space for women's media in mainstream media, with pockets of women's media developing in newspapers and other media, including television and new media, throughout the decade. Research building on the Women, Men, and Media studies has begun to track whether the introduction of women's pages made measurable progress or whether they acted to maintain the status quo by siphoning women and the redefinition of news off the front pages.

With at least one researcher still noting, "News is essentially a male domain," cross-media analysis of the 1990s should be undertaken to assess whether "Womanews" was indicative of a transitional phenomenon that characterized cultural transformation or merely a "commercial break" in media business as usual. The signal call of "Her Say" beyond the bounds of "woman" was to call for the ongoing redefinition of "news" and indeed to place "Womanews" and its sister startups across the nation in the position of being dependent upon successful transformation of "news" for survival into the 21st century.

The "Womanews" that "Her Say" guided was not a magic pill for industry. But it was a compelling call. What is called for on the academic side are new and better methods of assessment. Feminist media research is well positioned to further develop women's ways of measuring success. Recognizing the enormity of this task, this study nevertheless echoes the appeal of Fenton in citing the "need to examine production, content and reception as connected and integrated within transnational, national, local and personal socio-economic realities and in a way that is manageable within the practical constraints of empirical research". Guided by "Her Say," the section espoused the values of a second-wave feminist paradigm that had taken hold in the culture by the 1990s. It also heralded many of the concerns emerging in a third wave of feminism. The goals of the cultural feminist strategies would be best achieved by women taking individual responsibility and group action. In applying a cultural feminist theoretical perspective, this study has been able to identify the entrance of women's media into mainstream media and suggest the value, power, and promise of such an appearance.

This cultural feminist analysis of "Her Say" has argued that, strategically positioned by its editorial voice, the section constituted a women's space and through the women's culture cultivated in that space gave a mediated reality to a cultural feminist manner of understanding gender. Implicit in this understanding of gender was the need for cultural transformation through a reevaluation of cultural values; yet, as this study points out, this women's media relied on traditional news values to enable its privileged position as part of the media mainstream. Aligning the section with industry conventions, "Her Say" called for a reassessment of values in the larger news culture. "Her Say" heralded a women's culture complete with its vision, but through metathemes of difference and a middle-class construction of gender, it reveals the workings of its own demise. The tendency of a cultural feminist strategy to diffuse itself from a women-centered base located within patriarchy suggests diffusion as a phase of cultural transformation as the values of the women's culture take hold in the culture at large. But in this it also suggests a strategy easily derailed at this juncture since the reform becomes dependent upon the larger culture, once motivated, to act to sustain the momentum of the transformation.

"Her Say" announced that the baby was back, and 25 years later, editors showed that they were ready to nurture this section. The politically conservative mood that had taken hold of the country during the 1980s had squeezed out many of the women's voices that had broken into public discourse. With "Womanews," Dishon and Woodhull carved out a cultural feminist space that fulfilled a strategic need measurable by ready advertisers and eager readers, as well as subscribers to its "Womanews" news service, through which stories were sent to papers that might not otherwise have been able to sustain such coverage. Although its true measure of success may lie in further feminist analysis, its success was certainly evident in the fact that it was so quickly adopted as a model for the women's sections that sprang up across the country. Voice in sync with the times, "Her Say" was a cultural feminist manifesto of women, by women, and for women. Emerging from a women's culture within mainstream journalism, "Her Say" gave voice to a new generation of women's pages in the daily newspaper, with "Womanews" providing a care-giving inoculation to a flagging newspaper industry and reenergizing women's media.

7

Responsible Journalism

The news director of a television station in a mid-to-large market area explained why he denied my request to accompany his reporters as they gathered news. I would unobtrusively observe and occasionally ask journalists to explain strategies. He said he tells all his reporters to imagine that when their story comes up in the newscast, he is handing them a certain number of viewers. He cupped two big hands together as if to hold the audience. "When their story is done I want them all back. The last thing I want them thinking about are news values." The news director added that this wasn't his idea. He only wanted to keep his job. "In this business," he explained, "you have to think with a cash register in your head."

In that newsroom, and in four other local television newsrooms I observed, journalists--from reporters and videographers to news directors-were much more decision takers than decision makers. Their autonomy was bounded by three universal commands: Do whatever it takes to maximize audience; minimize cost; don't embarrass big advertisers or the owners' other interests. Only after satisfying these demands were reporters and editors free to practice journalism as they saw fit. As a consequence, content was designed more to sell than inform. Abbreviated reports of simple, visual, emotional, and obvious events displaced explanations of complex, significant, and underlying issues.

Contrast the freedom of action in these newsrooms--which now supply most Americans with their news--with the expectations of journalism's national codes of ethics. Most codes imply that the journalist is a "professional" free of any obligations except responsibility to enlighten the public. And so they place full moral responsibility for news on the shoulders of individual practitioners. The American Society of Newspaper Editors Statement of Principles, for example, holds that:

The primary purpose of gathering and distributing news and opinion is to serve the general welfare by informing the people and enabling them to make judgments on the issues of the time. Newspapermen and women who abuse the power of their professional role for selfish motives or unworthy purposes are faithless to that public trust.

No mention is made of executives of parent corporations with "cash registers in their heads" who might bend journalists to the wills of major investors, sponsors, and powerful sources.

This chapter argues that contemporary national codes of ethics are based more on the fantasy that journalists control what becomes news than the reality of control by owners. In fact, a long accretion of journalistic autonomy has stalled and appears to be eroding as corporations providing news seek to maximize return to shareholders. Journalism's national ethics codes, then become less relevant to practitioners and deceive the public by deflecting criticism from owners onto their employees.

The codes also are unethical themselves to the extent that journalists become decision takers rather than decision makers. We need a more realistic code that recognizes those who wield power and assigns them appropriate responsibility. The argument begins with an analysis of journalism's moral blueprints.

It compares their language to the research literature of reporter and editor autonomy, including recent court cases and surveys of American journalists in print and broadcast media. It concludes with a proposal for a "structural" framework for journalism ethics that takes into account the growing influence of forces outside the newsroom, such as the executives of corporations that own news media, the interests of corporate "siblings," and the markets for investors, advertisers, sources, and consumers.

ANALYZING CODES OF ETHICS

Although the question of who journalists are is not addressed in national codes, this analysis will count managers who supervise newsroom employees, but not those in other departments. And it includes all news department employees. In newspapers, everyone from the executive editor to contract or freelance reporters and photographers is considered a journalist. In television, everyone working in the news department--from president of the news division at the network and news director at a local station--down to production assistant is included.

Of the four most widely cited codes--enacted by the Society of Professional Journalists, the American Society of Newspaper Editors, the Associated Press Managing Editors, and the Radio/Television News Directors Association--three begin with plausible and lofty language about the role of journalism in a democratic society. The Code of Ethics of the Society of Professional Journalists, for example, begins: "Members of the Society... believe that public enlightenment is the forerunner of justice and the foundation of democracy. The duty of the journalist is to further those ends by seeking truth". Each code then lists more specific do's and don'ts intended to realise these broad goals. The oldest of American journalism's codes, written by the American Society of Newspaper Editors in 1922 and most recently revised in 1975, aims all of its moral injunctions at individual "practitioners," "journalists," and "newspaper men and women." No others are mentioned. Further, the code is cast as a covenant between two parties only, intended to "preserve, protect and strengthen the bond of trust and respect between American journalists and the American people".

The newest code, updated by the Society of Professional Journalists in September 1996, also places responsibility for news solely and directly on journalists. No other actors are assigned moral duties. The code is divided into four sets of moral commands, each of which begins with the phrase, "Journalists should."

The third such injunction says "Journalists should be free of obligation to any interest other than the public's right to know". That heading obliges journalists to "refuse gifts, fees, free travel and special treatment, shun secondary employment, political involvement, public office and service in community organizations" that might conflict with objective reporting. All of these lie within the control of the individual journalist.

He or she must give up some personal benefit to avoid an ethical breach. But parallel with these individual-level injunctions are others in which it is not the journalist's self-interest that must be restrained but that of the corporate or other owner. For example, journalists are obliged to "deny favored treatment to advertisers and special interests and resist their pressure to influence news coverage." Here journalists are asked to decide when the owning corporation must deny itself benefits, such as revenues from advertisers, to avoid an ethical breach. By making no distinction between individual and corporate levels of obligation, the code implies that journalists have this authority.

The Radio/Television News Directors Association code begins: "The responsibility of radio and television journalists is to gather and report information of importance and interest to the public accurately, honestly, and impartially". It contains 10 references to individual broadcast journalists and one to the "broadcasting industry." No other actors are mentioned.

The Associated Press Managing Editors' code, revised in 1995, departs from the others in naming an institution, "the newspaper," as the principal subject of moral injunctions. It commands that "the newspaper should report the news without regard for its own interests, mindful of the need to disclose potential conflicts. It should not give favored news treatment to advertisers or special-interest groups". This language reduces the asymmetry of a subordinate class of employees--journalists--making decisions for the corporation that owns the newspaper. But it may not achieve parity.

For newspapers (and television stations) which are part of larger corporations, the subordinate local unit is still being asked to decide an issue that affects the bottom-line of the parent corporation. Given the hierarchical structure of conglomerate corporations, it is more likely that parent corporations will impose policies on their subsidiaries than the reverse. Corporate financial pressures on subordinate firms have occurred despite the protests of the most influential editors. Gene Roberts resigned as executive editor of the Philadelphia Inquirer rather than accept continuing cuts in resources for reporting. Under Roberts the Inquirer won 17 Pulitzer prizes. The corporation applying the pressure was the chain with perhaps the nation's highest reputation for quality, Knight-Ridder.

Common to each of these four national ethics codes is the notion that journalists--individually or in the aggregate--are, or should be, free of business-related constraints imposed by those who pay them and distribute their work. In fact, the obligations are reversed. Corporations employing journalists are expected to conform to the demands of this special class of workers.

Such an arrangement reverses the usual direction of corporate authority. It deprives owners of their traditional right to use their assets as they see fit. Since the First Amendment's guarantee of press freedom has been interpreted as a privilege of the owner and not of the employees or of the community, this reversal might be seen as obstructing the spirit of the First Amendment. Before going any further, we should ask whether this unusual arrangement of employees making decisions for owners actually exists.

Historical evidence indicates that American journalists have been bowing to the demands of owners since the marriage of the steam engine and the printing press gave birth to news as an industry in the 1800s. According to Bates: Will Irwin, Upton Sinclair, George Seldes, Morris Ernst, Oswald Garrison Villard, Leo Rosten, and Robert Lasch all had analysed how profit-seeking interfered with truth-seeking in the press; so had several critics of the 19th century.

The tension between the owner's business interests and journalism was one of the primary reasons Pulitzer proposed professionalizing journalism through higher education at the turn of the 20th century. This struggle was also the centerpiece of the Hutchins Commission's critique of the news at mid century: "The press is... caught between its desire to please and extend its audience and its desire to give a picture of events and people as they really are". Several media historians have noted an accretion of authority for journalists beginning with the waning of the "Yellow Press" at the turn of the 20th century. They note that journalists have become much better educated and compensated than the "ink-stained wretches" of earlier periods of American journalism.

Indeed, two recent court decisions--one each in print and broadcast news--have re-evaluated the U.S. Department of Labor's 50-year-old classification of journalism as a trade protected by wage and hour laws. In December 1994, a federal court judge ruled that former Washington Post reporter Thomas Sherwood was exercising professional prerogatives and receiving a professional level of pay. In April 1996, a federal court of appeals ruled that writers, editors, and producers at NBC News must be classified as "artistic professionals".

The Sherwood case bears directly on journalistic autonomy. In her opinion Judge Norma Johnson noted: Sherwood's job... required him to originate story ideas, piece together seemingly unrelated facts, analyse facts and circumstances, and present news stories in an engaging style. The Court further finds that Sherwood's fact-gathering involved more than passively writing down what others told him. He was required to cultivate sources, utilize his imagination and other skills in seeking information, and continuously develop his finely tuned interviewing skills.

While the evidence that Sherwood was a smart and highly skilled reporter is undeniable, the judge passed over how much the journalist's exercise of authority required permission. The evidence also showed Sherwood's choice of topic and story angle, his choice of sources, his handling of quotes, and the time he had to cultivate sources and write stories all were subject to approval by his superiors. Sherwood worked not within a structure of collegial control but within a hierarchy.

Not even the Post's newsroom meets the standards of autonomy in journalism's national ethics codes. Even at a paper such as the Washington Post, by reputation a paper where reporters have unusual freedom, editors were not elected by their peers, but appointed from above. The most influential manager was selected by business persons outside the newsroom.

Similarly, the resources available to the newsroom were determined not by a committee of journalists but by the parent corporation's board of directors. Were Rupert Murdoch to buy the Post (God forbid!), he could change the operation of the newsroom as quickly as he did when he took over Britain's best-selling newspaper The Sun in 1974 and switched its orientation from labour to conservative.

As owner, Murdoch could dismiss any journalist disagreeing with his notion of news without any hearing or professional due process. And Murdoch could violate journalism's codes of ethics without fear of sanction because none contains enforcement language. The First Amendment would protect Murdoch from any government response.

Not even the Post's newsroom meets the standards of autonomy in journalism's national ethics codes. Like many educated and skilled whitecollar employees, these journalists enjoy some authority over their work product. They are not assembly-line workers. But their autonomy is clearly bounded by corporate superiors, not by allegiance to peer standards.

Ironically, during the same half century journalists were gaining those responsibilities Judge Johnson noted, scholars studying the question of who has influence over the news were locating control over the news further and further from reporters and editors. The notion of journalists as arbiters of news was implied in the famous "gatekeeper" study conducted by White. But the 1950s were only half over when Breed contradicted the notion at least of reporter autonomy with his classic survey of 120 journalists at northeastern newspapers. He described a newsroom culture established by management that--usually subtly--enforced management's orientation toward news. The reporters' choice was to go along or get out.

From the 1970s into the early 1980s researchers such as Epstein in network television, Sigal, Sigalman, and Fishman in newspapers, Powers and Bantz, McCorkle, and Baade in local television, Tuchman across several media, and Hirsch reanalyzing White early data, documented that newsroom routines-established more by their employers than by journalists--dictated news content and practice.

In the mid- 1980s Altschull argued that news has always been advertisers. Turow conceptualized journalists as holding only one of 13 power roles that determine media content. Bagdikian located most of the power to shape news well above the newsroom in corporate boardrooms. Soloski argued that professionalism is a widely shared myth in American newsrooms that is manipulated by managers to control news work.

In the 1990s Auletta, Squires, and Underwood described the economic rationalization of network television and newspaper newsrooms in response to profit pressures from owners and the stock market. McQuail proposed an array of social forces outside the newsroom as the determiner of news. Shoemaker and Reese offered a five-level analysis in which owners of media firms exerted the greatest control. McManus theorized that news results from an elaborate compromise among powerful market-driven influences outside the newsroom.

Similarly, scholars who analysed the application of journalism ethics in newsrooms found that journalists are more often the object than the subject of codes. Davenport randomly surveyed 100 newspaper managing editors and an equal number of local television news directors. Eighty per cent of respondents who had written codes said they were imposed on the newsroom by managers with little rank-and-file discussion.

In a review of research, Boeyink found that ethics codes were effective only when publishers decided they were important. Beam surveyed 300 top editors at 60 newspapers of varying sizes. He found that professional autonomy makes more sense considered as an organization level, rather than individual level, variable. Writing about reporters in the American news industry, Fink concluded: "Either you and the hand that feeds you agree on ethics in reporting or writing, or you (not your editor) will be a very unhappy employee--or unemployed".

RECENT TRENDS IN JOURNALISTIC AUTONOMY

Random surveys, each of more than a thousand U.S. journalists, con ducted every 10 years since the early 1970s suggest that journalism's century-long ascent toward professionalism has stalled and may, in fact, be reversing. The newsroom surveys show a strong trend toward declining journalistic autonomy. Weaver and Wilhoit, who conducted the last two surveys, wrote:

Compared to the early 1970s, journalists in the 1982 sample reported a significant decline in their freedom to decide news story emphasis and editing. The 1992 interviews suggest that newsroom autonomy has diminished further, and at a startling pace. For the first time in three decades, barely half of reporters see themselves [with] the newsroom clout of their predecessors. And the lessening autonomy is occurring at a time when many in the work force--who entered the profession during a tide of heavy hiring of young staff in the late 1970s and early 1980s--have been in the newsroom long enough to have established their authority.

Four of five journalists laid the loss of autonomy to profit-driven management decisions as well as pressure from government, advertisers, or a hostile public. A comment the researchers deemed typical read: "There is increasing pressure from large corporations, including my own, for bottom-line profit and gains at the expense of long-term quality". By contrast, only 8 per cent said they were hindered by professional standards of ethics, good taste, or objectivity.

Other surveys show a similar trend. A 1993 Associated Press Managing Editors survey of 627 newspaper journalists showed rising discontent from a survey 8 years earlier, particularly among the young, minorities, and best educated. Almost half the journalists with graduate degrees counted themselves dissatisfied enough to want to leave their jobs. "About half of these dissatisfied journalists say they do not have sufficient autonomy on the job," the report said, "they lack resources to do their jobs properly and they are not very impressed with the quality of their newspapers".

A 1995 Associated Press Managing Editors study of newsroom managers also showed less autonomy and greater stress than a similar survey in 1983. "Fully 66 per cent of responding editors said their news hole was reduced in the past year. Half reported losing news staffers who were not replaced. Eighty per cent reported that 'there is more work than I can complete in a normal day'". All of these limitations were imposed from above the newsroom.

Summing up these changes for newspapers in an article titled "The Thrill is Gone," Stepp concluded: "In the age-old battle between the editorial side and the business side, the editorialists have lost the upper hand". In local television--the part of the news industry growing A fundamental principle of ethics is that those with greatest power bear the greatest moral accountability.

Fastest over the past several decades in employment, consumer loyalty, and influence over news practice--the outlook for journalistic autonomy is more dismal still. According to Fink, "In television sheer perversity is at work-a sort of Gresham's Law of Journalism: poor quality, low-cost entertainment shows drive out high quality, high-cost news programming". If these assessments are accurate, journalists are more decision takers than decision makers. While they cannot disavow responsibility for their actions so long as they retain the option to quit their jobs, their authority to produce high-quality ethical news reports is circumscribed, tightly for some, loosely for others. A fundamental principle of ethics is that those with the greatest power bear the greatest moral accountability. Journalism's ethical codes have it backward.

A recent text on media ethics concluded: "[I]t's futile to discuss... efforts by individuals to practice ethical journalism without examining the corporate profit motive and its impact on those efforts". Major American journalism ethics codes, however, not only fail to examine the corporate profit motive, most don't even recognize its existence. Difficult structural ethical questions lie at the heart of journalism conducted by profit-seeking businesses.

Particularly in the modern newsroom where barriers between the business side and the news side have been lowered or eliminated, journalism ethics must speak to potential conflicts of interest with powerful news-shapers outside the newsroom. Drawing on theoretical work by Turow, McQuail, and McManus, at least eight such powerful actors can be identified. In each case there should be both a prescription of an optimal relationship and an enforceable ethical proscription to protect the news department's interest in providing news that maximizes public understanding from the media firm's narrow self-interest in serving the following constituencies:

- Shareholders/Owners. If they seek maximum short-term returns on their investment, they may balk at spending what quality journalism requires.
- Rational advertisers seek the largest audience of potential customers in a context that both lends their claims credibility yet encourages consumption, all at the lowest cost. In contrast, quality journalism seeks the largest audience regardless of customer potential--wealth-and freedom from bias toward advertisers and the ethic of consumption.
- Sources may manipulate the supply of raw material for news in order to gain favorable exposure to their ideas and often themselves. In contrast, ethical journalism gathers information without fear or favour and without regard to the information subsidies of public relations.
- Consumers: More people may be attracted to entertainment information. Further, quality journalism that challenges popular myths and prejudices may drive away some consumers.
- Government: In an environment where parent conglomerates of media firms own companies affected by government regulation or government contracts, or simply by government spending, there may be pressure for biased news in return for favors.

- Parent corporations may exert pressure to report favorably or at least not initiate negative coverage of corporate siblings and their business interests.
- Media firms, represented by the newspaper publisher or TV station general manager or network CEO, may not allocate adequate resources to their news departments given the greater profitability of other choices, such as entertainment programming, or entertainment-oriented sections of a newspaper, or other business interests.
- Pressure groups including social institutions may exert influence on the newsroom for content that does not offend the group's sensibilities or that furthers its agenda. Quality journalism, however, is independent, acting in the best interest of the entire community.

The details of such a structural ethics of journalism are beyond the scope of this chapter. Fresh thinking about how to define, measure, and enforce a new moral code for news is urgently needed. Even the most modest proposal is likely to be highly controversial because structural ethics must negotiate the First Amendment, and more importantly, intrude on the "forbidden," realm of ownership prerogatives of private enterprises. My purpose here has been restricted to demonstrating that the current expressions of national codes of ethics ignore or gloss over the most serious moral issues in contemporary journalism. As long as they do, journalism's codes of ethics are themselves suspect ethically. At best, they are incomplete. At worst, they confuse and discourage needed reforms by permitting those who control the news to deflect criticism from themselves onto their employees.

In Britain, lone motherhood is not a neutral nor an apolitical status; it evokes strong moral evaluations and therefore easily becomes a political symbol. Although the historical status and treatment of British lone mothers has varied over time, they have almost continually been at the centre of public debates about the state of society in general, but more particularly of 'the family' and the role of women.

Most recently, political and media attention has focused on the doubling of the number of lone parent families in Britain over the past two decades (reaching around 20 per cent of all families with dependent children, over 90 per cent of whom are headed by a lone mother), on the growth of unmarried mothers as a proportion of all lone mothers, and on their increasing reliance on Income Support (the social assistance benefit) rather than on paid work.

Debate has centred around whether lone mothers prefer to live off the state, and may even be created by such policy 'cushioning', or whether they want to be 'self-sufficient' but cannot because welfare policies are unsupportive.

Arguably both views are wide of the mark; research reveals that lone mothers' moral views about 'good' mothering, and how this does or does not combine with paid work, is the crucial issue. Lone mothers received particularly damning attention at the hands of new right politicians and the popular media in 1993, in the context of the then Conservative government's 'back to basics' campaign. Indeed, 1993 has been dubbed 'The year of the lone mother'.

Lone mothers were depicted as a threat to the fabric of society, supposedly rearing delinquent children without the guidance of a proper father, and scrounging benefits and housing off the welfare state. Social policies were called for that would deal with this menace. Lone mothers received further attention in the media as a legitimate cause for social concern during 1996, again functioning as a sort of symbol as part of a national debate about 'moral values', as policies concerning divorce law reform and working mothers were debated.

And towards the end of 1997, lone mothers were once again in the political and media spotlight as a result of the New Labour government's social reforms. Here lone mothers functioned as a symbol in the attempt to restructure social benefits towards welfare-to-work strategies.

Academics have played an important supporting role in media preoccupations with lone mothers. In particular, new right and revisionist/ communitarian academics have gained space in the national media, and have propounded what Judith Stacey calls 'virtual social science'.

Here categorical assertion, anecdote and selective readings of 'facts' are posed as unbiased and fault-free authoritative research, in this case purportedly showing that lone mothers are formative members of a British 'underclass'. The US academic Charles Murray gained particular space in the press in the early-mid 1990s, with Cassandra-like statistical and rhetorical predictions that Britain was heading down the same slippery slope as the US, to extensive urban crime, drug use and disorder-where all this was the result of increasing 'illegitimate' births supported by the benefits system. The answer, in this view, is to stop 'supporting' lone motherhood through social policies and instead support the traditional married family.

Such negative portrayals of lone mothers have not gone unchallenged. Attempts have been made by voluntary pressure groups, such as the National Council for One Parent Families, and liberal left professionals and academics, as well as leading figures in the 'liberal' establishment, such as Church authorities, to reinsert a public image of lone mothers as 'normal' women who are doing their best in externally constrained and unfavourable circumstances. In this view, social policies should be enlarged to properly support such women in bringing up their children.

Consequently, mainstream political and media debates about lone mothers in Britain-and corresponding policy proposals-have become polarised between seeing lone mothers as a threat to society or as victims of social problems. Each of these positions, their propagation in the media, the role of academics within this, and the social policies that accompany them, is reviewed in more detail below: particular attention is focused on the ways in which the media have depicted black lone mothers.

But these polarised positions are not the only ways of understanding lone mothers' situation, or of framing the parameters for social policies in response. Indeed, other views may more accurately reflect how lone mothers themselves understand and experience their lives.

These alternative views of lone motherhood are also discussed albeit more briefly, because they have not gained wider legitimacy or currency in national media and political debates, nor influenced policy frameworks to any great extent. The propagation of particular media images of lone mothers and their accompaniment by recommendations for particular social policies, is posed rather simply above. Clearly, the media increasingly inform public understanding and comprehension of the social world, and play a role in placing issues on the political policy agenda-as this volume attests.

Nevertheless, the relationship between mainstream media presentations of lone motherhood and the actual or possible social policies that address their situation is not a relationship of simple stimulus-response.

As in other policy areas, this relationship is more complex, not least because government and political agendas influence and inform media coverage. It is perhaps more useful to see ideological issues lying at the root of both, which relate to shared social understandings about the relationship between individuals, states, markets and families, and to how 'explanations' are constructed in dominant western and academic categorical modes of thought.

REPRESENTATIONS OF LONE MOTHERS AS A SOCIAL THREAT

One perception of lone mothers expounded in mainstream political and media representations sees them as a social threat: both morally and financially. They are formative members of an underclass that has no interest in providing for itself in legitimate ways. This position links into the underclass theory that has developed in the USA in particular, but has been imported into, and gained influence in, Britain-although it also has its roots in a longstanding British 'social pathology' view of the poor.

This theory posits that, in spatially segregated areas, there is a developing class that has no stake in, and is hostile to, the social order. Lone mothers are seen as active agents in the creation of this underclass. In Britain, young single (that is, never-married) mothers have been focused on as the central culprits.

Lone mothers allegedly choose to have children outside wedlock to gain welfare and housing benefits, and then, supported by the state, they choose not to get a job. Their sons, assumed to be without male authority or roles, are said to drift into delinquency, crime and the drug culture, while their daughters learn and repeat the cycle of promiscuity and dependency. Popular media depictions of lone mothers as a social threat use emotional symbolism more fully than more 'respectable' academic tracts. Media reports, however, both draw on, and are sometimes written by, academics. The American new right/republican academic Charles Murray has enjoyed particular prominence in the *Sunday Times,* to purvey his virtual social science.

Andrew Neil, when editor of this paper, claimed that he had introduced Murray to the British public and politicians, and sponsored his 'research' in Britain. During the early 1990s and especially in 1993, the *Sunday Times* and other right-wing broadsheets, along with the tabloid press, devoted considerable and regular editorial attention to stories about single mothers and the underclass. They also displayed some raw prejudice in doing so. An editorial in the *Sunday Times* for example argued that:

It is becoming increasingly clear to all but the most blinkered of social scientists that the disintegration of the nuclear family is the principal source of so much unrest and misery. The creation of an urban underclass, on the margins of society, but doing great damage to itself and the rest of us, is directly linked to the rapid rise in illegitimacy... It is not just a question of a few families without fathers; it is a matter of whole communities with barely a single worthwhile role model.

A headline in the same newspaper queried, 'Wedded to welfare-do they want to marry a man or the state?' The *Daily Mail,* with its ideological and political address to 'middle England', offered a similar viewpoint:

The Willenhall estate, on the outskirts of Coventry, houses a large number of single mothers. There are also a lot of young, single men, many living on the proceeds of either crime or benefit fraud and more or less attached to the young women... It is kept afloat by the niggardly (if costly) charity of the state and the local authority, that is to say the taxes paid by traditional two parent families.

The targeting of a particular public housing estate with a supposedly high proportion of young 'underclass' single mothers seems to be a virtual social science technique for delivering messages, and for concretising particular views, as used by Murray and journalists in the popular media. The flagship BBC television current affairs programme, *Panorama,* entitled 'Babies on benefit', broadcast on 20 September 1993, used a similar technique.

In this case it was the St Mellon's council estate in Wales that was portrayed as an underclass breeding ground. This estate had previously received critical attention from the then Conservative Secretary of State for Wales, John Redwood, in a speech arguing for policies that deterred young women from having babies outside marriage and supported by the tax payer. Indeed, the programme makers claimed that they were investigating his contentions. Both Redwood and the *Panorama* programme implied that St Mellon's was typical and could be extrapolated as representative of all lone mothers-despite more considered accounts revealing inaccuracies about the estate and lone mothers generally. Popular media presentations of lone mothers as a social threat link into a conservative new right political view of the state in society, where the welfare provision of housing, benefits and other social provision is castigated as encouraging state dependency, an underclass, and especially single (never-married) motherhood.

Peter Lilley's now infamous 'little list' speech at the 1993 Conservative Party conference, for example, alleged that single mothers were having children to secure welfare benefits and housing, while Stephen Green, Chair of the Conservative Family Campaign, argued that 'Putting girls into council flats and providing taxpayer funded child care is a policy from hell'.

But strands of an underclass discourse are also discernible in the communitarianism underlying the New Labour government's ideas about a 'stakeholder society'. The long-term unemployed, which includes lone mothers, are placed as 'socially excluded'; 'family values' are stressed as the key to a 'decent' and crime-free society, and an element of coercion is required to reintegrate the excluded back into society through paid work. New Labour's view that life in a married two-parent family is better for children and for social cohesion, most notably expounded by Tony Blair and Jack Straw, has been widely reported in the media since 1997.

Media, politicians and academics who promulgate this view of lone motherhood as a threat to society also campaign for social policies that do not reward or encourage such 'self-damaging conduct'.

Consequently, the New Labour government has implemented the previous new right Conservative government's proposal to remove the extra allowances available to (new) lone parents on both the universal child benefit payment and on targeted income-related benefits-with Harriet Harman (then Minister for Social Security and for Women) stating, 'Life is about work, not just about claiming benefit'. Other policy disincentives to lone motherhood advocated by those who hold a social threat view include restrictions on payments to lone mothers who have more children while receiving benefit (as is the practice in some American states). There are also suggestions that young single mothers on benefit should be placed in hostels where their sexual relations and children's upbringing can be supervised. This policy idea has been floated by the New Labour government, in linking hostels with job training-again revisiting proposals of the Conservative government.

Encouragement and reward for traditional male breadwinner/female homemaker couples is also stressed by social threat advocates, with policy proposals to redress the supposed benefit bias towards lone, as opposed to married, parents (another reason given by New Labour for its lone parent benefit cuts). Other policy proposals include a tightening of the divorce law so that fewer lone mother families are created in the first place, as well as advocating 'moral' family and parenting education-the latter being the remit of the government's new National Family and Parenting Institute to be launched in April 1999.

Black Lone Mothers as a Social Threat

Until recently, 'race' and ethnicity were muted features of British social threat representations of lone motherhood. In the wake of the heightened media attention to lone mothers from 1993 onward, however, articles about black lone mothers began increasingly to be reported in the white-dominated media. Under the headline 'The ethnic timebomb', for example, the tabloid *Sunday Express* noted that more than 50 per cent of black families are headed by a lone mother and argued that, 'Almost six in ten black mothers are bringing up children on their own, urged on by the benefit system', implying a direct causal relationship between the incidence of black lone motherhood and the growing social security bill. Such claims ignore the fact that black lone mothers are more likely to be economically active and in full-time employment than their white counterparts; research suggests they also provide healthier lifestyles for their children. The *Sunday Express* article also raises the spectre of 'babyfathers' who-in newspaper accounts-father worryingly large numbers of children with multiple female partners.

Stories about 'babymothers' young black women who are presumed to have children by multiple male partners) also received considerable attention in the broadsheet press. Mainstream radio magazine programmes, such as BBC Radio 4's *The Locker Room* and *Women's Hour,* have also featured discussions about black lone motherhood and its social implications. Much of this coverage has echoed the ongoing debates in black media, especially the tabloid daily, *The Voice*-self-styled 'Britain's best black newspaper'-but there are significant differences between these stories as they are reported in the black press compared with their coverage in the white-dominated media.

First, there are no scare stories about social security bills. Second and importantly, there is a sense of debate in the black press, with the black readership responding to 'personal opinion' columns through the letters page. By contrast, coverage of black lone motherhood in the mainstream press tends to be devoid of vigorous questioning or alternatives, with a flat presentation suggesting that 'this is how it is' in the British black population. It is argued elsewhere that the emergence of a focus on black lone mothers in the British mainstream press is linked to the broader social threat concerns discussed above. It is suggested, moreover, that it is through such 'exotic' media explorations of black family life that white people vicariously play out their fears about social breakdown and relationships between men and women.

REPRESENTATIONS OF LONE MOTHERS AS A SOCIAL PROBLEM

In contrast to the view of lone motherhood as a self-created threat to the social order, a second perception of lone mothers widely reported in mainstream media, presents them as victims of externally created problems and in need of help. Stress is laid on the 'facts': in Britain, the majority of lone mothers (just over 50 per cent) are 'mature' divorced, separated or widowed women, rather than young single mothers (with less than 9 per cent being teenagers). Similarly, there is no underclass in the sense of a self-reproducing distinct part of society which stands outside cultural, political and economic norms.

Rather, there is a growing number of people in poverty, including lone mothers, who have essentially the same ambitions as the rest of society, but who are stigmatised and marginalised. The economic and social causes of this marginalisation are beyond the control of those they affect, while the shrinking welfare state only exacerbates difficulties.

According to this perception, lone mothers are seen as social problems. They want paid work to provide for themselves and their children, but are hindered by the structure and nature of the welfare state. From this social problem position, the appropriate policy prescription signals that lone mothers should receive more, not less, state assistance to help them escape poverty and state dependency. By contrast with the social threat perspective discussed above, the social problem framing of lone motherhood is far less common in the tabloid press.

It is mostly limited to broadsheet newspapers with more left wing or 'middle ground' sympathies, such as the *Guardian*, the *Observer* and the *Independent*, which have given a platform to various commentators stressing the poverty and limited options of lone mothers. An article in the *Guardian*, for example, argued that: Reducing the number of single parent families is not an issue about the morality of feckless unmarried women who won't use contraceptives. Two-thirds of single parent families are caused by divorce. What is needed is a genuine political commitment to supporting the family. Better childcare provision for starters...

Despite these broadly sympathetic views, the broadsheets have also published reports by new right/revisionist commentators and, as we noted earlier, they have also been complicit in vicariously playing out social threat views through examinations of black lone motherhood.

Again, academics such as A.H. Halsey and Norman Dennis, taking a revisionist social-problem position, have been given a platform in the mainstream media to advocate a return of the political left to what they call 'ethical socialism', with its 'historic mission to spread the value of the family throughout all the relationships of society'. Indeed, Halsey was one of the commentators featured in the *Panorama* 'Babies-on-benefit' programme. New Labour's commitment to 'the family' as the source of social morality and obligation echoes this ethical socialism. The social problem view of lone motherhood, based on a concern with poverty rather than the fate of 'the family', is dominant among academic social scientists (especially in social policy), however, as well as among welfare practitioners and the British liberal establishment, such as church leaders.

This often reflects a Fabian political inheritance of enlightened state intervention. Jonathan Bradshaw, for example, an academic advisor to the Church of England's commission on the family, supported the Archbishop of Canterbury in arguing that 'lone mothers should be seen primarily as victims and get more help'.

Furthermore, the major lobby group for lone mothers in Britain, the National Council for One Parent Families, has also adopted this view of lone mothers. In contrast with the marginalisation of these arguments during the eighteen years of new right Conservative government, there has been renewed lobbying for intervention with the advent of the New Labour government-some of which was disappointed early on with the continuation of some Conservative policies such as the cutting of lone parent benefit.

In Britain, advocates of the social-problem view argue that day-care costs should be taken into account when calculating in work benefits for lone (and other) mothers. In 1994, under the Conservative government, an earnings disregard for formal day-care costs was indeed made available, although at a niggardly level. This suggests that, despite the prevalence of social threat representations of lone mothers in the media at the time, the social problem approach retained influence in British policy-making circles.

This disregard has since been increased by the New Labour government. Other policy suggestions within the social problem mould which have also been taken up by the New Labour government include measures to encourage lone mothers to pursue training and higher education under the New Deal welfare-to-work strategy.

Since autumn 1998, lone parents on income support with a youngest child over school age have been invited to an interview with a personal advisor in their local job centre to discuss 'upgrading' their job skills and/or finding paid work. An expansion of 'after school' care services for children is also part of this New Labour strategy (although this goes no way to matching the levels of public day-care in most other west European countries).

In championing the two-parent family, New Labour politicians are usually careful to say that they do not intend to demonise lone mothers. Jack Straw, for example, in a speech stating that strengthening the institution of marriage as a basis for bringing up children was a cornerstone of 'modern family policy', added, 'We are not in the business of making the job of lone parents more difficult by blaming them as some have done in the past'.

However, while it might be thought that the social-problem view of lone mothers' position had gained political ascendancy since New Labour's election victory in 1997, another suggestion under this perspective has not had such success in reaching the policy agenda. Rather than increase lone parent 'top up' benefits these have been cut altogether, as we noted above. Indeed, New Labour is effectively combining the social problem view of lone mothers with the social threat view as part of its communitarian approach (a manifestation of its 'third way' between old left and new right). Certainly, lone motherhood continues to be a potent political and media symbol.

There are two alternative views of lone mothers represented in mainstream British media. First, lone motherhood can be seen as part of a general change in family forms and lifestyle patterns, resulting from people's choices about how they live their lives and construct relationships, within a context of over-arching economic, social and cultural change. Policies would thus be predicated upon creating better conditions, and reconciling paid work and family life, for all families rather than focusing on lone mothers alone.

This view is strong at the national level in much of continental Europe, where lone motherhood is less commented on and is much less important as a moral or political symbol than it is in Britain and the USA. While such a lifestyle perspective on lone motherhood may be muted within national media discussions in Britain, appeals to such a view can be seen in the launch of the niche monthly glossy magazine *Singled Out* in 1995. This was aimed at the British 'lone parent' market and covered all aspects of lifestyle, from holidays and cookery, through conducting relationships and child rearing, to financial and legal matters. However, the magazine did not survive its first year-signalling either the lack of a large enough audience who saw themselves as living a 'lone parent' lifestyle, or lone mothers' inability to afford the cover price.

Second, lone mothers can be seen as women who are no longer willing to accept control over their lives by individual men and are thus escaping patriarchy, with access to paid work, contraception, divorce and so on giving them the practical means to be independent. Policies should thus support and encourage this autonomy (including, for some, state support through wages for housework). Such a radical feminist perspective is rarely represented in the national press in its own terms (other than in more marginal publications such as the now defunct *Spare Rib*). Rather, it gets caricatured and castigated as part of the social threat view, where feminists (and socialists) are blamed for supporting lone motherhood and thus social breakdown. Other media can portray lone mothers, particularly black lone mothers, as deriving strength from their embeddedness in supportive female networks.

The low budget black-British film *Babymother*, released in September 1998, thus tells the 'ragga to riches story of single mother Anita, bringing up her children on Harlesden's tough Stonebridge estate, and her struggles to make it as a deejay'. But journalists who are committed to a social threat view can take an entirely different perspective on the same story: *'[Babymother's]* aim seems to be to encourage immature black women to behave like aggressive, self-pitying trollops, bring up more and more illegitimate children very badly, with no visible means of finance except the taxpayer'. Bigotry of this calibre seems unmoved by facts such as black lone mothers' high rates of employment.

While alternative views may not have had much influence on mainstream media representations of lone mothers or on policy development, they do hold sway amongst lone mothers themselves. Research conducted by two of us draws on interviews with lone mothers in 1994, just after the furore in the media about the moral and financial threat lone mothers posed to British society.

The research revealed that most lone mothers from all social groups held opinions about their position that were congruent with the (nationally muted) escaping patriarchy position, while aspects of the lifestyle perspective were also much in evidence. They often valued freedom to do what they wanted without having to take account of a male partner and were proud of managing on their own. Some also understood themselves to be just a normal part of the diversity of family forms in contemporary British society, especially younger African-Caribbean and white 'alternative' lone mothers who held a more feminist view of families and society more generally.

Given the plethora of bad press that lone mothers have received, voluntary groups representing lone mothers in Britain-most notably the National Council for One Parent Families (NCOPF) and Gingerbread-have made concerted efforts to counter such negative portrayals. Various forms of media coverage, including both newspapers and television programmes, have been influential in shaping the strategies of such organisations. In fact, the NCOPF has emphasised the importance of negotiating the 'right' image of lone mothers.

While they maintain that they need to make a case for lone mothers' special needs, they stress that they must be careful to avoid potentially incendiary images that emphasise differences rather than commonalities with other families. Thus both lone mother organisations have been prominent in rebutting dominant social threat political and media images.

In particular, the NCOPF evidenced their concern about harmful media portrayals of lone mothers by challenging the content of the *Panorama* 'Babies-on-benefit' programme. This documentary purported to show the reality of lone motherhood, and alleged that feckless, young, single women were having a string of babies, and living off benefits and in council housing. These never-married mothers supposedly saw no point in gaining employment or in having long-term stable relationships with men as providers and active fathers to their children.

The programme also examined the 'effective' policy option of benefit capping to deal with this phenomenon. The NCOPF complained to the Broadcasting Complaints Commission and went to court over this documentary. As is evident from the press release the organisation put out at the time, they did this because of fears that negative media representations might fuel moves towards punitive social policies: 'At the time when Government is investigating ways to reduce the benefit bill, this *Panorama* has been a disastrous intervention into the debate.'

The NCOPF accused the programme makers and the BBC of presenting an 'unfair, misleading and irresponsible' image of lone mothers. Rather, they asserted, for the majority lone parenthood is an unexpected event in people's lives, and the typical lone parent is a responsible, caring, divorced mother struggling to provide for her children. Interestingly, neither the NCOPF nor Gingerbread responded to the treatment of black 'babymothers' in the mainstream press, for fear of promoting racialised debate about lone mothers that would cut across the 'safe' social problem image of their constituency that they wish to portray.

The dominant social threat and social problem views of lone motherhood in Britain, including discussion about black lone mothers, have been articulated strongly in the national media over the past few years. These perspectives, by defining issues and setting agendas around lone motherhood, are significant components in the policy process. They assign meaning and causes to lone motherhood and construct the parameters within which social policies towards lone mothers should be constituted or changed.

But this is not to imply any direct stimulus-response relationship between media representations and policy formulation; the two interact in complex ways. For their part, the media are highly diverse and, as we have seen, there are alternative ways to frame lone motherhood to those which are predominant in mainstream media: and these do find voice in some niche media (as well as amongst lone mothers themselves).

Relations between media and politicians are reciprocal. It is politicians, along with academics who share their political mission, who have provided copy for the media while, in turn, the media have fuelled public opinion and encouraged particular responses from politicians.

At one level, media and policy representations of lone motherhood as interlinked and mutually reinforcing can be seen simply as the result of a small but influential 'chattering class' of media workers and policy makers (and a few academics) who inhabit a restricted social and geographical world, and who define what is important and what is marginal. What happens in the 'real world' becomes little more than symbolic foils for various political groupings and regroupings. However, even if largely correct, this appealing caricature does little to explain why it is that the social threat and social problem views of lone motherhood are promulgated in the media and by politicians, and not alternative perspectives.

The reasons for this dominance are to be found at deeper social levels; first, at the level of shared social understandings about the relationship between individuals, states, markets and families, and second, at the level of how explanations themselves are normally constructed in dominant and 'educated' modes of thought.

On the first level, different welfare state regimes develop different sets of social policy in expressing their particular conceptions of the proper, and gendered, relationship between individuals, families, states and markets, not least with different implications for the position of lone mothers. In Britain, politicians and media workers increasingly seem to share a world view defined in terms of a liberal welfare state regime.

In the liberal welfare state regime (such as the USA) social policy is used to uphold the market and traditional work-ethic norms. Modest and means-tested benefits are aimed at a residualised and stigmatised group of welfare recipients such as lone mothers, and depiction of lone mothers as a social threat more easily attain dominance. Under the conservative welfare regime (with Germany as a type case) states intervene to preserve status difference-including those of traditional gender roles and family forms.

Here lone mothers become peripheralised as mothers without male partners, and the social problem view of lone motherhood more easily gains purchase. In social democratic welfare state regimes (where Sweden is a type case), social policy reforms de-emphasise the market and emphasise equality rather than the meeting of minimal needs. Both men and women-including lone mothers-are seen as independent worker-citizens who support themselves through participation in the labour market, and social problem and lifestyle views of lone motherhood merge.

Within this, Britain presents a complex, hybrid case, where some elements of the social democratic regime (classically in the NHS) have been inserted into a liberal welfare tradition. Thatcherism, however, marked a rapid return towards the liberal model and, whatever its political differences, 'Blairism' seems to share the same liberal assumptions about the proper relationship between states, markets, families and individuals.

It is the USA that is explicitly taken as a policy role model by both media commentators and politicians rather than the increasingly derided 'European model' (other than by marginalised 'Old Labour' politicians or maverick journalists such as Will Hutton, author of the best-selling book *The State of the Nation*).

On the second level, though, why is it that the dominant view of lone mothers is as a trope for welfare dependency, social marginalisation and even hopelessness? After all, people know from both personal experience and research that most lone mothers do not fit this caricature. Partly, this type of image building depends upon a particular method of explanation commonly used in western thought.

When they use the term 'lone mother' (or 'single parent'), politicians, the media and even voluntary organisations representing lone mothers themselves (such as the NCOPF) are attempting to invoke a particular categorical representation of a type of person-a ready-made classificatory package that serves as a short cut to reading off a particular social situation.

'Lone motherhood' is seen to stand for an a priori, unitary, fixed, coherent, inherent and essentialised set of attributes and characteristics-in other words, the category articulates a particular stereotype-which in Britain easily becomes a negative stereotype to fit in with the preconceptions of the liberal welfare state regime.

This short cut in image building, and in explanation more widely, is often completely misleading because it assumes that the taxonomic group accurately delineates a social group. Taxonomic groups, such as lone mothers distinguished as a particular parental family form, are often different from the real substantive social groups that actually carry through social relationships and actions. It is not just that lone mothers are not a homogeneous or unified population, so that different social groups of lone mothers may behave differently.

Rather, it may not be lone motherhood in itself that is substantively or causally most important for their social behaviour. It may, for example, be membership of a particular ethnic or class group, or location in a particular area, that explains why some lone mothers take up paid work and others do not. Underlying social divisions and differences, however, remain unspoken in taxonomic representations. Nevertheless, lone mothers are not the homogenous group, in terms of social characteristics, that media and politicians invoke when they use the term, and it is therefore extremely unlikely that, as a putative categorical group, they will hold similar views and respond to policy development in similar ways, as maintained by media commentators, politicians, and even many academics.

Such categorical thinking, and taxonomic modes of explanation, have their roots in Cartesian thought as a means to produce independent descriptions of social life that are generalisable. This type of conceptualising has received critical attention in a number of ways from philosophers of science such as Wittgenstein to the critical realist, postmodern and feminist theorists of today.

Nonetheless, as a model of understanding and portraying social life (and thus also as a mode of control) it retains enormous purchase and power, underlain as it is by the idea that experts, through their categorisations, have a correct and authoritative access to reality. This is why academics like Murray and Halsey are given media space to confirm stereotypes of lone mothers.

The media and politicians clearly also have greater access to image production and dissemination than most lone mothers. In this way they have the power to impose their categorical version of the reality of lone motherhood-and thus to assert a particular identity of lone mothers, their motivations and behaviour, and the causes of all this-as superordinate and exclusive. A particular image, such as that of lone mothers as a social threat, may be contested by less powerful lobby groups such as the NCOPF. But such attempts to insert an alternative identity for lone mothers into the categorical space still rely on the same unitary and essentialist mode of thought as that dominant in media and political portrayals.

They do not admit, or recognise, diversity within the category, or that the category itself may be cross-cut or even unimportant where other differences (like those of class, ethnicity or location) may be the more influential in explaining motivations, behaviour and causes.

This means, moreover, that the 'categorical identity' that ascribes a particular set of characteristics to the taxonomic group 'lone mothers' is not the same as the various 'ontological identities' of lone mothers themselves-how they think about themselves in relation to others and their situation. These ontological considerations have little authority or power, however, and largely remain invisible unless they are used by the media to support pre-existing categories of lone motherhood as a social threat or a social problem.

8

Crisis of Conscience

Journalism is going through a crisis of conscience. In this, it is not alone. One after another, institutions grope their way through an impenetrable gloom, their anchors adrift in the murky seas that encompass them. Like the others, journalism seems ready to pitch overboard the illusions that have accompanied it on its way to This Place, wherever it is. It is turning to new They are not the same. It isn't easy to distinguish among them, but there is one constant: the belief—no, the conviction—all is not well and something new must be tried. Jay Rosen, the chief spokesman for public journalism, said the world that journalism has inhabited for a long time has come to a dead end.

Like many other commentators, he notices some very important developments: the takeover of news organizations by disinterested corporate America, falling newspaper circulations, the melding of television news and the big budget entertainment industry. He concluded that the only way for traditional journalism to survive is by abandoning its model of dispassionate, objective detachment and re-emerging as a proactive force for social change. A number of other political activists want journalism to retreat from worship at the shrine of the First Amendment and lead an attempt to drive corporate oligarchy out of the news business.

Davis Merritt, senior vice president of the *Wichita Eagle*, a newspaper that has been on the front lines pioneering the cause of public journalism, correlated "the decline in public life" with "the decline of the efficacy of journalism" obligating journalism "to do more than tell the news". To stride firmly away from the old-fashioned press posture of objective detachment toward a stance of activism and corn mitted participation is, Merritt said, one way to shatter "an incestuous partnership of politics and the political press".

Merritt and Rosen, and their fellow visionaries launched their movement in an uncomfortable environment of public disgust with politics, a loss of a sense of purpose, a decay of public discourse, and steeply falling readership of the nation's newspapers. Merritt said, detachment has bred among journalists "a dangerous arrogance, a self-granted immunity [that] encourages us to ignore or demean outside criticism". Well, that's where we are now. The topic of public—or civic or *community or communitarian*—journalism has attracted my attention for a good many years, dating back to my days as a journalist for newspapers, magazines, news agencies, radio, and television. I have been a happy witness to the phenomenal gains in the stature and reputation of journalism that began with Cronkite and Brinkley and hit its height in the days of Woodward and Bernstein. I have been an anguished witness to the equally phenomenal collapse of the stature and reputation of journalism that reached epidemic proportions in the last decade or so. It is still with us.

The appearance of public journalism (let's call it that at this point) marks a serious effort to return journalism to the reputation it once had and, even more important, to restore the role of the press to its original purpose-that is, to serve as a breeding place for ideas and opinions, a place worthy of elevation to the honored position it was given in the First Amendment. I applaud the motives behind the campaign for public journalism. I have campaigned for it in my book, Agents of Power, in the original edition in the early 1980s and the new edition published last year. Except, I did not speak of public journalism but of participatory journalism.

A Semantic Jungle

Let me address briefly a semantic jungle, one that involves one of the three movements in the symphony of the press I addressed in Agents of Power as a metaphor for the role of journalism in all corners of the world. It is a semantic jungle because every name comes with its own heavyweight baggage. I called these movements market, communitarian, and advancing, which stand for value systems that exalt the role of the individual, the role of the collective, and the role of the community. The movement I name communitarian includes the values of Soviet Communism, the religious values of leaders like the Ayatollah Khomeini, and the messianic nationalist values of lands in Africa, Asia, and Latin America. I understand and sympathize with some ideas in communitarian doctrine spread today by thinkers such as the sociologist Amitai Etzioni.

Indeed, the doctrine can be found in all corners of the earth, in areas of the Third World and in our own market economic and social order. Much wrangling results from the slippery nature of words and definitions. As Clifford Christians, who like myself endorsed a move away from the ego centric world of today's journalism, observed, language is the marrow of community. Yes, indeed, but taming our words is among the most intractable problems we human beings face.

In this country, commitment to shared communities has stirred political movements for 200 years. Etzioni sought "a communitarian perspective" that avoids particular policies and instead aims at strengthening families.

Lamentably, for many but not all its supporters, communitarianism means the open use of the press as an avowed instrument of propaganda. I do not advocate this kind of communitarianism for the American press today.

Christians argued for journalism in the service of the public good, and I certainly agree with that end. But the means used worry me. And, as he correctly pointed out, there is always the risk that a community will turn its back on the outside world and root for only its own gods. The definitional jumble is further confounded by the fact that sometimes communitarianism is portrayed as the direct opposite of libertarianism and thus a philosophical support for limited government controls to challenge the might of media empires (a worthy enough idea but outside the scope of this discussion).

Nor am I comfortable with the ideas in the public journalism advocated by Merritt and Rosen. Perhaps the designation coming closest to my sense of values is of community journalism. So, let me settle on that, because I believe most strongly something must be done if we are going to salvage the traditions of journalism from the cesspool into which it seems headed. I have always been a news junkie and, like many of my colleagues I began my long career as a journalist and academic as an idealist. From the outset I believed wholeheartedly in government by the people; I was sure that democracy could be served only when journalists presented to the people the information--the news--that they needed if they were going to fulfill their duties as citizens of a democracy.

With diminishing enthusiasm during my years as a working journalist, I accepted and endorsed all the "truths" that permeate the world where journalists dwell: that the highest goal of journalism was to serve the public interest, to aim above all to serve "the people's right to know." After I switched to the research-oriented world of the Academy and no longer rushed to deal with time and space constraints of reporting, I thought longer and harder about what I had always known but had somehow ignored. In time, I came to realise what was wrong with my thinking. Like so many journalistic colleagues, I had ignored money.

My writing as an academic and freelance journalist has concentrated on money and how the quest for maximizing profits has done its insidious job. I have witnessed the fall of newspaper after newspaper, the rise of tabloid journalism, and the decline of competition as news began to vanish in the irresistible embrace of entertainment, and lamentably the switch of the public from veneration to disgust with their newspapers.

Still, the belief that fired my career as a journalist has not retreated. The appeal of Merritt and Rosen public journalism is it offers a thin, quixotic ray of hope that the mission of journalism may yet be restored in the forbidding world of Time Warner, Ted Turner, and Rupert Murdoch.

In my book, I call this belief the democratic assumption, and I believe those words are accurate. I embraced in Agents of Power the cause of participatory journalism in which Reporter and Reader could jointly agree on a definition of news and work together to provide the people the information they need to carry out their role in the democratic assumption. To some degree, this is also the goal of the public journalism movement.

If we are going to go on, I would like to go beyond what seems to me to be the modest goals set by Merritt and Rosen and Company. I am convinced that we cannot compete by ourselves but only in union with one another. We may not succeed. In my own despair, I don't really think we can. But the choice is there. Either we can give up and abandon the dream that undergirds the democratic assumption or we can join together as a community and take our place on the battlements.

A NEW DIRECTION FOR JOURNALISM

It is foolish, I believe, to reject the idea of a new direction for journalism. Some, like Merrill, fear that new direction will eliminate what tradition sees as the proper role of journalism, to be a fourth branch of government, a watchdog, to keep its eye on those who really wield power--the government, those who make law and those who enforce law; the corporations, the churches--and without fear or favour to report what they see. Objectivity simply does not exist.

Even if it did exist, it would be wrong because objectivity always works on behalf of the status quo. It is true that the typical American journalist perceives this to be his highest calling: To get the facts and to lay out the facts for the reader, who may or may not act on those facts, as he or she sees fit. But objectivity is a mechanism for ensuring the status quo. It is an instrument to guarantee the preservation of institutions and the social order. It permits criticism of individuals but not of the fundamental system, political, economic, or social.

The state of impartiality is, in fact, defensive of the system. That in this model the press retains the potential to challenge the social order is the element that poses a threat to those who exercise power. Inasmuch as the press fails to live up to its potential, it is carrying out the political role that is desired of it by those in power. To the extent that the press endorses the idea that it is above politics it is serving the needs of power.

Isn't it the business of journalism to help the public understand? High up there among the reasons why I have been so murderously disappointed in today's press is, if you'll pardon the expression, its know-it-all-ness. The First Amendment was not written for the benefit of the press. It was written for the benefit of the people. Under the First Amendment, everybody has the right to be heard. It isn't only for people with the resources to own the newspapers and the broadcasting stations and the fibre-optic bitstreams.

Why are the media so unpopular? They always come in at the bottom in public opinion polls along with the politicians. I don't know all the reasons, but one of them, I'm sure, is their arrogance, their assumption outlined every day in the newspaper columns as well as on the Sunday TV shows where Sam Donaldson and George Will let us know every week how clever they are and how stupid we are.

When I was a journalist in my arrogant mode, I used to think down, too. In Washington, we always used to report movement: Who was up? Who was down? That's what the dumbbells wanted, we told each other. They didn't want to hear about issues, certainly not the complicated ones.... Well, don't let me go too far. We did do the complicated stories; we did try to report what the Hutchins Commission recommended, that is, the truth behind the facts. Some newspapers still do. Some TV reporters still do. But they are all losing ground--to tabloid papers and tabloid television. Or to USA Today and its many clones. Short and very spicy.

The Voice of Money

One of the ideas behind what we cheerfully speak of as the freest press in the world is that it gives voice to those among us who are the hardest to hear. Of course, I am talking about the poor, the homeless, the Black, the gay, the Native American.

Mainstream journalists need to listen to them, too. I think the Finnish Television Network did the right thing when its reporters went out into the community and asked ordinary people what they wanted to know more about. When they learned what it was, they went out and produced documentaries giving everybody a chance to be heard.

Unfortunately, it has dropped the programme. Even in Finland, I guess, it's very difficult to challenge the bottom line. But why not here? What have we got to lose, except--aha!--Money? It wins every time.

Giving up is not the answer. Money is for the most part indifferent to content. Audiences will likely be stimulated to pay attention to substantive news when they have participated in defining what it is. Definition is the key. Reporters can and should be devoting time to finding out what matters to audiences and then laying out the story for them with suggested solutions. This is what participatory journalism is all about. News is no longer defined in terms of the journalist's amorphous news judgment.

Permit me to raise yet another counter-cultural idea (I am using that phrase here to refer to something that runs counter to the standard culture of journalism). Is it in keeping with the idea of democracy for us to invoke the First Amendment just to avoid engaging a tough problem? Journalists could, with profit, devote more time to making our world a better place to live in than to roll eyeballs, scramble for high salaries, and insist rigidly on our rights under the First Amendment. Whatever we write or broadcast has consequences. Don't we have to pay attention to those consequences? We also have responsibilities, don't we?

Let me get into what I believe community journalism demands of journalists, certainly of reporters and editors; I hope we can include publishers and owners, but this means they must lower their financial expectations. Community journalism demands putting the public interest ahead of the maximization of profit. Think about that. But working stiffs, no matter how high, can't force this formula on the people or the corporations that pay their salaries. That's a weakness in community journalism.

Utopians hope that weakness will go away. In my new mood of guarded optimism (I love that phrase), I would like to try to persuade the bosses that by bringing the people into the process of journalism, they can continue to produce earnings while serving the needs of the people.

It isn't enough. The community journalist goes beyond the facts. Beyond them. I have come to respect the research and analytical insights of the English sociologist, John Burton, who wrote that if we are to have a stable society--and that means for the journalist, his or her boss, and all the people who live in the community--then everybody, all the people, all the social units, must have equal access to the community's resources and the skills they need if they are going to act within the rules of society. Those denied this kind of access, Burton said, will turn to "alienation behaviour". And that means going outside the norms of society to a life of what we, who have that access, call crime.

There is a special role for community journalists here, maybe the most important of all. They could become a third party to conflict. It's an idea that appeals to me, an idea that makes people in the media real mediators.

LET THE MEDIA PEOPLE MEDIATE

Best of all, however, the community journalist can and should bring the two sides together. Let the media people mediate. Most problems can be solved, or at least alleviated. Here is the classical third-party role. Study the background. Recognize that you can provide the data that shows the antagonists don't have to play the zero-sum game, where one wins and the other loses. The mediator finds the places where the antagonists are in agreement, no matter how small the area.

After all, most of us believe in our personal survival. And most of us believe in the survival of the community. That's a start. It may not be the journalist's job to bring the two sides together, but ask yourself: Who else is going to do it? You can be the *link* that facilitates communication and decision making by the actors. The journalist is not the one who comes up with a solution, but certainly a solution is what is meant to be the end product of the process.

This role is an extension of the First Amendment. It speaks not of our rights but of our responsibilities. It is the positive side of freedom. Why not be responsible to the community and for helping it solve its problems? There are risks. Very serious risks. That arrogance I have been talking about is one. We don't need journalists in the pulpit, but they can help the people in the pulpit, and that's no mean role to play. To carry this fearsome burden, reporters must be what they should be under any circumstances, well educated and learned in analysis. Here journalism really plays a part in what matters most and becomes a true fourth branch of government.

Journalistic objectivity and detachment may have been fine once upon a time, but that doesn't bring communities together. It may even drive them further apart. The apathy of the public is well known.

It is going to grow deeper and deeper if the public continues to see itself as separate and disconnected, uncared for and uncaring. People need to care if they are going to tune in to and read the news. An active community journalism has a chance to reverse that course.

When the United Nations *Human Development Report 1998* appeared, it revealed a somewhat damning picture of the UK as one of the most impoverished nations of the developed world: the UK was ranked fifteenth out of the seventeen countries included in the poverty index used by the report. In the UK one in seven of the population was below the poverty line, and the country contained about 30 per cent of Europe's children in poverty.

This was not the image conjured by the sparkling glitter of new Labour's 'cool Britannia', its millennium dome ascending symbolically skyward from reclaimed London mudflats, and consumer spending running riot on digital television sets in the homes of a population who were now all middle class.

Something was amiss, and as ever it was in the working and reworking of popular cultural narratives provided by the news media that explanations could be forged and framed. When the 'new Labour' government of Tony Blair came to power in 1997, one of its primary targets in the battle to 'modernise' the British state was the social security budget.

Social security minister Frank Field, with a reputation for an independent and tough approach in this area after an early career as a 'poverty lobbyist', and several years chairing the Commons Social Services Select Committee, was charged with 'thinking the unthinkable'.

But this task, as always, had to draw on public and deeply rooted mythology and understanding. In this chapter I briefly review how this process was worked out in the 1990s by examining news coverage of poverty and social security, and its consequences for public beliefs and policy.

SHIFTING GEAR IN THE RHETORICAL BATTLE

In earlier work I have argued that contemporary understanding of welfare is drawn from three roots-'efficiency, morality, and pathology: efficiency of the labour market and the economy; morality of the work ethic and self-sufficiency; and the pathology of individual inadequacy as the cause of poverty'.

These three vary in intensity as conditions change. With rising structural unemployment, awareness of and familiarity with the circumstances and causes of unemployment became more diffuse through the population. But the increasing moralism of work as the only route out of poverty, and as the best cure for residual idleness, increasingly formed the core of a hardening set of political axioms arguing that duties as much as rights were the key to modern citizenship. This rhetoric became pivotal to the Blairite agenda, and to the welfare reforms the new Labour government began to pursue in office.

Samuel Smiles was back in favour. While the worthy toiled, 'Most wretched and ignoble lot, indeed, is the lot of the idlers'.

The intense 'scroungerphobia' evident in both press and public attitudes in the 1970s abates somewhat in this later period. But the rhetoric and vocabulary are by now set. Drawing on this three-part framework, news about social security now becomes merely a variant on the earlier period.

Within that a predictable and familiar set of motifs recur. First, the economic burden posed by social security expenditure, a restraint on growth and a punitive impost on the hard-working tax paying majority. Second, the need for control and punishment for illicit dependency on benefits, and especially for fraud.

Third, the clear and necessary boundary to be drawn between the deserving and undeserving poor, with single parents moving into greater prominence in the 1990s alongside the unemployed. Both receive vituperation as external to the social system, in association with the foreign or alien claimant. Fourth, the new moralism draws attention to the unduly pleasant 'lot of the idlers', when there is work to be done.

Tory Social Security Secretary Peter Lilley had the headline writers drooling in 1992 when yet another 'biggest crackdown ever against social security fraud' was launched at the party's annual conference. His gruesome adaptation of a Gilbert and Sullivan ditty ('I've got a little list/Of benefit offenders who I'll soon be rooting out/And who never would be missed...') had them rolling in the aisles and across the front pages.

As the *Mirror* warned of 'Dole scroungers facing new blitz', more simply in the *Daily Star* it was 'Stuff the spongers'. War was yet again declared on this outgroup of wasters, idlers, and loafers, a group set apart from the rest of society. The language of warfare underlines this imagery in two ways. First, battle is declared (as in the *Daily Mail* front-page spread, '£2bn blitz on dole cheats'.

Welfare claimants have endured more 'blitzes' than the Luftwaffe could ever have imagined possible. Second, readers are constantly reminded of their outgroup status by the recurrent and exemplary reporting of foreign spongers. In one brief period for example, from the *Mail* stable, we had 'A one man fraud factory', about a 'baby-faced 37-year-old' Nigerian who 'used Britain's benefits system like his own private bank' (*Mail on Sunday*, 21

September 1997); 'Thieving refugee sent benefit cash back home', about a Vietnamese caught shoplifting (*Daily Mail,* 25 July 1997); 'Irish fiddler takes British tax-payer for £1 million' (*Mail on Sunday,* 20 July 1997); 'First family of fraud' about a Pakistani family being tried for social security fraud in a Dutch court (*Daily Mail,* 20 April 1998); and an 'exclusive' exposé of the 'scandal of the illegal immigrant benefits industry' (*Daily Mail,* 30 June 1997).

Scorned for this scandalous exploitation of our softness and generosity as a nation, scroungers are as excoriated as other objects of social contempt, as hinted at by headlines like 'Fraud-busters make a dawn swoop on welfare scroungers', the comparison with drug dealers or child abusers not far from the surface.

Social security fraud, as I demonstrate below, remains a staple of reporting of the benefits system. Yet the arithmetic of this area of criminal activity remains riddled with anomalies. Calculations of annual fraud figures depend on presumptions that short-term fraud would have continued if undetected.

This indeterminacy gets played out in media reporting by the eternal refrain that '£1.4 bn benefit fraud is tip of iceberg' (*Daily Telegraph,* 10 July 1995). Dee Cook has carefully contrasted the policy and ideological response to social security fraud with tax evasion, which, as she points out, is equally a cost to the public purse resulting from criminal fraud. By 1995/96 the Department of Social Security was undertaking over 10,000 prosecutions annually, compared with 192 by the Inland Revenue. In the same year, even assumed benefit 'savings' (which include payment 'irregularities') arising from this action amounted to £1.2 billion, compared with £5.2 billion actually accrued from imposing 'compliance' on would-be tax evaders.

Yet the latter remains veiled behind either total invisibility or humorous disregard for what is seen to be a victimless and innocent piece of mischief we would all engage in, given the opportunity.

Blurring the dividing line between welfare dependency and criminality fuels the sense that an unnecessary burden is being placed on the public purse by all this largesse. The day after disabled activists chained themselves to the railings at Number 10 in protest at threatened benefit cuts, that voice of middle England, the decade's most successful newspaper, the *Daily Mail,* in its new conditional Blairite pose, argued that 'while those in genuine need will not be abandoned' the reforms would 'make sense of a welfare structure which creates a culture of dependency, fails to eradicate poverty, and yet imposes an ever-increasing burden on the economy'.

This was the welfare structure, as an earlier *Mail* lead article had pointed out, that 'has spawned a debilitating culture of welfare dependency, fecklessness, and fraud' (15 August 1997). The result, warned the *Sunday Times,* is that 'Benefit fraud is a way of life in Britain's sign-on society' (31 October 1993), a diagnosis echoed in the double page spread in the *Daily Mail* headed 'Sign up here for sick-note Britain' (14 April 1998).

This fecklessness arises from the alleged luxury of the lifestyles endowed by social security benefits, and from the indolence and ease with which the system is exploited. My clippings files bulge with annual examples of the, invariably misleading, summertime accounts of social security enriched holiday-makers. The *Daily Express* front-page lead 'Dole cheat's sun holiday' ('A dole cheat soaked up the Caribbean sunshine while still claiming benefit in Britain'), catches the flavour (16 August 1995).

But towering over all such narratives are those of the 'super-scroungers'. Among the more prominent such bogey figures recently was 47-year-old former pig worker and invalidity beneficiary Paul Booth, who in 1998 found himself getting more column inches than the resigning social security minister Frank Field. The *Daily Mirror* gave a double-page spread to Mr Booth and his two-family, eleven-children household (8 April 1998).

By the following week further investigation enabled the headline 'Scrounger and a liar' to be printed (14 April 1998). Not to be outdone the *Sun* topped its story with a mock-up medal, 'S.O.B.

Order of Scroungers of Britain', and invited its readers to submit details if they knew 'a bigger parasite than Paul Booth? We're looking for one to win our Scroungers of Britain gong' (8 April 1998). As the paper editorialised, 'Wasters like Booth are a huge millstone round our necks...layabouts who do nothing but breed should be cut off without a penny.' And it added archly, and none too elliptically, 'Perhaps we should cut something else off too'.

The same allusion had informed the paper's front-page lead a month earlier that 'Blair snips Jack the dads' as absentee dads were to find that 'Their pay packets or benefits will be slashed in a massive crackdown on scroungers and cheats'. The notion that social security was a drag of enormous proportions on the motor of economic growth had become prominent in political orthodoxy again by the advent of the new Labour government.

The 1998 Green Paper on Social Security in which Frank Field unveiled his unthinkable thoughts was rapidly distilled by the press into two congruent themes. First it was another 'War on cheats', in which 'Welfare cheats face spot fines' *(Express)* as the 'Shake-up in welfare hits the workshy' *(The Times).*

To help this policy along the *Sun* invited us to 'Shop a bad dad-Field war on spongers who cost us a fortune'. In fact criticised from left and right the Green Paper soon saw its two principal begetters, Field and Social Services Secretary Harriet Harman, both out of office, victims of hubris and the charge that 'Ministers fire welfare blanks'.

But the central message of modern welfare reform was well and truly forged. In a forceful front-page spread the *Express* shows a bewhiskered Field as Moses coming down from the burning bush, tablets in hand, alongside the divine full page headline 'Thou shalt not shirk'. The second theme continued to be the welfare burden which made all this necessary. As the

Mail had explained a year earlier, 'Labour's radical social security reformer Frank Field yesterday pledged to cut the Government's £90 billion a year welfare bill' ('Field sharpens the axe for a purge on welfare'-5 May 1997).

In fact, as many commentators have noted, UK welfare expenditure is relatively low by international standards. By 1995/96 UK expenditure on 'social protection' ranked ninth out of eleven in European comparisons, with only Italy and Portugal lower. Equally, as Hills points out, '...the UK is not a high tax country. Over the last twenty years the UK has moved from being slightly above the mid-point of the international range of tax as a share of national income to being clearly well below the international average'.

Nevertheless, the public rhetoric tells another story. Behind these 'unbearable' cost levels lies, of course, the excessive allocation of welfare generosity, not merely to too many recipients, but to quite clearly the wrong people. Maintaining a necessary cultural distinction between the deserving and undeserving poor remains one of the cardinal boundary sustaining functions of the public media, even though there are occasional shifts in the demographics of those two groups.

In the early 1990s, and occasionally thereafter, periodic out-bursts of puritanical outrage at single parents placed that large and rapidly growing group firmly in the firing line. Eventually the conclusion was clear: 'Lone parents are the biggest cheats: single mothers may be lying their way to £1 billion'. Not surprisingly, given both the popular and policy onslaught, we then find 'Fewer single mothers claiming benefit'. In contrast was the poignant tale of former legendary Liverpool soccer hard-man Tommy Smith, given a sympathetic treatment in his battle to regain his cancelled disability living allowance.

Equally sympathetic treatment is received by the 'genuinely' disabled, as in the case of an unambiguously 'deserving' woman whose plight was headlined in the *Sun* as 'No arms, no legs...but you're not disabled' (13 April 1998), in a story about a thalidomide victim whose Severe Disablement Allowance was stopped when the DSS found evidence of her selling puppies five years previously. By contrast our attention was drawn to the naivety and absurdity of Oxfam's venture into poverty in the UK. Real poverty is of course to be seen in the fly-encrusted faces of children lying helpless and starving on the dusty sun-baked ground of a far-away disaster zone.

As a *Daily Mail* feature, headlined 'Can you spot the difference', pointed out, 'generous people who wish to give to Oxfam are encouraged to do so by pictures of skeletal mothers and children in Africa'.

To help us understand the point, an accompanying photo of 'an African famine victim' is juxtaposed with a family snap of Paul Booth, the 'superscrounger', and his apparently rudely well-fed and voluminous family. This is not 'the poverty that means wearing rags or having no roof at night' (9 April 1998).

The durability of the deserving poor and the deeply-held foundational myths that sustain them enables a proud tradition of campaigning journalism to surface periodically.

In December 1997 the *Mail on Sunday* claimed a success in its 'campaign' on the much-maligned Benefits Integrity Project, with 'Benefits U-turn ends disabled mother's order' (28 December 1997) in a story about a woman crippled by multiple sclerosis whose Income Support had been withdrawn.

Even more emotively signalling a nostalgic search for its heroic campaigning past, the *Daily Mirror* produced a three-page 'Poverty-shock report' feature on the 'virus' which is 'spreading at an alarming rate... The name of this virus is poverty' (30 October 1998), with a two-column photo spread of a three-year-old girl clutching her doll in the bleak passage of a 'grim Liverpool estate'.

Only the relegation of the feature to pages 33-35 signalled a very different set of priorities from the barnstorming polemics of the *Mirror* under Bartholomew and Cudlipp half a century earlier.

Powerful myths about poverty, public expenditure, and the moral economy of welfare remain immovably planted at the core of public understanding of policies related to social security.

Since the 1980s some of these myths have been severely tested by changing economic conditions, yet their potency seems largely undiminished. These exemplars, however, should not disguise the very limited nature of news coverage of pertinent areas of public policy, and it is to that wider, and more calculated picture, that I now turn.

Small but Imperfectly Formed: a Measure of Social security News

To obtain a measure of social security coverage in the media this section extracts relevant data from a larger study of policy news undertaken at the Communication Research Centre at Loughborough University. The data summarised here cover all national UK news media throughout the year October 1996 to September 1997.

The first and most obvious finding is how little coverage social security gets. In that period there were just twenty-four stories primarily about social security on the BBC's main evening television bulletin, eleven on ITN, and in broadsheet newspapers not many more (twenty-six in the *Guardian,* twelve in *The Times*).

Social Security is not big news, even compared with other social policy areas such as education, housing and health. Health is by far the most regularly reported, even dwarfing education in a period when all the main parties were ostensibly committed to that field as a priority.

Social security, like other areas of social policy, is first and foremost about politics. Poverty, benefits, and welfare are refracted through the legislative cycle and the machinery of government, or at least that fraction of it which surfaces in media exposure.

During the same period the Prime Minister appeared in roughly 15 per cent of all such social security news items and other government ministers in 60 per cent. Claimants and non-political actors of any kind made up just 12 per cent of the total actors appearing in these stories.

When social security minister Frank Field published his Green Paper it received high-profile coverage, but nothing so extended and close focused as his ill-tempered resignation saga some weeks later. One facet of this less than comprehensive account of social security and poverty in the major news media is a diminishing attention to social policy news of any kind.

In recent years frequent charges of 'tabloidisation', not least from within journalism, have argued that the major news media, most especially broadcasting and the serious newspapers 'of record' had abandoned their traditional and honourable role of serving citizens with the essential diet of information required to perform their democratic role, and were instead moving to a more diverse and diverting fare with aspirations to entertain more than inform.

I have examined the empirical foundation of this claim elsewhere. It shows a clear trend in both titles towards a much greater proportion of crime stories, and a rapidly diminishing proportion of both social policy stories and indeed of foreign news. With such a diminishing scope for news about poverty and social security it matters more than ever what aspects of these issues are given prominence or attention.

It is not altogether surprising, given the historic confusion in the British psyche between the iniquities of the criminally indigent and the lifestyles of the merely impoverished, that social security and crime news occupy close quarters in the journalistic corpus. In the period of our content analysis we examined both crime and social security stories.

Of all stories that were primarily about one or other of these topics, 27.1 per cent (in the tabloid press), 16.6 per cent (in the broadsheet press), and 11.7 per cent (in broadcast news) were about both-that is were about criminal activity associated with social security.

As I have noted above, it would be difficult to attribute this to the prevalence or scale of social security abuse, but it does certainly register a consistent association between the two areas of activity in the public mind, as we shall see shortly. My concern throughout this chapter has been, of course, primarily with the news media.

Nonetheless it would be remiss not to recognise that the welfare state in its various guises forms a luminous backcloth for the fictional lives of much popular drama, and no more so than in the working class sagas of the soap operas. In the lives and doings of these twenty-seven characters, and others like them, are embodied powerful and rich evocations of the understandings which imbue public perception of issues like social security. In *EastEnders*, for example, Irene (who claimed unemployment benefit despite living with her boyfriend Terry), fell foul of Susan (who also lives in the square but works for the Department of Social Security), leading to an inevitable showdown in the Queen Vic pub.

There can be little doubt, though evidence awaits, that in such constructions lie the source of much of the imagery and explication deployed by people in responding to news and experience of major social issues like poverty and social security.

Responding to the 'Wretched and Ignoble': Public attitudes

There is some evidence that public attitudes have, in recent years, softened and extended to suggest a broader understanding of the ways in which sections of the population are being cut adrift from 'comfortable Britain'. Despite that, the more severe responses which lie deep-rooted in our culture, and on which much of the media coverage illustrated here is based, seem entrenched.

If anything the same surveys show that hostile attitudes to those who do not avoid dependency on the state have hardened. Although such attitudes soften in periods of recession, animosity to presumed fraudsters remains consistent, a pattern that offers circumstantial evidence, though no more, for a contrast between the fluctuating direct experience of people in the wider economy and their more constant exposure to the punitive odium attached to social security 'abuse' in the mainstream media.

The sturdy beggar and his cousins, the 'wretched and ignoble', live on in pre-millennial Britain. In the 1990s, theories popularised by writers like Charles Murray argued that a section of the population in the USA, and in other countries like it, notably in the UK, had become detached from the mainstream of society, primarily by virtue of its distinct culture.

What separated this group from the majority was its 'deplorable behaviour', making them a quite separate 'underclass'. The term, and the imagery and mythology on which it drew, became deeply rooted in the policy aspirations of social security reformers across the political spectrum.

It was, of course, but a renaming of that multitude whose 'vicious habits and destitute circumstances make it certain that... they must hunger and sin, sin and hunger' till death in the 'darkest England' where General William Booth took his Salvation Army a century ago.

While an alternative and more recent language of 'social exclusion' expressed the structural forces preventing the entry of large numbers into the benefits and delights of late-twentieth century society, both rhetorics established symbolic barriers between the consumers of the social security and benefits system and the larger majority whose labours and diligence provided that system's resources. The discursive battle to understand and encapsulate the mystery of severe and extensive poverty within the affluent communities of late-twentieth century society takes place in the pages of the daily press, and on the screens of the nation's living rooms, as much as on the floor of the House of Commons. That battle seems as flourishing and as critical as it was in General Booth's time, and no less is at stake.

9

Resistance and Repression

This study uses feminist standpoint theory to obtain and analyse the discourse of women journalists who quit newspapers. Many of the women expressed regrets over their unmet ambitions at newspapers and their lost identities as journalists. While their communication included regret and marginalization, resistance was also seen, as the women discursively continue to describe themselves as journalists, continue to pursue freelance journalism work, and as they express worth and meaning in the new roles they have assumed. Even so, these coping strategies leave the dominant masculine identity at male dominated newspapers intact.

Scholars and industry organizations have long recognized the disproportionately low share of female journalists at American newspapers. Despite that attention and years of progress, the levels of women in the newsroom seemed to reach a plateau in recent years. The latest national decennial survey of journalists put the total number of women newspaper journalists, and women journalists in all news media, at just 33 per cent. For newspaperwomen, that was down 1 percentage point from the authors' 1992 survey and down 0.8 per cent from the 1982-83 count.

The American Society of Newspaper Editors (ASNE) provides a higher count for women, finding they comprise about 37.3 per cent of journalists at daily newspapers. Even so, that is just slightly more than the 36.8 per cent share ASNE found in 1999, when it first counted female journalists. The Task Force on Minorities in the Newspaper Business found that women "comprise about 4 out of 10 newspaper employees, but are half of all departures". Weaver et al. (2003) similarly found that the news media has problems "attracting and retaining enough women" even though women with less than 5 years of experience in journalism outnumber comparably experienced men. Clearly turnover is a significant contributor to the moribund share of women in journalism.

Indeed, the poor retention of women journalists has been foretold for years by studies large and small, which have long found that a sizeable share of women working at newspapers said they did not expect to stay. One 2002 study found that 27 per cent of the nation's top female newspaper editors said they would "definitely" or "probably" depart the newspaper industry entirely. This was 4 times the rate of their male counterparts.

Feminist organizational communication scholars would say that the challenge goes deeper than a mere imbalanced share of female journalists. At organizations in general, adding and promoting more women fails to change the dominant masculine culture, power imbalances, the secondary status of women, or standard practices for working women. Buzzanell, in fact, wrote that bringing in more women may prevent a critical assessment of the problems that prompt women to leave.

"While traditional practices have opened some opportunities for women," she wrote, "they are still aligned with career rules, discourse, and organizational structures created for and by men". Indeed, she added, "We don't even notice how members construct jobs, tasks, occupations, and settings to sustain gender". Recognizing female journalists' perceptions about gender-sustaining construction in newsrooms is important to understanding turnover among women journalists.

According to Hochschild, women have entered the workplace on "male terms". And that male model, she found, is not one where family or personal life is "balanced" in comparison to the expected work commitment. Instead, she found that long hours are expected and rewarded, even when they are spent inefficiently. That is perhaps because when male employees work long hours they are usually considered to be able breadwinners selflessly climbing the ladder of success, while women employees working long hours are often seen as "selfish" or neglectful of their families.

Most organizations, meanwhile, wash their hands of the work/home demands dilemma by ignoring it or treating it as a separate-from-work, private matter for employees to negotiate. Such a separation especially hurts women, who are marginalized and exhausted by trying to meet both the demands of work and home. Kirby and Krone found that even when organizations adopt policies that would help employees with their non-work needs, there is often resentment from peers against those who use such programs, which pressures some employees who need the policies not to use them.

Individual competitiveness and achievement at the expense of others is also valued in organizations. At the same time, supportive and collaborative behaviors and interpersonal relationships—often prized by women—work against them. Additionally, women are seen as responsible for their lack of success in the workplace, despite doing a disproportionate share of the work at home and getting little help from community structures, and in spite of the fact that managerial roles are overwhelmingly held by males.

That is also true at newspapers, where long hours are common, as is the workplace stress and pressure of trying to produce or process news on daily deadlines in sometimes harsh conditions. In general, women (or men) who try to reduce their hours or work part time find such efforts are devalued and their careers suffer. This could be because organizational members of both sexes come to internalize the standard masculine practices and discourses found there, believing that the very alternative practices that may benefit them personally are without merit or practicality, or are just inconceivable. Suppressing such ideas serves to replicate patriarchal value systems.

Writing of the glass ceiling that prevents women from advancing in organizations, Reuther and Fairhurst (2000) wrote that language patterns, organizing practices, and ideologies "establish and reify this invisible barrier" to women's advancement.

The bureaucracy of organizations also serves to normalize the inequalities "behind a mask of rationality; behind discourse tangled with detail and stripped of emotion". It makes those standards seem normal and expected, and favors the dominant male group. Underwood found just such a bureaucracy of "manager-technocrats" well established at American newspapers.

No matter how competent women are, writes Valian, they are hindered in achieving their professional goals by what she calls "gender schemas." Even more so than stereotypes, gender schemas are ways in which we unconsciously make sense of the world based upon gender. Because of these schemas, she argues, men are more often expected to do well in a professional setting, more likely to be evaluated well for their efforts, and more likely than women to accumulate advantage from their efforts and inputs. As a result, some women, frustrated because their efforts do not accumulate advantage to the same degree that men's do, seek greater self-esteem through other pursuits.

Some women, Valian wrote, "faced with a clear picture of their personal situation, devalue the field they originally aspired to and relinquish a professional career or relinquish their high aspirations. They resolve the conflict by valuing other areas of their lives more highly". Gerson detailed a similar theme, finding that some women who lack a strong desire for motherhood or domesticity nevertheless grow to "see the home as a haven" after a dissatisfying career or work experience.

The objective of this study was to learn more about the turnover of female newspaper journalists from the retrospective discourses of women who have left the profession for a new role. Such scholarship is important given that, according to Bullis and Stout (2000), the exit of women from organizations is so little studied. It also adds another perspective that is apart from traditional institutional theory, which, Martin writes, "runs the risk of unreflexively duplicating the viewpoints of the powerful—those who initiate and perpetuate existing structures—without acknowledging that others with less power may consider widespread structures to be illegitimate". While journalist turnover and turnover intentions have been studied at newspapers, there is a dearth of studies on women journalists' turnover that utilizes and draws upon in-depth individual discourse. This study employs feminist standpoint theory, which rejects the idea of "universal, objective knowledge," as Lorber wrote, because it represents the dominant ideology that has typically excluded the experiences of women and various "others."

Here, the experiences of female former journalists were sought through individual in-depth interviews, in keeping with standpoint theory, which, rather than assuming a singular perspective exists to speak for all women, seeks out the standpoints of multiple women whose experiences, social locations, and characteristics may vary widely.

This ideology seeks to learn about the life experiences and perspectives of individual women who differ from one another based upon their social location. As Allen (2000) wrote, "Feminist standpoint theory endorses allowing women, as 'others,' to speak from and about their everyday experiences in order to discover aspects of the social order that have not been brought to light".

SECURING RESEARCH PARTICIPANT "VOICES" IN IN-DEPTH INTERVIEWS

Women journalists' narratives and experiences as they relate to their departure from newspapers were sought via in-depth interviews with 15 female former newspaper journalists. The women were selected using snowball sampling. Current and former reporters, editors, and columnists from several newspapers were contacted and asked to recommend women journalists they knew who had left newspapers and might be willing to discuss their experiences.

Many of those women agreed to participate and, in turn, recommended others. Some women who were contacted referred others even when the woman contacted did not wish to participate herself.

In the effort to represent multiple standpoints, participants representing a range of ages, work roles, and other demographic circumstances were deliberately sought. Therefore, the pool includes a Hispanic woman, 3 African-American women, and 11 white women, ranging in age from 28 to 49, living in 3 different states.

They worked between 5 and 27 years at large, medium and small daily or weekly newspapers, with stints at newswire services for 2 of the women.

At the time of the interviews, 9 were married and 8 had children, though 1 had been divorced and one had been widowed. While at newspapers, the women worked in a variety of reporting and editing roles. When interviewed, 5 worked in public relations jobs, 5 were stay-at-home mothers, 1 edited a trade magazine, 1 was a lawyer, 2 were in graduate school, and 1 was a freelance writer.

A semistructured open-ended interview format was followed, allowing for follow-up questions. The interview allowed participants to raise issues on their minds that were not imposed upon them, related to their newspaper experiences, turnover decisions, or subsequent roles. The women's personal narratives of working as newspaper journalists, leaving those jobs, and assuming new roles are relevant data and sources of knowledge that have been neglected in scholarly research.

As Lorber wrote, "Simply put, standpoint feminism says that women's 'voices' are different from men's, and they must be heard in the production of knowledge". This process, including an "in-depth contextual analysis of ordinary experiences", seeks to uncover and understand the meaning women make from their own turnover experiences.

After the interviews were transcribed, the 332 pages of text were deconstructed and analysed for themes, behavioral norms, and other understandings from the discourse of women journalists who had left newspapers and assumed new roles.

The interview text was closely examined multiple times, with notes written in the margins that were later used to facilitate the analysis.

Next, repeatedly heard concepts were grouped into categories that were organized with the use of file folders. Over time, it was found that some concepts had little support in the data and were discarded; other concepts generated so much data that they had to be subdivided.

Next, links, relationships, and patterns that were inherent in the emerging categories were diagrammed. Negative or contradictory observations and incidents were sought out that cast doubts or raised questions about the various categories and relations. Concepts were next joined into a sequential model, with all conclusions corroborated with quotations, descriptions, and events described in the interviews. Findings are presented in a structure that parallels the actual sequence of events from the women's turnover experiences to their post-turnover lives and the way that they retrospectively construct both through discourse and communication. Pseudonyms are used.

Buzzanell says exploring the emotion in women's experiences, such as career change decisions, can help us to understand women in organizations.

Therefore, this study seeks to understand, through the discourses of former newswomen, how these women construct and articulate their turnover experiences and transitions to new roles today. In so doing, males, particularly those at the top of newspaper companies, can come to understand how masculine norms, practices, and understandings may have contributed to female journalist disenfranchisement and turnover.

As Ashcraft wrote, this process "affords an outlet for men to learn from the concrete experiences of the 'other'". The following sections describe the themes found in the discourse analysis, drawing upon the women's words and experiences to illustrate them. The concepts are described in sequential order to the women's real-life experiences: their newspaper departures, their current lives, and, finally, their communication today to reconstruct both of those experiences.

FORMER NEWSWOMEN'S RETROSPECTIVE VIEWS OF TURNOVER

The women interviewed described how they came to decide to leave newspaper journalism and the duration of their decision. The analysis revealed that nearly all of the women communicated a "turning point," as other scholars have defined it, that precipitated their decisions to quit newspapers, which is portrayed in the first section.

The second section describes how most of the women interviewed discursively still construct themselves as journalists as a sensemaking or coping skill to explain their career change decisions and current selves. The third section describes the women's regrets or, alternatively, the justifications in their discourse to describe their perceptions about their lives today, post-newspaper work.

Turning Points

Three common turning points emerged that influenced the women's turnover decisions. While some of the women expressed developing a long, gradual, and growing dissatisfaction with newspaper work or with aspects of their jobs, most of them also described a turning point—such as having children or getting an unexpected job offer—that they said forced them to make a decision about whether to continue working in newspapers or not.

For many of these women, turning points emerged to influence their turnover decisions above and beyond their feelings of contentment or discontent about newspaper work. These turning points fell into three categories: having children, getting an unsolicited job offer, and having an attainable new full-time goal come to fruition.

Having Children. Having children prompted turnover decisions for six of the eight mothers in this group, but it was not an immediate influence. Three of the women did not leave newspapers until after the birth of their second children, one being swayed by the cost of childcare for two children and the expected increased stress of trying to leave work on time, despite lowering her hours to 30 a week after her first child was born.

As a result, the decision to quit newspapers made sense to Ruth. While Lynn had a less stressful caregiver arrangement for her first child in that her mother-in-law was available for the often unexpected overtime hours, she wanted to care for her own children at home after the birth of her second child.

Yet she also wanted to work and negotiated to work from home 20 hours a week, doing that for nearly a year. Still, Lynn found it hard to get her stories done in those hours and, as a part-time journalist, came to feel that she was no longer taken seriously in the newsroom. She recalled, It's not really worth it to me to have the stress and to feel that... people with whom you were working were really not as good as you in terms of the professional aspect of the job. It's just that they decided to do it full time. That doesn't make them better at it.

Within 11 months of this arrangement, Lynn quit working, went on to have a third child, and has not gone back to work because, she says, her husband has a good job. Darcy also worked at her newspaper for a number of years after adopting her daughter. While Darcy wanted to spend more time with her daughter, she also was extremely frustrated in the content of her newspaper work. She believed any effort to change her job content to something more enjoyable would have required more work hours than she wanted to give.

Kaye, Nancy, and Paula left newspapers to relocate for marriage or a husband's new job. But motherhood played a role in all their decisions, too. Because Kaye's fiance in another city was happy with his job and she was unhappy with hers, she never considered having him move and keeping her newspaper job, although she planned to get a newspaper job in his city after her honeymoon. Instead, she quickly became pregnant and decided to stay home, recalling, I knew that if I ever wanted to have a family, I would leave newspapers....

And after a while... working nights and weekends and split days off and stuff like that, it became apparent to me to spend more time with her daughter, she also was extremely frustrated in the content of her newspaper that precipitated their decisions to quit newspapers, which is portrayed in the first section.

The second section describes how most of the women interviewed discursively still construct themselves as journalists as a sensemaking or coping skill to explain their career change decisions and current selves. The third section describes the women's regrets or, alternatively, the justifications in their discourse to describe their perceptions about their lives today, post-newspaper work.

TURNING POINTS

Three common turning points emerged that influenced the women's turnover decisions. While some of the women expressed developing a long, gradual, and growing dissatisfaction with newspaper work or with aspects of their jobs, most of them also described a turning point--such as having children or getting an unexpected job offer--that they said forced them to make a decision about whether to continue working in newspapers or not.

For many of these women, turning points emerged to influence their turnover decisions above and beyond their feelings of contentment or discontent about newspaper work. These turning points fell into three categories: having children, getting an unsolicited job offer, and having an attainable new full-time goal come to fruition.

Having Children. Having children prompted turnover decisions for six of the eight mothers in this group, but it was not an immediate influence.

Three of the women did not leave newspapers until after the birth of their second children, one being swayed by the cost of childcare for two children and the expected increased stress of trying to leave work on time, despite lowering her hours to 30 a week after her first child was born. As a result, the decision to quit newspapers made sense to Ruth.

While Lynn had a less stressful caregiver arrangement for her first child in that her mother-in-law was available for the often unexpected overtime hours, she wanted to care for her own children at home after the birth of her second child. Yet she also wanted to work and negotiated to work from home 20 hours a week, doing that for nearly a year. Still, Lynn found it hard to get her stories done in those hours and, as a part-time journalist, came to feel that she was no longer taken seriously in the newsroom.

She recalled, It's not really worth it to me to have the stress and to feel that... people with whom you were working were really not as good as you in terms of the professional aspect of the job. It's just that they decided to do it full time. That doesn't make them better at it.

Within 11 months of this arrangement, Lynn quit working, went on to have a third child, and has not gone back to work because, she says, her husband has a good job. Darcy also worked at her newspaper for a number of years after adopting her daughter. While Darcy wanted to spend more time with her daughter, she also was extremely frustrated in the content of her newspaper work.

She believed any effort to change her job content to something more enjoyable would have required more work hours than she wanted to give. Kaye, Nancy, and Paula left newspapers to relocate for marriage or a husband's new job. But motherhood played a role in all their decisions, too.

Because Kaye's fiance in another city was happy with his job and she was unhappy with hers, she never considered having him move and keeping her newspaper job, although she planned to get a newspaper job in his city after her honeymoon. Instead, she quickly became pregnant and decided to stay home, recalling, I knew that if I ever wanted to have a family, I would leave newspapers.... And after a while...working nights and weekends and split days off and stuff like that, it became apparent to me that this would not work with a family life, or not the way that I wanted it to, because it was important for me to be there for things with my kids.

Paula was similarly drawn by the desire to be home with her children, although she--unlike Kaye--loved her career and newspapers and had numerous opportunities to advance on the male dominated sports staffs where she worked. Before having children, Paula had always expected to be a working mother, but those plans changed after having a child. She recalled, "I thought I'd have babies and work, [eventually] be the editorial page editor and... that would be great. But then the babies came and it didn't matter anymore." Paula wanted to leave work after having her first child, but her journalist-husband did not make enough money for her to stay home.

Two years later, when Paula's husband got a new job paying more, she quit, and went on to have three more children with him. Nancy also relocated with her husband to a new job. While he was for the first time also making enough money for her to stay home with their then-3-year-old, Nancy wanted to work at a newspaper part-time. When she could not find part-time newspaper work that paid decently, she threw herself into securing freelance assignments she could write from home, and she now works about 30 hours a week.

She is happy to still write and to have the extra income, but does not want to return to work full time. Unsolicited Job Offers. Three women left newspapers when higher paying job offers in public relations came their way unexpectedly. All said they had been open to a career change, although they were doing little or nothing to pursue a new job. Sally and Joyce believed there were no opportunities for advancement where they were, and Marian had been turned down in her effort at a promotion.

Sally recalled, "It was very flattering to be recruited. I'd never been recruited for a job and there was more money involved and the hours would be more regular and it wouldn't require physically moving." Marian decided she could not afford to turn down a job that doubled her pay and provided tuition benefits to her husband and children. Joyce's job offer also came with better pay, benefits, and hours, but she struggled over the decision: "I waffled back and forth for weeks actually because I didn't know what to do," she remembered. In the end, she decided that since she wanted to stay in the fairly rural community where she lived, new career options were always going to be rare and she took the offer.

Having New Attainable Full-time Goals. Five of the women left newspapers when they had another full-time option or goal they had been pursuing come their way. For Doris and Maggie, the option was a new job they pursued, in part, because of growing dissatisfaction with their newspaper jobs' long hours, stress, and, in Maggie's case, her perceived inequitable pay and lack of respect from editors.

DeeDee and Myra were accepted into graduate programs, which had been a goal of both women. Neither was unhappy with newspaper work; they simply had other goals that had grown in importance. DeeDee recalled, "I just think I was thinking, I'm gonna investigate other things. I had some other interests." She also acknowledged that a recent merger between her newspaper and its competitor had produced a significant adjustment to her worklife. She recalled:

I had a lot of... friends that lost jobs. That was sad and it was hard to come in. It was the same building, the same place where we had all worked, but all of the sudden I'm seeing all these different people because it's their place now. While Myra began to tire of newspaper deadline pressures, new non-career interests primarily influenced her decision to satisfy those goals. For several years, she had wanted to get her doctorate so she could teach in college and be a role model to budding minority journalists. Her non-career priorities also grew stronger to be closer to her family and to other Hispanics, even though she still loved her newspaper career.

Maggie, who achieved a longtime goal of getting her law degree while working nights as a reporter, initially hoped to remain with her newspaper or its parent company as a media attorney. When no opportunities came about, she left to practice law. For Carol, a false cancer scare prompted her to decide to seize new opportunities, one of which presented itself when Carol's sister invited her along on a 1-year international sabbatical, prompting Carol to take a leave of absence from her midsized daily. She always intended to return to her newspaper, but while she was gone the ownership changed and a new editor would not rehire her.

Because she--like Joyce--was unwilling to relocate for another newspaper job once she returned, Carol switched careers and found a job initially in television news. Only Lindsay did not have one of these three turning points influencing her turnover decision.

Growing job dissatisfaction and stress strongly influenced Lindsay's decision, as well as being denied a transfer to another job she felt she deserved at a different newspaper in the chain that employed her.

Leaving the turning points that precipitated the women's career changes, the following section turns to the present, and describes how most of the women interviewed discursively still construct themselves as journalists as a sensemaking or coping skill to explain their career change decisions and current selves.

"I Am Still a Journalist"

Seven of the women said their turnover decisions were made expressly with the belief that they would return to newspaper work, and an eighth still says that she might. After they had assumed new roles, however, some changed their minds about a career return.

Others unexpectedly found the door to newspapers closed to them, either because of a move or management change. While none of the women have returned to full-time newspaper journalism, 9 have either continued to practice journalism through freelance writing or editing or say they hope to do so. This allows them to continue to do something that most journalists find intrinsically satisfying. It also falls in line with research finding that journalists identify to a greater extent with the discipline of journalism than with journalists' media companies. Kaye, for instance, explained that during her career--mostly as a business copy editor--she edited stories that did not interest her. But she would leap at the chance to write the kinds of stories she wanted as a creative outlet. Paula felt similarly: "I feel like with all my experiences as a mother, as a working mother, as the mother of a whole bunch of kids, I am a widow--that I have a lot to say."

Some of the women do freelance journalism from home, and others said they want to do so. Nancy has made the largest commitment of any participant, doing regular freelance writing about 30 hours a week from home and "ticking away" at a novel. Sally said she has recently thought more and more about doing freelance writing, explaining that as a reporter she felt as though she were "going out and seeking the truth" within the parameters of deadlines and editing. "It is different being at an organization where your job is to present the organization in the best light.... I miss that about reporting," she said.

While she expressed no regrets about leaving her newspaper job, Sally acknowledged that she might have regrets about having left journalism in general. Joyce spoke happily of a new opportunity that had just come her way to host a monthly local talk show on cable television. There, she could revive her skills as an interviewer and make use of the in-depth community knowledge she acquired as a journalist. While many of the women continue to discursively or actively retain their connection to journalism, the third section focuses on two discursive practices that they also widely communicated: newspaper career regrets and post-career validations.

Regrets, Lost Identities, and Post-newspaper Solace

The 15 women reflected on their lives, both as newspaper journalists, and now in another career or life role. Some communicate being happier, both professionally and personally. Others say they have not been happier since their career change. Some wished they had left newspapers earlier. Others regretted not achieving bigger ambitions in their newspaper careers. These emerging concepts fell into the themes of post-newspaper regrets and lost identities, and post-newspaper solace.

Regrets and Lost Identities

Six participants readily spoke of their unhappiness about not achieving more in their newspaper careers, saying that they had held bigger, but unachieved, ambitions as journalists. Most of the women also offered that they felt they lost their identifies when they gave up newspaper journalism. Several harbored regrets about not meeting their earlier career aims.

Others described their ambitions but shrugged off the losses as the inevitable byproduct of life changes. Joyce, for instance, said that in order to get to a larger newspaper she knew she would have to leave her home region, but she was always satisfied to stay. Initially, she had expected to "end up working at a really big newspaper and travel all over the world." Doris said she still sometimes thinks about her former ambitions and wonders if she should have persevered. She explained,

There's that [journalistic] ethic that still kicks in and I feel like, gosh, I should've stayed in newspapers, and I was capable of doing that and rolling with it. It just seems... like wanting a personal life was not good--there could have been better reasons for me to leave newspapers.

At the same time, Doris also regretted having "given my 20s to my job." Marian, too, had strived to work at bigger newspapers, explaining, "You know, if I had been patient, maybe something else would have come up for me." A number of times during Nancy's interview, she also raised having had bigger newspaper ambitions, and having regretted leaving one large newspaper after just 6 months when her father died suddenly.

While she has been happy, Nancy recalled "feeling like I was almost settling... because [I wasn't at The New York] Times." DeeDee similarly expressed some regret about having turned down a job offer from a large newspaper that involved covering a beat she wanted and getting her own column. "That is something that comes back and haunts me occasionally," she said. During this interview DeeDee was struggling again over having just turned down a job offer from a major newspaper in favour of some part-time freelancing because she was studying for her medical school entrance exams. She explained:

Kind of in my days when I've struggled lately with my decision, I'm like, 'you idiot. You should have said, here I am.'... You know, this [was] the first time I've been in a newspaper office for a long time and... some things about it... felt like home. Eleven of the women said their identity was--and for some, still is--wrapped up in their work as journalists. For some, that has been one of the hardest adjustments about leaving newspaper jobs. Some described feeling lost when they could no longer call themselves journalists. Maggie recalled, "I mean, my whole life, for 20 years, I was defined as a reporter." Lynn described it this way:

I had done it for 12 straight years, and it was hard to just not do it anymore. I mean, it was like, what am I going to do? What is my identity now?... I'm not a reporter. I'm not an editor.' You know, it's like who am I? Am I morn?... It was a really hard transition.

Nancy also recalled feeling at a loss once the excitement of moving to a new house in a new city wore off. She said, "I felt like I'd had my underpinnings pulled out, because I realized I'd always had my work. My work had been something very vital."

For Darcy, her job as a journalist had connoted both identity and status. She said that journalists "tend to regard ourselves as a class apart.... Letting go of that was hard." Darcy recalled that a new acquaintance called her with lavish praise after she published a freelance story in her local newspaper.

"You know, it's gratifying on the one hand and on the other hand, it's like, 'Well, now you care,'" she related. Carol recalled feeling that she was no longer a part of her city's "action and activity" once she left newspapers. Now working as a magazine editor for a state research organization, Carol struggles to keep journalism at the forefront of who she is, even though one journalism organization accepts her as a member and a second one considers her to be in public relations.

Others said they still find themselves mentioning to people that they are writers or used to be newspaper journalists in an effort to cling to their journalist identity. Working as a freelance writer, Nancy explained, "I guess there's something in me that wants to let people know that, you know, I'm not just dabbling. I'm not just little housewife journalist.

I'm really bringing in a decent salary, but I mean, I don't say that." As a result, she continues to write occasionally for her local newspaper even though other clients pay better because "when you're working at a newspaper... you are somebody that people recognize. And I do think I miss that a little bit." Paula laughingly said that she still considers herself a journalist even though she has been a stay-at-home mother longer than she worked. Carol and Lindsay both corrected the interviewer when asked to talk about their decision to "leave journalism." Doris, similarly, offered that she still feels as though she is "a member of the media," even though she works in an advocacy role.

Post-newspaper Solace

Just as there were regrets, many of the women interviewed talked about their lives being more gratifying now that they are in another career or life role. Some said they are happier now, or more fulfilled. Some expressed having a strong belief in what they do now that sustains them. A few expressly stated that they do not miss newspapers or have regrets about leaving newspapers. Seven of the women offered that their lives are calmer and less stressed now that they do not work for newspapers.

They are better able to make plans and keep them, or better able to accommodate unforeseen events such as sick children. Some feel they have more balanced lives than before. While some have jobs that sometimes involve night or weekend work, they know in advance when it is going to happen and can plan around it. Lynn explained, I realise now when I did journalism I was frantically running from one place to the other all the time because I had to, you know, get it all in. But now I can kind of have down time and feel calm and not rushed around.

Nancy found that freelancing gives her the flexibility to have other interests and do what she needs to do for her son and household while also offering work satisfaction. Others said they have found more time for family and personal interests, with several of the married women offering that while working--and now they did far more work at home than their husbands, so now they are not as exhausted. Only Marian said her life is more stressful now than when she was at a newspaper. As the lone public relations official for a small private college, she often is required to work nights and weekends, travel frequently, and be on-call for unexpected events. She explained that as a feature writer her hours and stress were limited.

Now, if unforeseen events happen, she has to be there. Often, she said, "I pick my kids up from school and I go back to work. I take them to work with me on the weekends." Some of the 15 participants have had significant life changes since leaving newspapers, such as getting married, having children, losing a husband, moving to a new city, and more. So it was difficult for them to isolate a career change's effect on their overall satisfaction.

Yet about half of the women communicated certainty that leaving newspapers improved the overall quality of their lives. As a lawyer, Maggie said she is "very much happier with my life.... I would say that I'm more enriched. It's much more broad-reaching." Doris said she is happier having more personal time, and discovered that having a richer personal life was "just as satisfying" as her newspaper career.

ally is more content with her non-newspaper career primarily because of the lower stress and greater appreciation from supervisors and colleagues. Three of the mothers also said they are happier to be able to put all their efforts into their children rather than dividing their time between children and work. Kaye described her life as a stay-at-home mom as having a greater "payoff" than newspaper work. She explained, I can see when I go out to someplace and people say, 'Your kids are really... nice kids and your kids are really smart.' Well, that makes me feel like... I'm doing a halfway decent job at it. I never got praise at work or was told that what I did was making something better. It was just like you didn't hear anything if you did... a good job, and if somebody disagreed with what you did, then you caught hell for it.

Other participants were more ambivalent in their commentary. Some said they were not unhappy at newspapers, so their satisfaction levels now are about the same. Others said they are making changes that they hope will lead to something that will make them happier than newspapers did. Joyce said that while her personal life is not so stressful as it was while editing a newspaper, she is not as satisfied working in public relations as she was in newspapers, explaining,

There were only a few periods over the years [at newspapers] that I didn't really get up in the morning and look forward to coming to work.... There've been more periods with this job when I didn't get up and look forward to coming to work. It's just not as exciting.

Lindsay, who was both unhappy at newspapers and is also disappointed and disillusioned in the PR job she has held for 6 years, distinguished one telling difference between the two: At least [at newspapers], when you've got a great story there's a big rush, and your public and your sources love it, and your editors loved it.... And here you don't get that. You just mostly get resented for... trying to make people talk to the media and come clean. And sometimes you get told to spin something that conflicts with your value system.

Marian spent much of the interview discussing the advantages of her new public relations job. But later, she acknowledged that she is not more satisfied, in many ways, by the career change: she feels that she deals with too many "abrasive" people, gets little respect because of her young age, has had little positive feedback, and has significantly greater stress in her family life as a result of the added travel and hours. Despite some regrets, several of the women articulated a belief that what they do now is important and benefits others, be it in their current careers, voluntary pursuits, or rearing children. Kaye summed it up best:

In the big picture of things I just feel like... I can contribute more to this world in being a decent mom to my kids, and a wife and a decent person helping other people in my neighborhood that may have had a baby, or had an operation, or whatever.

Many of the women interviewed readily offered similar assertions about their current lives. Next, I will discuss how the commonly held themes revealed in the women's communication articulated some broader conceptions related to identity, home/work demands, and coping strategies to mitigate some unattained ambitions and losses. Discussion

The discourse from nearly all of the women in this study suggests three similar turning points that precipitated their decisions to quit newspaper journalism. All except one of the women quit newspapers because of the birth of a first or second child, getting an unexpected job opportunity, or seeing another attainable full-time goal come to fruition.

Nearly all of the women also expressed dissatisfaction over the long and erratic hours and low pay of newspaper work, and, as found in a separate study, a patriarchal newsroom culture, while several described a lack of opportunities to advance. Nearly all were exhibiting both their resistance to a workplace culture that worked against them as well as their search for an alternative role to sustain them. For some the alternative role came in caring for their families at home full time, which is in keeping with the findings of Valian and Gerson that, after an unsatisfying work experience, some women come to find the home as a haven, or come to devalue their original career intentions.

Additionally, these decisions reflect the long-established difficulties and exhaustion women endure by working full time and bearing a disproportionate load at home. For others of the women, the new role became additional schooling, which has helped many women access male dominated careers. Indeed, according to Chambers et al., access to women occurred in the practice of journalism in the U.K. after higher education became a requirement for newspaper journalists. Until then, people were hired to the "craft" of journalism mostly on the basis of personal connections, which most often benefits males.

For other study participants, the alternative role entailed a new job in public relations, an overwhelmingly female dominated profession. All but one of the 5 women who had left newspapers for a PR job said that the new job came with better pay and hours, and in some cases, the perception of greater appreciation from supervisors. Two of the women found it flattering to be recruited for a new job. Meanwhile, obstacles abounded for the women who tried to remain in newspaper work.

Three of the women with children tried to continue working at newspapers part time, but one found little respect for her work, two found it hard to keep their hours within the parameters for which they were being paid, and the third found available part time work to be low paid and secretarial in nature, trends that Hochschild documented in her book, The Time Bind.

Two other women participants tried but were unsuccessful in being rehired at newspapers after a staff change, and a third was denied in her attempts to transfer to a larger newspaper in the chain that employed her. Nearly all of the women described how they had enjoyed, and now miss, their close relationships with colleagues at newspapers, where large, open newsrooms more easily allow for relationship building at work.

Indeed, one participant described the time before she left the newspaper as emotionally difficult after a number of colleagues had been laid off in a newspaper merger. Here, their communication articulated Hochschild's findings that women are more likely than men to find their social connections at work. Interestingly, half of these women left newspapers believing they would return to the profession. Given that the communication from all of them, even the most dissatisfied, described aspects of newspaper work that they had greatly enjoyed, the perception could have helped to ease their departure.

Myra, who had worked in managerial roles at very large newspapers, best illustrated this dynamic, stating, "What calmed me in that first year [away from newspapers] when I thought--am I ever going to make the transition?--is the knowledge that I could always go back if I wanted to."

After being away from the newsroom and in some cases finding the door closed to their return, more than half of the women offered that they were either currently doing freelance journalism work or were trying to.

Discursively, most of the women were still constructing themselves as journalists, an identity that was highly important to most of them, even years after assuming a different role.

Even years later, most of the women in this study communicated regrets about those lost identities or about the newspaper career achievements they had hoped for but were unsuccessful in attaining. Some blamed themselves, stating that they should have "persevered" or "been patient" or were still "haunted" by lost opportunities, even though the costs to those goals were high for women who also wanted fulfilling personal lives. As Doris recalled,

You know, my friends were all ready to go [on] Fridays at 6:00, but I was maybe three-fourths of the way through with my workday at that point.... I look back and I got a lot out of it, but I really regret that there were so many things in my personal life that I feel like I gave short shrift because [my newspaper job] just demanded everything.

At the same time, many of the women were adamant in communicating a post-newspaper life that was less stressful and also offered fulfillment equal to or greater than their newspaper careers had been.

The mothers in the group all described being torn by the demands of caring for children and homes, which is no surprise given the finding that women are more distressed by family stress than are men. The discourse of the women who expressed conviction or contentment in their new roles is also not surprising given the limited choices for women.

Their communication expressed validation, but with their quest for ambitious goals and life balance unfulfilled, the women who left newspapers express marginalization. These are the once sequestered stories of women who reside behind the many newspaper industry studies depicting rapid turnover and stagnant shares of female journalists.

While much scholarship and industry writing discusses the need for more balance in journalism work, they do not depict the regrets of women journalists who enjoyed much about their careers but found them unsustainable in the long run. While considerable scholarship on female journalists has focused on the difficulties in balancing a personal or family life with the long and erratic hours of daily journalism, these and other women could perhaps have been retained with balanced workplace policies that allow for more than paid work. The long-hours ideology has become an unquestioned discourse that relies upon the unexpected, always changing nature of news and the perceived need for daily, or with the Web, even hourly, published updates of information.

That discourse has long been entrenched at daily newspapers, yet the continuation of such an ideology has not helped the industry to stem its rapidly shrinking readership and declining profits.

Other types of news outlets, such as newsmagazines and weekly newspapers, have been successful without the need for all-hours updates by their employees. Most of their content provides broader reaching explanations of the news, while eliminating the often-changing minutia of most "breaking" stories. The erratic and long-hours discourse at newspapers also often excludes the fact that additional staff working additional shifts could help journalists to leave work at a more predictable hour. In her research, Hochschild found that companies with family friendly policies do not attract workers who work less or are less productive, and such policies make recruitment and retention easier, both for males and females.

While many of the women said that they missed the work they did at newspapers, most of their discursive practices also sought validation in expressing the belief that they are doing good for other people or for a worthwhile organization. Given their expressions of regret and lost identity, this could be, in part, a strategy for coping with the loss of their unmet goals in journalism.

By leaving newspapers, the women in this study failed to change the dominant ideology, and feminist scholars might contend that they abandoned similarly situated women by not staying on to collectively challenge the patriarchal culture at newspapers.

As women exit the news business, their voices for changed work policies and culture at newsrooms most likely depart as well. Indeed, "retreat" is one of the ways that Melin-Higgins and Djerf Pierre, as reported by Chambers, et al., concluded that women journalists in Scotland "cope with sexism in the newsroom".

Here, many would say, we saw retreat in the women's decisions to quit the profession they once chose, continuing a patriarchal cycle that persists in leaving women under-represented in the newsroom. At the same time, however, the women's quest for freelance journalism work articulates resistance to the long hours and lack of control that predominate in daily newswork.

Chambers et al. (2004) noted that alternative work options such as freelance writing or working at feminist Web-based publications has improved the lives of female journalists who can better combine journalism work with family or other personal commitments.

Despite their marginalization, the women have, in one sense, challenged the dominant ideology through their discourse about their experiences. They continue to call themselves journalists or writers, refusing to become invisible, and reproducing honour in the years they gave to the profession.

To be sure, the end result contains both viewpoints: abandonment and challenge. As several scholars have noted, though, feminist resistance is often contradictory. In their discourse, the women articulate resistance outside of the control of the news organizations, and their search for justice came in terms of a better, less stressful personal life.

They quit in order to resist being overwhelmed and dissatisfied by work, but left the patriarchal newsroom norms intact. For those who are not as happy in their new pursuits or miss newswork, their struggle does not overcome their repression. They refused to continue to give in to the way newspaper workplaces function, but at the same time imposed punishment on themselves.

10

Then and Now

When one seeks to understand the place of public relations in our country's history, one immediately runs into at least two problems: What exactly is public relations? Once you have defined it, how can you show public relations actually shaping developments? For the purposes of this chapter, the first problem will be looked at briefly there is at least one definition that will suit our needs. Since the academic study of public relations began in the 1920s, professionals have struggled with finding an adequate definition. Said Edward Bernays, the first individual to teach a class in public relations: Men in the profession of public relations are as little ready or about to define their work as is the general public... [yet] this profession has developed from the status of circus stunts to what is obviously an important position in the conduct of world's affairs.

Many occupations are unhappy with their coverage in the news media. In the past, most complaints alleged superficiality or distortion. Now the demands of promotional culture can make no news even worse than bad news.

A high 'corporate profile', often used by government as a key indicator of effectiveness in the quasi-market competition for public funds, has become crucial for public sector agencies and organisations. While high-visibility groups like the police try to improve their image, low-visibility players like HM Customs and Excise work to establish their social importance through 'fly-on-the-wall' documentaries.

Few occupations, however, have had their sense of grievance about media treatment given official endorsement. The Inquiry Panel on the death of Kimberley Carlile made a 'Reasoned Decision' to meet in private on the basis of hostile press coverage; and the government Command Paper reporting the Butler Sloss inquiry into allegations of widespread familial child sexual abuse in County Cleveland contains a specific section on the role of the news media in the crisis.

During the mid-1980s articles in social work trade journals frequently reflected the preoccupation of both managers and frontline staff in local authority social services departments with media responses to their work.

Since 1990 this kind of semi-public anxiety has diminished, though the private concerns of social workers and departments may not have done.

A review of *Community Care* for the period January 1997 to August 1998 produced only one major article on the news media, and that related to the possible damage caused by the portrayal of people with a mental illness.

Nevertheless, 1998 research into reader attitudes still showed that 'The majority of those surveyed felt that the way the media covers social work issues makes their jobs more difficult to do'.

Social workers' fears about the impact of hostile reporting on public attitudes may be exaggerated since few areas of social research are as hotly contested and inconclusive as studies of media effects. As we shall see, the episodes engraved in the social work collective memory are of press coverage, while survey data regularly report that most people regard television as their primary source of news. But television and radio are fugitive.

Archives of news and documentary are few and are not accessible to the public. In contrast, dramatic or distressing press coverage can be retained and referred to both by consumers and producers.

A key aspect of media routines when dealing with new events is to interpret them through previous, similar events, often by looking back to earlier news coverage ('going to the cuttings'). Nor do news media operate independently; in conditions of intense competition other media are a cheap and accessible source of news. Once established, therefore, interpretive frames tend to persist.

Even more importantly the UK press, unlike broadcasting, is free to be politically partisan. Dealing with family breakdown, young people in trouble with the law, elderly people struggling to maintain an independent household, or people in poverty: social workers and their employing agencies are always operating on the terrain of political conflict.

When social work becomes news, it is unlikely to be bland and in the intensely reflexive world of news media, even impartial broadcast media can reinforce and amplify the interpretive frame placed on an event by reporting its press treatment as a topic in its own right. Empirically, then, social workers' concerns about press reporting should not be dismissed as of no consequence.

More sociologically, their belief that it is important is, as W.I. Thomas classically formulated it, 'real in its consequences'. To put the 'problem' of social work in the press into perspective we must deconstruct it: this prompts a number of questions. Are we talking about local as well as national newspapers? Are we taking into consideration all national newspapers?

Local authority social services have a range of responsibilities: for child protection, for the care of adults who need support because of disability, mental illness or the consequences of aging. Is there a difference in the press response to these different facets of state social work? Do we take into account the wider politico-historic context?

Although social workers have come to fear that any controversy will cause a cascade of press abuse the reality is more complex.

There are even circumstances in which social work gets a 'good press', for instance, when doing 'griefwork' in situations of loss and bereavement. Social workers' support for survivors and those bereaved in the Clapham rail crash of 1988 and the Hillsborough football stadium disaster of 1989 was reported briefly but approvingly in the press.

SOCIAL SERVICES IN THE PRESS: CASE STUDIES

When social workers recount their adversarial relationship with the news media, the critical precipitating event is usually said to be the 1973 criminal trial and official inquiry that followed the death of Maria Colwell and the subsequent official enquiry. Maria, aged seven years, was killed by her stepfather while she was in the care of the local authority.

The case attracted very extensive publicity both nationally and locally and established a template of news coverage which was applied again when three similar cases occurred over a short period in the mid-1980s.

Essentially the deaths of Jasmine Beckford, Tyra Henry and Kimberley Carlile were represented as preventable, if only the departments concerned had been better managed and co-ordinated and the workers involved had been more expert, more experienced and better supervised. In short, social services should have intervened more.

Yet the Cleveland crisis of 1987 (when suspicions of sexual abuse within families led to large numbers of children being taken into care) and similar events in Rochdale and the Orkney Islands resulted in the excoriation of social services for taking children into care by intervening too much.

In none of these cases was there any suggestion that the staff or departments had acted in other than good faith. By contrast, during the 1990s there has been real scandal: a series of court cases in which social services staff have been accused of serious, long-term, sexual abuse of young people in their care. Surely the combination of breach of trust, policy failure and sexual wrongdoing would attract the most vitriolic press coverage? In fact these dreadful events have been downplayed or ignored, particularly in those papers which social workers fear most, the mass tabloids.

This may, at least in part, reflect the legal prohibition against naming either the perpetrators or survivors of abuse, but this neglect also suggests that it is not simply the intrinsic characteristics of an event that determine whether and how the news media will take it up. The explanation lies in the economics and politics of newspapers themselves.

NOT LOW PROFILE BUT NO PROFILE

The fact that all the instances mentioned above relate to social work with children is not haphazard, but fundamental. Social work becomes news because it is about the politics of the family as we can see from a major aspect of social services work that is almost entirely ignored by the press, even when mistakes are made, like the care of elderly people.

For instance, when the local government ombudsman criticised the London Borough of Hammersmith and Fulham for failing to meet the needs of a confused elderly resident, only the *Guardian* covered the story.

After a resident had lain dead for six weeks in her Wirral Borough Council sheltered home, the council ordered an inquiry but only the *Daily Telegraph* reported it. An 'important test case' in the High Court in which a group of residents in local authority homes tried to establish their rights seems to have been entirely ignored by the national press.

Why then, was the possible closure of several local authority elderly persons' homes the subject of a very high-profile campaign in the Nottingham *Evening Post* from late 1991 to mid-1992? Two aspects of the news treatment provide the key. First, that it was never placed within a 'social work' frame. The dispute was reported as a matter of local politics, while the staff were portrayed as quasi-family 'carers'. (Social services management hardly got a mention.)

Second, the elderly people at the centre of the furore were rendered almost entirely passive in the construction of stories, the use of language and in pictures: '"Tearful pleas from Beattie, 99"; "Why can't they leave us alone?"'- a resource to trigger an emotional response.

The 'address' was not to readers in the same situation but to younger people in their capacity as voters, employees or family members. When the issue re-emerged during the summer of 1998 the *Evening Post's* focus was on closure as an employment dispute. This time residents were almost invisible.

'He Let Her Die'

Social workers dread that, whatever the complex actuality, the death of a child in care will lead to sensational press coverage organised round 'the search for blame'. This belief has some foundation. Between 1985 and 1987 some of the newspaper treatment at the conclusions of three very highly-publicised trials represented the supposed errors of social workers as almost equivalent to the guilt of the convicted person.

Martin Ruddock, as the child's social worker, gives a paradigmatic account of being a key witness in the Kimberley Carlile case: massed photographers outside the court, the 'door-stepping' of his family, and 'fishing expeditions' for background information.

At the end of the trial, he writes, the *Daily Star* published a seven-page shock issue in which his picture was placed alongside those of her stepfather and her mother with the caption 'He let her die'. Reports on the earlier death of Tyra Henry had attributed supposed blame in less personal terms, but nevertheless all sectors of the press assumed that there had been avoidable errors: 'Life sentence for Tyra's father' was the front page-lead in the *Daily Telegraph* with a subsidiary story headed 'Row over who was to blame'.

The *Daily Express* devoted its first three pages and entire editorial to the trial outcome, including an item headlined 'Probe reveals basic blunders'. The editorial talks of 'bumbling amateurism' and workers being 'fobbed off or fooled' while the *Sun* had a banner across pages two and three in white-on-black: 'Our deadly blunders'.

Like the Kimberley Carlile case, the interpretive frame in the Tyra Henry coverage closely matched that of the Jasmine Beckford trial in early 1985. This is not, however, to be understood simply in terms of lazy journalism or unimaginative editorial mind-sets.

The intensity and tone of the coverage was crucially linked to the political context of the mid-1980s, when the Conservative government under Margaret Thatcher was at its most confident and radical. Local government was the crucial terrain of conflict as a number of very vocal Labour-led local authorities were pursuing left-wing policies around issues of 'race', gender and sexual orientation. These 'loony left' councils provided a perfect ideological target to mask the more prosaic central government goal of reducing central government contributions to local authority spending in order that direct taxation could be reduced.

All three cases referred to above took place in left-wing London boroughs; in two of them the local politics of 'race' was central. Both Jasmine Beckford and Tyra Henry were African-Caribbean.

The professional and organisational conflicts and confusions surrounding their lives and deaths reflected intense controversy over how child protection practice should adapt to a multi-ethnic and multi-cultural population.

Antagonisms between elected members, senior officers and staff in the London Borough of Lambeth, culminating in a strike by frontline staff, enlarged the news value of the Tyra Henry case well beyond the trial, particularly in the broadsheets. In the tabloid sector the racialisation of the case took a variety of forms from the pseudo-analytical 'Are black power politics costing the lives of children?' to the crude 'Animal gets life', simultaneously illustrating the discourses of otherness and dangerousness then being mobilised to legitimate the reconstruction of local government and social policy. If professional 'failure' was the sole driver of newsworthiness, condemnatory press treatment similar to that recounted above might be anticipated every time a child in care comes to harm.

The pivotal importance of the political context is demonstrated by cases where, though they were apparently similar to those discussed above, media attention was low-key, short-lived, or even non-existent. Charlene Salt died in Oldham, Lancashire despite multi-agency involvement. After the trial verdict in October 1985, although there was extensive coverage in 'how could this happen?' mode, responsibility was placed firmly at the door of Charlene's parents. Later that year, the parents of an African-Caribbean boy were tried for manslaughter at Nottingham Crown Court.

It was reported that his mother had unsuccessfully approached social services for help, but despite the potential 'race' angle, national press coverage consisted of small factual items on inside pages.

Sudio Rouse was in the care of the Conservative-held London Borough of Croydon when she died. The subsequent murder trial in 1991 was covered extensively in the national press (perhaps because of its geographical accessibility and some of the grim details of the child's death) but with no editorial comment and general acceptance of the director of social services' assurances that an internal inquiry had resolved any problems of practice.

'Simply a Terrible Botch'

Between March and September 1990 Rochdale Social Services took legal measures to protect seventeen children from suspected ritual abuse. In mid-September it was announced that there would be no prosecutions, for lack of criminal evidence. The social services committee asked for a report on practice from the central government Social Services Inspectorate (SSI). In March 1991, after a case in the High Court lasting three months, ten of the fifteen children still in care were returned to their parents. The court judgment contained very adverse comments on aspects of the social work intervention.

Nearly a decade later, many of the positions taken up during the Rochdale events seem less secure. While Jean La Fontaine found no evidence of links between Satanism and child abuse, the uncovering of the systematic sexual abuse of children and young people has occurred with ghastly regularity.

As Kitzinger claims, however, the contemporary hysteria about paedophilia has constructed it as 'stranger danger' rather than involving family members. In Rochdale parental rights were being challenged. The Rochdale events raised very complex issues of law and evidence. What is particularly notable about the press coverage is the drive to simplify and to accept 'common sense' attitudes and explanations, even in newspapers addressing a sophisticated professional audience, like the *Guardian*.

The coverage in the *Daily Telegraph* was more even-handed, providing a very detailed account of the legal judgment and allowing a 'voice' not only to aggrieved parents but also to members of the social work agencies involved. Two factors may account for this curious reversal. First, the *Guardian* was originally based in Manchester and still has a strong presence (and source of intelligence) in the north west through its sister the *Manchester Evening News*. Over Rochdale, it adopted the style of a local paper, identifying with the local community.

Consequently, second, it may have responded more sympathetically to several pressure groups representing parents which pursued a well-organised media relations strategy, possibly including the leaking of the SSI report. Its response to the High Court judgment was harsh and unequivocal 'Rochdale: simply a terrible botch'. The paper interprets the judgment as establishing that there had been no abuse. In fact social services were criticised for their failure to produce an evidentially sound basis for their actions in most (but not all) cases-hardly the same thing. The *Daily Mail* had no problems with complexity. From the start its accounts were inscribed with support for the parents and scorn of the local authority's actions: '"Satan case"' parents in clear, say police', another instance of treating lack of robust proof as equivalent to disproof.

The SSI report was represented as having been demanded by central government and being utterly condemnatory, whereas it was neither. On 8 March 1991 the High Court judgment was given most of the front page, supported by editorial drawing parallels with the 'scandalous oppression of innocent parents' which had previously occurred in Cleveland.

Alongside the editorial was a feature about allegedly Trotskyite councillors in the London Borough of Lambeth. Neither the *Sun* nor the *Daily Mirror* covered the case as extensively as the broadsheets and mid-market tabloids, nor in such partisan terms.

'Four pages of Utterly Compelling Reading'

After several separate police investigations over more than a decade, in 1991 Frank Beck was tried (with two other defendants) on sixty charges of rape, buggery and sexual assault against young people resident in the local authority homes that he had worked in and managed. His victims included staff as well as residents, women and men.

Beck was sentenced to life imprisonment (and died of a heart attack in prison). Leicestershire County Council had already set up an independent internal inquiry. At the end of the trial the Secretary of State ordered a national inquiry and a further internal investigation. The matter was also referred to the Police Complaints Authority.

The Beck case demonstrated that social workers could be not merely 'amateurish' but criminal wrong-doers and that their managers might have failed to stop them. Given previous denunciations of state social work in the press, the logical inference would be that the trial and its aftermath would be-literally-front-page news.

Moreover, earlier the same year investigative journalism for a television documentary and by the *Independent* had uncovered inhumane (but not criminally deviant) practices in Staffordshire children's homes, also accompanied by ignorance or tolerance on the part of managers and elected members. News of Alan Levy and Barbara Kahan's report on the 'pindown' affair had been extensive and, in a well-established pattern of news media operation, had 'sensitised' newspapers to similar controversies elsewhere in the UK. Residential social work was on the news agenda. In fact, the press treatment of the Frank Beck trial was relatively low-key in relation to its implications. While the ten-week case was in progress, national press interest was sporadic, triggered by Beck himself giving evidence and by allegations about a local MP.

Despite the sensational nature of the charges, there was more consistent reporting of the trial in the broadsheets than either mid- or mass-market tabloid newspapers. At the beginning of the Beck trial there had been legal restraints on reporting (as there had in Rochdale) the lifting of which was news in itself. As far as can be established, however, after the verdict and sentencing there was no reason not to print the kind of background and 'colour' stories typical of other major trials, like the cases of Charlene Salt and Rikki Neave.

In the Leicestershire scandal, moreover, much useful material was presented readymade to the news media by the publication of the Newell internal inquiry report, a detailed saga of management incompetence.

The *Leicester Mercury*, which had covered the case extensively almost every day under a linking logo, produced a pull-out supplement: 'Today we publish the secret report on the Beck years of evil; four pages of utterly compelling reading'.

In the national newspapers sampled, however, only the *Independent* put the case on page one, where it appeared as a descriptive 'hard news' item, without editorial comment. Nor did the *Daily Mail* make any explicit comment, although its page-two coverage gave more space to 'Blunders over Beck' than to the case itself. The *Daily Mirror*'s presentation was dramatic, but on page nine, while the *Sun* provided extensive text but also in hard news format only and on page seven.

TEN YEARS ON PROBATION

During the mid-1980s, when other agencies of state social work found themselves with a high and very unwelcome media profile, the probation service in England and Wales was almost invisible. In two of the instances of the death of a child in care referred to above the accused man was under the supervision of the service, but neither the work done, nor the effectiveness of probation itself were questioned.

Only once has a probation officer been subjected to media accusations of personal responsibility for an avoidable tragedy. The conviction of Colin Evans, in December 1984, for the sexual assault and murder of Marie Payne (aged four years) was given very extensive coverage in all the national newspapers. At the end of the trial the *Sun* devoted five pages to it and the *Daily Star* nearly six.

At the trial it emerged that Colin Evans had a very long record of sexual offences yet his supervising probation officer had introduced him to a Christian voluntary organisation without informing them of his record. This conferred respectability with other social work agencies and users which allowed Evans to set up a babysitting organisation (unconnected, however, with Marie Payne's death).

All the newspapers criticised the probation officer in trenchant and personal terms; all but three printed a photograph of him. The case also reverberated politically, with members of parliament demanding that a register of sex offenders be set up.

While most of the national press followed up the policy and politics of the case, only the *Daily Mail* news and editorial treatment questioned the *idea* of probation work. It located the issue in a much wider frame: the 'scandalous leniency' of the whole apparatus of social control: 'Our courts, our probation and social services, our schools and education authorities cannot toy tolerantly with violators and corrupters of youth'.

In a classic example of the *Mail's* technique of imputing guilt by juxtaposition this editorial shared the page with a feature claiming that London supply (temporary replacement) teachers were left-wing failures and misfits. Condemning the probation service as practitioners of social work has been a unique theme in the *Daily Mail* which has been pursued relentlessly ever since. The paper is the most loyal in its support of the Conservative Party and a consistent advocate of conventional values, notably the patriarchal family and the strong state. According to the *Mail* almost all players in the criminal justice system are 'soft' and/or 'out of touch'.

Given the high political salience of law and order, the probation service's quiet life could not continue. Despite the Thatcher administration's well-cultivated reputation for toughness in relation to crime, Home Secretaries of the period favoured relatively liberal policies, including the wider use of 'community disposals'.

Consonant with the party's traditional position, however, a series of government policy documents and speeches from 1988 onwards required that probation work be more focused on concepts of punishment and control. No more 'clients', but 'offenders'. Both locally and nationally the probation service was directed simultaneously to toughen its image and to increase its visibility in the local community.

The Association of Chief Officers of Probation (ACOP) and the National Association of Probation Officers (NAPO) both responded by developing their media relations work. Given its greater financial resources and structural freedom as a trade union, NAPO had more success.

Among local probation areas the importance attached to promoting the service's work was very variable (and remains so). When it was actively pursued, though, it could generate just the kind of 'good news' in local media that had been demanded. In a three-month period of 1991, for example, a probation public relations officer working in the south west of England collected thirty-six items about his area, of which thirty-three were neutral or positive. When Michael Howard became Home Secretary, however, priorities changed dramatically.

From 1993 he played a key role in trying to re-establish Conservative credibility over law and order, under the slogan 'Prison works'. Clearly a policy centred on imprisonment has profound implications for the probation service, but Michael Howard's strategy was much more radical, not just uncoupling the probation service from social work, but eroding its autonomy by dismantling its training.

Inevitably his attempt to discursively reconstruct probation training and practice as flawed and the profession's response were pursued in part through the news media. Neither the Home Secretary nor probation professionals, ironically, gained the extent or type of press attention that they desired. 'More former soldiers and police officers are to be recruited to the probation service to dilute its "liberal do-gooding ethos"', reported the *Guardian* in response to a Home Office briefing, as the future tense construction clearly indicates. An announcement about the new form of professional training was expected by the autumn but did not appear. As subsequent events showed, the Home Secretary was finding that few interested parties shared his views about the probation service, so classic techniques of news management were deployed.

In the 'slow news' hiatus between Christmas 1994 and the New Year, the *Daily Mail* printed, across two pages, an 'exclusive' by the political editor headed 'Howard calls up the probation troops'. Doubts as to whether his proposals would gain public endorsement seem to have persisted.

As the *Guardian* pointed out the announcement was 'buried' by appearing on the same day (22 February) as the publication of a major policy document on Northern Ireland. Apart from the faithful *Daily Mail*, the only papers that reported the issue were *The Times* and the *Daily Express*, both in neutral hard news style, and the *Guardian* in a report dominated by dissenting voices.

Unfortunately for those in the probation service, this lack of press response continued during their campaign against the dismantling of their training system. Like the Home Secretary, NAPO and other stakeholders were attempting mobilise support.

Their hope was that the broadsheets would take up the issue and stimulate a response from politicians and other sections of the 'policy community'. Though unlikely, coverage in the tabloid press would be very welcome as it would confirm that probation training was a public issue that might result in political embarrassment.

Even NAPO did not expect active support from the real 'public': as so often the press reaction was being used as a surrogate for public opinion. The campaign lasted for most of 1995, but neither a major House of Lords debate featuring three former Home Secretaries, and expressing almost unanimous hostility to the training proposals, nor a mass lobby of parliament by probation staff attracted significant national press coverage. The demonstration was widely reported in local media which, though important for morale, is not significant in terms of national policy and politics. NAPO's final tactic was to challenge the Home Secretary's proposals through judicial review but it lost the case in February 1996.

As this deviated from a run of defeats for Michael Howard in UK and EU courts, it had a certain novelty value and was reported in all the broadsheets. The probation training saga was arcane, protracted-lasting over three years-and appeared to affect directly only a very small number of people. It was never going to be newsworthy for mass tabloid papers. According to NAPO, even the broadsheets seemed to find it 'dry', despite its significance for other professional groups in a close relationship to the state.

Looking back, it is likely that the real problem for the defenders of probation training was that it remained an abstract policy matter. It was never transformed into party politics, a domain deeply incorporated into the structures and daily routines of newspapers where, vitally, issues can be dramatised and personalised. The Labour party, then in opposition, resisted the Home Secretary's attempts to dismantle probation training without a House of Commons debate, but it maintained an ominous silence on the substance. In government Labour, far from reversing the training changes, carried out a review of the whole probation service.

The resulting consultation document appeared in August 1998 proposing far more swingeing changes than those pursued by Michael Howard, including making probation officers into civil servants and thus directly answerable to central government.

The preoccupation with corporate profile persisted: a key part of the review process had been the search for a new, 'tougher' name for the service. Apparently Jack Straw had thought better of his earlier enthusiasm for 'reviving the old-fashioned title "corrections service"'. Instead, finding a name formed part of the public consultation process. It appears, however, that the probation service remains stubbornly lacking in news value.

Of the papers sampled on 7 August 1998 the government's announcement of the policy and consultation process was covered by the *Guardian* with a news items and adverse opinion piece, only as straight news by the *Daily Telegraph* (page 2) and the *Daily Mail,* not at all in the *Sun,* and on page 15 of the *Mirror* where a two-sentence box headed 'Name is on probation' opens 'Ministers are asking the public to think up a new name for the Probation Service, because they can't'.

Even the *Daily Mail,* under the heading 'Probation service gets a macho makeover' expresses an uncharacteristic mix of irony and scepticism. In the reflexive world of postmodern promotional politics, even senior ministers cannot guarantee a result.

UNDERSTANDING SOCIAL WORK NEWS

National and local newspapers in the UK are run for profit and are free to be politically partisan. Indeed, the political sympathies of national daily papers are a crucial aspect of their identity and position in the market. The interplay of these two factors explains nearly everything about the press treatment of state social work. Obviously a newspaper needs readers. They pay directly for the product; the size and spending power of the readership determines advertising revenue.

No newspaper, therefore, can address itself primarily to sections of the population with little to spend. Even the mass tabloids, specifically pitched at 'ordinary folk' (a code for working class) are filled with news of and for people between young adulthood and middle age. They may not be well off but, typically, they are setting up households and having children.

Money is being earned and spent. Newspapers, in other words, have a powerful commercial interest in the family-based household which, by itself, explains their greater responsiveness to child protection work than to social work with elderly people or those with a mental illness.

As well as being economically crucial-and ever more so in a society driven more by consumption than production-the family is a key site of political cleavage, over the potentially competing rights of women and men, children and adults. This is the terrain on which state social work operates, so it is inevitable that professional practice will often be newsworthy, justified or not and skilful or not. The *Independent* is positioned as supporting children's rights and addresses a professional audience, hence the very extensive resources invested in the 'pindown' affair.

While the *Daily Mirror* concentrated only on the personal experience of those involved, it, too, implicitly supported a welfare system in which children are seen as having rights as well as needs.

Conversely, the *Daily Mail* powerfully and consistently promotes the conventional, patriarchal family where parents' (particularly fathers') rights prevail. The parents of the children subject to pindown did not feature as an organised voice in the controversy (unlike Rochdale) so the *Mail* showed little interest in this instance of social work failure.

If state social work were as accessible to families in difficulties as the NHS is intended to be for the sick, the cost would be commensurately huge. Most of the Conservative changes to the welfare state in the 1980s were intended to reconstruct welfare services as a minimal system of containment for failure and deviance, in which resources were concentrated on the 'dangerous'.

Apart from the struggles over local government and the politics of difference, already referred to, the cases of Jasmine Beckford, Tyra Henry and Kimberley Carlile were also politicised in this sense. Social workers were being accused of lack of expertise in identifying and controlling the 'other/

them' on behalf of 'us'. Taken together with the very real drama and tragedy at the centre of the cases, extensive and melodramatic media coverage was not merely likely, but over-determined.

So social work with children will always be contested, but in recent years its significance as a political symbol and metonym has diminished. Cambridgeshire Social Services was heavily criticised during and after the trial in 1996 of Ruth Neave for the murder of her son Rikki (of which she was acquitted). It could not have been otherwise: social work's alleged failings were part of the defence case; the department had itself declared its practice as falling short; and further inquiries into its operation were ordered by central government.

Most press comment, however, did not target individual social workers, nor enlarge the issue any more than might be the case where, say, a health authority's failings were in the news. The *Daily Mail* devoted most of its two-page coverage to the allegedly obvious 'dangerousness' of Neave, including the curious accusation that 'By 16 she was having sex with men'.

Arguably, however, the Neave trial was big news because of other features of the case, notably allegations of drug use, witchcraft, threats and intimidation. At the conclusion of a much more brutal child murder case, the judge said 'The social services [Northeast Lincolnshire] have already instigated a wide-ranging internal inquiry into these matters-I don't think they are thorough enough'. Although all the papers sampled reported the verdict and sentence in the case, only the *Daily Mail*-'Boy of 4 taken off "at risk" roll killed by couple'-gave the social work and 'preventable death' motive prominence in its report.

The Rikki Neave trial also illustrates the different interpretive frame applied by local newspapers. While the national papers all reported the first and last day, there were only occasional reports during the intervening four weeks, ranging from six in the *Daily Mirror* to none in the *Daily Mail*.

The Peterborough *Evening Telegraph* covered the story every day, sometimes prominently and in detail. The outcome took up all of the front page and seven inside pages. A local paper, however, must appeal to the whole population, not a section defined by age, class and politics.

Accordingly, the editorial comment emphasises not individual blame but community responsibility for the events and for recovery: '...a shadow hangs over our city'. Everyone is given space to justify themselves, including social services. It is clear that Ruth Neave was a controversial figure: she pleaded guilty to five cruelty charges and was sentenced to seven years' imprisonment.

Nevertheless, the background features on her life and behaviour are complex and sympathetic. Similarly the material on Rikki Neave resists the 'tragic tot' reflex in favour of an account of a sad little boy from a difficult background.

Frank Beck's wrongdoing extended over many years beforehand, so the case failed to provide the staple materials for constructing satisfactory news stories. His victims had grown up and dispersed, making it very difficult to produce 'background' and 'colour' featuring either them or their parents. Nor did the young people comfortably fit the frame of innocent 'tragic tot'. One reason that it took so long for Beck to be challenged, according to the Police Complaints Authority report (1993), was that his victims had already been written off as deviants.

In the last analysis, however, the key to the mysterious silence over the Frank Beck case is that he raised too many questions about the solidity of the social and institutional order. This applied as much to the *Guardian,* with its investment in the possibility of professional trust and rational policy-making, as to the *Sun*. Cheeky irreverence cannot work without stable authority structures as both butt and boundary.

Deviance and conflict are central to news but newspapers' place in parliamentary democracy-to say nothing of their capitalist rationale-relies on social stability. That a well-respected local authority manager, local councillor and consultant on childcare methods could be behaving as Frank Beck did was too chaotic to be contained within conventional press narratives which, among other things, require a reassuring 'closure'.

Recent events have, unfortunately, simply verified this interpretation of the press response to the Frank Beck trial. A succession of similar cases, involving men working both in local authority and voluntary agency homes, has gone almost unreported in the national press, even though the Conservative government was worried enough to set up a tribunal chaired by a retired High Court judge. The Waterhouse enquiry began on 21 January 1997 (and heard evidence for a year and a half). As the *Independent* reported (22 January 1997) on its front page it was 'Britain's biggest child abuse enquiry: 650 cases, up to 80 staff involved at 30 homes'.

The other broadsheet reports were relatively low-key accounts of opening speeches, placed on inside pages. The *Sun* ignored it while the *Mirror* gave it three paragraphs and the *Daily Star* two. The *Daily Mail* devoted most of page 12 to the tribunal, foregrounding the possible culpability of social services management even though the remit covered the role of the Welsh Office and other agencies. The outcome of the Waterhouse enquiry will undoubtedly be a matter of profound public interest. As we have seen, though, this does not help us predict how the press will treat it.

That will be determined by a judgement as to whether it will interest their public. Politically and commercially it is safer to entertain and titillate, even to make readers indignant, than to take risks with their ontological security. Consequently, literally dozens of definitions for public relations exist in the literature. However, it is my contention that Bernays provided the best definition in his early writings. Bernays describes PR's key function as "the engineering of consent," or the ability to get diverse individuals with varying perceptions and values to come to a "consent to a programme or goal". Newsom, Scott and Turk have similarly referred to PR as a "broker for public support of ideas, institutions and people".

And there were plenty of opportunities for PR to attempt to build consensus among American publics in the late 1800s. Rex Harlow points out the mix of increasing industrialization (e.g., the railroads) and "expansions in science, invention, commerce government, and communications" helped contribute to rising complexities. Then, Harlow makes an unmistakable allusion to how PR developed in great part to address fissions within American communities:

Under the impact of these swiftly moving... developments, individuals and institutions of all kinds were broken loose from their moorings and cast adrift upon a tide of uncertainty and uneasiness... the elements of fear and uncertainty made demands that brought public relations to the fore. Cutlip, Centre and Broom address how PR rose to the occasion:

To state that public relations has evolved from press-agentry, though a gross oversimplification (my emphasis), contains a kernel of truth. Systematic efforts to attract or divert public attention are as old as efforts to persuade and propagandize. Much of what we define as public relations was labeled press-agentry when it was being used to promote land settlement in our unsettled west.

However, when addressing the push westward and the related need to build new western communities, PR faced an almost paradoxical situation; the westward move emphasized individualism. Says McDougall, "There was a struggle for existence, and the fittest did survive. Self-reliance... did flourish. Pioneers had to look to their own resources and efforts".

How could PR address the need for community-building in the new West, yet still respect individualism? One answer could be found in PR's attempts to further settlements near expanding railroad lines. PR's attempts to reach large groups of individuals and persuade them to move west would literally establish a public - a public of individuals. John Peters refers to this persuasion when he wrote, "...These representations can then invite [a dispersed people] to act as a unified body. This is where rhetoric comes in: it is the means of articulating common identity and belief".

It would be difficult to pick one moment where public relations established its presence and value within the railroad industry. However, one can make the case that the 1869 completion of the transcontinental railroad at Promontory Point, Utah, was PR's first high-profile opportunity. As guests and media were entertained with speeches, alcohol and the whistles of four locomotives, a golden spike was driven into the last tie.

The news was immediately telegraphed coast-to-coast. Notes Stover in The Life and Decline of the American Railroad, "A seven-mile parade began to move in Chicago, dozens of firebells rang out in San Francisco, and a magnetic ball dropped from a pole on top of the Capitol dome in Washington, D.C." Coming off of this success, PR was seen as a valuable aid to the railroads as they moved west and needed to sell government-granted lands to settiers. In fact, at one point shortly after the Promontory Point celebration, the railroads had full title to more than 133 million acres, the majority of it in states west of the Mississippi.

The railroads also understood, from earlier westward movements, that "many people traveled in caravans and settled as communities, although each family claimed its own plot of land". They also understood what historian Ray Allen Billington noted that these individual communities could be persuaded to act in an almost concerted manner: The migrations that peopled California and the Oregon country in the 1840s were induced not only by the usual impulses to escape an uncongenial homeland - but by one of the most effective promotional campaigns in history.

Historian J. Valerie Fifer refers to the same power of PR, when she says: Together the transport, tourist, and information industries played a crucial role in Western development... All brought new settlement... into the West... and stimulated the growth of a new spirit of American nationalism.

Many of the early persuasive approaches taken by the railroads in the 1870s were covert. The railroads used lobbyists and secret press agents to make their claims for routes and the related lands. Both the Burlington and Illinois Central railroads paid for books and newspaper and magazine articles that were to appear to be unbiased accounts. These lines would also pay for making reprints of the favorable articles and having them sent to thousands of media and VIPs - one mailing list had more than 30,000 "influentials."

A shift happened in the early 1880s. Because of the secrecy, efforts to reach key opinion leaders and media were highly complicated, and a little too narrow. So, it's no surprise that Railway Age, a trade journal, established a "Bureau of Information," that would send settlement-related information to both the targeted "influentials" and the general public. The railroads moved toward increasingly overt contact with the media and began setting up their own 30-to-40-person staffs to crank out stories, advertisements and pamphlets.

The desire to reach outward for as large an audience as possible slowly became the practice. Burlington's Charles Russell Lowell said, "We are beginning to find that he who buildeth a railroad west of the Mississippi must also find a population... We wish to blow as loud a trumpet as the merits of our position warrants."

Consequently, Burlington built a PR campaign through the writings of J. D. Butler, a newspaper correspondent and lecturer. Butler was a late-1880s version of Charles Kurault. He would travel extensively throughout Iowa and Nebraska and write about the common man's life. His letters were not only shared with the media in the eastern U.S., but also shipped over to the

British press. Burlington also took his writings and turned them into pamphlets, circulars and posters. These writings were also given to advance men in England who shared the news about the good life in the American west with roomfulls of emigrants who "paid for their night's lodging by attending" the speech.

The Atchison, Topeka and Santa Fe (ATSF) took these approaches and added a few innovative touches. They worked with European colonization agencies, land companies and steamship lines to attract European immigrants. The ATSF started a branch office in London and distributed more than 300,000 pamphlets in various languages throughout Western Europe.

Stateside, pamphlets and brochures extolling Kansas were given to dozens of agents, who would distribute this info in Illinois, Iowa and other nearly states. ATSF would also hold "colonization meetings" where it offered free or low-cost trips to Kansas. In fact, ATSF was able to get a delegation of 225 journalists to proclaim the ATSF lands as the "Garden of the West."

Even more innovative was ATSF's use of the Philadelphia Centennial in 1876: The ATSF sent a large display of Kansas crops to the fair, and a new pamphlet was issued for circulation in Philadelphia. Forty-six pages long, "How and Where to Get a Living. A Sketch of `The Garden of the West"' sang the praises of the land grant.... President J.A. Anderson of the Kansas State Agricultural College praised the land, and urged farmers to see it for themselves because it was "the best thing in the West".

Further north, the Northern Pacific (NP) Railroad was not going to fall behind. As early as 1870, the NP held a special promotional ride for 150 VIPs from New York to San Francisco. NP set up a small printing office on the train and, when local, general and world news was telegraphed in at a designated stop, the printing office would compose a small newspaper and hand it out to all on board. The NP also took the newspapers and mailed them to other influentials across the country, generating significant publicity.

Where ATSF had emphasized the natural attraction of their lands, NP preferred to focus on the need for colonization. When Congress, in 1871, passed a homestead act for veterans, NP set up a bureau of immigration. This bureau handed out pamphlets extolling the need to organize colonies.

NP also offered to assist veterans with reduced transportation rates, the selling of building materials at wholesale prices and even offered to build reception houses! Essentially, NP's promotional literature was designed to appeal to an individual's desire for a new beginning that would not only be a good move, but an economically smart move. NP's pamphlets emphasized the benefits of colonization; the Guide to the Lands of the Northern Pacific Railroad offered: The Boston colonists who are rearing their homes on the shores of beautiful Detroit Lake in Minnesota can ship their grain to market at as low rates as the farmers who live in Dubuque, 188 miles from Chicago.... With cheap transportation, with [fertile] soil... there must be a corresponding increase in the value of the land, and the settler who secures a farm of 160 acres now may be sure of an advance of several hundred per cent for his investment a few years hence.

Another major player in the growth of railroad PR was the Union Pacific (UP). UP took many of the same approaches as Burlington and ATSF within a "Go West" promotion. Its emphasis on affordable, productive land as the basis for new communities attracted many immigrants, including those seeking religious freedom, like Mennonites (Nelson, 21). UP also hired one of the best publicists of the westward movement Robert E. Strahorn.

A former Indian wars corespondent for the New York Times and the Chicago Tribune, Strahorn also had done some freelance publicity writing over the years for the Denver and Rio Grande railroads. UP's Jay Gould hired Strahorn to start a publicity bureau in both Denver and Omaha. Under Strahorn's guidance, the bureau put out The New West Illustrated, full of information tailored for westward emigrants. He also insured the bureau wrote publicity pieces to papers throughout the country - in one summer alone, the Omaha Republican printed 45 columns from his bureau. Strahorn's approach emphasized the new West as the place to build a new world, with resulting new wealth. Says historian Oliver Knight:

Strahorn's emphasis on guidebooks differentiated him from other publicists. His job was not to publicize the Union Pacific but the entire West, not to sell UP lands but to attract settlers who would create freight tonnages and passenger revenues. His propaganda... was the kind that contributed to the urbanization and industrialization through which the developing West was absorbed into the economic nationalization of America.

More than 2,000 muckraking articles appeared in magazines that reached a distribution of about 5 million copies (during a time when there were only 20 million families in the U.S.). Riding a wave of the disaffection, and the economic disenfranchisement, of the common man, muckrakers sought out more than corruption and malfeasance in the business world.

These journalists reflected a concern in the U.S. that the absolute power of the few was disintegrating society. Said Chalmers, "They described a condition in which all of the individual parts seemed to conspire against the whole.... The muckrakers seemed to be explaining... the moral disintegration of a whole society".

The railroads, with their extensive web of political and economic power, were seen as prime targets by the muckrackers. In fact, the muckrakers unveiled the seamy side of the railroads - the rate inequities, their setting rates for farmers' products their influence in setting land values and their bribing of politicians. Reporters for Leslie's, The Nation, The Arena and The Science Monthly also detailed scandalous problems concerning railroad accident rates. Ray Stannard Baker, writing for McClure's, found that the massive trusts built their wealth on the ownership of the highly profitable railroads. In fact, Baker believed that, unless Congress passed some effective restraints, the railroads might be ripe for government takeover as the only sure way to eliminate abuse.

In sum, the more the muckrakers looked, the more they discovered. Christopher Connolly, writing for Collier's found: That the railroads were involved in corruption. Where they did not cause it, they at least sought a share of the profits. They were everywhere exploiting mineral resources and seeking possession of public lands. In West Virginia... the Baltimore and Ohio railroad dominate the legislature.... The Southern Pacific was the real government of California. In the face of such massive exposes, the railroads were rightfully nervous. If the public continued to see only pictures of railroad corruption, could nationalization of their industry be far behind?

Accordingly, their use of PR changed. Gone were the days of using PR to disseminate information to the public in an attempt to build western communities. In its place came advocacy PR, best exemplified by the railroads' turning to the Publicity Bureau to fight off government regulation. The railroads retained this Bureau, considered the forerunner of the modern PR agency. The Bureau, which opened branches in several major U.S. cities, and also stationed employees in South Dakota and California, attempted to directly reach reporters and editors with railroad propaganda. This approach, say Cutlip, Centre and Broom, shows one of PR's first attempts to use "the tools of fact-finding, publicity, and personal contact to saturate the nation's press... with the railroad's propaganda".

Ivy Ledbetter Lee, considered by many experts to be the father of modern-day public relations, assisted in efforts to defend the railroad industries. While retained by Pennsylvania Railroad, Lee wrote a Declaration of Principles that clearly show the new advocacy approach. A key part of the Principles reads: We aim to supply news... In brief, our plan is, frankly and openly, on behalf of our business concerns and public institutions, to supply the press and public of the United States prompt and accurate information concerning subjects, which is of value and interest of the public to know about.

From this course of events we can see in action the adage "for every action, there is a reaction." In essence, the rise of the muckrakers, and their relentless attacks against the railroads, caused the railroad industry to seek out PR as a way of defending itself.

When this happened, PR as a community-building instrument became a secondary concern. Henry Adams, in 1902, writing on the railroad's dilemma, best summed up their thinking when he said, "The task of publicity is to allay [the public's] suspicion... Indeed for whatever point of view from which the trust problem is considered, publicity stands as the first step in its solution." Kruckeberg and Starck observe that:

Thus, what really prompted the birth of contemporary public relations... was the reaction against the muckrakers with their new power to communicate with the masses.... If publicity was being used to effectively to attack business, why could it not be used equally well to explain and defend business?

What of PR and Community-Building Today? In the case of the western expansion of the railroads, we've seen that PR helped attract settlers and build communities through widespread publicity techniques. We've also witnessed how railroad PR abruptly changed course toward corporate advocacy in the face of the muckrakers.

At this late date, is there a case that can be made for PR to once again assume a community-building role? There are some recent developments that point to that very possibility, especially if one looks at the recent rise of another phenomenon -public journalism.

First, the sense of community that was once known in this country is slowly crumbling, say Kruckeberg and Starck. Modern U.S. society, with its high premium placed on technology, is witnessing a corresponding isolating effect. Technological communications developments like the television, the computer and the telephone all tend to move individuals away from community interaction. Two-way communication, however, can help make sense of the information flowing within a community and can help develop a healthier social structure.

PR, with its firm grounding in communications approaches, is well positioned to take an active step in facilitating the two-way flow of communications within a community. Kruckeberg and Starck maintain that the modern PR practitioner can through being an effective communication facilitator - successfully overcome the weaker sense of community. However, for now, PR, according to Kruckeberg and Starck, hasn't recovered from the defensive "information-dispensing" role adopted in the face of the muckrakers' assault. They speak of this when they write:

The transmission view of communication connotes doing something communicatively persuading? advocating? - to someone else.

The competing model, which indeed probably predates the other, stresses the "communal" or "communitarian" aspect of communication.... This model connotes doing something with someone.... Public relations early adopted and has continued to apply - the transmission model of communication... rooted in persuasion and advocacy rather than principles based on social involvement and participation.

With PR abdicating the role it once played in mixing communication with community-building, another powerful entity has recently stepped forward to begin filling the gap. Communication historian Robert E. Parks has written that "the newspaper... is the great medium of communication within the city, and it is on the basis of the information it supplied that public opinion rests." However, other communication theorists, including John Dewey, have written that printed communication alone is but a precursor to community-building around an issue or event.

Hence the recent public journalism (PJ) movement among several newspapers in the U.S. With PJ, the newspaper attempts to be more than "information-dispenser." PJ is an attempt by newspapers to be part of the dialogue within a community, essentially facilitating discussion and helping to mold consensus and further decision-making. Recently, James Carey, professor of journalism at Columbia University, described PJ in this way:

If journalism is not actively engaged in enhancing and forming a democratic public in debate, disputations, arguments and... things done outside of the realm of surveillance - it's at odds with its original purpose (Klotzer). And Cole Campbell, the editor of the St. Louis Post-Dispatch, has identified a similar way of looking at PJ's role, which sounds very close to some of the opportunities Kruckeberg and Starck have identified for PR:

I like what Buzz Merritt of the Wichita Eagle has said about a successful community. He says a successful community is one whose members know what's going on and take responsibility for it. So to me public journalism is a way of making both of those things happen.... You also need to get below the event-driven news agenda to find out what's truly happening in a community (Bishop). How does one get a clear idea of just what PJ is? Campbell's definition seems to be mostly accurate.

However, at this early stage, PJ is mostly visible through certain "event-driven" activities. The Akron Beacon-Journal asked readers to sign racial progress cards vowing to work for racial harmony. The Spokesman Review in Spokane enticed communities, by offering pizza, to have backyard gettogethers to discuss the issues that concern their neighborhoods. Several California dailies promoted gang peace summits to try to find an answer to escalating violence.

Without too much imagination, one can easily picture a business, government organization or non-profit group offering any of these PJ activities as a PR programme (and many similar-sounding programs have been offered through PR involvement - the award-winning gun buy-back programme held a couple of years ago in St. Louis immediately comes to mind). What is likely happening here is that PJ has identified both the continuing need for dialogue facilitation within a community, as the part this dialogue plays in community-building. In the meantime PR has not, in large part, made a turn off the road of "information-dissemination" first widely followed in reaction to the muckrakers. The earlier use of PR to build communities along the westward railroad develop-ment shows that PR can fulfill what Baskin and Aronoff describe as the third stage of development - mutual influence and understanding:

In this most recent stage, public relations accepts the responsibilities of [information dissemination], but also provides information and counsel to management of the nature and realities of public opinion and methods by which the organization can establish policy, make decisions and take action in light of public opinion (my italics). It's this interaction with the community (and the related community-building) that PR needs to investigate. Otherwise, PR might have to resign itself to continue primarily with information-dissemination. If so, the media, through public journalism, is already preparing to fill the need for dialogue facilitation and related community-building.

With an awareness of the numerous and widely varied sources of political violence, one should proceed cautiously to consider more narrowly why some individuals or groups choose terrorism as a form of political violence. A clear concept of what constitutes terror and how terrorism functions must be obtained at the onset. To illustrate, terror is a superlative form of fear, and fear is a human emotion that pertains only to the living. The helpless victims who were massacred by the Abu Nidal group at the Vienna and Rome airports in December 1985 were not terrorized. They were simply murdered.

Those who survived the massacre, either physically present at the airports or miles away learning of the atrocities through media depictions, were those who were perhaps terrorized. While the above illustration is overly simplistic, one is well advised to approach the study of political terrorism by recognizing that the "victims" of political terrorist atrocities are not normally the "targets."

Herein lies an important distinguishing feature that separates political terrorism from other forms of terror such as psychopathic.

The psychopath's victim is likely to be first terrorized and then killed, and is the principal object of the psychopath's atrocity. The terrorizing and elimination of the victim is both method and goal.

In contrast, the political terrorist's victim is symbolic. A victim is chosen who is representative of a target group that is strategically involved in the terrorist's political goals. When the Iranian-backed hijackers of TWA Flight 847 beat and killed U.S. serviceman Robert Stethem and threw his body on the tarmac at the Beirut airport, his death was not a direct objective of the terrorists. His demise was not their goal; rather, their goal was the elimination of U.S. influence in the Middle East in general and Lebanon in particular. Stethem was their victim, but not their target. Their target was the American public who observed the atrocity through the international media. The strategy for their target selection was based on the notion that the American public had the power to force a change in the Reagan administration's foreign policy for the Middle East and Lebanon.

TRANSMITTING THE TERROR OF THE ATROCITY TO THE TARGET

Obviously those present in the Vienna and Rome airport terminals during the Abu Nidal group's shooting and grenade explosions were more "terrorized" than those who later witnessed the atrocities through the international media. Further, of those learning of the atrocities through the media, it is likely that only those who were considering international travel, personally or by friends or associates, experienced some degree of fear.

The association between the symbolic victim and the target audience is indeed a critical aspect of political terrorism effectiveness. However, regardless of the degree of association, a means of transmission must exist to make the target audience aware of what has happened before an atmosphere of fear can be created. Those who might not yet have heard of an atrocity are in no way terrorized by it. Given that one understands the basic rationale for the terrorist's tactical selection of a symbolic victim associated with the strategic target audience, the next item for consideration is how the terrorist transmits the terror of the violence perpetrated on the victim to the target group.

The focus of this analysis is necessarily the perpetration of political terrorism by groups and individuals not in power. However, it may be instructive to deviate briefly and consider how the transmission of terror as a superlative form of fear might be accomplished by a regime.

For this examination, a regime is considered to be a government in power that has at its disposal all the forms of physical force normally associated with that position. It seems that the characteristics of the target population are a primary determinant in a regime's selection of the most efficient method of transmitting terror. The modern media's transmission to the public of information about political terrorists includes processing and disseminating as well as gathering that information. Students of communications identify several significant problems normally associated with those functions.

For example, the problem of distortion normally abounds in the processing and dissemination of any information. This major problem and others are passed from the communicator to the consumer of information. In the case of the media's coverage of political terrorists, the end result could be the formation of erroneous perceptions by the public.

It should be recognized that the modern media, while seemingly a giant impersonal apparatus, is indeed composed of individual persons, each seeking to achieve personal aims, and each susceptible to human failings. The transfer of information by the media to their audience is, in its basic essence, the communicating of information from one human being to another. All the frailties and failings of humanity are involved in this process. As a simplistic example, the recipient is subjected to the interpretation of the information by the communicator, which may or may not be factual, and at best reflects the values and biases of the communicator.

The numerous difficulties involved in the accurate transmission of information have plagued literally every profession, and studies in this area are voluminous. A review of the literature allows one to more directly focus on those communications issues of importance in the media's coverage of terrorism. Prominent among processing and dissemination issues is the media's portrayal of terrorists and their atrocities.

In democratic societies with political systems based on plurality, the public's perception of events may determine which policy alternatives are available to the government. To the extent that the images of political terrorism, as portrayed by the media, affect the public's perception, those images are of significant concern to the society as a whole.

The importance of this issue has been illuminated by the Task Force on Disorders and Terrorism of the U.S. National Advisory Committee on Criminal Justice Standards and Goals: "Depictions of incidents of extraordinary violence in the mass media are... a significant influence on public fears and expectations." In discussing the importance of the public's perception of terrorists and their atrocities, Miller has centered on the proposition that sensational terrorist acts publicized by the media can make the public so amazed at the terrorists' description of reality that it will question its own assumptions of morality and the political system.

For Miller, such a redefinition of values holds the seeds of revolution. If one accepts the hypothesis that the public's perceptions of events can influence policy alternatives, then it follows that disseminating factual, nondistorted information on important domestic and international events is vital to the stability of a society.

INFLUENCING PERCEPTIONS THROUGH LABELING AND TERMINOLOGY

When reviewing the literature on terrorism, one becomes quickly impressed with the semantic problems of labeling and terminology that apply directly to the media's influence on the public's perceptions. Biased images and false perceptions can be created as simply as with a choice of words.

Referring to a group involved in political violence as "guerrilla" imparts an image far different than referring to it as "terrorist." *Guerrilla* is the term for irregular armed forces involved in political violence through the conduct of combat operations against military targets, whereas terrorists do not attack the military strength of their political opposition but rather hit symbolic targets that are most often innocents. Similarly, referring to the killing of a person during an act of political violence as an execution imparts a far different image than if it is referred to as a murder. If the news media choose terminology provided by the terrorists, they may inadvertently transmit terrorist arguments sympathetically to the public.

11

The Process and Effects of Mass Communication

Between about 1930 and the early 1980s, a number of studies were published that led to significant advances in understanding the process and effects of mass communication. Sometimes referred to as *milestones,* these were well-funded, large-scale efforts, conducted with important objectives in mind, and based on standards of methodology respected in their time. A few were much more modest in scale, but whether large or small, they yielded important concepts, generalizations, and theories that are now part of the accumulated knowledge of how the U.S. media function and the kinds of influences that they have on individuals and society.

Since that period, there has not been a similar level of production of such seminal studies. No widely heralded investigation has been produced in nearly two decades-one that provoked wide discussion and changed the way scholars think about the mass communication process. Many noteworthy studies, even hundreds of well-conducted and interesting investigations, have been reported. However, most focus on restricted topics or hypotheses, or are efforts to explore issues raised by the earlier milestones. When asked by my publisher to revise a book summarizing the existing milestones and adding new ones, I could not identify even one that fit the same criteria as the earlier investigations.

It is the purpose of this chapter to suggest some of the reasons why the field of mass communication has changed in this respect. The reasons advanced include a change in the agendas of the social sciences, a lack of a programmatic approach by media scholars, a shift to nonquantitative and critical modes of analysis by many writers, and changes in the work conditions of the professorate.

THE CHANGING RELATION BETWEEN THE MEDIA

A number of trends in U.S. society would seem logically to lead to a prediction that important research on the process and influences of mass communication would have increased, rather than decreased. Specifically, the media have expanded and become more complex; their labour force has grown considerably; and colleges and universities now offer far more instruction related to work in the media labour force than ever before. Yet, as already mentioned, there has been no corresponding increase in the production of ground-breaking studies.

THE GROWTH OF THE MEDIA LABOUR FORCE

It is now widely understood that over the last half-century the United States increasingly became an information society. In the older manufacturing-based economy, blue-collar employees worked on factory floors producing things with their hands and machines. However, after midcentury, more than half of our workers were manipulating words and numbers to provide both products and services. With the coming of the computer revolution and the increasing globalization of the economy, the pace of that change has accelerated.

One reason that the percentage of the workforce manipulating symbols, as opposed to things, has increased greatly is that our media system has continued to expand. Before midcentury that system included only telegraph, telephone, print, radio, and film. Today, it includes not only all of the earlier media, but also fax, cellular phones, video-cassette recorders, television, cable, satellite television delivery, and the Internet — with its e-mail, local networks, and World Wide Web. As the media system expanded, a corresponding need for communication specialists and practitioners grew. This, in turn, increased the need for media-related education and has expanded the number of communication professors, scholars, and researchers.

THE GROWTH OF MEDIA-RELATED CURRICULA

Preparing a well-educated labour force for the media industries posed a new challenge for colleges and universities. At the close of World War II, there was a very limited relation between the mass media and the U.S. academy. Journalists had been educated on campus for decades, but that was not the case for other media professionals. Only a limited number of fledgling programs existed to prepare students for careers in movie making and radio broadcasting or other media employment. No degree programs existed in such fields as advertising or public relations. As television usage spread, a similar situation prevailed. Institutions were slow to offer industry-related curricula. In the more general field of mass communication studies, there certainly were no advanced academic programs designed around studies of research and theory development. The 1960s saw the beginnings of a gradual and long-term expansion in the number of programs, departments, schools, and other academic units with curricula focused specifically on the mass media. Some were theory- and research-based programs. Others were professionally oriented, providing for media-related career training. At present, undergraduate, master's, and doctoral degree programs in mass communication exist on many campuses. Professional programs prepare students with the skills needed in such fields as advertising, public relations, film production, and broadcast news. Some programs remain theory oriented, preparing students to conduct basic research on mass communication. In the professional schools, in particular, many of the courses are now taught by part-time professors, often brought in from the media. In such settings, the study of research methods and theory development may be marginal at best or simply ignored.

Today, students can graduate with a degree in, or at least a major in, media-related communication at the majority of U.S. institutions of higher learning. The numbers rise or fall from time to time, but somewhere between 5 per cent and 10 per cent of all undergraduate and graduate degrees now granted in the United States are in various fields of media-related communication.

That change has not always been a smooth one. Media-related studies are still regarded with suspicion by many traditionalists on campus. They are not always respected by professors, or even administrators, from the physical, biological, and social sciences. Nevertheless, course work in such fields as advertising, public relations, marketing communication, magazine publishing, film and television production, broadcast journalism, and the use of the Internet as a medium for public communication are now providing an annual pool of college graduates that can be hired to exercise the many specialized skills that are at the heart of those industries.

THE DECLINE IN THE PRODUCTION OF RESEARCH MILESTONES

From these three trends one might logically predict that there would be a corresponding increase in significant research on the process and effects of mass communication. Few would disagree with the conclusion that the growing presence and importance of mass communication in the lives of individuals has increased the need to understand their nature and influences. It follows, then, that scholars in the communications disciplines should now be formulating and testing more and better theories, many with practical importance, to explain how the media function and how they influence people, both individually and collectively.

However, in fact, that has not been the case. The development of media theory seems stalled. For a time, earlier in the 20th century, scholarly inquiry and the development of research-based theories to explain the process and effects of mass communication did increase at a rapid rate. Starting even before World War II, and continuing until the early 1980s, scholars conducted a number of seminal studies aimed at understanding the nature, functions, and consequences of mass communication.

As the scientific study of media influences got underway, it was psychologists and sociologists who provided leadership. Some of the Payne Fund studies concluded that movies had powerful influences on children. Later, in 1938, a quantitative study reported that a radio programme prompted millions of people to panic. These findings reinforced beliefs in the *magic bullet* theory, an earlier and now discredited formulation explaining that the media had immediate, uniform, and powerful effects on all who were exposed to their messages. Later, as additional studies were reported, the concept of powerful media began to be questioned.

The results from studies of the influences of training films by the U.S. Army led to a new formulation, now termed the *selective and limited influence theory*. It explained that the media could change beliefs, opinions, attitudes, or behaviour for only some people under some circumstances. The classic Erie County study of media influences on a presidential election campaign showed that belief in powerful, immediate, uniform, and widespread effects was no longer tenable. This milestone also led to important theoretical concepts, such as the two-step flow of communication and personal influence. Clearly, empirical research was beginning to reveal with greater accuracy the complex relation between the mass media and their audiences.

Additional milestone research revealed that the media were not particularly powerful, that the audience was highly selective, and that the process of shaping people's beliefs, attitudes, and behaviour with mass communications is very complex. Studies now regarded as classics yielded such insights as the *uses and gratifications theory,* explaining that audiences used content from the media as guides for their personal choices and derived many psychological rewards from exposure to mass communications. Another modest experiment led to *modeling theory,* which explained the influence of media-depicted models of actions or situations on acquiring new forms of behaviour.

A study of Iowa farmers in a relatively obscure journal provided the foundation for *adoption of innovation theory,* describing the pattern followed when people begin using new products or processes after obtaining information from the media.

Other classic research yielded theories of persuasion, explaining how the structure and other features of a message were related to changing beliefs, attitudes, and behaviour. A study of a small community showed how personal influence was exercised in the two-step flow of communication from the media to opinion leaders, and from them to others who did not attend directly. More recently, *agenda-setting theory* was formulated to explain how levels of prominence selected by the media in forming their agenda play a part in setting personal agendas among their audiences. At one point, attention to television almost crowded out research on other media. Its influences on individuals and society were addressed in literally thousands of studies. A major focus was on the relation between portrayed violence on TV and aggressive conduct in children and youth. This issue was a special focus for psychologists. Their interest was not so much on the process of mass communication, as such, but on media-provided stimulus factors that produce aggressive or violent behaviour. By the end of the 1970s, it seemed clear that under certain circumstances, the portrayal of violence in television content could increase somewhat the probability of aggressive behaviour in some kinds of children. That generalization still represents what we now know about that issue.

In retrospect, then, the decades from the 1930s to the early 1980s, appear to have been a kind of golden age of research on mass communication. During that period a significant number of studies had especially high theoretical yield. Some were large-scale efforts like the massive Payne Fund studies; others were methodological masterpieces, like the Erie County investigation. Few were programmatic — an exception being the Yale studies of persuasion. Others were small in scope, but theoretically important.

Early in the 1980s, however, the golden age all but came to an end. That is not to imply that research on mass communication ceased. During the last two decades thousands of studies have been published. However, most explored very specific issues or narrowly focused hypotheses; some retested or studied extensions of ideas generated by the original milestones.

Perhaps many scholars will challenge these conclusions, or claim that their personal research, or their favourite recent study, should be regarded as truly seminal. Perhaps they would be right. Overall, however, there has been a conspicuous decline in theoretical advances in the study of mass communication compared to the earlier period.

A major question is, Why? Are today's researchers less creative? Are the questions of media functioning and influences any less important? Are members of the public apathetic and uninterested in how mass communications influence them and their children? Is research on mass communications unrewarding, either in terms of personal interest or academic advancement? The answers to all of these questions seem to be a resounding "no." Today's researchers are equally smart and energetic; they have research methods and computer tools at their command that the older generation lacked; the public is still concerned; scholars still need research to develop reputations for career advancement. Where, then, have all the milestones gone?

The answer to why there has been a decline in theoretical productivity in the study of the mass media has no easy answer, but a case can be made that it lies in a complex set of changes that have taken place, both in society as a whole, and in the academy more directly. The sections that follow discuss those changes in an attempt to provide an explanation of why the production of influential research has slowed, or even stopped.

One factor has been the withdrawal of social scientists — who conducted most of the early milestones — from the mainstream of media research. A second is the failure to develop and establish a programmatic approach to the investigation of media processes and influences. A third is the shift away from science to qualitative studies and a focus on criticism within the communication disciplines. A fourth factor is the loss of talented researchers who leave the low pay of the academy to earn high salaries elsewhere. A fifth is that funds for studies of mass communication, especially from federal sources, are more difficult to obtain at present than was the case during the golden age of media research.

Sixth, and finally, there have been changes in the work environment of college and university professors in the field of mass communication that may limit their ability to conduct research resulting in significant scholarly publication. Each of these factors can be discussed more fully.

THE SHIFTING AGENDA OF THE SOCIAL SCIENCES

At present, the study of mass communication and its influences on individuals and society is not at centre stage in the social and behavioral sciences. It was at an earlier time. After pioneering the investigation of the influences of mass communications, such fields as social psychology and sociology went on to pursue other agendas.

To illustrate, between 1940 and the end of the 1950s, among the most respected media scholars were sociologists Lazarsfeld and Merton. Both of these world-class researchers made the study of mass media central to their discipline. Similarly, in social psychology, Hovland was conducting his classic experiments on communication and persuasion.

During the 1960s, many psychologists were focusing intensely on the relation between television and violence. By the 1970s, however, their participation declined and their influence waned. Other kinds of scholars were undertaking media studies and distinguished sociologists and psychologists were no longer the central figures pushing forward the cutting edge.

That does not mean that research on mass communication ceased. For a time, the issue of violence and children continued to be almost a one-dimensional concern. What happened was that the social science agenda changed. For many in those disciplines, the level of importance assigned to the study of media effects was reduced by attention to other concerns.

As the late 1960s and early 1970s came, sociologists and psychologists turned to studies of deviant behaviour, such as the causes of the rising crime rate, youthful violence, drug use, the influences of the counterculture, the roots and consequences of social inequalities, such as racial and ethnic discrimination, and the unequal status of woman in society. The study of devip'ant behaviour and the problems of disadvantaged people have always been central in social science.

Even many of the early studies of mass communications were conducted as a means of furthering these objectives. In other words, social scientists who had conducted media studies earlier returned to their traditional concerns, leaving basic research on the process and influences of mass communication to others.

THE LACK OF A PROGRAMMATIC APPROACH

Even during the golden age, when a series of well-known studies yielded significant theoretical advances, mass communication research was never conducted programmatically. With few exceptions, each study was a one-shot enterprise, done independently for its own sponsor's reasons. Such research sought short-term objectives that were deemed important at the time. There was no theoretical trail being followed, or accumulative refinement of concepts leading from the results of one study to the design of the next. In contrast, programmatic research and concept refinement is often the case in the physical and biological sciences, where one investigator's results yield insights or theoretical advances that open pathways taken by subsequent researchers. Even today, mass communication research seldom follows a programmatic approach, holding back the pace of theoretical development.

The lack of integration between studies is also reflected in the methodology employed in mass communication research. For example, concepts are often defined in a multiplicity of ways from one study to the next, with each researcher conceptualizing variables differently from the definitions of previous investigators. Such basic procedures as measurement, sample selection, and statistical analysis are conducted differently from one investigator to the next, even when researchers are studying essentially the same phenomena. Such a lack of methodological standardization makes it difficult to replicate studies of a particular process or effect, reducing the ability of investigators to accumulate evidence related to specific generalizations, hypotheses, or theories. It seems likely that this unintegrated approach will continue to be a handicap to the development of future milestones.

THE SHIFT TO NONQUANTITATIVE AND CRITICAL MODES OF ANALYSIS

In earlier years, when social scientists managed the research agenda of mass communication, the accepted epistemology for research was defined by the rules of natural science. Empirical observation of independent and dependent variables within a system of controls was required. Evidence was gathered within well-understood requirements for valid and reliable measurement. Quantitative analysis of data was assumed. Statistical probability provided the accepted criterion for making decisions about results. As social scientists began to turn to different agendas, other kinds of investigators, using other approaches to the accumulation of knowledge about the media, took their place. Today, many media scholars are not well-trained in, are not committed to — or indeed are openly critical of — the postulates, procedures, and requirements of science.

Such scholars often use a qualitative and intuitive approach to describe the nature of various features and processes of mass communication. Although such an approach has merit in many cases, it is not likely to produce significant milestones in research that will provide a foundation for theoretical breakthroughs or definitive assessments of existing formulations.

The reasons for that pessimistic conclusion are not complex. Whatever the merits of qualitative research, it lacks some of the features of science that for centuries made it the acceptable mode of analysis employed to advance knowledge in a for jobs in a nonexistent critical cultural industry, but they contribute little to the development of a tested body of explanations of the process and effects of mass communication. That is not to say that the voices of those specializing in critical cultural perspectives should not be heard. Robust discussion of claims and conclusions is one of the great strengths of the American universities. John Milton said it well in *Aeropagitica,* his treatise on freedom to publish without prior consent by the Crown: "Let Truth and Falsehood grapple; whoever knew Truth put to the worse, in a free and open encounter". Thus, the marketplace of ideas seems likely to allow those who rely on the scientific method to prevail. Those who limit their analyses of the media to ideological criticism are likely in the long run to be relegated to the sidelines. The bottom line, then, is that the milestones of the future will be products of carefully conducted scientific research, as opposed to qualitative writings or ideological criticism.

CHANGING WORK CONDITIONS OF ACADEMICS

Three additional factors have appeared in recent decades that seem likely to limit progress in understanding the nature of mass communication. One is that many of the bright young people who do attain a mastery of the scientific method in doctoral programs may never use it to conduct basic studies of the influences and functioning of the media. Another is that since the period in which the last milestones were produced, funding for research on mass communication has become increasingly difficult to obtain. Still another is that the academy itself is changing in ways that may discourage rather than encourage difficult and large-scale investigations.

THE MOVEMENT OF CAPABLE RESEARCHERS FROM THE ACADEMY TO INDUSTRY

A clear trend among media-related industries is that they have discovered research. This happened because clients who hire advertising firms, public relations agencies, or other groups that offer services or consulting on communication problems want to see what kind of results they are getting for the fees that they pay.

Promotional efforts are expensive, whether for selling a product, improving an image, or getting elected. Earlier, practitioners would show their clients that they had placed their ads, public relations messages, or election campaign announcements in various media. Both parties would then assume that lots of people would be exposed to the messages and would thereby be influenced by them.

Today, no such assumptions are entertained. Research milestones, produced over the decades discussed earlier, have shown that achieving effects through mass communication is not that simple. Clients want empirical evidence that people are not only aware of their ads or campaigns, but also that they have been influenced by them. This means that they want research to be conducted to provide a factual basis for claims made by communications practitioners. For this reason, an applied communication research industry is growing in the business, industrial, and commercial world. Surveys, focus group studies, content analyses, and opinion polls are now routinely conducted to provide answers to practical problems and to assess potential outcomes. These may be as mundane as what is the best colour for a package of cereal, or as complex as deciding what attack ads are most likely to provide an edge in an election without backfiring on the candidate who uses them.

One of the most difficult aspects of conducting such research is locating and hiring research specialists who are fully trained in the techniques that are required for planning studies, gathering the needed data, performing the appropriate statistical analyses, and preparing reports that can be understood by clients who are not sophisticated in research methods. There is, in any realistic sense, only one category of persons who can provide effective leadership to a team that does these things.

That person is a talented product of a doctor of philosophy (PhD) programme, preferably in mass communication, who has mastered the mysteries of quantitative research methodology and who has the writing and speaking skills required. Those who take such employment, as opposed to toiling in the vineyards of academe, are likely to make salaries that make the pay of an assistant professor seem like a begrudged welfare check.

Pay levels that are double, or often triple, those paid to PhDs who elect to teach are not at all uncommon. For this reason, a mini-brain-drain appears to be starting — a drain that channels capable researchers out of the professorate. If this continues, many of the brightest and best scholars — PhDs who might have produced the next milestones — will be drawn away to the more practical and more lucrative world of applied communication research.

DECLINING FUNDING FOR BASIC MASS COMMUNICATION RESEARCH

During the 1960s and 1970s, public interest in the effects of mass communication was at an all-time high. Massive funding became available from such federal agencies as the National Institutes of Mental Health after Congress identified the issue of violence and the media as one that deeply concerned parents. Moreover, rising rates of crime, delin-quency, civil disturbances, substance abuse, and other forms of deviant behaviour were widely attributed to media influences.

Since that time of abundant government funding, however, the amount of financial support for media-related research has clearly declined.

There has long been some funding available from private foundations, but even here there is a decreasing interest in supporting basic research on the process and effects of mass communication. The limited support that exists tends to be in areas where the media are thought to play a role in promoting behaviour that poses a public health hazard.

For example, studies of such issues as the influence of liquor advertising on the consumption habits of youth, or the role of media models in prompting children to begin smoking, are projects that have recently been funded. Theoretical research, focusing on the ways in which media content is shaping nonproblem behaviour or central values in the U.S. culture would be difficult to fund. Finally, current changes within the academy itself seem designed to limit the interest of the bright young people who might think about entering the teaching profession. This may place limits on the prospects for the future production of truly significant research milestones.

One ominous situation is the great increase in the number of part-time instructors that are now offering courses to communication students. According to Walker, this is a national trend that is by no means limited to the communication disciplines.

Although part-time instructors are often wonderful people, they do not spend the time on campus required to advise students, serve on departmental committees, help students plan and conduct theses or dissertations, participate in student organizations, and all the rest. Typically, the part-timer arrives at his or her class, offers a lecture, chats briefly with students for a short time, and then departs. A related trend is that undergraduate enrollments are rising and are predicted to soar in the years ahead as a result of earlier changes in the birthrate. With more part-timers and fewer full-time faculty available to take care of nonteaching duties, and more students to deal with, less and less time will be available to plan and conduct research.

Challenges to tenure offer another ominous situation. Professional schools, in particular, are easy targets for legislators and administrators who seek to abolish this traditional protection for academics. Some opponents see tenure mainly as a matter of undeserved job security for professors, but there are abundant cases every year to show that instructors are at risk in some institutions if they speak out or publish facts, state views, or reach conclusions that are not approved — either by central administration, by some large donor to the institution, or by a controlling political figure.

Moreover, tenure offers not only protection in the area of academic freedom, but also the ability to pursue a long-range project — such as a milestone in mass communication research — that may have no tangible results for several years. In a situation where some sort of scholarly product has to be produced every year to gain extension of a short-term contract, abolishing the protection of tenure may very well inhibit a researcher from undertaking the kind of time commitment required to produce a major contribution.

A golden age of research productivity in the study of the processes and effects of mass communication appears to have existed from the decade just before World War II until the early 1980s. During that time a number of studies yielded most of the theoretical perspectives explaining the influences on individuals and society that are at the heart of our understanding of the process and effects of mass communication.

Since that time, milestone studies have not been produced at the same rate. This slowdown seems inconsistent with the increase in the number and reach of media, the growth of their labour force, and the expansion of media-related curricula on U.S. campuses. Those trends would seem to predict a corresponding increase in significant media research and further theory development.

There appear to be a number of complex reasons why the development of knowledge about the process and influences of mass communication has stalled. For one thing, social scientists, who were responsible in large part for the earlier surge in media research, have returned to their traditional agendas and media research is no longer at centre stage in either psychology or sociology as once was the case. Among those who continue to study mass communication, new epistemologies have in part replaced those central to science.

Qualitative research is now a more accepted strategy than it was earlier, even though this approach is not likely to produce additional milestones. Furthermore, many media scholars have little interest in — or indeed are openly hostile to — the methods and epistemology of science. Instead, they are committed to criticism of the media, following the dictates of an ideology rather than the implications of findings based on empirical data. These writers are quite unlikely to produce additional milestones. In addition, the conditions of work in the academy are undergoing change. Those who become well-trained in quantitative research now have opportunities open to them for well-paid employment in nonacademic and applied settings. In such roles they are unlikely to produce milestones yielding additional theories.

Another limiting situation is that sources of funding for many of the milestone studies are not now supporting media-related research. Finally, part-time instructors teach many courses, leaving an additional workload of advising, departmental chores, and other responsibilities to those who teach on a full-time basis. With rising enrollments ahead, this will limit the time that professors have for research. All of these factors, taken together, are likely to slow rather than promote additional milestone investigations that will advance theoretical understanding of mass communication and its influences.

12

Success in the Mass Communication

There is little doubt that mass-mediated communication has become both more visually oriented and more technologically complex in recent years. Sophisticated graphical interfaces on the Web, seamless photo imaging in TV and print advertisements, and intricate colour information graphics in newspapers are evidence of this emphasis on presentation and its technologies.

This marriage of presentation and technology, however, is not a new phenomenon. Advances in one historically have gone hand-in-hand with advances in the other, from the invention of half-tone technology and new photo equipment to the introduction of colour television. More recently, the arrival of digital imaging technology has strengthened the marriage, and a much-anticipated move toward newsroom "convergence" points to the integration of technological and graphical knowledge with traditional journalistic knowledge.

Anecdotal evidence suggests media managers aggressively seek staffers with the skills to operate today's new technologies, and this demand necessitates training. Training may be gained in school or in the work place, but for those just out of college, school experiences may be the only option.

This study explores the relative importance of knowledge of presentation technologies gained in school to the job-finding success of graduates of journalism and mass communication. The study seeks to determine if level of technological skill predicts job-finding success even after accounting for more traditional school-related predictors such as grade point average, internship experience and curriculum sequence. As such, the study extends earlier work on the predictors of success in the journalism and mass communication labour market. In so doing, it draws on the sociological literature on the relationships between the skills of prospective employees and their likelihood of being hired. The hypotheses generated come from what is termed screening theory, which helps to contextualize the hiring decisions made by communication employers.

TECHNOLOGY AND MEDIA PRESENTATION WORK

Work involving presentation technology is not only becoming more advanced, it is apparently making this type of activity more central to overall work processes in media organizations by facilitating the integration of job tasks. Tasks are integrating because new technologies allow the bundling of work routines from previously separate tasks.

Digital technologies seem especially to facilitate convergence of tasks and roles within media organizations because the underlying language - information as a series of 0's and 1's-can be used in the production and networking of a variety of communicative symbols. Text, photos, video, sound, and the juxtaposition of all of these symbolic elements may all be translated into digital language. A convergence of broadcast, print, and Web technology is already taking place in isolated newsrooms around the country.

In addition, so-called WYSIWYG ("what you see is what you get") software such as pagination programs, photo-imaging programs, and Web-editing programs facilitate task integration.

They do this by allowing those who write and edit text also to visualize and shape page designs, graphics, and photos, all at the same work station or at least in closer quarters. In Web work the tasks of presentation and content creation are perhaps most thoroughly integrated, as Web editors often design and produce images and pages, troubleshoot technical problems, edit copy, and write headlines. Of course, technological change is not the only explanation for task integration. Organizational size and structure are also strong influences.

Industry trade publications, anticipating technological convergence in newsrooms, are abuzz over a perceived need for journalists who can write, research, design graphics, shoot video, and build Web pages. Research also indicates media managers and staff value knowledge of technology highly. Relevant studies include the following findings: computer skills are considered highly important in assessing applicants for reporting, editing, and design positions; newspaper editors who design list technological knowledge as the skill they most wish they possessed; and "digital darkroom skills" are second only to "good portfolio" in hiring criteria for photojournalism positions.

Technological expertise appears to be rivaling professional journalism knowledge in online work. A 2000 survey of online news managers found managers value both traditional journalism skills and Web knowledge such as the ability to write HTML. A 1999 study found that managers in online newspaper publishing give multimedia skills and computer knowledge greater weight than journalism experience in hiring decisions.

SKILLS, SCREENING, AND HIRING DECISIONS

Hiring is a highly uncertain activity, and frequent turnover and retraining are costly. According to sociological literature on skills and hiring, this in part explains why employers value specific skills learned through job experience, such as technological skills, more highly than a candidate's broader educational experience. Screening theory provides a framework for examining employer assessment of candidates' credentials. In contrast to human capital theory, in which education is viewed as increasing individuals' productive capacity, in screening theory educational credentials are viewed as a tool for employers. As a tool, however, they are inexact. These credentials are merely a proxy for reducing uncertainty in the early stages of the hiring process.

Employers do not focus on specific educational credentials but instead roughly correlate notions of job competencies with a general assessment of educational attainment. In addition, employers view educational attainment as much less important when evidence of productive capacity through on—the-job experience is available.

Often educational attainment is used only in the initial sorting of the candidate pool, while specific job experiences, if available, are used both in the initial sorting and as criteria in the final hiring. Employers for professional and technical jobs tend to focus on technical skills more than behaviour or trainability. Previous job performance and technical expertise have been found to be more important than educational record or personality traits in hiring decisions. However, a number of studies suggest personality fit plays a role as well, especially in the final hiring stages. In these final stages, employers tend to rely heavily on a less formal, but more specific, assessment of "fit" between a candidate, the hiring criteria, and organizational culture. Employers look among the final pool of candidates for highly specific elements of skill, experience, and personality fit called "hot buttons." A hot-button match may be more a result of good fortune than of successful preparation by the candidate.

Previous research findings on hiring for mass communication jobs are largely consistent with the findings of the broader sociological literature. Studies show that job candidates who have tangible experience in the media fields they are pursuing have more success finding work in these fields. Success in the classroom alone-as measured, for example, by grade point average-does not strongly predict job-finding success.

Internships and college media activities provide graduates with practical media work experience, and graduates with these experiences are better positioned in the job market. Other research has shown that media employers value results of practical skill-based tests by prospective employees more highly than they do classroom achievement. Studies also show that graduates who specialize in the media fields in which they seek work have more success finding jobs than those with a more general background or than those who specialize in something other than the field in which they seek work.

Research Questions and Hypotheses

The literature suggests the media are becoming more visually sophisticated and more technologically complex, and that managers may value technological know-how in a job candidate more than professional knowledge about media content. This makes sense from an organizational standpoint. In order to function at all, media organizations must first reduce uncertainty by ensuring that they control the technology necessary to produce and disseminate content. The urgency of this first step heightens in an atmosphere of technological ambiguity. Ensuring quality of content is an important step, but it is not as crucial as the first. The news media, for example, whether print, Web, or TV, do not require staff-created content to function. They may fill all of their pages, Web space, or airtime with syndicated content.

In addition, knowledge of presentation technologies is a specialized knowledge; both the sociological and mass communication literature on hiring indicate that job candidates who have job-specific skills and knowledge are most likely to find work. Therefore it is proposed here that skill with presentation technology should significantly impact degree of job-entry success by those seeking media positions.

This study focuses on the potential benefit of learning such skills in school prior to entering the job market. While screening theory suggests employers only rely on educational attainment (e.g., GPA and type of degree) for sorting the initial pool when evidence of job-specific experience is unavailable, schools do play a role in training candidates for highly specialized skills. Students' experiences beyond the classroom, such as internships and involvement with campus media activities, provide more exposure to job-specific skills. By its very nature, technological skill is highly job-specific, thus rendering the issue of where the skill was learned less important.

For example, computer programs comprise specialized rules by which work is accomplished, thus making it unnecessary for media organizations to teach these procedures and routines if they have been learned in school. In contrast, the procedures for tasks like writing headlines or conceptualizing the design of information graphics, while also embodying routines, are less constrained by rules and involve more uncertainty. These more malleable, content— oriented tasks allow, or even require, more specific shaping by the hiring organization.

Technological skills, therefore, are more likely to meet the specific "hot-button" needs of employers, especially when technology in the school and in the work place are identical or similar. Experiences tailored to specialized "hot-button" needs of the industry are most valuable to employers, whether learned during school internships or on the job.

Transferred to the individual level of the employee, these arguments suggest that graduates with specific skills will have more success in the job market than those without those specific skills. Consequently these specific skills will explain variance in job-seeking success once other less general skill sets are controlled for. This argument can be restated as the following two hypotheses.

*H*1a: The greater the degree of skill with presentation technologies possessed by graduates, the greater the degree of success the graduates will have in the job market.

*H*1b: The greater the degree of skill in presentation technologies possessed by graduates, the greater the degree of job-finding success graduates will have, even after controlling for traditional school-related predictors of job-finding success.

This study also addresses several other research questions, which are of a mostly descriptive nature. These include: Are those graduates who have knowledge of particular presentation technologies upon graduation likely to use these technologies in their work after school? And, in which media jobs are these particular technologies likely to be used?

Method

Data used in addressing these questions come from the 1999 Annual Survey of Journalism and Mass Communication Graduates, which tracks the experiences of a sample of graduates of journalism and mass communication programs once they leave their universities.

The surveys are conducted at the Henry W. Grady College of Journalism and Mass Communication at the University of Georgia. Each year a sample of schools is drawn from those listed in the Journalism and Mass Communication Directory, published annually by the Association for Education in Journalism and Mass Communication, and The Journalists' Road to Success, published annually by the Dow Jones Newspaper Fund, Inc. Selection of schools is probabilistic, so that those chosen represent the population of schools listed in the two directories. In 1999, 102 schools were drawn from the 456 unique entries of four-year programs in the United States in the two directories.

A questionnaire was mailed to the 6,613 spring graduates receiving either a bachelor's degree or a master's degree from the selected programs. Two follow-up questionnaires were mailed to graduates as necessary. Included in the instrument were questions about university experiences, job seeking and employment, salaries and benefits, and experiences with media technology.

A total of 2,826 usable questionnaires were returned, producing a return rate of 47.4 per cent. Return rate, when computed as the number returned divided by the number mailed minus the bad addresses, was 50.8 per cent. Data used in the present study only include results gathered from full-time employed bachelor's degree recipients. Bachelor's degree recipients are the majority of graduates of journalism and mass communication programs each year.

The independent variable, "skill in presentation techno-logies," was operationalized via self-reported level of proficiency by survey respondents with five different types of presentation software: pagination, graphic illustration, photo imaging, Web-site building, and nonlinear editing. Degree of job-finding success, the dependent variable, was operationalized as the number of job offers graduates report receiving upon graduation. The traditional school-related predictors used here as controls were grade point average, sequence specialization, involvement with campus media activities, and involvement with media internships.

Specialization in media presentation was not common for graduates of the schools of journalism and mass comm-unication. In 1999, just slightly more than 1 per cent of bachelor's degree recipients reported selecting graphic design as a major, and roughly the same per cent reported photojournalism as a major. These figures have changed little over the last ten years.

Not only did few graduates report graphic design as a curricula specialization, few reported being proficient with presentation technology at the time of graduation. Data also showed that a relatively low percentage of bachelor's degree recipients reported using presentation technology in their current full-time jobs.

For four of the five software types measured in the graduate survey, one in five or fewer graduates reported being proficient. The percentages of those actually using these software in their current jobs were similarly low. The notable exception was page-design software. About half of the graduates reported being proficient with page-design software while more than 80 per cent reported being at least somewhat proficient. Nearly 60 per cent reported using this software for their jobs. It seems that the technological skill of assembling elements for print layout on computers is widely diffused in the work place.

For most software types, close to half of the fulltime employed graduates who reported proficiency with a software upon graduation ended up using this software on their jobs. Again the exception is page-design software for which more than three-quarters reported use on the job. The chart reveals a substantial difference in actual use of software by all graduates and use of software by only those who said they were proficient upon graduation. This chart gives the first hint that the acquisition of expert technological skills in school may predict future use of these technologies in the workplace.

SOFTWARE USE ACROSS MEDIA TYPES

The work in each type of media industry involves unique technological processes, therefore necessitating the use of some graphic software programs more than others. The data show that skill with page-design software is highly important to the work processes of graduates working at all media types, with the single and not surprising exception of television. Somewhat surprising is the high percentage of online-publishing workers who use page-design software. This may be explained by the fact that designers sometimes first design Web pages in page-design software and then use these designs as templates in Web-site building programs. It may also be that many respondents who categorized their work as online publishing actually design print material as well. Graphic-illustration software is most heavily used by those in online publishing. Once again, the percentage of graduates working in television who use this software is the lowest.

Similarly, the percentage of graduates working for online publishing companies who use photo— imaging software was much higher than the percentages for other media types. Graduates working for newspapers, public relations, and advertising reported using this software in fairly high percentages, relative to percentage use of other software types.

The results for questions about non-linear editing software, which is used in television work, may reflect a measurement problem. While the percentage of those working in television using this software was the highest, followed by use in online publishing, the relatively high rate of reported use in newspapers is not tenable given the nature of print-media production processes (and most newsrooms aren't "converged" yet). It seems likely that the word "editing" in the question choice "non-linear editing" may have led to confusion by some respondents.

Not surprisingly, the percentage of graduates working in online publishing who reported actually using Web-site building software was much higher than were the percentages of those working for all other media types. The percentage of graduates working in public relations and in advertising who use Web-site building software was low, but it was higher than the percentages working for print media and TV who use this software.

It is clear that knowledge of presentation technology is more necessary to online publishing work in general than to work in the other traditional media industries.

Presentation technology may be more intricately woven into the fabric of the overall work process in online publishing organizations than in the work processes of print media, television, public relations, or advertising. The fact that Web work converges media forms-video, sound, photos, and text-is also a likely explanation.

REGRESSION ANALYSES: SOFTWARE PROFICIENCY AND JOB-FINDING SUCCESS

In order to test the hypotheses and determine the impact of technological knowledge on job-finding success, a zero-order correlation analysis and several regression analyses were conducted. To obtain the overall measure for the independent variable software proficiency, measures of proficiency in four of the five software types were summed.

Non-linear editing, which did not scale well with the other measures, was excluded from the scale for two reasons. First, there is a conceptual distinction between this technology and the other four.

Non-linear editing deals with moving imagery only, while the other software types are largely oriented toward still imagery and design. Second, as previously mentioned, results indicated some respondents might have been confused about the meaning of the term "non-linear editing." The alpha coefficient for reliability among the remaining four items was.

The dependent variable, degree of job-finding success, was measured by the number of job offers graduates reported having upon completing school. The analysis includes only the 1,897 bachelor degree recipients who sought employment with a communication employer, which is 72.7 per cent of the total sample. The mean of the dependent variable was 2.19 (number of jobs offered) and the standard deviation was 1.85. To test H1a, number of job offers received by under-graduates who sought communication jobs was correlated with degree of presentation software proficiency. The coefficient was.064 and was significant at the.01 level. H1a therefore received support.

Overall, the model shows these variables explain a significant though small amount of variance in job-finding success-2.6 per cent of the variance. The finding is consistent with the earlier work in the field of journalism and mass communication both in terms of the predictors and the relatively small amount of variance explained. Having an internship, participating in campus media and being a public relations major are the strongest predictors. The only other significant predictor is being a broadcasting major, and this relationship is negative.

In the next model, the variable Degree of Presentation Software Proficiency is entered as a second block. The increase in variance explained is fairly small-from 2.6 per cent to 2.9 per cent-but the incremental change in R-square is significant at the.05 level. H1b receives support, as Presentation Software Proficiency does prove to be a significant predictor, even when accounting for the traditional predictors. Internships, Campus Media Activities, and Public Relations Major continue to be the strongest predictors. In neither model is GPA or Advertising Major a significant predictor.

While the model was significant, the amount of variance explained was quite small. In an attempt to clarify the role of proficiency with presentation technology in job success and improve the overall predictive model, regression analyses next were conducted to test predictors of receipt of a job offer in only the online publishing field. It was anticipated that proficiency with presentation technology would be a better predictor of success finding work specifically in online publishing than it was as a predictor of general job-finding success. This should be the case both because of the apparent importance of presentation software knowledge to Web work and because the model is more specifically targeted.

In the models predicting job-finding success in online publishing the dependent variable was scored as a dichotomy because variance was minimal beyond the 0/1 level. One is equal to receipt of at least one job offer in online publishing work at graduation, and zero is equal to the absence of such a job offer. Only the 300 bachelor degree recipients who sought work in online publishing were included in this analysis, and this number was 12.4 per cent of the total sample. Among these, 38.3 per cent received at least one job offer in online publishing. Because the dependent variable is dichotomous, both OLS regression and logistic regression models were used to assess predictors. There were negligible differences between the models, and OLS regression results will be shown here to make comparison with the earlier regression analysis easier.

The first model includes the traditional predictors of job-finding success, entered as a block. The R-square of the model is not significant. In the next model Proficiency with Presentation Software is entered as the only variable in a second block, and it and Campus Media Activities have the highest beta weights, at.089 each. The R-square of the new model is.026, but neither the change in the R-square nor any of the model's predictors test as significant.

Next, job-finding success in online publishing is regressed on more specific predictors-Campus Media Activities and Proficiency with Presentation Software are replaced with Campus Web Activity and Proficiency with Web-site building Software. In the first model only the traditional predictors are entered as a block (including Campus Web activity), and the R-square is.037. In the second model Proficiency with Web-site building Software is added as a second block, and this second model's R-square is.052. Proficiency with Web-site building Software, with a beta of.131, is the strongest predictor, followed by Campus Web Each of these predictors are significant, and change in R-square is significant as well.

It appears then that as independent variables are tailored more narrowly to the criterion variable, they become better predictors. It also appears that the nature of online publishing work is such that it requires a particularly high level of skill with the requisite presentation software.

However, it may be that Web work is no more demanding of software skills than other media work and that any model made more specific would predict more successfully. To assess this possibility, a final regression model was run for comparative purposes. This model also predicted receipt of a specific type of media job offer, but here the offer was from a daily newspaper job. Included in this model were GPA, sequence, internships, campus newspaper involvement, and proficiency with page-design software, the software most likely to be used by newspaper staffers. While being a print journalism major and working with a campus newspaper were the most important predictors, proficiency with page-design software was not a significant predictor. Neither was the model improved significantly. The results of this comparative analysis lend support to the conclusion that the importance of software proficiency to landing Web job offers is due at least in part to the nature of Web work, and not entirely to specificity of the model.

Study results show that degree of skill with presentation technologies matters to the job-finding success of journalism and mass communication graduates. Skill with presentation technology stands as a significant predictor of job-finding success, even when controlling for GPA, sequence specialization, number of internships, and campus media activities. If media technology and media processes continue to converge, as many industry experts predict, it seems likely presentation software skill will grow in importance.

For those seeking work in online publishing, knowledge of presentation software for the Web surpasses the importance of all the other school-related predictors traditionally associated with job-finding success. Given recent findings from the Annual Survey of Journalism and Mass Communication Graduates that the percentage of graduates taking jobs in online publishing is growing faster than all other media, it seems advisable for journalism and mass communication programs to increase technological instruction for their graduates. Yet the present study finds that proficiency in online publishing technology (or any presentation technology) is not widespread among graduates of journalism and comm-unication schools. The recent downturn in the economic fortune of tech industries should be acknowledged here, and this focus on technological competence in hiring may change as media industries evolve. On the other hand, it is hard to imagine the industry becoming less visually oriented.

This study lends support to previous findings that media employers-and employers in general-tend to favour job candidates with jobspecific skills. According to screening theory, employers only rely on educational attainment when candidates in the pool lack job-specific, or so-called "hot button," skills. Educational credentials such as GPA serve only as a less-than-perfect proxy for assessing candidate fit. However, skills with presentation technology are job-specific by nature, and they may be taught through school curricula. The rules and routines embodied in these software are the same in school as in the workplace. As a result, employers may view skill with presentation software as a more reliable measure of evaluation than other credentials gained during schooling. Employers may be more likely to hire candidates with these skills because it is a convenient way to reduce uncertainty in the highly uncertain hiring process.

Study findings may also reflect the importance of technological processes to organizations undergoing technological change and indeterminacy. Online publishing is a relatively new field with relatively new technologies that are presently in flux. But as with the production of most mediated information, online production involves time constraints. In Web work, content may be disseminated on a constant, ongoing basis, and increasingly Web-savvy audiences expect sites to be always accessible. Securing the means of production necessarily takes priority over ensuring quality of content: the newspaper must come out, the show must go on, and the site must stay up. Technical skills and knowledge of production would be prioritized over skills and knowledge involved with crafting content. After all, it is possible for a Web site (or any media product) to be produced without using locally generated content. In fact many Web-site producers choose to fill their sites with nothing but "repurposed" text and images and links to the content of other sites.

Perhaps then it is not the degree of technological complexity of a media form that determines how important technological skills are to the operation of a media organization, but rather the degree of uncertainty about technological processes. Older, more established media forms have been able to routinize technological processes and the learning of these processes to a greater degree than has the new field of online publishing. The structural framework for the instruction of older technologies (i.e., school curricula and training sessions in media and professional organizations) has been in place longer, and the principles and conventions adopted for instruction are more established. Such structures for learning are only now being established in online publishing. Once these structures are in place and processes are more routinized, employers in online publishing should be able to turn more attention to content quality.

The study does not directly address the issue of where graduates learned these skills. They may have learned them in classes, in internships, in campus media activities, or even in the privacy of their dorm rooms. Analyses not tabled show that graduates with media internships reported slightly higher levels of software proficiency. This issue should be addressed more directly in future studies.

While this study addresses the importance of technological knowledge to finding jobs, it does not explore the relative quality of such jobs. Knowledge of the software may be enough to help a graduate get hired, but not enough to put the graduate in a good job and foster promotion. There is some evidence to suggest that tasks involving presentation technology eat into time spent performing occupational tasks of a more conceptual nature. Workers relegated to routine technological procedures are less likely to control their work than those whose work knowledge is more abstract and less tied to specific technologies. Findings here suggest schools of journalism and mass communication benefit students through rigorous training in technological skills, but this need not be a zero-sum game. Ways must be found to teach skills in conjunction with more conceptual curricula.

Finally, while the data presented here suggest that job specific skills contribute to the success of graduates in the labour market, and that the more specific the skills the better they predict to success, these skills clearly play only a small role in the hiring decision. In fact, the analysis conducted here show that the vast majority of the variance in hiring is not explained by the job specific skills identified here or even by the more general attributes such as scholastic performance, represented by grade point average.

As noted, the hiring process involves not only an assessment of specific skills, but also an assessment of personality fit, the extent to which an individual will mesh with the organizational culture, and the extent to which candidates are able to match the highly specific and hard— to-anticipate "hot-button" needs of employers. How the applicant presents herself or himself in the interview situation is not measured by any of the variables included in the analysis here. As a result, it is possible to argue, based on the data at hand, that specific skills are important predictors of job market success for journalism and mass communication graduates, but it is not the case that these are the main determinants of success. The main determinants of success will be identified only with additional research in this area.

In recent years, radio and television stations consistently have offered entry-level news salaries below those provided by daily newspapers, public relations, and advertising employers. Yet the broadcast industries report no difficulty in finding people willing to take their jobs. One possible explanation for low salaries in broadcast news is that universities are producing a surplus of graduates, holding down the salaries that are offered. Another explanation is that the lure of jobs in radio and television - the appeal of being a part of these "glamour" industries - is enough to fill the jobs available and keep wages low.

This chapter draws on roughly parallel surveys of hiring patterns in the daily newspaper, radio, and television industries to provide a test of these expectations. The results of these surveys are linked to data on recent graduates of journalism and mass communications programs to make assessments of the fit between the demand for labour and the supply of labour in these industries.

The Annual Survey of Journalism and Mass Communication Graduates, conducted at The Ohio State University, has shown a consistent gap between the entry-level pay of graduates who found full-time work at radio or television stations and those who found work elsewhere in communications. Survey respondents graduated about a year before being surveyed, so the term "entry-level workers" here describes new college graduates taking their first job after graduation. In 1994, only those graduates going to work for weekly, biweekly or triweekly newspapers earned salaries as low as those in television and radio.

The evidence available shows that the low entry-level salaries continue through the career of broadcast journalists. Drawing on data from his surveys of radio and television news directors over the last ten years, Stone shows low pay across almost all job categories in both types of organizations. Television pays well in the large markets and particularly well for anchors. Radio news directors even in large markets earn only about half as much as their TV counterparts. A disparity between the pay for broadcast and print journalists has appeared in the last twenty years. Although a survey conducted in 1971 by Johnstone, Slawski, and Bowman found journalists in television earning slightly more than those at newspapers, later surveys by Weaver and Wilhoit found broadcast journalists' pay lagging behind pay for print journalists. In 1991, the highest median salaries were earned by journalists at news magazines and wire services. They were followed by journalists at daily newspapers, television, weekly newspapers, and radio. Theoretical Issues Stone offers at least two explanations for the low pay in broadcasting. First, in the view of news directors, there is an excess supply of applicants. Second, broadcasting is seen as an attractive field, and people are willing to work for low pay. It seems likely that the attractiveness of the field encourages the excess supply in the first place, but there may be other factors that add to the excess supply as well.

The news directors' notion of excess supply is consistent with the general economic theory that demand and supply work in the labour force as well as the marketplace. According to the labour market application of the demand and supply model, the low pay reflects the fact that there are too many qualified individuals seeking a limited number of jobs. When there is a surplus or excess supply of labour, employers offer low wages, and the supply decreases.

The labour supply curve is a positively sloping straight line illustrating an increasing supply of workers as wages offered increases. The labour demand curve is a negatively sloping line illustrating a declining demand for workers as the wages increase. The intersection of the demand and supply curves is the equilibrium wage, which is what the industry should offer.

The argument that the field is attractive and therefore pay need not be high is frequently heard for various occupations and should not be dismissed out-of-hand. Professors, for example, do not earn salaries comparable to what persons with their education or training would earn in industry. They accept positions at the university, however, because of other benefits. In American society, few institutions are as prominent as television. Broadcasting offers public visibility and star status not provided by many other occupations. These are "benefits" that may compensate for low pay, at least in the view of young persons seeking entry-level work. In the language of labour economics, these "benefits" must be offset with higher wages by competing media industries. The newspaper industry, if this interpretation is correct, must offer its employees a "compensating wage differential" since broadcasting is such an attractive alternative.

These are two explanations for the low pay in broadcasting. If the excess supply argument holds, the higher pay earned by entry-level hires at daily newspapers compared to broadcasting should result from differences in the supply of trained graduates. If supply is not the determinant of salaries, but rather the perceived attractiveness of broadcasting, then supply should be unrelated to salary. It is possible that both supply and the attractiveness of broadcast jobs work together to hold down wages in broadcasting. If supply is comparable for newspapers and broadcasting, the observed differences in wages may be explained as a "compensating wage differential." If supply is greater for broadcasting than for newspapers, both supply and compensating differentials may be at work.

Data allowing for a comparison of the supply and demand for entry level jobs in broadcast news versus the daily newspaper industry were obtained for the first time in 1991. Stone incorporated items dealing with hiring practices in his annual survey of news directors of television and radio stations. Similar items had been included in the 1991 survey of daily newspaper editors conducted for the Dow Jones Newspaper Fund. The 1991 newspaper survey, was, in turn, a replication of a study conducted by the Newspaper Fund at irregular intervals beginning in 1970. These surveys provide parallel data on demand for labour. Data on supply can be inferred from the 1991 Annual Survey of Journalism and Mass Communication Graduates.

In the broadcast news survey, questionnaires were mailed in the summer of 1991 to all 960 nonsatellite commercial television stations in the United States and a probability sample of 810 commercial radio stations drawn from the population of 6,600 stations. Joint AM-FM news operations were counted as a single station. After two mailings, responses were received from 506 television stations (53 per cent) and 315 of the radio stations (39 per cent). News operations existed at 412 of the responding television stations and 275 of the responding radio stations. Only broadcast stations with a news operation were used in these analyses.

Editors at 1,590 daily newspapers in the United States were sent a questionnaire in January of 1991. After two mailings, 704 (44 per cent) responded. The survey paralleled one conducted by the Newspaper Fund in 1986 and dealt entirely with hiring practices.

In the broadcast survey, news directors were asked how many newsroom staff were hired in the past twelve months and how many of those were hired directly out of college. In the editor survey, respondents were asked to indicate how many persons were hired for the newsroom staff in 1990. Staff hires were broken down by position. In each case, the number of hires directly from college was determined.

The annual survey of graduates of U.S. journalism and mass communications programs is conducted each year by the School of Journalism at The Ohio State University. A sample of schools is drawn from those listed in the Journalism Career and Scholarship Guide, published each year by the Dow Jones Newspaper Fund, and the Journalism and Mass Communication Directory, published annually by the Association for Education in Journalism and Mass Communication. To be included in the guide, the college or university must offer at least ten courses in news-editorial journalism including core courses, such as an introduction to the mass media and press law, as well as basic skills courses such as reporting and editing. Schools list themselves in the AEJMC Directory.

Administrators at the selected schools are asked to provide the names and addresses of their spring bachelor's and master's degree recipients. As the second step in the annual survey, a questionnaire is mailed in November or December to all spring graduates receiving either a bachelor's or a master's degree from the selected programs. A second questionnaire is sent to nonrespondents in January or February.

In the autumn of 1990, the survey was mailed to 5,002 individuals whose names and addresses were provided by the administrators of the eighty programs sampled. A total of 2,948 respondents returned the questionnaires by the end of May of 1991. Of the returns, 2,596 were from students who reported they had actually completed their degrees during the April to July 1990 period. A total of 223 questionnaires were returned undelivered. Return rate computed as the number of questionnaires returned divided by the number mailed was 59 per cent. Return rate computed as the number returned divided by the number mailed minus the bad addresses was 62 per cent.

The graduate survey includes detailed questions on types of jobs sought and obtained by the respondents as well as type of curricular specialization. The data can be generalized to the population of graduates for that year, estimated by Becker to be approximately 33,300 bachelor's degree recipients and 2,700 master's degree recipients.

Becker reported that 57 per cent of the 1989-1990 graduates of journalism and mass communications programs actually completed their studies in spring of that academic year, i.e., spring of 1990. There is no reason to believe the graduates completing their studies at times other than spring would engage in different job hunting tactics or have different curricular specialization while in college.

A comparison of the schools in the OSU surveys and data obtained via a U.S. Department of Education census of four-year degree-granting institutions of higher education shows the appropriateness of the OSU data for this project. The Department of Education reported that 41 universities offered degrees in radio/television news broadcast in academic year 1990-91. All but 9 (78 per cent) are in the corresponding OSU survey. Of the 131 universities reporting degrees granted in radio/television (news broadcast and general), 93 (71 per cent) were included in the corresponding OSU survey. Of the 329 universities offering degrees in journalism/mass communi-cations, 260 (79 per cent) were included in that year's OSU survey.

In terms of degrees granted, however, the distortion is even smaller. Of the 6,641 degrees the Department of Education says were granted in radio/ television (news broadcast and general), all but 14.1 per cent were granted by schools included in the OSU surveys. Of the 12,173 degrees granted in journalism, all but 6.2 per cent were granted by schools included in the OSU surveys.

The methodology of the Department of Education census is distinct from the OSU methodology. A student receiving a degree from a journalism school would almost certainly be classified as receiving a journalism degree, though the student might well have specialized in broadcast journalism. The OSU Survey also includes data from schools not reporting communications degrees to the Department of Education. In sum, the OSU data allow for more precise designation of degrees granted by subfield of communication. The OSU Graduate Survey, based on reports of the graduates themselves, provides data not only on curricular specialization at the university but also types of work sought.

By combining the graduate data from the Annual Survey of Journalism and Mass Communication Graduates with the data on degrees granted, it is possible to make an estimate of the number of persons in the labour pool. This estimate can then be matched to the labour needs obtained from the news director and editor surveys.

Radio stations hired an estimated 5,444 persons for their news operations in 1990-91, 39.4 per cent of them from other radio stations. Another 34.0 per cent were hired directly from college. Of these college hires - or entry-level hires - 76.9 per cent had a journalism major, a little over half of them specializing in broadcast journalism. Some of these entry-level hires will have completed a master's degree; others will have earned a bachelor's degree. Becker projects that only 7 per cent of the journalism and mass communications degrees granted in 1989-90 were at the graduate level.

The questions on hiring were less detailed (with less information obtained on the majors of the graduates), but the comparison shows that number of hires in radio has declined markedly from 1984 to 1990-91. The percentage of hires in radio coming directly from college, however, has increased about 11 per cent, a statistically significant change (at the.05 level). This offset a decline in radio hires from jobs outside broadcasting. Total radio news staffs were estimated at 19,700 in 1984 and 16,900 in 1991.

Television hired an estimated 5,069 persons for their news staffs in 1990-91, 64.9 per cent of them from other television stations. Television news directors report hiring 18.1 per cent of their 1990-91 employees directly from college. Of these, 91.1 per cent came from journalism and mass communications programs. The 1990-91 television hires are an increase of just over 1,000 persons from the number hired in 1984. The percentage being hired directly out of college in 1990-91 is statistically comparable to 1984. Total television news work force was 17,100 in 1984 and 23,100 in 1991.

Because of differential return rates by newspaper size in the 1990 survey of daily newspaper editors, the returns were weighted so as to accurately reflect the population of newspapers stratified by size. The sample data were then used to project the number of hires at the full population of daily newspapers. The daily newspaper industry hired an estimated 8,941 persons in 1990,55.0 per cent of them from other newspapers. The second largest group of hires came directly from college. These are entry-level hires. Of the daily newspaper hires directly from college, three-quarters came from journalism programs. Just under 16 per cent of the new hires at daily newspapers in 1990 came from nonmedia jobs, and 7.1 per cent were hired away from other media. The 8,941 new hires for 1990 represent 15.7 per cent of the 56,900 newsroom employees estimated to be holding jobs in daily newspapers at the end of 1990.

The 1985 data have been weighted to reflect the population characteristics of 1990 so as to make the data sets comparable and correct for sampling bias in that earlier survey. Comparisons of the 1985 and 1990 surveys show the dramatic decline in hiring at daily newspapers during that period. The decline in hiring is accompanied by a decline (significant at the.05 level) in the percentage of hires coming directly from college, and, among the new hires, a slight (and statistically nonsignificant) decline in the percentage coming from journalism programs. In actual numbers, there were 2,221 fewer hires directly from college in 1990 than in 1985, or a decline of 53.0 per cent.

Clearly, not all entry-level hires in radio, television, and daily newspapers come from journalism and mass communications programs. The data presented here, as well as earlier research by Becker, Fruit and Caudill, Giles and Stone, indicate that the bulk of them do. Consequently, it is reasonable to turn to the Annual Survey of Journalism and Mass Communication Graduates for 1990 to estimate the supply of graduates for these jobs.

Respondents to the annual survey of graduates are asked if they had sought employment in radio, television, or daily newspapers since graduation. Among the 1990 bachelor's degree recipients, 18.0 per cent reported looking for a radio job, 25.7 per cent reported looking for a job in television, and 22.4 per cent sought daily newspaper positions. Based on the estimated 33,331 journalism bachelor's degrees granted that academic year, this would translate to 6,000 bachelor's degree recipients seeking work in radio, 8,566 seeking work in television, and 7,466 seeking work in daily newspapers. If master's degree recipients are added, the gross estimates are 6,090 in radio, 9,087 in television, and 8,239 in daily newspapers.

These estimates of the labour supply are gross in that they do not take into consideration the basic requirements of journalistic work in radio, television, and daily newspapers. A student with a degree in advertising and an internship with an advertising agency would not be qualified for the news positions of concern here. Qualification for the job has to do minimally with curricular specialization within journalism and mass communications, internships, and work for the appropriate campus medium.

In the view of news directors and editors, an applicant who has not learned the basics of writing and reporting for that medium is not qualified. Similarly, an applicant who has had an internship in the medium would be viewed as more qualified than one who has not. Work for the campus radio station would provide the applicant with more of the skills needed for radio work and more experience in the routines of that medium than a student without that experience. Students in television obtain relevant experience working for the campus television station; print students obtain their relevant experience with the campus newspaper.

5.2 per cent of the respondents in the graduate survey specialized in radio/television and sought a job in radio, 8.9 per cent of the graduates specialized in radio/television and sought a job in that medium, and 9.3 per cent specialized in print journalism and sought a job with daily newspapers.

The extra qualified graduates are those who did two of the following: specialized in the relevant curriculum, interned for the relevant medium, or worked for the relevant campus medium. The highly qualified graduates did all three. Only 648 graduates of 1989-90 would be labeled as highly qualified for jobs in radio, 1,008 would be considered highly qualified for television, and 1,619 would be highly qualified for daily newspapers. There were 3.29 persons seeking each of these jobs. The ratio of extra qualified persons to jobs available, however, was 1.17 to 1, while the ratio of highly qualified persons to jobs in radio news was 0.35 to 1.

For television, the ratio of persons seeking jobs to jobs available was 9.9 to 1. The ratio of extra qualified persons to jobs available was 3.8 to 1. The ratio of highly qualified entry-level applicants to jobs available was 1.1 to 1. For daily newspapers, the ratio of graduates seeking daily newspaper jobs to entry-level jobs available was 4.18 to 1. For extra qualified persons, the ratio was 2.06 to 1. For highly qualified persons, the ratio was 0.82 to 1.

In sum, regardless of criterion used, television has an excess supply of applicants to entry-level job openings. At the gross level, this is nearly 10 persons for each job available. At the extra qualified level, the ratio is nearly 4 to 1. Neither of the other media enjoy this type of excess supply. In fact, when the OSU survey is compared to Department of Education data, all but 14.1 per cent of degrees granted in radio/television are included in the calculated labour supply for this study, compared to all but 6.2 per cent of journalism degrees.

Thus, the labour supply of radio/television graduates is probably even proportionately larger than the supply of journalism graduates. The data support the argument that television does not have to pay high wages because supply is outstripping demand.

For daily newspapers, there also is an excess supply of persons seeking jobs. That excess supply is 4 to 1 if job seekers are used as the criterion, and 2 to 1 if moderate qualifications are imposed.

If daily newspapers want the graduates who specialized in news-editorial journalism, had an internship with a newspaper, and worked for the campus paper, they will find that demand outstrips supply. This might explain the higher wages paid by daily newspapers in contrast to television news operations.

Radio presents a complicated picture. Wages in radio news were the lowest among the three employers examined here. Yet radio has the lowest ratios of supply to demand. There are three times as many jobs as highly qualified persons seeking them - using the criteria enumerated above.

The ratio of extra qualified persons to jobs available is close to 1 to 1. If radio reaches over to the television pool - as it may do over time - an even larger number of graduates is available. Many graduates may see radio as a steppingstone to television and readily make this transition.

It is also important to keep in mind that graduates with degrees in other fields compete with the graduates of journalism and mass communications programs for entry-level jobs. Radio and daily newspapers report filling nearly 25 per cent of their entry-level jobs with these graduates.

That supply is almost limitless. Based on the data examined here, there is no evidence to support the argument that newspapers would have to pay higher salaries to compensate for the attractiveness of broadcasting. All three have adequate supplies of graduates. It does seem reasonable, however, that the gross excess supply in television serves to hold down salaries in the newsrooms.

SUPPLEMENTARY ANALYSIS

The idea that radio does not hire the same type of applicant as the other two media, and, more generally, that salary differentials among the three media can be explained in terms of differences among those hired, can be tested with data from the annual graduate survey. To do this, 1990 graduates with full-time work in radio, television, and daily newspapers were singled out for analysis. The basic strategy was, via hierarchial regression analysis, to examine if salary differentials among the three media types remained after various characteristics of the respondents with jobs in those media were first eliminated or controlled for.'

A total of 240 graduates, either with a bachelor's or a master's degree, were used in this analysis. First, racial or ethnic classification of the respondent was entered into the equation, along with sex. As can be seen, this block of variables explains a significant amount of variance in salary. When only these two variables are in the equation - that is, when there are no controls - being a minority is associated with higher salaries; being a woman is not significantly associated with earning less. (The effect of minority status is decreased after subsequent controls, but it remains slightly positive in the final equation.)

Next, population of the community in which the graduate was working was entered into the equation. Not surprisingly, those persons who found work in large communities received higher wages than those who did not.

The next block of variables measures the experiences of the graduates at the university. Graduates who had a high GPA in college earned more when employed than those with a low GPA. Controlling for other factors, internships are associated with higher pay. Master's degree recipients earned more than those with a bachelor's. Having a second major or having prior work experience with the employer did not contribute to pay, other things held constant. Working for the campus radio station was negatively related to pay received, working for the campus newspaper was positively related to pay, and working for the campus television station was unrelated to pay.

The explanation for the differential effect of college media experience is simple: Those who worked for a college radio station were more likely to take a job in radio, which pays less than television and newspapers. Working for the college newspaper is associated with taking a job in newspapers, which pay more. Even after these experiences are eliminated, however, type of employer still explains a significant amount of variance. Type of employer was entered as the final block in the regression equation.

Those people who found work in radio received less pay than those who found work in television and newspapers not because they were different in terms of their training, but because they worked for radio. Similarly, those who found work for newspapers received higher wages not because they were different in terms of training or characteristics, but because they found work in newspapers. The media pay differently, holding constant differences in the characteristics of the people employed.

The data reported here suggest that excess supply of labour exists in radio news, television news, and daily newspapers. That excess supply probably serves to hold down salaries generally and to explain the lower pay in television news in comparison with daily newspapers. Television in particular has many more persons seeking entry-level jobs than there are jobs available.

The daily newspaper industry also has an excess supply of entry-level applicants, but the ratio is about half of what it is for television. If daily newspapers want to hire persons who specialized in print journalism, had a newspaper internship, and worked for the campus newspaper, they are going to encounter a competitive labour market. There are not enough graduates to go around. Obviously, employers are going to have to compromise to fill positions.

Radio presents a complicated picture. Among the three media studied, the ratio of supply to demand is lowest for radio. Yet radio pays the lowest salaries. One explanation is that radio is meeting its needs by reducing the qualifications sought among its entry-level hires. Another explanation is that radio reaches into the television labour supply, which might mean that radio and television labour markets are more closely related than many have thought. Radio also is highly competitive and generally less profitable than television, and this may increase the scope of the search in radio and serve to explain lower pay than would be expected based solely on supply.

If the economic theory of supply and demand in the labour market is at work here, then the supply should decline and the salaries increase as college students gravitate to better paying jobs. If the attractiveness of the field is the primary draw for aspiring television journalists, then there is no reason to believe that the supply of applicants, and the wages offered, will change. This is the critical difference between the two explanations for excess supply offered here. Even when we control for qualifications of graduates, newly hired persons in broadcast news earn less than those in newspapers.

In looking at the labour supply for media outlets, it is important to note that there are a significant number of graduates looking for work in each of the three media who have taken measures to increase their qualifications for a job. At one end of the scale, 14 per cent of all journalism graduates have no specialization. They have not specialized their degree in a prospective medium, taken an internship in the medium, or worked at a college outlet of that particular medium. On the other hand, 36.1 per cent of all graduates took advantage of at least two of the three options and significantly increased their qualifications in the eyes of most media managers.

Caution is in order in interpreting the results of this analysis. The fit is far from perfect between information available and information needed for a fool-proof test of the relationship between labour supply and labour demand. We have provided an examination of the labour supply and labour demand relationship at one point in time. These types of analysis should be replicated across time. In a competitive labour market, salary adjusts itself to supply and demand over time. It is not possible to see that dynamic with the static data available for these analyses.

Despite these limitations the data provide a more detailed examination of supply and demand than has previously been possible. The analyses have been conducted in the context of an analysis of salary differentials between those hired for entry-level positions in radio, television, and newspapers. The data argue that television is able to pay less than daily newspapers in part because of a huge surplus of supply of labour to demand. This excess supply seems likely to continue to deflate salaries in television for the near future.

13

Commitment to Journalistic Work

Commitment to the occupation of journalism has been declining during the past twenty to thirty years. Studies show that a relatively small and decreasing number of journalists plan to retire in the field.

The percentage of journalists saying they planned to leave the field nearly doubled from 1971 to 1982, and then nearly doubled again in 1992, as more than one-fifth of journalists reported they were likely to change careers. Commitment levels have been especially low among those recently entering the field. Recent surveys of journalism and mass communication school graduates show that around 20 per cent expect to retire in the field. Though studies have shown that longevity in the field increases commitment, many are leaving the field before longevity becomes a factor.

Commitment to an occupation also should be the result of the socialization activities associated with the education and training that prepares entrants for it. For entrants to the occupations of journalism, training is most often offered in journalism programs at a college or university. However, this study proposes that participation in high school journalism should play a role in the socialization of the journalism career entrant and to commitment to that occupation. This study focuses on recent entrants into the field of journalism to examine if precollege and college experiences with journalism-e.g., involvement in journalism activities and classes-have an impact on later level of occupational commitment. Factors that are specific to journalists' first workplaces are also examined. In addition, analyses are conducted to assess commitment and predictors of commitment in other fields of mass communication-i.e., public relations, advertising, and telecommunications-in order to provide context for the analysis of commitment to journalism.

Commitment is conceptualized as containing both an affective and a nonaffective component. The affective component, which has been dominant in the journalism literature to date, focuses on such feelings as loyalty and a sense of mission. The nonaffective component focuses on the accumulation of investments made in pursuit of an occupation and involves a recognition of costs of leaving. The implications of this conceptual distinction are discussed.

COMMITMENT TO JOURNALISM

Commitment to an occupation is conceptually distinct from commitment to the organization. It is possible to feel stronger attachment to a particular organization than to a profession, and the reverse is also possible. Also, factors that explain greater commitment to occupation are likely to differ from those that explain commitment to the organization. This distinction is particularly important to the study of journalism because of the occupation's dependency on organizational resources.

Despite this distinction, experiences in news organizations have an important impact on journalists' perceptions of their occupation. Journalists, as members of a "semi-profession," are heavily influenced by the needs and resultant routines peculiar to their individual organizations. Journalists are socialized to the norms of the profession through subtle critiques of managers and conversations with workplace colleagues and they commonly define their goals by using those most immediately around them as a reference group. News workers often generalize conditions of their field from conditions of their specific workplaces, a shortcut pursued because of constraints on time and relative lack of audience information. Other media occupations such as advertising and public relations are also strongly influenced by organizational factors.

Researchers have frequently conceptualized journalists' commitment as an affective characteristic-as loyalty or pride in one's work. The committed journalist is assumed to have a sense of calling to the field and a recognition that the social consequences of work outweigh economic gain. Job satisfaction and evaluation of one's work organization-also affective factors-have been found to be highly predictive of commitment to the occupation, a finding that is consistent with studies of occupational commitment beyond the field of journalism.

Concrete characteristics of the workplace also have been examined as predictors of occupational commitment. Weaver and Wilhoit and Wilson found salary was influential, while Becker, Sobowale, and Cobbey found salary to be of little importance to occupational commitment but of some importance to organizational commitment. Salary has proven to be an important predictor in studies of other occupations, but the predictive power of this factor is dependent on occupational type as well as on age, socio-economic status, and length of time in the field.

In several studies journalists have been asked to give their own reasons for wanting to leave their occupation. Among the top reasons, respondents have listed low salaries, work schedule and hours, and stress level. Journalists have also said interest in other fields was important. This factor has been phrased in a variety of ways, such as "opportunities elsewhere," "need for a new challenge," and "interests changed," but each phrasing signals a belief that opportunities beyond the occupation exist and are reasonably within reach. Continuance Commitment. Both the psychology of work and sociology of work literatures discuss attitudinal, or affective, commitment, a type of commitment that reflects positive identification and positive experiences with the occupation. Another conceptualization of commitment is "continuance" commitment, which is an accumulation of investments made in pursuing an occupation and involves recognition of the costs of leaving the occupation. When journalists or others look at "opportunities elsewhere," they exhibit lower levels of continuance commitment. When alternative lines of action are open and recognized, continuance commitment to an occupation becomes less stable. Availability and attractiveness of other options are important to level of commitment. They shape the decision-making environment so that choosing another career is seen as more legitimate, or thinkable.

Studies of journalists' commitment have found that individual and background characteristics generally do not explain variability in commitment very well, but length of time spent in the occupation is highly predictive. According to Kornhauser:

To incur a commitment is to become more or less unavailable for alternative lines of action... A commitment consists in the various relations which are formed in the process of acting in a certain direction, so that to shift the line of action requires changing these relations... the strength of a commitment can be measured by the number of social spheres for which it enforces lines of action.

Commitment involves pursuing a path with consistency to the exclusion of other paths. Such a pursuit consumes resources, and these resources are perceived as investments "when they are made in anticipation of future returns and the expenditures are not returnable." Changing occupational lines may mean forfeiting considerable time and effort spent learning skills that are of little or no use outside the original occupation.

Decker suggested that individuals increase commitment to an occupation because they stake things they value in the pursuit. The higher the stakes, the greater the commitment to the occupation. Such stakes are placed either by personal choice or result from simply passing through the social structures of work and playing by the rules. For example, accruing pension plan money over time makes changing one's line of work more difficult later on.

Stakes also may be placed in the realm of personal interaction. Citing Goffman's facework theory, Decker said, "Having once claimed to be a certain kind of person, [individuals] find it necessary to act, so far as possible, in an appropriate way... A person will often find his activity constrained by the kind of front he has earlier presented in interaction." For example, an individual who has gained public recognition in a field has an investment in the public perception accrued from such recognition. To drop out of the profession after receiving and accepting acclaim would be to squander the investment. Longer tenure in an occupation also strengthens personal identification with the occupation.

It may not be necessary to have longevity in one's field before the effects of these stakes, or investments, are felt on level of commitment. Certain investments are made early in one's career as well, during education and training. Involvement in the early tasks and trappings of an occupation in college and high school represents investments of time, effort, and money by the individual and the individual's parents. Also, the role of "future journalist" may be supported by parents and other mentors, thus creating a constraining interpersonal structure.

Alutto, Hrebeniak, and Alonso found that commitment among young professionals in teaching and nursing was high. Commitment then dipped in midrange years and increased in later years. Citing Becker and Carper, they speculated that enthusiasm among neophytes in the profession was high because "formal socialization experiences" were fresh in their minds. Socialization in the form of formal education has proven to be a salient factor in other studies of occupations, and studies have shown that the learning of occupation-specific skills by adolescents in part-time jobs strengthens intrinsic orientation toward work. Early socialization has proven less important in studies of journalists' commitment. Weaver and Wilhoit found that years of education and being a journalism major correlated positively with commitment, but that the strength of prediction was weak in comparison to longevity in the field and such job-specific variables as job satisfaction and salary.

Concepts and Hypotheses. Following Becker's46and Kornhauser's conceptualizations, occupational commitment is defined in this study as a desire to engage in a consistent line of occupational activity to the exclusion of other occupations. The literature differentiates between continuance commitment, or the recognition of stake in investments made, and affective commitment, or the emotional attachment to an occupation. The definition used here is closer to continuance commitment than affective commitment, but it does not entirely preclude an affective dimension.

This study assesses three sets of predictors of occupational commitment. The first set of predictors relates to the nature of the work environment, including both perceptions of work such as level of satisfaction, and concrete characteristics of work such as salary.

As discussed, workplace experiences have proven important in socializing journalists to the field, and journalists use workplace colleagues as a reference group for deciding on appropriate practice.

Literature on newsroom decision making suggests influences from characteristics of individual news workers are strongly constrained by higher-level influences such as those at the organizational level. The second set of predictors represents investments made through involvement with the occupation during undergraduate study. These investments, or stakes, should constrain choice and encourage commitment to an occupational direction.

The third set of predictors includes investments of time, effort, and social role attachment made prior to college. Workplace predictors are introduced first, so that the possible contributions of individual-level school experiences may be assessed in the context of presumably dominant organizational influences.

This study offers a simple model to explain level of commitment to journalism among recent entrants to the field. It is expected that sentiments about job environment and concrete benefits from the workplace should have an impact on level of occupational commitment, but it is also expected that greater investments made in pursuit of a journalism career during precollege and college years should lead to a higher level of commitment to the field after controlling for workplace-related factors. Finally, greater investments in pursuit of journalism made during precollege years should lead to greater investments made during college.

Thus:

- *H*1: Positive sentiments toward one's job environment lead to greater occupational commitment.
- *H*2: Accrual of benefits from a job leads to greater occupational commitment.
- *H*3: Investments in an occupation made during college lead to greater occupational commitment.
- *H*4: Investments in an occupation made prior to college lead to greater occupational commitment.
- *H*5: Investments in an occupation during high school lead to a greater level of investment in the occupation during college.

These hypotheses were tested for the occupation of journalism, since declining commitment to journalism has received much attention in the scientific and professional literatures.

Predictors of commitment to public relations, advertising, and other media fields are also assessed for comparative purposes. The focus in all cases is on commitment of persons just entering the occupation, since investments in the occupation made prior to entry are of primary concern here.

Method and Measures

Data come from the 2000 Annual Survey of Journalism and Mass Communication Graduates, a standardized survey monitoring employment rates and salaries of graduates of journalism and mass communication programs in the United States, including Puerto Rico, The survey also tracks the curricular activities of those graduates while in college, examines their job-seeking strategies, and provides measures of the professional attitudes and behaviors of the graduates upon completion of their college studies. Each year a sample of schools is drawn from those listed in the Journalism and Mass Communication Directory published annually by AEJMC, and The journalist's Road to Success: A Career and Scholarship Guide, published by the Dow Jones Newspaper Fund, Inc. Selection of schools is probabilistic, so that those chosen represent the population of schools in the two directories. In 2000, 103 schools were drawn from the 463 unique entries of four-year journalism programs in the United States in the two directories.

Administrators at the selected schools provide the names and addresses of their spring bachelor's and master's degree recipients. A questionnaire was mailed in November 2000 to all spring graduates receiving either a bachelor's or a master's degree from the selected programs. A second questionnaire was sent to nonrespondents in January 2001 and a third mailing was sent in March 2001.

The survey was mailed to 6,670 individuals whose names and addresses were provided by the administrators of the 103 programs. A total of 3,139 returned the questionnaires by the end of May of 2001. Of these, 2,880 were from students who reported they actually had completed their degrees during the April to June 2000 period. The remaining 259 had completed their degrees either before or after the specified period, despite their inclusion in the spring graduation lists. A total of 446 questionnaires was returned undelivered and without a forwarding address. Return rate computed as the number of questionnaires returned divided by the number mailed was 47.1 per cent. Return rate computed as the number returned divided by the number mailed minus the bad addresses was 50.4 per cent. Of the 2,880 usable questionnaires, 2,734 (94.9 per cent) were from bachelor's degree recipients and 146 were from master's degree recipients.

The respondents included graduates working for a wide variety of media and nonmedia occupations. For initial analyses, only respondents performing tasks commonly considered journalistic and who also work for organizations that traditionally have a journalistic function were selected for analysis. Specifically, respondents who said they performed tasks related to editing, writing/reporting, design, graphics, photography, audiovisual production, or on-air work, and who also reported working for newspapers, magazines, wire services, radio stations, TV stations, or online publishing organizations were selected. Among these, only recipients of undergraduate degrees who reported working fulltime were selected. The final sample consisted of 449 respondents.

Consistent with other studies, the dependent variable Commitment to Journalism is operationally defined by measuring desire to spend one's working life exclusively in journalism. Four survey questions were used to measure this variable: "I expect to retire in this occupation" (1=disagree, 2=neutral, 3=agree, M = 1.81, s.d. =.78), "Do you think of the work you do as a job or as a career?" (job=1, career=2, M = 1.59, s.d. =.49), "Do you wish you had prepared for a career other than in journalism?" (yes = 1, no = 2, M = 1.77, s.d. =.42), and "The work you do is meaningful" (1=disagree, 2=neutral, 3=agree, M = 2.49, s.d. =.73). The first three measures represent the continuance element of commitment, while the final item adds an affective dimension. These four measures were standardized and summed into an index, with an alpha of.68, which was considered appropriate given the distinctiveness of the affective and continuance elements. Each measure was analysed separately as well.

The first set of independent variables derives from the respondents' jobs. These include the job perceptions of job satisfaction and pride in the organization, as well as the tangible job benefits of salary and work schedule (extent to which nonreimbursed overtime work was demanded). Job Satisfaction was measured on a 4-point scale (4 = very satisfied, 3 = somewhat satisfied, 2 = somewhat dissatisfied, 1 = very dissatisfied, M = 3.05, s.d. =.84). Pride in Organization was measured by presenting respondents with the statement "I am proud to be working for my firm/organization" and possible responses of 3 = agree, 2 = neutral/not sure and 1 = disagree (M = 2.67, s.d. =.59). Salary is measured by asking respondents to report their annual salary (M = 28,508.73, s.d. = 9,634.72). Work Schedule is measured on a scale in which a more beneficial combination of schedule and pay structure has a higher score. Respondents are presented with the statement "I must work beyond a 40-hour week" and given the following possible responses: 3 = "I am not required to do this," 2 = "I must do this, and I am paid or reimbursed" and 1 = "I must do this, but I am not paid or reimbursed" (M = 2.34, s.d. =.82). Pride in the Organization and Job Satisfaction are considered job sentiments, and in the hypotheses they are conceptualized separately from salary and work schedule, which reflect tangible job benefits. All four variables are included in the same block because of their chronological relationship relative to college and high school predictors and because they each reflect experiences with a particular organization rather than with the entire occupation.

Investments representing involvement with journalism during undergraduate study serve as the second set of independent variables. These are measured through questions about participation in journalism-related college activities (newspaper, TV and radio broadcasting, online publishing, magazines, and yearbook) and in journalism-related internships (newspaper, magazine, and TV and radio broadcasting). Each of these measures was scored as dichotomous (1 = participated, 0 = did not participate), and they were summed to create two continuous predictor variables, College Internships (M = 1.06, s.d. =.65) and College Activities (M = 1.27, s.d. =.88). Role attachment is measured by asking respondents if they were encouraged to study journalism by college teachers and counselors (0 = not encouraged, 1 = encouraged). Measures for these two types of mentors were summed to create the variable College Encouragement (M = 1.18, s.d. =.86).

Investments in time, effort, and social role attachment made by respondents prior to college represent the third set of independent variables.

These include involvement in high school journalism classes, and with high school newspapers, broadcast operations, and yearbooks. Respondents were asked if they had engaged in these activities in high school, and each individual measure was scored as dichotomous and summed to form the continuous variable High School Involvement. Strength of role attachment during high school was operationalized by asking respondents if parents, high school teachers, and counselors encouraged them to pursue journalism. Encouragement was scored as "!,"lack of encouragement was scored as "0," and responses for these three types of mentors were summed to form the continuous variable High School Encouragement. Respondents were also asked how early they decided to study journalism or communication (4 = before or during high school, 3 = after high school but prior to undergraduate education, 2 = during undergraduate education or 1 = after their undergraduate education). The variable is named Time of Decision. It is expected that respondents who decided early to study journalism would have developed a more substantial network of "social spheres" that involved journalism, which should have increased commitment.

For sake of comparison, commitment in communication fields other than journalism was assessed. Respondents consisted of all those not selected for the journalism analysis. In addition, commitment in advertising and public relations was assessed in order to provide a specific comparison with another major communication field (respondents for this sample were also part of the nonjournalism sample). Respondents included only those who said they worked in PR or advertising departments of firms and who also said they performed tasks related to ad production, ad sales, product or company promotion, corporate communication, graphic design, photography, and video production.

Data were examined to see if they fit assumptions of multiple regression. College Activities, Internships, and Salary had outliers, and these values were changed to equal the closest value not determined to be an outlier by the box plot. However, because regression results were not significantly changed by the substitution of these altered variables, and because outlying values did not represent coding errors, the original unaltered variables were left in the model. The regression models' Durbin-Watson statistics fell between 1.86 and 2.14. According to Ott, Longnecker, and Ott, uncorrelated residuals are evidenced by a Durbin-Watson statistic between 1.5 and 2.5.51 Residual plots also do not suggest nonconstant residual variance. Intercorrelations among independent variables ranged from.001 to.530, and no correlations reached a level suggesting redundancy.

Bivariate analyses of the journalism sample were conducted first as a preliminary assessment of the relationships among independent and dependent variables. The scaled dependent variable Occupational Commitment, along with the four measures used in this scale and the ten independent variables. Occupational Commitment correlated significantly with both Organizational Pride and Job Satisfaction. Contrary to expectations, neither the salary the entry-level journalist received nor the work schedule were related to occupational commitment.

Also inconsistent with expectations, the number of college media activities engaged in, the number of internships, and the amount of encouragement received to pursue the occupation did not correlate significantly with Occupational Commitment once the journalists were on the job. Similarly, the investments the entry-level journalists made in the occupation while in high school were unrelated to Occupational Commitment once they had taken a job.

Hypotheses were tested using multiple regression analysis. The indexed Occupational Commitment variable was regressed on predictors, which were clustered into three sets and entered in three different blocks. The four workplace-level predictors were entered first, followed by college-level predictors and then high-school-level predictors, reflecting the temporal ordering of possible effects. As each block was entered, its importance to the explanatory power of the overall model was assessed. Importance of individual predictors was also assessed.

The final R-square for the regression analysis was.326, which is statistically signficant at the.05 level. H1 received support, as perceptions of the workplace were important predictors of commitment. The model had an R-square of.310 with only the workplace variables entered into the equation. However, H3 and H4 received no support in the analysis of the overall model, as neither college nor high school experiences made a significant contribution to understanding commitment once job-specific predictors had been entered into the equation.

Job-specific predictors remained important after the subsequent variables were entered. In fact, all four job-specific predictors tested as significant (at the.05 level) in the final equation. However, H2 received no support, as the signs of the beta coefficients of Salary and Work Schedule were both negative, contrary to prediction. In other words, once Organizational Pride and Job Satisfaction are considered, Occupational Commitment actually is higher for people low in salary and for those with unfavorable work schedules. It may be that the Commitment is an expression of justification for working in a negative compensation situation.

Time of Decision is a significant, though not strong, predictor of Occupational Commitment in the final regression analysis. Consistent with H4, the earlier one decides on journalism as a career, the greater the commitment later on.

To determine if individual items in the Occupational Commitment index were related to investments made by entry-level journalists, analyses were repeated for each of the four measures in the index. In general, findings remain largely unchanged. Pride in the Organization and Job Satisfaction are the key predictors of each of the four items in the Occupational Commitment index, though they predict the more affective measure Work is Meaningful most strongly.

In the bivariate analysis, college and high school investments are related to the Plan to Retire in Occupation measure of Occupational Commitment, but not consistently to the others. Only High School investments significantly change the amount of variance explained when Plan to Retire in Occupation is regressed on predictors.

Findings for commitment to PR/advertising and for nonjournalism jobs are highly similar to the findings on commitment to journalism. For both the PR/advertising and nonjournalism samples, Job Satisfaction and Pride in the Organization are the strongest predictors of the indexed commitment variable. Pride in the Organization tested as somewhat more important in both of these analyses as in the journalism analysis. Having college internships tested as significant in the nonjournalism analysis, though the correlation is not strong. The significance of this factor may be attributable to the large N in this analysis. No other college or precollege factors were predictive of the commitment index for PR/Advertising or for nonjournalists.

Does this mean early experiences with the occupation are of no consequence? Analysis of bivariate relationships between college and high school investments suggests otherwise. These findings show that those who get on the journalism track prior to college are more likely to be involved in journalism activities once in college, thus lending tentative support to H5. Involvement in journalism in high school also significantly predicts degree of encouragement received from journalism teachers and counselors in college, which suggests precollege socialization to the field makes college students more comfortable establishing relationships with mentors in the field. Though precollege socialization does not directly predict involvement in internships, the moderately strong correlation between campus media involvement and internship involvement (r =.325) suggests early socialization may work indirectly on the decision to apply for internships. Not surprisingly, results show that students who become involved in campus media are more likely to land internships later on.

Previous studies show that internships and involvement with campus media also significantly enhance chances of pursuing journalistic work and of finding work. An additional analysis was conducted to assess the effects of college and precollege socialization variables on looking for journalistic work (1 = looked for journalism job, 0 = did not look for journalism job). This analysis was conducted on the entire data set of 2,804, and just under half of the respondents reported looking for a journalism job (newspaper, TV, radio, wire, popular and trade magazines). Both OLS and logistic regressions were conducted with similar results. The R-square of the OLS model was.141, which is not strong but is significant at the.01 level. Internships and Campus Media Activities were the strongest predictors, with beta weights of.275 and.128, respectively. Encouragement from college teachers and counselors was also a significant predictor of looking for journalistic work, as was Time of Decision. The addition of precollege predictors in a block had a significant, but small, effect on the predictive power of the model, as the R-square rose from.137 to.141. It appears college-level socialization is an important predictor of the decision to pursue journalistic work, and precollege socialization has a direct, but weak, effect.

Overall findings suggest precollege socialization predicts involvement in college, which in turn predicts looking for journalistic work. Despite the importance of the high school investments in explaining some of the subsequent investments made in college, neither investments in high school nor investments in college make much difference in explaining Occupational Commitment once the journalist or other communication worker starts the job. The initial job experiences are what have impact on the commitment the individual feels toward journalism at that time.

Findings demonstrate some support for the proposed model but offer only limited support for the concept of continuance commitment-that pursuit of a career path to the exclusion of other paths is encouraged by nonreturnable investments made along the way. As expected, affect for one's work environment was an important predictor of commitment, but college and precollege experiences, conceptualized as investments, have little direct influence on commitment. This finding reinforces prior literature on news work that suggests organizational influences trump individual-level influences. The same pattern is seen in advertising and public relations and other nonjournalism communication fields, and the similarity of this pattern challenges the idea that journalism experiences are unique occupationally.

For both journalists and nonjournalists, job satisfaction and pride in the organization are the strongest predictors. Respondents appear to be extrapolating positive experiences from their specific organizations to the wider occupation. For journalists, salary and work schedule are only weakly related to commitment, and the relationship was unexpectedly inverse. Apparently perceived long-term commitment is highly related to less tangible aspects of the job such as, perhaps, the enjoyment of performing tasks, or camaraderie with colleagues. Poorer tangible job benefits such as salary and work schedule may predict higher commitment because they reflect an expression of justification for being poorly compensated in a concrete way. It also may be that higher salary predicts lower commitment because it reflects higher marketability, which may increase the availability of alternative lines of work. Such opportunities may lure recent entrants away from the field.

It is disconcerting that despite years of socialization to the field-and presumably, to the occupation's social and political importance-so many graduates should judge the work of journalism in an organizational rather than in an occupational context. This finding reinforces the view that journalism has a relatively weak professional orientation. However, occupational commitment may have more salience for longtime journalists. Journalism may begin to look more like an occupation for those who have accumulated more substantial investments in time, energy, and role attachment, as well as concrete investments such as mortgages and pensions.

There are some effects from socializing early to the field, but these are indirect and incremental. These factors operate in the short term, with one link in the chain leading only to the next:

High school involvement leads to involvement with campus media and relationships with mentors in college, which lead to internships, which lead to the pursuit of journalism jobs. With the exception of Time of Decision, effects do not reflect cumulative investments made over the span of one's college and precollege years.

The significance of Time of Decision for journalists lends limited support to the concept of continuance commitment, though this was not a significant predictor for nonjournalists. Deciding early proves significant as a predictor of the commitment index and of planning to retire, each of which are closely related to continuance commitment. Making an early decision to pursue journalism apparently has no impact on finding journalism to be a meaningful pursuit. In contrast, the affective factors of satisfaction and pride in one's organization were most highly related to finding meaning in one's work. These findings recommend treating affective commitment as distinct from continuance commitment.

One highly relevant investment that may be indicated by the early decision variable is choice of college. Individuals who know prior to college that they wish to study journalism are more likely to select a college because of its journalism programme. For such an individual to consider leaving the field is to consider the possibility that family money was wasted, and that a mistake was made in an important life decision. In contrast, an individual who picked a college on vague criteria and decided to study journalism only after entering college has not risked as much and may have been entertaining alternative lines of work all along.

There are implications from this study for the news industry. The importance of pride in the organization suggests early entrants value the quality of the work produced at their organization, and that this pride connects with perceived long-term commitment to the field. Managers should be sensitive to the importance of journalistic quality to employee commitment, as well as to the value of intangible rewards such as work assignment, colleague camaraderie, and pride in publishing work. The importance of deciding to pursue journalism early and the indirect effects of early socialization suggest industry leaders should support opportunities for young people to learn about journalism prior to college. Educators should also look for ways to collaborate with the industry.

Findings also have social relevance, within a public interest framework. Though the efforts of individual news workers and the effects of such efforts are constrained by factors on higher levels of analysis, it seems logical that a more committed and more thoroughly socialized work force should better serve the public. Of some concern is the finding that recent entrants to the field dwell more on their organizational experiences than on the broader purposes of journalistic work. Results here suggest that journalism education may be failing to instill the idea that journalism transcends particular work environments, though it may be too much to expect recent entrants to have this broad perspective. Studies of commitment by long-time journalists would shed more light on the implications of reduced commitment.

14

Traditional Media and the Internet Influence Credibility

While the debate over whether the Internet as a whole should be judged as a credible source of news and information has ebbed as more users have flocked to news sites sponsored by traditional media, the question remains of how much faith users should place in certain online components such as Weblogs (also known as blogs).

Weblogs, diarystyle Websites that generally offer observations and news listed chronologically on the site as well as commentary and recommended links, surged in popularity after the events of 9/11.

Bloggers (those who create blogs) and traditional journalists argue over how much faith to place in messages posted on the blogosphere (the blogging universe). But while several studies have examined credibility of online media, scholars have paid little attention to how credible users judge Weblogs. Metzger, Flanagin, Eyal, Lemus, and McCann argue that one weakness of online credibility studies is that they examine only the Web and ignore other Internet components.

Alternative sources of news and information, such as Weblogs, have been ignored. However, their credibility deserves attention for several reasons: First, they are a growing phenomenon, increasing from an estimated 30,000 in 1998 to at least three million by the beginning of 2004. Second, while the number of blog users is small (only 17 per cent of Internet users have ever visited a blog), their influence may exceed their readership. Because many blog users are politically interested and active, they are wooed by tech-savvy politicians. For instance, blog users may have given a boost to presidential hopeful Howard Dean. Also, many journalists consider blogs a trustworthy source of information and rely on them for information and story ideas. Blogs have been credited for bringing to light stories ignored by the traditional media, such as racist remarks by Senate Majority Leader Trent Lott that led to his resignation.

This study surveyed Weblog users online to investigate how credible they view blogs as compared to other sources. This study will also explore how reliance on Weblogs, as well as traditional and online media sources, predicts credibility of Weblogs.

TRADITIONAL MEDIA AND CREDIBILITY

Beginning in the 1940s, many researchers studied the impact of the credibility of sources on interpersonal influence, examining what characteristics made a speaker persuasive. Similarly, researchers examined characteristics of persuasive messages. Studies of the credibility of a medium, however, arose from concerns in the newspaper industry first about the rising number of people turning to radio for news and then about the number relying on television. The rise of the Internet has led to a host of recent credibility studies comparing traditional sources with this emerging medium.

NONTRADITIONAL MEDIA AND CREDIBILITY

Credibility research has focused almost entirely on mainstream media, particularly newspapers. Many of these studies were conducted by news organizations that feared that falling credibility would signal further decline in readership and advertising profits.

CREDIBILITY OF NONTRADITIONAL MEDIA

Several studies have explored the impact of nontraditional media such as talk radio and late night talk shows in the last three presidential elections on voters and on the campaign itself while others have explored the content of such nontraditional media. While scant attention has been paid to how credible voters find information in nontraditional media, anecdotal evidence suggests that users judge them as more credible than mainstream media.

For instance, scholars have noted that talk radio and talk television emerged as forces in the 1992 presidential campaign because the public was dissatisfied with media coverage. Users could talk directly to candidates or to talk show hosts, rather than have information filtered through the press.

While traditional media attempt to balance coverage, talk radio hosts openly attack both opposition candidates as well as what they perceive as liberal media coverage. Political talk show hosts present themselves as true authorities on political issues while claiming traditional media hide or lie about facts, a suspicion apparently held by talk show listeners.

Finally, listeners may trust the information they receive from talk radio because they believe the hosts are more open about their biases than traditional journalists who subtly interject their views into their stories. Early Internet Users and Credibility. Some of the earliest Internet credibility studies were conducted before traditional media became established in online publishing. During the mid-1990s the Internet was compared to a frontier outpost where discussion was "free, sometimes pointed, often blunt, and frequently rebellious." Critics suggested several reasons why the Web should be judged as a less credible source of information than traditional media: Anyone could post information to the Web, and these sites created by individuals spouting their views often appeared as credible as those hosted by reliable sources.

Such sites lacked editorial oversight and did not have the professional and social pressures to provide accurate and unbiased information. Also, the Internet was rife with rumors and misinformation, and several parody sites, which looked like official sites, sprouted up on the Internet.

However, the public, particularly Internet users, did not share these fears. While some studies found that the Internet lagged behind traditional media in terms of credibility, most found Web information just as, or more, credible. Many of these studies only examined Internet users. However, when studies compared users to nonusers, findings indicated that those who relied on the Internet for news and information were more likely to judge it as credible.

Weblog Credibility

Clear lines have been drawn between blog users and traditional journalists on the question of blog credibility. Critics advance the same arguments made against the Internet in its earliest days. Anyone can create a blog, and bloggers are not bound by ethical and professional standards of trained journalists. Indeed, a leading blogger, Sean-Paul Kelley of the Agonist, was accused of stealing information from a subscription intelligence service and posting it to his Weblog. Similarly, bloggers are not bound by standards of objectivity; most have strong views that they express openly.

As Instapundit blogger Glenn Reynolds says, "A blog is a disclosure of the blogger's biases." Weblogs do not undergo gatekeeping or editing to cull misinformation, sharpen prose, and ensure what is written is fair. Finally, many bloggers use pseudonyms such as Loco Parentis, Big Arm Woman, or No Watermelons, making it difficult to judge the credibility of the information, on their site.

Blogs do rely, however, on peer review of other bloggers to point out mistakes that can be easily and prominently corrected. Users may find Weblogs more credible because they are independent rather than controlled by corporate interests; bloggers may discuss issues traditional media shy away from because they might hurt corporations. Blogs also run stories from around the world that were unavailable or ignored by traditional media. Like political talk radio listeners, then, Weblog users are likely to consider blogs a highly credible source of information.

TRADITIONAL MEDIA USE AND WEBLOG CREDIBILITY

Observers relate the rise in blogs to growing distrust and dislike of the traditional media, particularly after 9/11, which saw the number of blogs increase due to the perception that traditional media coverage was overly sympathetic to Arab nations and their peoples. Most bloggers and their readers are conservative, viewing the media as liberal, and tend to see blogs as a new and better journalism that is opinionated, independent, and personal. While studies of traditional media suggest that opinionated writing lowers credibility, bloggers and blog readers contend that Weblogs contain thoughtful analysis of the news events missing from mainstream media. Bloggers and readers criticize the media, and some sites, such as talkingpointsmemo.com, buzzmachine.com, and asmallvictory.net, are devoted to critiquing media coverage. Bloggers and readers routinely fact check stories in traditional media and gleefully point out errors.

While bloggers and blog readers are critical of traditional media, they do not ignore them. Instapundit's Reynolds notes that to be a critic of the media means that you must pay attention to them. Because most bloggers are not independent newsgatherers, they must rely heavily on the Web for their content, and much of that comes from traditional media. Also, bloggers often try to lend authority to their sites by providing links to traditional media sites.

Conversely, although journalists may perceive bloggers as "wannabe amateurs badly in need of some skills and editors," they increasingly rely on blogs for story tips, information, and access to stories from media throughout the world. Further, while many political blogs are written by armchair observers spouting their views, many journalists and some news organizations like MSNBC host their own blogs.

Studies consistently show that heavy media users judge the Internet as highly credible. Indeed, traditional media use in some studies is the strongest predictor of Internet credibility. Those who go online for political news and information tend to be political junkies, heavy users of traditional political sources of information such as CNN, Sunday morning public affairs shows, and newsmagazines. The Internet supplements rather than replaces traditional sources of political information. Also, traditional media users tend to be highly media literate, knowing what sources to trust and what to discard, and have learned where to go online for credible news.

INTERNET USE AND WEBLOG CREDIBILITY

Studies of mainstream media suggest that the more people rely on the media for news and information, the more they will judge that information as credible. Similarly, people judge their preferred news source as the most credible. Many studies examining Web credibility also find that the more people go online the more credible they rate the information they find. Greer discovered that amount of time online was the strongest predictor of whether an online medium would be judged as credible. On the other hand, Johnson and Kaye discovered that for both political and sports news, amount of Web use failed to predict online credibility, a finding supported by others. Johnson and Kaye found that Internet users were not heavy users of traditional media and speculated that because of their limited experience with traditional media, they were not well trained to judge which Internet sources are credible.

Anecdotal evidence suggests that Internet use would predict Weblog credibility. First, blog users are heavy Internet users. Blog users are likely to be media literate and know what sources they trust and do not trust.

Blogs and Political Attitudes

With the exception of trust in the government, political variables have not proven strong predictors of online credibility. For instance, Johnson and Kaye found that political trust was the second strongest predictor of credibility of online newspaper and TV news, and strong partisans tended to judge online media as believable.

Political attitudes may have little influence on online credibility because studies suggest that online users, rather than being socially isolated and apathetic, are politically interested and are more likely to seek out information from the media than the general public. However, researchers are split on whether they are more knowledgeable than the average citizen. While trust in government initially was not a strong predictor of credibility, it has emerged as a stronger influence as the audience has become more mainstream and trust in government has increased.

Political variables may have a limited effect on credibility judgments of blog users because many are strong political activists. While some Weblogs and blog readers lean toward the left, the blogosphere is predominately right of centre, either conservative or libertarian. Blog readers are also political junkies. The American Demographic survey found that political sites were the second most visited type of Weblogs behind personal or family blogs.

Blogs and Demographics

Studies of the Web offer conflicting findings about the influence of demographics on Web credibility. Earlier studies found that those who judged the Internet as credible were, paradoxically, those who tended to use the media the least: young females of lower education and income. Demographic influence, however, sometimes declined after controlling for other factors. Some recent studies have also found fewer connections between demographics and credibility, particularly after controlling for other factors. Johnson and Kaye speculated that as the Web has moved from being a bastion of young, white, wealthy, well-educated males to one that is more demographically mainstream, the influence of demographics has declined. However, Flanagin and Metzger reported that men rated both message and site credibility significantly higher than women. Johnson and Kaye, in a study of how online experience influenced credibility judgments, found that demographics proved to be the strongest predictor of credibility, with young men with lower education rating the Internet as less credible. The authors speculated that because men had been online longer than women, spend more time online, and engage in more activities, that experience may help them judge which sites are credible and which ones are not. Demographics should predict Weblog credibility because, like the Web in general during the mid1990s, the blogosphere is populated with younger white men of high incomes.

Research Questions

This study poses the following research questions:

- *RQ*1: To what degree will Weblog users view Weblogs as a credible source of information?
- *RQ*2: Will Weblog users judge Weblogs as significantly more credible than other online sources?
- *RQ*3: Will Weblog users judge Weblogs as significantly more credible than traditional sources of information?
- *RQ*4: To what degree will reliance on Weblogs predict Weblog credibility after controlling for demographics, political attitudes, interest and knowledge of nonpolitical news, as well as reliance on traditional and other online media?

Method

A survey aimed at Web log readers was posted online from 23 April to 22 May 2003. The survey was linked from 131 Weblogs of diverse ideologies and 14 Weblog-oriented bulletin boards/electronic mailing lists. Respondents also learned about the survey from announcements sent to Weblog-oriented chat rooms and to bloggers who agreed to post the survey URL. Additionally, a "snowball" technique was used where respondents could automatically forward the survey to fellow blog readers.

Generating a random sample of Weblog users would be very difficult because there is no central registry of blog readers or any way to identify them from Internet users who do not access Weblogs. Unlike telephone and mail surveys, samples cannot be produced through census lists or random digit-dialing-type techniques such as random e-mail generators. Therefore, this study employs a convenience sample. Although the findings cannot be generalized to Internet or Weblog users as a whole, they do present a picture of the 3,747 survey respondents. Dependent Measures. Media credibility is generally defined as the worthiness of being believed, and it is often measured as a multidimensional construct consisting of believability, accuracy, fairness, and depth of information. Respondents were asked to rate on a 5-point scale the degree of believability, fairness, accuracy, and depth of Weblogs. The 5-point scale ranged from "not at all" to "very" (believable, fair, accurate, or in-depth). Scores were combined into a Weblog credibility index (Cronbach's alpha =.79).

Independent Measures

Credibility of Traditional and Online Sources. Respondents were asked to compare traditional and online media in terms of believability, fairness, accuracy, and depth using the same 5-point scale.

Respondents marked their assessments of traditionally delivered broadcast television news, cable television news, newspapers, radio news, talk radio, and news magazines, and of the following online sources: broadcast television news sites, cable television news sites, newspaper sites, radio news sites, and news magazines sites.

Scores were combined into a credibility index for each traditional and online medium (alphas for traditional media range from.87 to.92 and for online media from.83 to.89).

Source Reliance. Past studies indicate that the credibility of a medium or source of information is strongly related to reliance on a source. Using a 5-point scale ranging from "heavily rely on" to "don't rely at all," respondents assessed their levels of reliance on the same six traditional media and five online sources.

Political attitudes: Respondents assessed their knowledge and involvement in politics and in nonpolitical issues in relation to their Weblog use. Using a 5-point scale ranging from "greatly increased" to "greatly decreased," respondents judged whether Weblogs influenced their involvement in politics and their knowledge about political and general news issues. Respondents also indicated their degree of interest in politics, in general news, and in current events on a O to 10 scale.

Trust in the government was measured as a summated index of three items from the National Election Studies conducted by the University of Michigan: "Most of our leaders are devoted to service," "Politicians never tell us what they really think," and "I don't think public officials care much about what people like me think." The polarity was reversed on the second and third statements to create the index (alpha =.75).

Demographics. Gender, age, income, and education data were also collected.

Data Analysis: First, frequencies were run on the Weblog, online sources, and traditional media credibility indices. second, paired f-tests were calculated to compare the credibility of Weblogs to each online and each traditionally delivered medium. Lastly, hierarchical regression was conducted to examine whether reliance on Weblogs predicts credibility of Weblogs after controlling for demographics, political attitudes, general news interest and knowledge, and reliance on traditional media and online sources. The predictors were entered into the regression models as blocks, with demographic variables entered first, followed by political and general news variables. Measures of reliance on traditional media were entered third, followed by reliance on online sources.

Results

Respondent Profile. The online survey was completed by 3,747 respondents. Almost 9 out of 10 Weblog readers are white (89.3 per cent), and 76.5 per cent are male. The respondents are highly educated, with 92.6 per cent reporting some college or higher, and 41.8 per cent earning more than $65,001 per year.

Just over half (52.5 per cent) credit Weblogs with increasing their levels of political involvement. Almost 9 out of 10 claim that they have become more knowledgeable about politics (87.3 per cent) and about general news and current events (88.7 per cent) since they started reading Weblogs. Almost threequarters of the respondents are very interested in politics (64.9 per cent) and general news and current events (67.8 per cent).

They are politically interested and knowledgeable, but only moderately trusting of government. Slightly less than one-half (47 per cent) report high to very high levels of trust in the government, 30.9 per cent are moderately trustful, and 22.1 per cent claim low to very low degrees of trust.

Respondents have been online for just over 71/2 years, spending about 9.1 hours per week interacting with bloggers, reading comments, and following links to additional information, and have been doing so for 1 year and 9 months on average, which coincides with the post 9/11 popularity surge of Weblogs. Additionally, 64.5 per cent seek information from what they consider conservative or very conservative Weblogs, whereas only 16.3 per cent turn to liberal or very liberal Weblogs, and the remaining 20.2 per cent look for more moderate information. The demographic profile of the respondents and the types of Weblogs they visit closely mirror Weblog reader profiles reported by others.

CREDIBILITY OF ONLINE AND TRADITIONAL SOURCES

Weblogs

Almost threequarters (73.6 per cent) of Weblog readers view Weblogs as moderately to very credible and only 3.5 per cent consider them "not at all" or "not very credible".

When the credibility index is broken into its four components (believable, fair, accurate, depth), depth of information emerges as a Weblog's strongest attribute; 72.2 per cent of respondents think of Weblogs as "moderately" to "very" in-depth sources of information.

Weblogs are judged moderately to very believable by 59.6 per cent. Blog users seem to acknowledge that accuracy of Weblogs may be questionable; 50.2 per cent consider them "somewhat" or "not very" accurate. Additionally, respondents seem aware of Weblog biases with 61.6 per cent claiming that Weblogs are "somewhat" or "not very" fair.

Online Media Sites

Weblog readers rated online newspapers the most credible of online media, although all online sources were generally thought of as only "somewhat" credible. However, only 42.7 per cent rate online newspapers as "moderately" or "very" credible. Online radio news sites and broadcast television sites were judged as the least credible with 26.7 per cent and 29.0 per cent, respectively, considering them as "not very" or "not at all credible."

Traditional Media

Traditional media do not fare much better. Printed newspapers and news magazines had the highest percentage of respondents rating them as moderately to very credible sources, 46.5 per cent and 43.7 per cent, respectively; however, both had an almost equal percentage rating them as "somewhat" credible. Generally, Weblog users view traditional media as only "somewhat" credible.

Weblogs Compared to Online Media Sites. RQ2 asked whether respondents view Weblogs as more credible (M=14.3) than other online sources. Paired sample t-tests were used for comparisons. Weblogs were more credible than any other online source: online broadcast television, online cable television news, online newspapers, online news magazines, and online radio news. Online broadcast television and online radio news have the lowest mean (M=10.3, M=10.4, respectively) credibility scores, whereas online newspapers had the highest (M=12.0).

Weblogs Compared to Traditional Media

RQ3 involved comparing Weblogs to traditionally delivered media. Weblogs were judged significantly more credible than any traditional medium: broadcast television news, cable television news, newspapers, news magazines, radio news, and talk radio. Broadcast television (M=9.4) and over-the-air talk radio (M=9.8) are the two least credible traditional sources and newspapers (M=12.3) and newsmagazines (M=12.2) the most credible.

Predictors of Weblog Credibility

RQ4 asks whether Weblog credibility can be predicted by Weblog reliance after controlling for reliance on traditional media and other online sources, and political attitudes, general news interest and knowledge, and demographics.

Even after controlling for other variables, reliance on Weblogs is a strong positive and significant predictor of perceptions of Weblog credibility. The more users rely on Weblogs, the higher their assessments of credibility. Reliance on Weblogs explains between 12.7 per cent and 14.6 per cent of the perceptions of Weblog credibility. Reliance on five of the six traditional media and on the online sources also significantly, but weakly, predicts Weblog credibility; however, all but two of those relationships were negative. Reliance on traditional media accounts for an additional.1 per cent - 1.8 per cent of the variance, and reliance on online sources for an additional 1 per cent.

Political involvement, political knowledge, political interest, and general news knowledge are weak, but consistent, predictors of Weblog credibility, but general news interest is not. Trust in government is also a weak, but significant, predictor. The political and general news variables, however, explain a greater percentage of the variability (about 15 per cent) than do the online and traditional reliance measures and about the same amount as the Weblog reliance variables. None of the demographic variables predicts Weblog credibility.

Reliance on Broadcast Television and Online Broadcast Television Websites

Perceptions of Weblog credibility are significantly, but negatively and weakly, predicted by reliance on broadcast television news and their online counterparts. The less Weblog users rely on broadcast television news and broadcast news Websites, the more they rely on Weblogs and, thus, the higher they rate Weblog credibility.

Reliance on Cable Television News and Online Cable Television Websites

Reliance on cable television news significantly, but weakly, predicts credibility of Weblogs. The more a Weblog reader relies on cable television news the higher the credibility of Weblogs. Conversely, less reliance on cable television news sites leads to perceptions of Weblog credibility. Those Weblog readers who view Weblogs as credible are more likely to watch cable television news than to connect to cable television news online.

Reliance on Newspapers and Online Newspapers

Reliance on both printed and online newspapers predicts Weblog credibility, respectively. Less reliance on newspapers and their online sites leads to higher Weblog credibility.

Reliance on Radio News, Talk Radio, and Radio News Site

Over-the air talk radio is a significant and positive predictor. The greater the reliance on talk radio, the higher the Weblog credibility. Online radio news, on the other hand, is a significant but negative predictor. Weblog users who rely on talk radio but not on online radio Websites for news and information are more likely to judge Weblogs as highly credible. Reliance on broadcast radio news is the only medium, traditional or online, that is not a significant predictor.

Reliance on News Magazines and Online News Magazines, Reliance on both print and online news magazines significantly, but negatively and weakly, predicts Weblog credibility. Weblog readers with low levels of reliance on news magazines are more likely to rate Weblogs as highly credible.

This study surveyed Weblog users online to discover how credible they viewed blogs and how judgments of Weblog credibility compare to traditional and online media sources. This study also explored the degree to which reliance on Weblogs, as well as traditional and online media sources, predicts Weblog credibility. Almost three-quarters of respondents view Weblogs as moderately to very credible and only 3.5 per cent rate them not at all or not very credible. An important reason users say they rely on blogs is because they provide more depth and more thoughtful analysis than is available in other media.

On the other hand, fewer than four in ten thought blogs were fair. However, while fairness may be considered a hallmark of traditional journalism, bias is likely seen as a virtue by blog users. The majority rate themselves as conservative and almost two-thirds said they sought information from conservative or very conservative sites. Blog readers are seeking out information to support their views and are likely to consider conservative information they receive from blogs as highly credible.

Users view blogs as a new and better form of journalism than the mainstream media, one that is opinionated, analytical, independent, and personal. Not surprisingly, then, Weblog users judged blogs as significantly more credible than other media. However, this does not mean that bloggers do not consider some mainstream media credible. The plurality considered both online and traditional newspapers, traditional news magazines, and online cable television news as moderately to very credible and both online news magazines and traditional cable television news also recorded moderate credibility scores. These ratings for print media and cable television were similar to those found in a study of politically interested Internet users. The moderate scores for print media and cable news may reflect bloggers' and blog readers' paradoxical attitude toward traditional media. They may distrust the media, but bloggers link to media sites and pay attention to media content, even if only to hunt for mistakes and look for what they consider bias.

Weblog reliance was the only strong predictor of Weblog credibility. These results parallel studies of traditional media that the more one uses a medium, the more credible one judges it. Amount of reliance may also be a strong predictor of Weblog credibility because media consumers determine the credibility of a source by using various cues such as reputation of the medium and style of delivery. For newbies, Weblogs may not appear credible. Most are a series of short journal entries with links to other information; they do not look like traditional media. Furthermore, the personal, opinionated writing style that attracts blog users may put off some newcomers used to the more balanced, disinterested writing style of traditional media. Finally, while traditional media claim to be nonbiased, most news Weblogs make no apologies for being conservative, liberal, or libertarian. Visiting blogs of a different political stripe than one's own may be particularly off putting for a new user. But as the user finds a blog with views matching his or her own and adjusts to the style of reporting, subsequent greater use of the blog may mean he or she will judge it credible.

Past studies have found that reliance on traditional media consistently is the strongest predictor of online credibility. This study found that both online and traditional media reliance were weak predictors of Weblog credibility. More important, most relationships were negative, meaning that those who rely little on traditional media are more likely to view blogs as credible.

Past studies have found that the Internet has served as a supplement to traditional information for news and information. Internet users are news junkies who judge online and traditional sources as equally credible and rely on both to survey the news environment. However, blog users distrust traditional media and see Weblogs as a viable alternative.

However, the more blog readers use talk radio, the more credible they view Weblogs, even though blog users did not rate talk radio as highly credible. In many ways, Weblogs are online versions of talk radio. Talk show listeners can talk directly to talk show hosts or guests; Weblog users can either e-mail the blog host directly or post comments to the blog. Both blogs and talk radio are dominated by conservative hosts who openly attack political opponents and what they perceive as liberal press coverage. Blog users may trust information they receive from Weblogs because they believe the hosts do not hide their biases. Similarly, while blog readers praise Weblogs for their depth of coverage, talk radio also is applauded by its users for depth. While early studies suggested that talk radio listeners were socially isolated and politically alienated, later studies presented talk radio listeners as politically interested and active, with high levels of political involvement and political knowledge, but low levels of trust in government.

This study's Weblog users also were politically interested, involved, active, and knowledgeable, but with only moderate trust in government. Furthermore, these variables positively, though weakly, predicted credibility of Weblogs.

Weblog credibility was also positively, though weakly, predicted by cable television use. Blog users who tire of the so-called liberal leanings of broadcast news may be taking shelter in cable networks such as Fox who have aligned themselves on the right end of the political spectrum.

The study has limitations, of course. Reaching the small population of Internet users who have visited blogs is a challenge because traditional methods of data collection do not readily apply to the Internet.

Though posting a survey online is recognized as an effective method of collecting data, limitations arise from the lack of random selection. This study relied on a self-selected convenience sample, and, therefore, results cannot be generalized to the Internet as a whole or even to blog users. As Babbie noted, however, in situations where random probability sampling is not possible, nonprobability sampling is acceptable.

The Internet is conducive to purposive sampling, as subsets within the larger population of users can be identified and solicited through announcements posted on message boards, sent out to special mailing lists, and through hyperlinks posted on key online sites, as employed here. Careful use of this type of purposive sampling generates results that may be representative of a specific subset of Internet users, but not the larger population. Still, the demographic profile of the Weblog readers who responded to this study and the types of Weblogs they visit closely mirror the Weblog reader profiles reported by others.

This study suggested that demographically, Weblog users resembled early Internet users: white males with high incomes and high levels of education. Past research indicates that as Internet users became more representative of the demographic mainstream, credibility scores for online and traditional media rose. Future studies could find if Weblog users follow a similar trend, or whether blog readers remain a distinct group of Internet users who maintain their dislike and distrust of the traditional media.

Elizabeth Custer's publicity efforts are examined here through the theoretical and historical lenses of image restoration and public memory. Public relations did not exist as an occupation at the time of Custer's death in 1876, but Cutlip has shown that Americans had experimented with propaganda, press agentry, and publicity since Europeans founded the colonies. Beginning in the 1820s, women promoted abolition, temperance, and women's suffrage by developing a broad range of publicity tactics. Amos Kendall served as a proto-press secretary for President Andrew Jackson during the 1830s, railroads used press agents, and P.T. Barnum created innovative publicity tactics to promote his circus and museum from the 1840s to the 1880s. Such diverse organizations as Westinghouse, the University of Michigan, churches, and the executive branch of the U.S. government established press bureaus or officers by the turn of the century. Because of the controversial nature of General Custer's death-some blamed him for the massacre, others praised him as a hero-Elizabeth perceived a need to protect his memory. Her campaign is, then, another example of the nineteenth century's burgeoning attempts to influence public opinion through publicity, in this case undertaken to repair an image.

The theory of image restoration was unknown during Libbie Custer's lifetime, but understanding it can help shed light on her efforts. As articulated by Benoit, image restoration theory suggests that when mistakes are criticized, "our image is threatened, we feel compelled to offer explanations, defence, justifications, rationalizations, apologies, or excuses for our behaviour." Benoit identified five strategies that are commonly used in order to try to restore one's image following a transgression: denial, evading responsibility, corrective action, mortification, and reducing the offensiveness of the event. Accompanying tactics include bolstering, or relating positive attributes or past actions; minimization, which suggests the transgression was not as bad as it first seemed; differentiation, or comparing the action to something worse that could have been done; transcendence, which means providing a different frame of reference; attacking one's accuser; and compensation, or remunerating the victim to offset negative feelings."

Scholars have recognized a connection between publicity and public memory, which Bodnar defines as a "body of beliefs about the past that help a public or society understand both its past and its present, and, by implication, its future." Lang and Lang have noted elements upon which the "durability of reputation" depends, including not only the efforts of the notable person, but "the availability of others" who "have a stake in preserving or giving a boost" to that person's reputation after death. The retention of social memory, according to Gross, "is not accidental, but purposeful, intentional, and institutionally supported." Schudson noted that "memory is sometimes located in collectively created monuments and markers: books, holidays, statues, souvenirs.... These are dedicated memory forms, cultural artifacts explicitly and selfconsciously designed to preserve memories and ordinarily intended to have general pedagogical influences."

The endurance of Custer's memory can be explained, in part, because he fits a heroic mold. "No matter the era or continent, heroes exhibit similar attributes: distinctive physical skills, an exemplary response to a set of challenges or a particular challenge, and admirable moral characteristics," according to Winfield. The hero, she argued, "must exhibit a greatness of soul in the connection with a particular pursuit." Custer's "particular pursuit," though a spectacular failure in military terms, represented a very public sacrifice. Boorstin noted that American heroes also possess a "common touch" and must "embody popular virtues." The republican hero of the nineteenth century was "marked not by the exceptional intellectual ability or elite birth of the founding fathers," Winfield explained, "but rather as a publicly spirited, sacrificing citizen, regardless of origin."

Despite the many studies focusing on memory and American journalism, little attention has been paid to the influence of publicity efforts of people who fall outside a traditional definition of "journalist." One of the powerful institutions credited with influencing American public memory is the press, which uses commemorations, historical analogies, and historical contexts in its reportage, according to Edy. She argued that "journalists' depictions of the past have repercussions for the ways in which a community relates to its past." The widow Elizabeth Custer was not a newspaper reporter or editor, but her voice was often represented on the pages of U.S. newspapers and magazines, and her writings regularly appeared there. Research has examined the activities-and the public image and memory-of self-promoters of the era such as William F. "Buffalo Bill" Cody and Carry Nation. However, this study is the first to examine a personal publicity campaign and its simultaneous contribution to the construction of the collective memory of a heroic figure. How did Elizabeth Custer's publicity campaign, as reflected in the press, contribute to the image restoration and public memory of her husband, a controversial figure?

To answer that question, this study examines newspaper and magazine articles that reflect Elizabeth's efforts. Press coverage of George and Elizabeth Custer was located via keyword search of newspaper and magazine indices from 1876 to 1934. In all, 265 articles were examined for this study, including those Elizabeth Custer penned, reviews and excerpts of her books, announcements and coverage of her lectures and charity benefits, brief items in social or "personals" columns, reports of her travels, coverage of her attempts to secure military pension for herself and others from her husband's regiments, coverage of her thoughts on anniversaries and memorials, her opinions about the frontier, and finally her obituaries and reports of her donations of Custer relics as part of her estate.

Elizabeth Clift Bacon, known as Libbie, was born on April 8, 1841, in Monroe, Michigan. She graduated from boarding school in 1862 and the following year met George Armstrong Custer, who had been born in New Rumley, Ohio, on December 5, 1839. A controversial character even in his youth, he had graduated-at the bottom of his class-from the U. S. military academy in June 1861. As a cavalry officer he was promoted numerous times for gallantry and meritorious services during the Civil War, achieving the wartime rank of major-general at the age of 25. He married Elizabeth in 1864, and throughout most of the twelve years of their marriage she followed him to military posts, first in the South then throughout the American West-Kentucky, Texas, Kansas, the Dakota territory, and ultimately Montana. At Little Big Horn, Custer made a fatal error in underestimating native forces; he attacked without realizing he was badly overmatched or knowing that another portion of his troops had already been turned back by Sitting Bull's men, leaving him without reinforcements. Custer and his men are often portrayed as heroes for fighting to the last man, but the battle was in reality a "stunning victory" for the natives, in the words of one historian.

Taken in context with the attitudes of the day, this disconnect is not surprising. Custer lived in an era of great geographic expansion. Many Americans believed in "manifest destiny" and they began to define what it meant to be American, creating a national identity related in part to the shifting frontier. Some discussed publicly their common interest in creating national social unity. Custer's role as "hero," and the Native Americans' role as "enemy," certainly fit with the era's larger national narrative.

Elizabeth likewise exemplified an important narrative, that of the traditional wife and woman. Nineteenth-century women had a particular position in American society, one uniquely feminine and domestic. De Tocqueville wrote in 1831 that they were responsible for the morals and strength of the nation. Women, he said, sacrificed pleasure for duty, and through the power of public opinion were relegated to the "circle of domestic interest, forbidden to step beyond it." Elizabeth's skill in the role of wife only heightened her husband's success. "Charming, polished and physically attractive," one biographer noted, "she cemented ties with crucial congressmen and senators and ingratiated herself with [Custer's] superiors." In fact, Leckie argued, "To a far greater extent than historians or biographers have previously noted, George Armstrong Custer's career was based on the efforts of two people."

With the disaster at Little Big Horn, Libbie Custer's life changed. At 34, with virtually no family, she was no longer a military wife, and she had to forge a new life as well as a living. This she did with a pen. She had not previously sought independence or a career, and becoming an author was not easy for her: only after nine years of widowhood was she able to begin writing about her husband. "Oh what intense anxiety I felt for fear my crude, inexperienced pen could not so frame a little story of his home life that anyone would be willing to read," she confessed to a friend. She wrote three books, published in 1885, 1887, and 1890, describing her life as an Army wife and, not incidentally, humanizing and glorifying her husband. She found this work debilitating, leading to sad dreams at night and a preoccupation with the past during her waking moments. Despite this difficulty, "Elizabeth transformed her domestic role as a widow," Leckie wrote, "into a publicly sanctioned profession." She was not alone. With the enormous success of mass-circulating women's magazines, which featured many women contributors, women's authorship had become professionalized and women's public voices increasingly accepted, if not commonplace. In this climate of both tradition and change, Elizabeth Custer would find an audience for her message.

In many ways, Mrs. Custer's efforts tell us as much about her as they do about her husband. Benoit has suggested that image restoration is directed first at an external audience, but he also notes that such efforts are also geared at making one feel better about oneself. In this sense, Elizabeth Custer's lifelong mission served not only to defend her husband but also to protect her own image. To have allowed others to pin the blame on Custer would have diminished not just him, but also his widow.

Her role in building her husband's legacy is often taken for granted. According to one of Custer's biographers, "ever present in the background of the controversies" surrounding Custer was his widow. "The tragic figure in black, widowed at thirty-four, prompted silence in many who might have spoken in criticism." Leckie, whose biography offers the most nuanced portrait of Elizabeth Custer, asserted that "she played a critical role in making and sustaining the Custer myth." However, Carroll rejects the claim that Libbie spent nearly six decades perpetuating her late husband's memory. His life and accomplishments counted more than anything she ever wrote, Carroll argued; "Libbie's only difference was that her memoirs were written by a woman in love." Although almost every Custer scholar, or aficionado, seems to have an opinion about Libbie, none has undertaken a systematic analysis of her campaign.

Had George Custer lived, he might have attempted to restore his image by evading responsibility, begging for forgiveness, or seeking corrective action. But he died, and Libbie's options were limited: she could not deny the slaughter had taken place, nor could she refute Custer's responsibility for the men under his command. She therefore used strategies associated with reducing offensiveness. In a few instances, she sought compensation for other Last Stand widows and children, but her primary weapons were bolstering, promoting positive aspects of Custer's past, and transcendence, suggesting a different frame of reference-that offered by a grieving widow. Toward the end of her life she also made a somewhat surprising gesture toward mortification.

Review of press coverage of Mrs. Custer reveals that she made frequent attempts to bolster George's image, first by making donations of historical artifacts to remind people of his service to the country. She gave to a museum a piece of the "truce towel" used at the end of the Civil War, for example, and gave a portrait-style photograph of the general to a Grand Army of the Republic post named for Custer. The photograph, according to the New York Times, displayed Custer "as the dashing cavalry man that he was, with his broad-brimmed hat, his velvet coat, his flaming necktie, and his brave, honest-looking countenance." Her most spectacular donation was the table reportedly used by General U.S. Grant to write the terms of surrender for the Confederate Army at Appomattox Court House, which she sent to the War Department in 1905.

She also bolstered his image by positioning him as a courageous, manly war hero, romanticizing one of the most brutally violent periods in history. When West Point erected a statue of the general, she was disappointed to hear (she never saw it for herself) that it was a poor likeness and that it made Custer, a national hero as a cavalry officer, look ridiculous in a pose in which he stood holding both a sword and a pistol and nary a horse in sight. "As a work of art it was a failure," the New York Times later wrote. The widow would have none of it. When she opposed the erection of a statue in Washington, D.C., because it would be sculpted by the same artist who created the statue at West Point, the Congressional bill died in committee. Moreover, her continuing entreaties led to the West Point statue being removed entirely. She then began a campaign to commission a better statue, one depicting Custer astride his horse, which was placed in her hometown of Monroe, Michigan.

She tempered this militaristic image with a more homespun vision of Custer as husband. At times, for example, she presented Custer as a gentle man who was kind to animals, as in an anecdote in the Christian Science Monitor about how Custer's entire cavalry unit had avoided trampling a bird's nest on a march. His domestic side was most evident in the widow's books and public speeches. Her first book, Boots and Saddles, quickly sold out its first printing of 2,000 copies, and ultimately sold more than 5,000. Its popularity led to two additional book contracts as well as public appearances in which she promoted the book, and her late husband's memory, in person. Her talks, with titles like "Buffalo Hunting," "Garrison Life on the Frontier," and "Life on the Western Plains," were well-received. The New York Times praised an appearance in 1891, noting that her delivery benefited "from the total absence of any trait of the experienced lecturer," but also complimenting her facility at handling the applause and laughter of her audience. The following year the Chicago Daily Tribune predicted that her two readings in that city would be among the most interesting and novel events of the season, noting that invitations would be limited. Afterward, the paper reported that "an audience of 150 women and a fair sprinkling of men greeted Mrs. Custer."

Elizabeth Custer also utilized the image restoration tactic of transcendence, which promotes a different frame of reference for the offense. In essence, Libbie herself literally lived her image repair efforts by becoming the kind of person who must have been married to a hero. In 1885, the Atlanta Constitution noted that "the wife of General Custer used to wear sometimes at a fancy dress ball a wig made from the golden rings of curly hair cut from her husband's head after the war, when he had given up wearing long locks." A few years later the Constitution further opined about the "lovable widow": "The tenderness and beauty of Mrs. Custer's character are so great that every person who meets her succumbs at once to her gentle, womanly charm." Other papers noted that she declined the assistance of an 1877 theatrical benefit in Chicago but later helped soldiers' widows and children with money from her books. The New York Times mentioned that "she has made a habit of answering all her letters personally in her own handwriting," despite receiving "several hundred of these communications a year, mostly from old soldiers." The implication of such articles seemed to be that only an extraordinary man could inspire such devotion.

She also constantly reminded people of the personal cost of her husband's sacrifice. "Mrs. Custer lives quietly and works hard on her books, going over and over her pages with extreme care," the Constitution reported in

1889. "She is absorbed in these labors, which serve to keep her so clearly in the presence of her great loss that it is as present and fresh...as years ago." She decided against getting together with his old Army friends because, as the Chicago Daily Tribune reported in 1891, "We get to talking over old times, and they get to crying, and I cry, and then I am ill for a long time afterward." When she visited one of Custer's military colleagues, the Washington Post reported: "His generous praise of his old commander and the many touching anecdotes told more than once brought tears to the eyes of the widow, who cherishes the gallant soldier's memory as fondly as if he had died but yesterday". And she continued wearing widow's garb publicly long after any traditional mourning period, as was noted in the Chicago Daily Tribune: "Mrs. Custer, widow of the General, has never taken off her widow's weeds. She dresses plainly in lusterless black, relieved by a white collar and deep white cuffs." The specter of the dead general was apparent every time his black-garbed widow appeared and spoke of his deeds.

Late in her life, Elizabeth Custer made a statement that might be interpreted as mortification. In 1927 she wrote in Outlook that after many years she had concluded "the Indians were deeply wronged," reflecting the changing American narrative. Yet even this change of heart would not detract from Custer's reputation. The general, she said, wanted the government to keep its promises to the Indians. He "respected a true nobility in the Indian character, and respected their feelings of attachment for their land." Although she seemed sorry for the way the natives had been treated, she never deviated from her efforts to build Custer's reputation.

MAKING THE MEMORY HEROIC

The most striking thing about Elizabeth Custer's efforts to restore George's image is that she situated the general in exactly the ways that modern scholars have identified as necessary for the maintenance of reputation and for survival in American memory-the designation of "hero," the connection to a larger American story, and the establishment of cultural artifacts. Indeed, Elizabeth's task of protecting her husband's image was made easier because his narrative resonated publicly, almost as a myth or archetype, which Lule calls an "eternal story." As Lule noted, "The Hero may be humanity's most enduring archetype and the basis for its most pervasive myth." This section relates Elizabeth's publicity efforts to public memory, analyzing published discussions of Custer's heroic qualities, both elite and common; reiteration of his ties to the American frontier, other icons, and the Civil War; discussions about the establishment of memorials and monuments; and public reminders of the hero's youthful and fateful death.

Elizabeth Custer's books heralded her husband as a heroic figure in myriad ways. Published reviews or notices of these books dutifully repeated what she deemed as his heroic qualities. For example, a decade before he became president, Theodore Roosevelt reviewed Following the Guidon for Harper's Bazaar, fairly gushing that Custer "was one of the most gallant and picturesque figures with which our history -or, for the matter of that, any contemporary history-has had to deal." Roosevelt added, "It was most fortunate that he [Custer] should have found the best of all possible biographers in his wife." In its notice of the book, The Literary World pointed with approval to Elizabeth's "hero-worship of her husband" and wrote that "General Custer appears the loyal knight, chivalric to women, protector of the weak, and tender to dumb creatures." Current Literature suggested that it was Mrs. Custer's "minuteness of detail" and her "utter subservience" that "gave pictures of him which will live in memory."

But, as Boorstin has noted, the American hero displays qualities of the "common" man, and while Elizabeth Custer's first book, Boots and Saddles, painted a picture of Custer and his brothers as "great souled, brave, handsome, dashing fellows," it also said their "home life was characterized by sincere affection and appreciation." In fact, as reviews of all three of her books noted, Mrs. Custer's feminine perspective and personality brought out her husband's tender and down-to earth qualities, both at home and in his military service. The Critic observed, "He is not only the gallant soldier, but the gallant lover-husband; not only the impetuous hero, but the tender son; not only the friend full of jollity, but the friend who takes care that no jollity shall hurt even his enemy" Such reviews repeated the general's qualities, both great and common, including descriptors such as "brave," "gallant," "noble," "handsome," "dashing," "easy strength," "magnanimity," "great physical powers," "daring," "exquisitely thoughtful," "model frontiersman," "boyish," "exuberance," and "beloved." Yet, the Spectator reassured in 1888, "While you feel in every page how [Elizabeth Custer] adores her heroic husband, not a syllable is set down which violates good taste or savours of mere sentiment." The New York Observer and Chronicle and The Dial noted that Mrs. Custer's books would be good reading material for young people, as her stories about Custer would "keep fresh the memory of one of the most picturesque and gallant characters of the Civil War and of the Indian campaigns that followed."

Elizabeth Custer repeatedly reminded Americans of her husband's place in the larger American story. In speeches, she described his efforts to open the frontier, his service in the Civil War (a watershed moment in American history that was being recalled and celebrated publicly, particularly during the last two decades of the nineteenth century), and his connection to notable figures of the era. For example, in a lecture on buffalo hunting, she noted his relationship with "Buffalo Bill" Cody, then an iconic frontier figure in his own right, and with Civil War generals. As the Chicago Daily Tribune noted, "Mrs. Custer's talk was full of reminiscences of the great Generals of the war, nearly all of whom she had known, and about whom she told many pleasant bits of gossip." Her correspondence, often reprinted verbatim in the press, also linked her husband to the Civil War and to the frontier. The New York Times, for instance, published a letter to the governor of Montana, in which she wrote, "He dearly loved the West, and counted it no sacrifice to spend nine years out of his young life in defending her borders and protecting the frontiersman's home."

Elizabeth Custer became intimately involved with the establishment of cultural artifacts that not only constructed a positive image of the general during her own era but that would help make him a memorable public figure for future generations. Long before her death, she made public the instructions in her will to donate Civil War relics. When she died, the Chicago Daily Tribune reported: "Portraits and photographs of Gen. Custer, his arms, accoutrements, uniforms, souvenirs of war and the frontier, books and trophies of the chase were left by the will to a public museum which is to be erected on the battlefield of the Little Big Horn, Montana."

Of particular note was her well-publicized dissatisfaction with the statue at West Point and its potential duplication in Washington, D.C. The New York Times and Washington Post noted her disapproval of the age and unmilitary dress of the Custer represented in the statue, as well as his being "armed like a desperado." She said: "It seems as if I could not endure the thought of this wretched statue being repeated." Her letter to a member of Congress, reprinted in the Times, implored: "You know what intense individuality Gen. Custer had. His quick movements, his active step, his riding, the very way he wore his clothes, were so totally unlike any one (sic) else." Recalling the general's distinguished appearance was important to her. In an article about the dedication of the Michigan monument, she wrote: "His hair waved in loose curls on his neck and still had the golden tint of childhood. His mustache was darker in colour and his face ruddy. Heavy eyebrows shaded clear blue eyes."

For decades Mrs. Custer used the annual anniversary of the Battle at Little Big Horn to keep alive the memory of her husband's public sacrifice. For example, on the forty-fifth anniversary she wrote an article for the New York Times, noting that communities around the battle site had formed an association and sponsored a "three day round-up" of pioneers and Indians, "with events descriptive of those adventurous days," as well as the unveiling of a monument in the Hardin, Montana, city park. These activities, she wrote, "showed evidence of patriotism when these young communities, forging ahead in all the splendor of their youthful vigour, pause to look back and honour those who 'opened the way.'"

Even in her declining years, when she did not grant interviews, Mrs. Custer and her work in preserving her husband's memory were noted. The 1931 anniversary, observed the Times, "was an uneventful day for the General's widow...who remained in seclusion in her apartment at Park

Avenue. Mrs. Custer accompanied her soldier husband on many of his expeditions and despite her declining years shows a keen interest in historic associations." The next year, the Times reported that Mrs. Custer listened to a broadcast reporting the unveiling of a memorial in New Rumley, Ohio, of the town's "most famous son." The article listed Custer's numerous achievements in the Civil War and Indian wars, and though it noted the "terrible affair on the Little Big Horn, in which he was overmatched," it reassured readers, "The controversy that followed left no blemish on his fame." She became so associated with memories of Custer that more than twenty years after she died, the Chicago Daily Tribune began its eightieth anniversary story by describing Libbie's final farewell to her husband: as Custer and his men rode off, the regimental band played "The Girl I Left Behind Me."

As reflected in the 265 articles examined for this study, Elizabeth Custer capitalized on her role as widow to create a living publicity campaign. Using bolstering and transcendence, and to a lesser degree mortification-all strategies associated with reducing offensiveness-she contributed to the image restoration of her husband, a controversial figure. Too, her actions exemplified what scholars have identified as important ingredients for situating a person or event in public memory.

She reminded book, magazine, and newspaper readers of Custer's contributions to the "taming" of the West and to the Civil War; she had a hand in ensuring particular cultural artifacts would survive through the generations; and she reminisced publicly about her husband's heroic qualities-his feats, his personality, his fateful death, and even his physical attributes. In other words, Elizabeth Custer's attempts to restore George's image during her own time simultaneously worked to promote particular attributes for his public memory.

Of course, other people also memorialized Custer. When word of his death spread, according to Paul Andrew Hutton, "the poets, the writers, the painters, and the popularizers of every stripe seized on the story" Rosenberg points to more than 950 paintings and illustrations of Custer, nearly all with sword in hand. John Mulvany's 1881 painting "Custer's Last Rally" was exhibited around the country for a decade. "Buffalo Bill" Cody re-enacted Custer's last stand as the climax of his famous Wild West Show.

Yet the widow's position gave her a special influence on his memory. For example, only she could plan his funeral, and she planned it with his public image in mind. When his remains were recovered from Little Big Horn in August 1877, she had them placed in a receiving vault in New York and held until October, when a suitable funeral could be held at West Point. In August, the students and many of the officers were on furlough, so a funeral held then would be sparsely attended and certainly not the public pageant Elizabeth believed her husband deserved.

Because of this careful attention to her late husband's image, biographer Lawrence Frost has described Elizabeth Custer as a "press agent." Her campaign continued for decades. "I have my hands full this summer," she wrote in 1913, "of schemes or plans to keep him [Custer] before the public. I never want to let an opportunity to go by to write and thank whoever writes an article or book, a play or a poemor whoever paints him."

Libbie Custer's campaign has not proved as eternal as her devotion. As Leckie concludes, "much of her work has been eroded." In 1991, for example, the name of the Custer Battlefield National Monument was changed to the Little Big Horn National Monument at the request of Native Americans. Nor have her efforts prevented George's excoriation by military historians for the calamitous defeat at Little Big Horn, as in a 1996 biography which concluded that Custer's decisions "resulted in a tragedy for himself and over 250 members of the Seventh Cavalry and he bears the primary responsibility."

Too, his designation as "hero" ebbs and flows, influenced in part by America's growing unease with its historically violent relationship with native populations. But George Custer is also remembered for his storied "Last Stand," and he has often been called an American hero. This is true at least in part because Elizabeth connected her hero with the Civil War and the taming of the Western frontier. Moreover, she understood the importance of establishing memorials and of the need for the general to be remembered in particular ways visually as well as verbally. Indeed, the cultural artifacts that typically designate a heroic figure have survived, even flourished.

Elizabeth Custer was certainly not the only one involved in the preservation of Custer's memory, nor could anyone single-handedly create an icon. But Libbie's reminiscences of her "boy general," his feats on the battlefield, and his human qualities beyond were regularly repeated for the readership of American newspapers and magazines. Through publication in the mass press, his legend was magnified for Americans who might never have read her books or attended her lectures.

She was, without doubt, the ultimate guardian of her husband's memory, a devoted wife wrenched from her "circle of domestic interest," as de Toqueville might say, by tragedy. With pen, voice, and deed, she recalled for Americans the dashing young hero who, in her view, made the ultimate sacrifice for his country.

As Lule noted, "Every society likely has dramatized and personified its core values and ideals in stories of a hero." It would have been difficult for anyone in her day to criticize the military widow, particularly such a devoted one, who continued to wear black mourning garb decades after her husband's death. Indeed, as the Langs noted in their study of reputation, durability depends not just on the efforts of the hero, but also on the works of others who have a stake in preserving the hero's memory after death. Libbie Custer was a tireless preserver of her husband's reputation.

Libbie lived her image restoration campaign, but she also lived her life. Her experiences and literary career led to her being treated as an expert on life in the Army and in the West. This role spanned the remainder of her life. Hence, her obituary writers and some biographers have not been entirely fair to Elizabeth Bacon Custer.

Although she did spend a lifetime working on behalf of her husband, she also grew into her own. In 1896 she was featured as the guest of honour at an Illinois Women's Press Association meeting on "Opportunity of Women Writers." She traveled extensively and spoke about her experiences in other countries-a topic totally unrelated to her husband. She even wrote a reflection on "If I Were a Man." Still, her personal accomplishments were usually linked to her husband. The Chicago Daily Tribune noted in 1894, for example, that Mrs. Custer "is a brilliant billiard player," but also explained it was a skill she learned with him on the frontier, where there was little other entertainment. She positioned herself, and was known as, the general's widow. As the magazine Outing noted of one of her books, "[It] shows plainly that the hero and the historian were ideally wedded, and proves the truth of the dedication - 'To my Husband, the echo of whose voice has been my inspiration.'"

15

Journalism in a Time of Great Change

The traditional mass media model-characterized by relatively few media creating and controlling content disseminated to large, mass audiences-has been replaced in the past decade by a new model that features many media disseminating content to smaller, niche audiences who are active, purposive, and more in control of their media choices. This evolution has had a profound impact on traditional mass media, which have been forced to change the way they do business and strategically reposition themselves in the rapidly changing media marketplace.

For the newspaper industry, the mandate for change has been apparent for more than a decade. Concerned by a dwindling base of readers and the impact of the Internet and emergent technologies, the industry has repositioned itself by developing new information and service products in electronic markets and focusing on the interests of potential readers in its print products. These changes have shifted priorities and resources at the organizational level, as newspapers become more reader-oriented, market-driven, and technologically savvy. Ongoing change efforts since the mid-1990s have seen newspaper organizations become more integrated, as news and business managers and staff collaborate on inter-departmental teams charged with the strategic development of information products. Newsrooms are also being restructured, and team-based newsrooms, with flatter organizational hierarchies and different roles for newsroom managers, have replaced or supplemented the beat system, especially at larger newspapers. As newspapers become more market-driven, traditional definitions of news values have been called into question. However, despite the uncertainty associated with markets, technology, readership, and news values, profit expectations remain high.

These changes create a different environment for editors as managers, who are required to accept new organizational roles and expectations. Journalism skills and judgment must be supplemented with a greater marketing consciousness and collaboration with non-news departments. The union of journalism and marketing has not been a harmonious marriage for many editors (and journalists), who see a stronger marketing orientation as a loss of editorial control and an affront to journalistic "professionalism." The "duality" of purpose for news organizations, as journalistic and commercial enterprises, has been shown in numerous studies to create a tension borne from conflicting values."

This duality adds to the complexity of managing change. Organizational integration has important implications for organizational decision making, including access to resources and how they are used, and for how influential journalism values are to be as newspapers try to respond to industry uncertainty. To date, there have been no attempts to measure how integration is occurring in newspaper organizations. Top editors (journalists in the highest positions in their organizations' hierarchies) are positioned in news organizations as the primary source of journalism expertise. To the extent that editors perceive they have organizational influence, they should be effective advocates for journalism throughout the organization.

This study, a national survey of top editors, measures editors' attitudes toward concepts drawn from theories of organizational development and organizational support that are important to explaining the ongoing changes in the newspaper industry. It introduces two concepts-organiz-ational integration and perceived organizational influence-that advance an understanding theoretically and practically of what it means to be the editor of a U.S. newspaper in a time of considerable uncertainty and rapid change.

NEWSPAPER CHANGE

The clamor for change increased in the mid-1990s as leading editors asserted the need to "blow up" the newsroom and recreate an organizational culture that was not so adversarial, competitive, and isolated from the business interests of the organization. Newspapers turned to outside consultants to lead efforts at organizational change; common to these efforts were initiatives to create more reader-driven content, restructure newsrooms into team-based systems of reporting, and integrate organizational decision making by having editors serve on strategic cross-departmental teams.

The restructuring of newspaper organizations has occurred on two levels: the creation of inter-departmental teams that pair news and business personnel in efforts to develop new strategic products or content, and the reorganization of newsrooms from a beat system to a team-based system of news coverage. "Organizational integration"-the extent of collaboration between historically autonomous units-conceptually describes inter-departmental restructuring and how the collaboration of journalism and business is occurring. Editors appear to recognize the value of working with non-news departments. Sylvie found editors were significantly more likely to say that more cooperation is needed between departments than advertising and circulation department heads. An Editor and Publisher study found that 63 per cent of responding editors agreed there should be more cooperation between news and business/ marketing departments. Campbell, who as editor led broad change initiatives at the Norfolk Virginian-Pilot and Si. Louz's Post-Dispatch, said that editors should welcome integration as opportunity to "colonize other departments with the values of the newsroom."

The reorganization of newsrooms into team-based structures gained momentum throughout the 1990s. A 2000 study found 53 per cent of newspapers with more than 100,000 circulation used reporting teams, and 37 per cent of papers surveyed used primarily a team-based system of news coverage. Only 8 per cent had teams in 1992. Team-based systems require journalists to have a broader base of skills; however, this structure should provide flexibility for newspapers to respond more quickly to marketplace opportunities. Russial found reporting teams produced more content that got more prominent play in the paper than the beat system, and concluded that teams represent an important realignment of newsroom resources. No studies of editors' perceptions of teambased newsrooms have been done. However, the few studies of journalists working in news teams indicate that journalists perceive less job-related authority and less success getting their story ideas in the paper, and team-based systems require more managers and do not improve the quality of the newspaper.

Changing organizational structures and attempts to be more market-oriented have raised questions about editors' organizational influence. Readers have become the "invisible giants" of the newsroom, with near equal decision-making power as journalists; editors, a trade journal suggested, were losing influence in their newsrooms. Harris, a journalist and former publisher of the San Jose Mercury News, asserted that the era of editors as "philosopher kings" in the newsroom is over, replaced by editors who team players with other organizational leaders are. Because these leaders have little knowledge of journalism norms and values, "editors need to speak regularly and articulately about the professional and ethical responsibilities of journalism, and also be respectful teachers and patient listeners on these subjects."

Newspapers have historically enjoyed high profits, and despite losses in circulation and advertising revenue, profit levels remain comparable to pharmaceutical and oil industries. The emphasis on maintaining high profits has been linked to recent waves of cost-cutting, fewer newsroom resources, and greater marketing focus, often at the expense of journalistic performance. Studies have consistently found that investments in newsrooms are related to increased circulation and profitability. However, newsrooms have endured a litany of cost-cutting measures, including staff reductions of about 3,500 journalists since 2000, about 7 per cent of all newspaper journalists. Meyer asserted that newspapers have maintained high profits by investing less in their newsrooms, putting out cheaper products, and raising advertising and subscription rates. Lacy and Blanchard found that higher profits were negatively related to the number of full-time journalism employees, and "the relationship became much stronger for newspapers with profit margins above average." Beam found newsroom managers acknowledge the profitdriven nature of news media, and when they believe profit interferes with the journalistic mission, their job satisfaction suffers. In earlier research, he concluded that efforts to make newspaper organizations more marketoriented have eroded journalists' capability to maintain control over the values that guide their work, resulting in a "deprofessionalization" of journalism.

Journalism is guided by professional values, including public service, allegiance to truth, journalistic autonomy, and social responsibility. Newsroom managers report higher levels of professionalism at larger papers, which make fewer errors, do more investigative reporting, and win more professional prizes. Efforts to change or redefine the values associated with professionalism often face resistance. Change has been associated with lower morale, a desire to leave the newspaper industry, corporate mandates for 20 per cent profit margins, and a sense that public service is dying as the sine qua non of journalism. Several studies found that journalists tend to blame newsroom managers-their editors-for mismanaging change. However, some studies also found that editors are conflicted by the motives and values associated with change.

Managing the internal organizational tension that arises from a duality of purpose is a core challenge of newspaper management. Sylvie and Moon found from three newspaper case studies that management "via sheer will"-pushed through initiatives to change the organizational culture. They concluded that management's approach "does not signify improved management or-in the case of newsrooms-a smooth marriage of journalism and marketing concerns." Russo found that editors have trouble acknowledging traditional values when organizational priorities are not consistent with professional expectations; newspaper journalists going through organizational change had higher levels of professional identification than organizational identification. She concluded that journalists' professionalism "served as a source of collective inspiration, energy and strength."

Organizational Development, Integration, Support, and Influence

To be competitive in changing markets, organizations must be innovative. Larger organizations have more complex and bureaucratic structures that tend to slow their ability to exploit market opportunities. However, they have greater resources, expertise, and market power, thus providing more strategic options for innovation. Organizational development is the process of organizational change and learning that assumes firms must find ways to adapt and innovate to be competitive.

The process of organizational development is not easy because change requires giving up what is known and routine for something new that may not be understood. Scholars agree that a key to development is organizational integration. Integration breaks down organizational barriers, creating opportunities for exchanges of knowledge throughout the organization. Inter-departmental teams are examples of organizational integration. These teams are expected to contribute to innovation because they create structural mechanisms for fresh thinking. However, this restructuring requires a different managerial mindset. Managers need to give up their "span of control" and forge a "span of relationships," sharing power and accountability with other departments in the organization. Managers must act more as "learners than knowers, listeners than tellers, partners than adversaries." This change is not easy for many managers, especially those accustomed to being the primary authorities.

Within these shifting organizational boundaries, managers are expected to be influential because their position in the organizational structure provides opportunities for leadership.

Management, especially during times of change, is expected to articulate a vision of the organization's mission and the values that support it. Effective managers show organizational leadership, which some scholars have called the "management of meaning." Managers have organizational influence when they are successful at identifying what is important and have the ability to induce others to behave a certain way. Organizational influence is related to a manager's sense of organizational support. Managers who perceive they are valued by their organizations sense they have greater support to take risks, and greater influence to initiate changes that redefine organizational norms. Employees recognize managers who have influence in important organizational decisions, and respond by increasing behaviors that benefit the organization.

Newspaper organizations are becoming more integrated, and news managers are increasingly working with non-news departments to strategize, plan, and market. Managing requires stronger business awareness, increased collaboration, and more subtle leadership skills. Editors are positioned in integrated organizations to be a voice for journalism professional values throughout the organization; however, change has been associated with transforming the newsroom culture and diminished editorial influence. Editors' perceived organizational influence begins to explain the extent that editors can be effective advocates for journalism values throughout the organization. Organizational integration and editors' perceptions of their organizational influence have not been studied.

- *RQ*1: To what extent do top newsroom editors perceive their organizations are integrated?
- *RQ*2: How influential do editors perceive they are in their organizations? In other words, what is their level of perceived organizational influence?

Newsrooms are being reorganized into team-based structures of news coverage, especially at larger newspapers. Team-based newsrooms are a tangible change that requires training, re-ordering of work and routines, and a different management approach. The few studies of newsroom teamwork indicate that journalists have not embraced this structural change, although no studies exist regarding newsroom managers' attitudes toward team-based newsrooms.

- *RQ*3: What are editors' attitudes toward team-based newsrooms?

Large newspapers exhibit more journalistic profess-ionalism than smaller papers, and to be the editor of a large newspaper reflects a high degree of professional achievement. Larger organizations are more complex and have greater resources, market leverage, and reservoirs of expertise. Accordingly, news managers in large organizations are respected professionals who have more strategic tools and options as they consider innovative responses to market uncertainty.

- *H*1: Organizational size is a significant predictor of editors' perceived organizational influence.

  Managers in integrated organizations are sources of specialized knowledge, exchanging their expertise across organizational boundaries. They are expected to be sources of innovation and leadership, developing spans of influence throughout the organization. Their sense of organizational influence should be shaped by the extent of their organizational integration.

- *H*2: Organizational integration is a significant predictor of editors' perceived organizational influence.

  Newspaper industry emphasis on profit is well-established. Editors acknowledge newspapers are market-driven, and staffs are becoming smaller. In an era of market uncertainty and much experimentation with new products and new media, editors have fewer newsroom resources. Editors react negatively when they perceive profit motive interferes with the journalistic professionalism.

- *H*3: Emphasis on profit is a significant negative predictor of perceived organizational influence.

This study sought a representative group of top editors at U.S. newspapers that included an adequate number of editors from large papers. The Editor and Publisher International Year Book (2003) listed 1,457 daily newspapers. This population was divided into four circulation strata for sampling: less than 25,000 (1,044 newspapers), 25,000 to 49,999 (194 newspapers), 50,000 to 99,999 (114 newspapers), and more than 100,000 (105 newspapers). Top editors were defined as having titles of executive editor, editor, managing editor, editor in chief, and vice president for news. Because larger papers often have two newsroom managers with one of these titles, the top two editors at papers with more than 50,000 circulations were included when there were two people with one of these titles. A census of top editors at papers larger than 25,000 was included in the sample. This meant that the initial sample included 194 editors in the 25,000 to 49,999 range, 200 editors in the 50,000 to 99,999 range, and 197 editors from papers with more than 100,000 circulation. Because there were about 200 editors in each of these strata, a similar-sized random sample (one-fifth) was drawn from the 1,044 papers with circulations less than 25,000 (n = 208). The initial mailing list included 799 editors.

The survey was sent postal mail in June 2004. A pre-notification e-mail was sent to potential respondents to increase the response. Subsequently, 36 editors were removed from the sample because they had left their jobs and their replacement could not be identified by searching the papers' Web sites. This left a sample of 763 editors. Dillman's tailored design method for postal surveys was followed closely.

Variable Measures. Respondents expressed agreement or disagreement with statements on a five-point Likert-like intensity scale. Organizational integration explores the extent to which organizational boundaries are changing, and how the integration of journalism and business is occurring. Perceived organizational influence measures the extent to which editors think they are influential and journalism values are important in their organizations. Team-based newsrooms measures editor attitudes toward news coverage teams in terms of newsroom efficiency and journalism quality (two statements, alpha =.S7). Profit measures editors' perceptions of organizational emphasis and their personal attention to profit. Organizational size is measured by newspaper circulation. Demographic data were also sought.

Responses were coded so a positive response indicated support for the concept (e.g., positive responses indicated high organizational integration, high perceived organizational influence, high profit emphasis). Construct quotients (the mean response to the set of statements measuring the concept) measure respondents' attitudes toward the concepts. To determine whether the quotient and statement means are significantly different from the neutral point (3.0 on a five-point scale), the standard error of the mean was used to calculate confidence intervals for each measure. Response means more than +1-2 standard errors from the neutral point are significant at the 95 per cent confidence level. Accordingly, means significantly above 3.0 indicate positive agreement with a concept, and means significantly below 3.0 indicate disagreement.

Of the 763 editors surveyed, 274 completed surveys were returned, a response rate of 35.9 per cent. Respondents managed 243 newspapers in 46 states and included top editors from 142 of the 219 U.S. newspapers with circulations above 50,000. About three-fourths of responding editors were men, 87 per cent were white, their average age was 50, and they had been the top editor for about six years. The first research question asked to what extent do top editors perceive their organizations are integrated. The quotient mean is 3.63, which is significantly higher than the neutral point, indicating that top editors show significant agreement that their organizations are integrated. Assessing the individual statements, all eight statements are significant, with seven indicating positive attitudes toward organizational integration.

Editors show strongest agreement (means noted parenthetically) that it is important for them to communicate the values of the rest of the organization to the newsroom, and their jobs as editors make them organizational team players who work with other departments to guide operations. Editors strongly agree that they are as confident in their management abilities in a business sense as they are in their abilities in a journalistic sense. Editors also agree that the newsroom must be supportive of the company's attempts to aggressively pursue emerging business opportunities, and that cross-departmental teams (pairing news and non-news personnel) have improved organizational decision making. Editors are committed to changes that increase collaboration between news and business interests.

However, they show mild, but significant, disagreement that the news and business interests of their newspapers are essentially the same. Together, the responses reveal that editors are active managers in integrated organizations. They are confident working outside the newsroom and they value their work with non-news departments. Editors perceive their role is to advance a stronger business consciousness in the newsroom; however, they recognize a tension between news and business, although this tension is not strong for many editors.

RQ2 explored the level of the editors' perceived organizational influence. The construct quotient is significantly different from the neutral point, showing editors agree they have a relatively high level of perceived organizational influence. Six of the seven statements have significant levels of agreement or disagreement. The editors showed strongest agreement that exhibiting an open passion for traditional journalism values is an effective method to gain influence in their organizations, and that their ideas regarding the newsroom and newspaper are valued throughout the organization. They disagree strongly that they are losing influence in their newsrooms. They also disagree that business interests think they should have a say in deciding how the newsroom operates, and that the journalistic interests of the newsroom are becoming less central to the mission of the news organization. Despite this optimism, editors indicate they recognize limits of their influence, responding that the decisive power in newspaper organizations is exercised by capital investors more than newsroom managers. Taken together, editors perceive they have moderately strong influence in their organizations and newsrooms, and they associate their influence with advocacy of journalism values. They appear optimistic about their personal influence in managing the tension that arises between journalistic and business interests in the organization, but they also perceive that their ultimate influence might not be as powerful as investors from outside the organization.

The third research question asked about editors' attitudes toward team-based newsrooms. Although several statements were written to test this concept, only two statements produced acceptable internal reliability (alpha =.87), and editors indicated significant disagreement with both of them, disagreeing that newsroom reporting teams are a more efficient use of newsroom resources (2.50) and that newsroom reporting teams produce better journalism than the traditional beat system (2.45). These statement means yield a team-based newsrooms quotient of 2.48, which indicates a significantly negative attitude toward the construct. Clearly, the benefits of newsroom teams are not apparent to the editors in this study.

To test the hypotheses, perceived organizational influence was regressed on the predictor variables-organization size, organizational integration, and profit, controlling for the impact of demographics and attitudes toward team-based newsroom structures. The model predicted about 30 per cent of the variance; none of the control variables was significant.

H1 anticipated that organizational size would predict perceived organizational influence. H1 was supported, as organizational size was a significant predictor (beta =.219) that explained 6.4 per cent of the variance. The data indicate that as organizational size increases, editors perceive themselves as more influential in their organizations; they are managers who think their views are more respected and valued throughout the organization, including among business interests outside the newsroom. As such, editors at larger papers perceive themselves to be in a more effective position to advocate journalism professionalism, they have greater resources at their disposal to meet the challenges of uncertainty and change, and they have more success buffering the newsroom from market influences that conflict with journalism values.

H2, which proposed that organizational integration would predict editors' perceptions of their organizational influence, was supported (beta =.230), explaining about 5% per cent of the variance in the model. This result supports the idea that editors see the importance of their roles outside the newsroom and think their organizational influence is enhanced by these expanded roles. Editors understand that their integration and collaboration with non-journalistic interests in the organization provides them opportunities to be influential beyond the newsroom and throughout the organization, forging spans of influence as part of the organization's management team. This finding speaks to the extent that the organizational culture of newsrooms has changed in the past decade, and editors perceive the "wall" that separated the newsroom from the business interests of the organization is no longer an effective organizational boundary. Editors see themselves as key leaders in this cultural transition. They acknowledge that journalism and business interests differ, yet accept that competing values must co-exist. Their influence as editors is based in part on their ability to advocate journalism interests throughout the organization while pushing the newsroom to accept a more market-oriented culture.

H3 predicted that an organizational emphasis on profit would have a negative impact on editors' perceptions of their organizational influence. This hypothesis was supported, as profit was the strongest predictor in the model (beta = –.441), explaining more than 19 per cent of the variance. This finding shows that editors think an emphasis on profit, relative to the other variables, is a powerful restraint on their organizational influence. They think their organizations favour profit over non-profit goals. Accordingly, although the editors see themselves as leaders and sources of innovation, their ability to respond to industry uncertainty is hampered by an emphasis on profit, a shrinking pool of resources, and smaller newsroom budgets. The data support the idea that editors perceive that profit emphasis reduces their organizational influence outside and inside the newsroom: as ambassadors throughout the organization, arguing, first, that quality journalism is good business and, second, that business interests must be better accepted and understood within the newsroom.

This study sought to better understand what it means to be the editor of a U.S. newspaper at a time the industry is in a period of fundamental organizational change. Newspapers have found their business model is antiquated and seek innovative answers to maintain readers and attract new customers. Editors, as the organization's top newsroom managers and journalism professionals, are a key source of organizational knowledge and competency, and accordingly should be important organizational leaders in crafting responses and a vision to meet the challenges facing the industry. Yet all agents work within an organization's structure, and the integration of newspaper organizations-the strategic synthesis of the news and business interests-raises some doubt about the values that will continue to guide newspaper organizations and the importance of traditional journalism values.

The responding editors perceive themselves as important managers throughout the organization, not just in the newsroom. They are confident of their ability, and they value their roles outside the newsroom. They acknowledge increased collaboration between the newsroom and non-news departments and are generally comfortable in these roles. They see themselves as a bridge between the newsroom and non-news departments, and one of their roles is communicating the values of the rest of the organization to the newsroom. The editors report moderately strong perceived organizational influence, and a basis for this influence is their advocacy of journalism values throughout their organizations. The predictors of perceived organizational influence-organizational size, organizational integration, and profit-illustrate both the scope and limits of editors' influence. Editors at larger newspapers are more likely to manage news organizations that are respected for their journalism professionalism. Larger papers have greater resources to pursue journalistic goals (e.g., enterprise and watchdog reporting), and are more likely to win prestigious journalistic awards. Accordingly, the papers are important arbiters of social and political influence in largely urban and regional settings. The top editors of these large, complex organizations have generally reached a level of professional accomplishment that surpasses their peers at smaller papers. This begins to explain why these editors perceive greater organizational influence than their colleagues.

Organizational integration suggests that editors who work with other departments-striving to create spans of relationships, as opposed to intra-departmental spans of control-perceive greater organizational influence. This finding should bode well for editors who are striving to advance the journalistic interests of their papers throughout their organizations. However, it is important to note that organizational integration creates structural opportunities for influence to flow in multiple directions. The integration of journalism and business raises the dual questions of the impact of business interests on the editors' journalism values and whether the editors' advocacy of journalism values is diminished or diluted in the exchange of ideas. In a related way, the data suggest a somewhat inconsistent optimism: editors think they can be influential voices for journalism throughout their organizations, while being effective at limiting the influence of business interests inside the newsroom.

Profit was the strongest predictor of perceived organizational influence; editors who think their organizations place more emphasis on profit have lower levels of perceived organizational influence. Editors appear to accept profit emphasis as an expectation they cannot manage (it is beyond their control), but they acknowledge that profit expectations impact their ability to influence people and affect change. This suggests that editors facing higher profit pressures are less influential advocates of journalism values, and they recognize that emphasis on profit cuts into their resources for creating stronger products and better employees. They see that external forces-their corporations and investors-are pushing them in uncomfortable directions.

The benefits of team-based newsrooms are not readily apparent to most editors in this study. Editors don't see teams as a better use of their resources, nor do they think the team system produces better quality journalism. These results hold for editors at all size newspapers. Although surprising given editors' embrace of organizational integration and cross departmental teams, this finding fits well with the small body of research that indicates rank-and-file journalists have not embraced team-based newsrooms. Team-based systems require training and new, broader skill sets. Reporting teams require more staff coordination and planning, which reduces time spent on information gathering, writing, and editing. These are tangible changes that editors don't see as an efficient use of limited resources or as resulting in better journalism.

Change is a process, and survey research is limited to capturing a snapshot of respondents' attitudes at one point in time. Since this study was conducted, the newspaper industry has endured noteworthy changes that are not reflected in these data. Also, asking editors about perceptions of their influence carries a risk that they might inflate their value through self-reports.

However, perception is an important concept in management and organizational literature; organizational members' attitudes and actions are shaped by their perceptions. In this study, editors appear to be quite candid, acknowledging the limits of their influence. Future research could ask other organizational members-both in and out of the newsroom-about sources of organizational influence and news managers' effectiveness as organizational advocates for journalism and as advocates for non-news interests in the newsroom. The study of organizational integration strives to understand how the boundaries and structures of organizations are shifting. Organizational development and the innovation that integration is expected to nurture often occurs along these shifting boundaries, where ideas and their advocates compete for organizational influence.

Editors realise that their newsrooms can no longer be isolated from the interests of other departments in the organization. But, most important, this study illustrates the unique position editors hold in integrated news organizations -that of primary advocate for journalism values.

Editors recognize that they must get out of the newsroom and engage other departments in the news organization. In this sense, they are organizational bridges and buffers, attempting to advance journalism professionalism throughout the organization while protecting the newsroom from marketing schemes at odds with journalism. These roles appear increasingly important to preserving journalism values in the twenty-first century, as newspaper organizations, facing ongoing threats to their core business, will continue to experiment with new products, technologies, and business partners to reach out to audiences in ways that often appear at odds with journalistic principles.

Index